ADDITIONAL PF

"Driven is brilliantly written! I know few people
their inner-most feelings with the candor, courage, and ~~~~
have done."

Alan Schwartz
Chairman Midtown Athletic Clubs, tennis court construction

"As a friend, doubles partner, and teammate of Julie Heldman, I thought I knew
so much about her. But once I started reading the chapters she sent me, I became
amazed at how much I was learning about her, and at how much of her inner
turmoil she had previously kept hidden. As I consumed each new batch of
chapters, I kept craving more.
Thank you, Julie, for sharing your remarkable journey. Your book touched me
on so many levels.
Whether or not you're a tennis player, Julie's path through life will surely
captivate you."

Peaches Bartkowicz
Winner of a record 17 U.S. national junior tennis titles, and former World and U.S. Top Tenner

"Julie Heldman has written a fascinating book about growing up as the daughter
of the extraordinary Gladys Heldman, founder of "World Tennis" magazine and
a driving force in the foundation of the Virginia Slims Tour in the early 1970s,
the precursor of today's WTA Tour. Unfortunately for Julie, the Gladys who bore
and raised her was not the same Gladys the tennis world knew and loved. Instead,
Julie describes her as a highly narcissistic perfectionist with a cruel streak that she
took out on Julie.
Instead of dealing with Julie's tennis career (she was ultimately ranked as high
as number 5 in the world) in a kindly, supportive manner, Gladys undermined
her. Julie never knew what was coming from her mother, rages, unrealistically
extravagant praise, or put-down humor. As a result, Julie was left with a lifelong
curse of extreme insecurity and a constant need to try to fill the emptiness inside
of her with successes. Yes, Julie became a highly driven achiever, but at quite a
cost. In the book, Julie is unsparingly honest about her emotional journey, as she
takes the reader for quite a ride."

Allen Fox
Psychologist, former top U.S. player, and former tennis coach at Pepperdine University

First Publishing, August 2018.
Second Edition, February 2019.

ISBN 978-0692172483

Photos:
Cover sourced from New York World Telegram and Sun; August 14, 1965.
p.12 copyright Ed Fernberger.
pp. 14, 424 sourced from WTA.
pp. 28, 66, 78 sourced from The Heldman Family.
pp.78, 307, 308 copyright Art Seitz.
p.99 sourced from The Globe and Mail, Toronto; August 13, 1958.
p.99 sourced from New York Times; August 1958.
p.236 sourced from AP Wire Photo.
p. 436 copyright Filip Osowski.

Cover design and typesetting by Filip Osowski.

DrivenADaughtersOdyssey.com

DRIVEN
A DAUGHTER'S ODYSSEY

By Julie Heldman

CONTENTS

CONTENTS

CHAPTER 1
CONFRONTING MADAME SUPERSTAR

My heart is thumping, which means I'm ready to do battle. I'm standing by the locker room door of the West Side Tennis Club, in Forest Hills, New York, itching to go, waiting to be called for my third round match against Billie Jean King at the 1973 U.S. Open. For many reasons, this is no ordinary tennis match.

For a start, Billie Jean's hyped-up match against Bobby Riggs, dubbed the "Battle of the Sexes," is looming over all of women's tennis. The contest will take place in just a few weeks at the Houston Astrodome, with a hundred grand up for grabs. That's a lot of dough.

But the match is far more important than the money. Bobby has dubbed the event "Male Chauvinist Pig Versus Women's Lib!" and he keeps whipping up a frenzy, pitting men against women as he spews outrageous nonsense over the airwaves, such as "women belong in the kitchen" and "women need to be shown their place."

Bobby was once a great tennis player, but now he's a 55-year-old with a soft belly and a loud mouth. He amassed a pile of money playing tennis, even when he competed as an amateur, because he bet heavily on his own matches, and he's still so addicted to gambling that he's known to wager on two spiders crawling up the wall.

When Bobby first challenged Billie Jean earlier this year, she turned him down, so he lured Margaret Court, an all-time-great champion, with the prospect of a $10,000 winner-take-all payday in a match on Mother's Day. Margaret is susceptible to nerves, and when Bobby arrived for the match carrying a bouquet of flowers, she got so flustered that she collapsed her long arms and legs into an ungainly curtsy. She never recovered, and once the match began, she crumbled. Bobby, joyous in victory, proclaimed to the world that he could beat any woman.

To prove his claim, Bobby yet again challenged Billie Jean, who had a change of heart. She realized that she'd have to play him to shut him up. Over the years, Margaret has won more matches than Billie, but Billie is better in the clutch. And while Margaret can stumble over her words, Billie Jean is magical with the press, and in her own way, she's as riveting as Bobby. Two years ago, she was the star of the first women's pro tour, winning most of its tournaments. That produced a few inches of ink, but not enough. So she announced her goal to become the first woman athlete to win $100,000 in a year. The press stood up and took notice, and so did the paying public. How do you reach the collective American heart? Talk money.

In every corner of the country, people are ablaze with speculation over the outcome of Billie vs. Bobby. They've become larger-than-life symbols. He represents men who belittle women, and she embodies women's freedom. Everyone seems to be taking sides, and betting on the match has become a national obsession. Rumors abound that Bobby is gambling big time—some say he's betting that he'll win, others say he's betting that he'll lose. Every woman's fear is that Bobby will beat Billie Jean, just like Margaret, which would make the male chauvinists unbearable.

I may be the only woman tennis player who doesn't give a damn about the outcome. All I care about is trying to beat her today.

"Billie Jean King and Julie Heldman! Your match is ready to go."

Billie Jean is standing near me, as always wearing her big eyeglasses and decked out in a Teddy Tinling dress. He's the world-famous tennis dress designer, a six-foot-six, thin, gay Englishman in his 50s, who wears outrageous clothes and has an over-the-top personality. When Billie Jean was first rising in the rankings, he despised her because she wouldn't wear his dresses. Now that she does, he's reversed course, becoming her greatest fan. He calls her "Madame Superstar." The name fits. She embraces the limelight.

During the years that I wore Tinling dresses, he adored me too, but everything changed when he became the official designer for the women's pro tour, whose biggest sponsor is Virginia Slims, a brand of cigarettes. The tour announced that all Tinling dresses would display the "Ginny," the tour's logo of a flapper girl holding a racket in one hand and a cigarette in the other. That's when I stopped wearing Tinling designs, and he stopped talking to me. I was enormously grateful to Virginia Slims for supporting our tour, but I refused to be a walking billboard for cigarettes.

I miss my Tinling dresses. They fitted beautifully, showed off my small waist, and made me feel attractive. My new dresses are fine, but they aren't in Tinling's class, and worse, my clothing contract requires me to wear a bulky, sun-protecting mesh cap. I need protection from the sun, but the cap makes me look dowdy.

Billie Jean and I walk out of the locker room, and just a few yards further is the Clubhouse court, where we'll play. Scuttlebutt has it that Billie Jean is seething because she's been scheduled far away from the Stadium and the Grandstand, the show courts, where she thrives. She's won the U.S. Open title on these grounds for the last two years, which makes the 14,000-seat Stadium akin to her home court. The atmosphere on the Clubhouse court, where space for spectators is severely limited—maybe a few hundred fans, max—is more like a club tournament. On the Clubhouse side of the court, seating is reserved for the outdoor lunch crowd, who sit at tables and chat noisily, smoke, and drink iced beverages that tinkle their glasses. The Stadium side of the court, the only one open to the public, has a knee-high fence lined four-deep by craning onlookers. That's it. No more room for fans. Few will get to watch our match. The Clubhouse court must seem like tennis Siberia to Madame Superstar.

The tournament director must have chosen to send us to tennis Siberia because he's certain that Billie Jean will win this match. He's wrong. I've beaten Billie Jean twice, although I've lost to her 14 times, plus I've been ranked in the world's top 10 for three out of the last five years. That makes me a threat to any player, although I'm a step shy of being a Great Player. I feel belittled by the tournament director's decision. Why he sent us out here is beyond me.

As we stride onto the mushy grass court, Madame Superstar looks all light-hearted and cocky, waving to her fans. Photographers are tripping backwards to snap a quick one of us. Well, actually, they're ignoring me. Everyone wants a piece of Billie. Wherever she goes these days, from her hotel to her practice court to her packed press conferences, she's mobbed by a circus of tennis fans, media, and curiosity seekers.

Both of us are acting nonchalant, trying to hide the enormous impact of the combined high-90s heat and the crushing humidity that have held New York in their grip for the last five days, sending one player to the hospital with heat stroke, and forcing two others to retire, sapped.

Billie Jean and I march steadily forward, both carrying five tennis rackets crooked under our left arms. Each racket head sports a canvas cover advertising the manufacturer's name. I also bring a small bag filled with necessities, such as extra socks and sweatbands, and potions filled with salt and sugar that are purported to help against the heat. Now we reach the umpire's stand, divvy up the changeover chairs, and organize our gear to be ready when we change sides after every odd game. She wins the coin toss and chooses to serve first. I elect to start play at the north end of the court, and the three-minute warm-up begins.

I use the warm-up to get a smooth rhythm, by swinging loosely from the shoulder and making sure to follow through. "Lobs, please." As I smack a few overheads, I feel my muscles come alive. I try to look relaxed. If I telegraph nerves, Billie Jean's belief in herself will be reinforced. I need to focus on the familiar. Sink into the soft grass courts. Smell my newly washed, white tennis dress, crisp against my skin. I'm proud of the way I look before I get soiled with sweat and dirt and grass stains.

Oh, great, another bad bounce. The warm-up isn't over, and already I've had three errant bounces. Even before the tournament begins, when the club's grass courts are bright green and pristine, they're so soft that bad bounces are common. Once play starts, it only gets worse, as players chew up the lawns by stopping and starting and dragging their feet. Billie Jean is a serve-and-volley specialist, and her terrific record on grass reflects her ability to rush the net and hit balls before they bounce. That gives her a definite advantage on grass over me, a dyed-in-the-wool ground stroker. But I won't just roll over. At all costs, I'll need to keep her away from the net. If she sneaks in too close, I'll lob over her head. And I'll rely on my Chip and Dip strategy—I'll chip my sliced backhand and dip the ball low with my topspin forehand, to make my shots sink after barely clearing the net. My goal is to force her to use more energy bending, and to make her hit tougher shots. I want her to pop up her volleys—high and soft would be nice—so that I can stomp on them with my forehand, my best shot.

When the umpire announces the end of the warm-up, I take a moment to scout the crowd, searching for familiar faces. I spot several friends who've traveled from far away to cheer me on. It really helps to have their loving support. I also know that Mom, the famous Gladys Heldman, the editor of *World Tennis*, the world's largest tennis magazine, is sitting at a table on the terrace with Pancho Segura, the Ecuadorian-American tennis genius, but I don't see them, even though her ever-present dark glasses should be easy enough to spot.

I catch myself looking for Vincent, but of course he's not here. Over the last two years, he loved me and dominated my life. He's a lawyer, a journalist, a TV broadcaster, and a musician, and I felt overwhelmed by his brilliance, his many skills, and his desire to change me. He's also way too cocky, and he thinks nothing of instructing experts in their very own specialties. I was drawn to him because he's the very first person to truly believe in me. But he also harmed me in many ways, the worst being the way he pushed me relentlessly to compete on a badly damaged knee.

Two weeks ago, my world blew up. Vincent was due to meet me in Newport, Rhode Island, where I was competing, but he didn't show and he didn't call. Desperate for news, I phoned a mutual friend in London, who said "Don't you know?" No, I didn't know that he left me for another woman. He didn't give me even the smallest warning. Shattered and adrift, I still had a tournament to play. Off the court, I let myself grieve, but once I suited up to play, I was a different person. Starting when I was very young, I learned how to compete when I was hurting by putting on my proverbial blinkers and concentrating even harder than usual. In Newport, I locked my sorrow away, put myself through grueling workouts, and reached the semis by beating two women in the world's top 10. I plan to wear those same blinkers today.

Without Vincent, and with very few friendly faces, I'm mostly on my own against Madame Superstar. Playing her is tough, because she's such a terrific player, but it's even harder because there's bad blood between us. We used to get along just fine. Back in 1966, she was a generous teammate when we played on the U.S. Federation Cup team. We even roomed together that year during Wimbledon, when she won the Ladies' Singles for the first time.

Our relationship turned south with the advent of the women's pro tour. In 1970, tennis was changing rapidly. Men were earning more and more money, and women's tennis was being marginalized. In August 1970, when the Los Angeles tournament announced that its prize money would be skewed 8-1 in favor of the men, the women began to rebel. Several top players turned to Mom, one of the greatest tennis promoters of all time. She organized a tournament in Houston for the following month, concurrent with the Los Angeles event. The United States Lawn Tennis Association tried to put a stop to the Houston event by threatening to suspend the nine women participants, including Billie Jean and me, which would have harmed our ability to make a living playing tennis. To protect the Houston players, Mom signed us to a professional contract, and she brought in Virginia Slims as a sponsor. The tournament was a big success, and the Women's Pro Tour was born.

Once the tour started full time in January 1971, Billie Jean was its biggest star. Every player on the tour was committed to solidarity and grateful for Billie Jean's commitment to the tour's success. But she was under phenomenal pressure, from playing and winning so many matches—she won most of the tournaments—and she became the tour's chief publicist. The unrelenting stress changed her. Where previously she was mostly sunny and pleasant, she often became difficult and demanding. Mom too was overworked, holding down two jobs, each requiring an extraordinary commitment: as the editor and publisher of *World Tennis*, her baby, and as the force behind the tour, building it and making sure that it succeeded. With both Mom and Billie Jean stretched to the limit, it was inevitable that something would snap. Mom reached her breaking point when Billie Jean made statements to the press that sounded like she was taking credit for Mom's hard work. Mom had never been any good at dealing directly with emotional situations. So instead of picking up the phone to talk it over with Billie Jean, she became increasingly distressed, and phoned me again and again, complaining about Billie. I couldn't help her. It wasn't my place to tell Billie Jean off on Mom's behalf. Besides, healing emotional rifts wasn't my forte. My occupation was competing in tennis tournaments, the same ones as Billie Jean. Mom's phone calls, which made me the dumping ground for her rage and hurt, rendered me miserable. Billie Jean became her enemy, and I was the collateral damage.

Out of this tinderbox, I became increasingly angry with Billie Jean, and we began to have little squabbles, which grew unchecked. Once, after I told her that her husband was making a mess of the tournament he was running, she said nothing, but she whipped me mercilessly in a match. I learned a lesson. I should have shut my mouth. Another time, because I speak French, she asked me to help her recover her French Open prize money check, which she had lost at the Paris airport. I was happy to help, and pleased to discover that the check had been turned in. But I got in hot water when I suggested that she give a reward to the Good Samaritan. Like Mom, Billie Jean didn't show her anger to me. Instead, she sent her friend and doubles partner Rosie Casals to tell me "You shouldn't have said that to Billie Jean."

Now, whenever Billie Jean and I play, emotions run high. I hope that our match on the Clubhouse Court won't produce unnecessary drama.

"Ladies and Gentlemen, this is a third-round match between Mrs. Billie Jean King on my left and Miss Julie Heldman on my right."

Miss? I'm 27 years old, not some 14-year-old in pigtails. Try "Ms."

So, here we are getting ready to play, and I can't get Vincent out of my mind.

How could he? STOP! I have to bury those thoughts!

"Mrs. King to serve." Billie Jean's been ambitious since she was little. You can tell by the strokes she developed. She catapults herself forward on her serve, which bounces high so that she has enough time to reach the net and prepare to volley. Net rushers' games take more time to mature, so she didn't reach her peak in the juniors. But she stuck with those strokes through some tough losses, and her greatness has come from her will, her athleticism, and her technically superb volleys that make her an unrelenting force, as she charges the net, extends her arm forward, lays her wrist back, and jabs.

I was taught to play in an entirely different way. Starting when I was eight, I spent seven summers at the Hoxie tennis camp in Hamtramck, Michigan, where Mr. Hoxie believed in huge forehands, lots of dropshots, and the will to fight to the bitter end. He also warned us to stay away from the net. Early on, I taught myself spins, and I developed a knack for point construction. I still play an unusual style of tennis, in which I throw in the kitchen sink, interspersing a wide variety of shots—hard and soft, low and high, flat and with spin—and I even approach the net occasionally. My style is rather like a junk ball pitcher in baseball. I've started calling myself Junkball Jul, and Bud Collins, the effervescent and ubiquitous reporter and TV announcer, has taken a liking to the moniker, which he uses on the air.

The match begins. On the first point, Billie Jean gets her first serve in and gushes toward the net, where she hits a leaping, lunging backhand down-the-line volley. 15-love. Second point. She thumps a crosscourt winner, short and wide. 30-love. Bam, another serve and volley for her, and I have no play on the ball, because it dies in the grass. 40-love. Then she serves to my backhand, and I dump it in the net.

"Game Mrs. King. She leads 1-love."

"Miss Heldman to serve." After the shellacking I received in the first game, an old fear crops up, that I'll lose 6-0, 6-0. That's happened to me twice, both times when I was a kid, but I still cringe at the memory. Whoa cowgirl! I must not go there. I have to yank my mind around, wipe it clean of those fears, and concentrate point by point. I will believe that I can beat her. I have done it in the past, and I can do it again.

My serve. I've never had a great serve, but I try to place it well. I smack my very first serve in the forehand corner of her service box for a winner. 15-love.

On the next point, Billie Jean takes my second serve on the rise, sprints forward, and knocks down a volley, 15-all. I must fend her off by serving deeper. Back and forth we grapple, parry and thrust, and I squeak out the game. It's 1-all. Whew, I'm on the scoreboard.

Billie Jean wins her serve easily, and we change sides, 2-1 for her. I use the minute's rest to force liquids to fight the heat. Damn it's hot. At least I don't feel as badly as I did yesterday, when I nearly lost to a player who's ranked much lower than I am. At one stage, I was sure I heard a train going by, but then I realized it was the blood pulsing past my ears. So I poured ice water on the back of my neck at each changeover, trying to cool down my spine. When I was two games away from losing, I tore after a ball from deep on my forehand side to short and wide on my backhand side, a very long run. I dove the last few feet and landed face down on the grass as I stabbed at the ball, which went for a winner. The drama of my effort and my lucky thrust sucked the steam out of my opponent, and from that moment onward, I ran away with the match.

Strangely, surviving yesterday's match and the horrific weather have immunized me against the worst of today's temperature assault.

But I'm not immunized against Billie Jean's style of play. It's 2-all. On her service games, she's relentlessly picking me apart. We reach 3-all, but then she cranks up her energy and comes to net on every damned point, whether I'm serving or returning. Nothing I try stops her from volleying winners. I remind myself to Chip and Dip. At least I'll extract some of her energy in this severe heat.

Billie Jean wins the first set, 6-3.

On the one-minute break I sit quietly, facing the Tudor Clubhouse. My mind floods with memories of coming here for the first time when I was seven. Mom had recently started *World Tennis*, and she decided that it would be cute to have me and my sister Carrie (who was nine) running the *World Tennis* booth under the Stadium. When crowds streamed out of the stands, we had customers galore. We sold magazines and tennis books, and I worked hard at making change and screaming "*World Tennis*, get your *World Tennis*, 25 cents a copy." When the booth was shuttered at the end of the day, I was bored, because there was nothing for me to do. I had never played tennis, so I sure didn't want to watch it. For me, the best thing about Forest Hills was Dad buying me a Good Humor ice cream bar.

Back then, waiting to leave the grounds was torture. I spent untold hours silently at Mom's side, as she talked endlessly to everyone she knew in the tennis world. When she'd finally say "Let's go get the car," and we'd start down the long walkway from the Clubhouse to the Stadium parking lot, I'd let myself believe we were actually getting out of there. Far too often, my hopes were dashed, as she continued to engage in lengthy conversations with people she met along the way.

Seven years later, when I was 14, I competed in the tournament (then called the U.S. Nationals) for the first time. They let me in at such a young age because I was a local and I'd just won the National 15s. My opponent in the first round was Billie Jean Moffitt (yes, the same Billie Jean), who at 16 was muscular and chubby, and she wore her white socks pulled up high, like a boy. I was still a flat-chested kid, which I tried to hide by wearing falsies, which stuck out in front of me like beacons. Billie Jean was already adept on grass, and I wasn't, so she smoked me in straight sets.

On the Clubhouse court, the one minute is up, so we start the second set. I've drunk as much liquid as I can force down, and I'm ready to go. I need to make an immediate statement, to stop the tide of her victory. But the second set begins the same way the first set ended, with Billie Jean jumping all over me.

I'm being deluged, and I can't stop the flow. I try to hold my serve, to hang in there, but Billie Jean is dominating me. I should slow down, but I can't. "Come on, ball boy," I say. "Give me the ball give me the ball give me the ball. Hurry up." Shit, shit, shit.

The tide is roaring against me. I'm down 2-1, then 3-1. I give it everything I've got, and still I lose the game. It's 4-1.

Changeover. I grit my teeth and decide to switch tactics. I'll still do my Chip and Dip, but I'll also start rushing the net. I'll get there before she does. And I'll go after her serve. In the first point of my new master plan, Billie Jean serves to my backhand and comes in, but I twinkle a few steps to my left to take it on my forehand, which I slug for a winner. That's better. I'm still 4-2 down, but I'm fighting.

My serve. Once again, I slice my first serve wide to Billie Jean's forehand, her weakness, and she hits it out. 15-love. I decide to pound on her forehand, and I win my service game running away. I'm hitting hard, but I have control. If only I could have control over my love life. 4-3 for Billie Jean.

What will I do without Vincent? He said "I'll love you forever." What a liar! Come on, block it out! My forehand is on fire. I know I'm hitting it correctly when my knee hurts. That's been true ever since my knee operation last year. I close my mind to the constant discomfort. Athletes play through pain.

"Game Heldman. The games are tied at 4-all in the second set."

My serve. I hit an ace and three winners. I can't miss.

Billie Jean serves at 4-5. On the first point, I charge the net and put away a volley, giving her some of her own medicine. Love-15. I smother my forehand on two points in a row. Love-40, set point. She staves off the first set point with a brilliant volley, 15-40, but then I catch her flat footed with a topspin lob that lands just inside the baseline, with lots of action.

"Miss Heldman wins the second set 6-4. The match is tied at one set apiece."

People are falling over each other to find a place to watch the match. The word must have spread that she's in trouble. When fans sense an upset in progress, they congregate from all over the grounds like buzzards drawn to a kill.

Final set. First game. Billie Jean's serve. She puts extra oomph into it, pinning me back. 1-love for her.

Changeover. I sneak a peek at Billie Jean. I sometimes do that when I'm playing her, to see if she's doing something unusual, like pushing the edge of the rules. For instance, last year, during the tour's winter swing, Billie Jean took to stamping her feet sporadically during play, which reverberated loudly in the small indoor arenas where we played. It was a ploy to make her opponent think that she was storming the net, even when she wasn't. That's illegal. A player isn't allowed to make noises during a point, yet the umpires weren't stopping her, and that pissed me off. So I complained to Vincent, who's a lawyer, and he hatched a plan, which I used the next time I played her, in Washington, D.C. Early in the match she served and made a rat-a-tat noise with her feet, consistent with rushing the net, yet she stayed back. Instead of playing the point, I caught the ball after it bounced, turned to the umpire, and said "That was a distraction. I claim Rule 15B." The umpire looked bewildered. No one ever makes a legal claim in the middle of a match. Plus he didn't seem to know the contents of the rule, so I said "If you think she did it on purpose, you should give me the point. Otherwise, we should play the point over." He cleared his throat and opined: "The point will be played over." Then I turned the screw, smiling sweetly at Billie Jean and saying something I hadn't planned: "I know you didn't mean it, Billie Jean." I went on to win the match. I stood up to her, and I won.

I wish I hadn't made that smarmy final remark. It just came popping out. I didn't break any rule, but I left the court feeling slimy and nearly as culpable as she was.

That match took place over a year ago, but it weighs on my memory. I wonder if it weighs on Billie Jean's.

After the one-minute changeover, it's my serve. I make her run all over. I take charge of nearly every point, and I win my serve. It's 1-all. I keep fighting and I break her serve. 2-1 for me.

This is a key game, and neither one of us backs down. It's deuce, my ad, deuce, her ad, and more, back and forth, a monumental struggle, with the heat wearing us down. I alternate between my Chip and Dip strategy and all-out attack. 3-1 for me.

Billie Jean's serve. First point, she rushes the net, and I make her bend for a low volley, which she misses. Love-15. What's this? She's near the net, bent over double, and she's not moving. Is she pulling a trick? My body is holding up well, but maybe the heat and humidity are getting to her. I ask "Are you all right, Billie?" What a dumb thing to say. She doesn't look all right. I don't really care how she feels. I just want to win. I should keep my mouth shut. She resumes playing, but not well. I break her serve to go up 4-1.

We sit for the changeover, and I'm roaring to go, but the umpire hasn't called time. I walk to the baseline to serve, but nothing's happening. The umpire isn't taking control of the match, so I ask her, "Is the one minute up yet?" She remains mute, but Madame Superstar stands up, slings her racket against the drinks cooler, making a resounding crash, and then she says something that I can't hear as she storms off the court. I won. I WON. 6-4, 3-6, 4-1, default. It's an ugly score, but the match is mine.

Eat your heart out Vincent. I won the big match, and I'll get the glory. You missed it all.

Marilyn Barnett, Billie Jean's assistant, enters the court and gathers up Billie Jean's rackets and belongings.

I feel simultaneously elated, confused, and weirded out. With no time to reflect, I'm deluged with reporters who're pressing so close to me that I can barely move, and they're barraging me with insane questions.

"Julie, what did you do to Billie Jean to make her quit?"

"Now that Billie Jean lost to you, do you think she'll lose to Bobby also?"

Beyond the crush of reporters, I see my buddy David Gray, the tennis scribe for the Guardian. Desperate to get information from a level head, I yell to him "What did Billie Jean say?"

David yells back: "She said 'If you want the match that badly, you can have it.' " What? I don't get it. I just asked if the time was up.

David adds: "I heard that Billie Jean took more than three minutes on that final changeover." Madame Superstar didn't just break the one-minute rule; she obliterated it. And when she was nabbed, she blamed me.

A man approaches me and says "I'm in charge of the press room, and we'd like you to meet the reporters right away." He guides me on the long walk from the Clubhouse to the Stadium, the one I took so often as a child, and into the jam-packed interview room. There, craziness continues to reign. No one asks me my strategy or about the ebb and flow of the match. Instead, I'm assaulted with accusations that I did something to harm Billie.

After my victory over Billie Jean, the press conference
was pandemonium.

The situation has me revved up and muddled. Asked what I think about the way the match ended, I say: "I wanted the match anyway I could get it. I thought I'd have to break her leg to win. This was as good." As soon as I say it, I realize that I've made a big mistake. Why the hell would I talk about breaking her leg? The entire press conference is torture. I thought I'd enjoy this moment, but I just want to get out of here.

Finally, I return to the locker room, where Billie Jean has been sleeping. Her story is that she's sick, and that's why she quit. She didn't look sick when she stormed off the court. And why did she quit at 4-1 down in the third? No one does that.

You just stand and take your medicine. The press should be writing about that.

After I shower and change, Mom comes into the locker room, and invites me to dinner. Vincent's gone, and I'm being unjustly attacked. I need protection and sanity, but I get neither. Towards the end of dinner, Mom asks me go outside to the newsstand and buy tomorrow's newspapers, which are just arriving. She's obsessed with seeing what they're writing about my huge upset. But other than Bud Collins's article in the Boston Globe, few give me much credit. Mostly they blame me for forcing Billie Jean to quit. Still, Mom reads every word out loud. I feel like I'm being eviscerated.

The day after my victory, the tournament gives me a day off, but I still head out to Forest Hills to practice. Standing on the Clubhouse terrace, I'm accosted by the Associated Press reporter, whom I've known for years. He omits the niceties, because he's on a mission, asking "Were you wearing a bra when you beat Billie Jean?"

I've had enough. I respond: "I don't remember."

*   *   *   *

Two days after I beat Billie Jean, I lose to Helga Niessen Masthoff, the six-foot-tall German who's a perennial world's top-tenner and often my nemesis. She tells players in the locker room "I didn't beat Julie. She beat herself." Actually, I imploded. I was angry at butterflies for existing.

Seventeen days after I beat Billie Jean, she plays Bobby Riggs in the Astrodome, surrounded by the biggest hoopla tennis has ever seen. Madame Superstar, wearing a lavish Teddy Tinling dress, garnished with a giant collar, is carried in on a divan, hoisted by half-naked, male athletes. Bobby enters wearing a bright yellow jacket that says "Sugar Daddy," the name of his sponsor's candy. Never has a tennis match drawn a larger live crowd (just over 30,000) or a bigger TV audience (estimated at 90 million worldwide).

I don't watch the match. I want Bobby to lose, but it's hard for me to root for Billie Jean so soon after the Forest Hills fiasco. My anger still burns.

Billie Jean has trained assiduously for the Billie vs. Bobby match, which is three out of five sets. She wins in a blowout, dispatching Bobby in three straight sets.

Bobby hardly practiced for the match. He was having too much fun with his instant celebrity. Rumors are raging that Bobby placed a large bet on Billie Jean to win. I believe that didn't affect the outcome of the match, because no matter how hard he trained, no matter how much money he gambled, Billie Jean would have won anyway. She's simply a better player.

Billie Jean King being carried into the Houston Coliseum, on her way to beating Bobby Riggs

I wonder if I could have beaten Bobby Riggs in front of 90 million people. Madame Superstar was able to do it because she believed in herself and she's always been focused and brilliant in the clutch. I'm an incredible fighter, and I'm younger, stronger, and fitter than Bobby. In front of 100 or even 1,000 fans, I might well have whipped him. But starting in my early childhood, I've absorbed some fearsome emotional blows, which always lurk within me and hammer at my self-belief. If I'd played Bobby in the Astrodome, he probably would have psyched me out.

CHAPTER 2
"BRING ME MY SCOTCH"

It's 6:30. Pull out the celery, fill it with cream cheese. 6:32. Turn on the broiler. 6:34. Pour water into two pots, the larger one for corn, the other for peas. Turn the burners on high. Put in the right amount of water—I hope—so that they'll boil soon, so I won't get in trouble.

Pour Mom the J&B. Choke back the nausea. Two shots, exactly to the line. No lower, or it won't be enough. No higher or she might get drunk too quickly. Walk carefully so it won't spill. Bring it to her room at 6:36. Perfect. 24 minutes to dinner, just the way she likes it.

She's sitting on her bed, naked from the waist up, adjusting the TV's rabbit ears and smoking a cigarette. The ashtray's filled with butts. "Where are the hors d'oeuvres?" Run to the kitchen, bring back the celery. Relief—she doesn't yell at me. 6:44. Cut the iceberg lettuce and mix ketchup with mayonnaise for the Russian dressing. Laura shucked the corn and shelled the peas before she went home, so this isn't too hard, and it's going well. Except for the celery.

6:46. Lay the lamb chops in the broiler. Use the oven glove the way Dad taught me. He won't be home until later, so I get to prepare dinner on my own. I'm 10, old enough to do it myself.

"Bring me my scotch!!" Mom bellows. Oh no! It's 6:50 and I'm two minutes late. I rush, and a few drops of the horrible stuff dribble on the shot glass and down my hand. I rub the glass on my shirt so she won't feel the wetness.

"I'm sorry, I'm sorry."

Furious, she takes the full glass from me, hands me the empty. Scurry back to the kitchen. Pour the peas into their pot at 6:52, turn the lamb chops over at 6:54, drop the corn into their pot at 6:55. Double check the dining room. The mats are out, so are the forks and knives and napkins.

7:00. Dump everything on the plates, make sure she gets the crispiest corn and the juiciest chops. 7:02. Race to Mom's room to tell her dinner's ready. She throws on a blouse, takes a last drag on her cigarette and stubs it out. She brings the shot glass with her. There's barely a drop left in the bottom.

7:03. Poke my head into our room and tell Carrie it's time. She doesn't like to cook. So it's my job. She gets going double time. Dinner's always at 7:00 and Mom doesn't like to wait, because then she'll get too tight.

Carrie was born a year, four months, and three days before me, but she looks a lot older. She's tall and thin with long legs, and I'm squat. Not fat, just strong. She doesn't like to play with me. She prefers to read.

Mom sucks the shot glass dry, eyes the food on the table. "You're the best! You're the most wonderful, magnificent, fabulous," she says. I glow. The pressure's off.

Carrie ignores me. She too craves that praise.

Mom hasn't slept in two days. She says she drinks so she can eat, that liquor calms her stomach. She doesn't eat much. She's five feet five and weighs 115. Exactly. She weighs herself 5-10 times a day. Her designer clothes have to fit. Before lunch she drinks two double vodkas—so her breath won't smell. And the two double scotches before dinner. More if there's a party. Mom started drinking scotch when she was 11, because her father did. Scotch is vile.

The lamb chops are pink, just right. The corn's crisp. I leave Dad's meal in the oven, where our cat Putty can't get it. I hope Dad doesn't catch hell for being late. He works in Rockefeller Center, and when it's raining the traffic stinks.

7:37. Dad's key turns in the lock. Mom explodes. "You're late! Did you conveniently forget the magazine has to go to press tomorrow? I've never been late. Ever. How could you do this to me?"

Mom's magazine, *World Tennis*, is scheduled to go to the printer in two days. The magazine is the most demanding child in the family. She started it after she quit playing tournament tennis. She runs it. She writes lots of articles and edits the others. She makes the whole thing tick.

Dad's the magazine's proofreader. Mom says he's the best, no one else will do. He has to work for Mom tonight. "I'll just eat my dinner and get started."

Dad's a great tennis player. One of the best in the world, even though he works full time. He has a PhD in physical chemistry. Mom says he should be a bigger star at Shell Oil but they don't like Jews.

Mom goes to the office on weekdays during the daytime and sometimes on weekends, when it's crunch time. That's when Dad, Carrie and I bring vodka and lunch to her office. Mom puts us to work. We do the work of Mom's secretary Mattie. Mom says she doesn't need Mattie when we're there. "You're smarter than Mattie. We're Heldmans. We're the smartest."

At age seven I stamped 3,000 subscriber stencils on the addressograph for the very first edition of the magazine. I finished at 10:45 at night. Mom told me I was the best in the whole world. Afterwards, I dropped a box of 200 stencils. They all flew out. "I'm sorry, I'm sorry, I'm sorry. I didn't mean to."

"Oh my god. Shit. Shit. Shit. WHY DON'T YOU WATCH WHAT YOU'RE DOING!"

I cried, and then she laughed at me for crying. I had to stay up alphabetizing every last one of them. It took days to get the black ink off my fingers.

Mom works from home at night and most weekends. Tonight she's doing the paste ups on her bed (her second office). Carrie and I cut the galleys and photos just right. It's our job. Mom loves a job well done. The bed's covered with all her papers and half-empty pots of rubber cement. At his bedtime Dad gingerly pushes aside the mess and crawls under a few inches of blankets. Sometimes in the middle of the night I hear her typewriter clacking. Or the TV blaring.

7:58. We wait at the table until Dad finishes his dinner. Guess what we talk about? You got it—tennis. I bet you don't know the name of the Polish woman who served underhand in the 1930s. Jadwiga Jedrzejowska. Or that it's pronounced "Yen-jay-ofshka." Or the full names of Big Bill and Little Bill (answer: William "Big Bill" Tilden and William "Little Bill" Johnston). You couldn't survive dinner at my house without instant recall of these tidbits.

8:14. Dinner's over. Carrie and I do our homework in the living room. We fight over who gets the wingback leather chair. I jump in first. Mom hears us screaming at each other and tells us not to make so much noise.

8:32. Mom yells "Julie M." Almost everyone but Mom calls me "Julie." They named me after Dad, whose official name is Julius David Heldman. She calls him "Juli." My name is Julie Medalie Heldman, so our first names sound the same. She uses my middle initial to avoid confusion. I hate being called Julie M. I never tell anyone my name is Julie M. But I know never to complain when Mom calls me "Julie M." I keep my mouth shut.

I'm halfway through a math problem. Carrie and I go to an unusual school. The teachers are loosy goosy. They let me teach myself math. Every year I go through three math workbooks. Last year I was in the fifth grade and finished math books for the fifth, sixth, and seventh grades.

"Just a moment, I'm finishing a problem."

"Julie M. Come here now!" I grudgingly uncurl myself, wary that I might lose the chair. I run in. "Darling, please make me some popcorn." Let me explain. That means "Make me popcorn right now, or I'll be upset." Mom weighs herself after dinner. Depending how much she's under 115, she has either popcorn or a Häagen-Dazs coffee milkshake made by Dad or me. The kitchen makes her nervous.

8:43. I bring her the popcorn—a little salt, a little melted butter—and a Tab. "Thank you, thank you, thank you. Come here—Tis Tis." That means 'Give me a kiss, but not too hard because I bruise easily. And be careful not to mess my hair.' Mom's hair looks just right. She has it done twice a week. She does the New York Times daily crossword puzzle—in ink—while she's having her hair washed. I don't know how she writes when she's leaning back. She likes to stay busy.

8:53. I get stuck on a math problem, so I ask Dad for help. He's working at the dining room table. He puts down the galleys and says "Let's work that out together." Dad doesn't get mad at me for interrupting him.

9:15. Mom comes into the dining room. I'm returning from the bathroom. She starts screaming really loud.

"LOOK AT YOU. YOUR SHOULDERS ARE HUNCHED. STAND UP STRAIGHT!" Her posture's great. Mine stinks. "If you don't stand up straight you'll have to be strapped in a corset until you can balance a book on your head with your back straight as a rod."

My eyes well up.

"Why are you crying?"

"I'm sorry. I'm sorry."

Dad says nothing.

CHAPTER 3
THE MAKING OF A REBEL

Mom had a rocky childhood. She grew up rich, but her highly educated, absentee parents failed to give her a secure foundation of love and guidance.

She adored her father, George Z. Medalie. He wasn't handsome, but he was brilliant, charming, witty, and magnetic. The son of a rabbi, he'd come up from poverty in New York City's Lower East Side to become an exceedingly successful lawyer. By the time Mom was born, her family had moved into a 10-room apartment on Manhattan's Upper West Side, replete with four servants.

George Z thrived in both private practice and the public domain, moving seamlessly between them. He grew very rich representing large corporations, such as Safeway, MGM, and American Tobacco, and also criminals, such as the infamous mobster Legs Diamond. But he also frequently took a giant pay cut to work for the government. In 1931, President Herbert Hoover appointed him U.S. Attorney for the Southern District of New York, basically the chief federal prosecutor for Manhattan. There, George Z succeeded brilliantly at combatting election fraud and snaring gangsters, including the same Legs Diamond whom he had previously defended. As U.S. Attorney, George Z hired and mentored Thomas E. Dewey, who later became Governor of New York and then the Republican Party presidential candidate.

George Z was very, very busy, and he was rarely home. And when he did spend time at the apartment, either in the afternoon or before a party, he'd often nap, and the family would need to tread lightly, or else he'd scream "BE QUIET! I'M SLEEPING!"

Mom enjoyed being around her father, whom she always lovingly called "Daddy," and she would eventually adopt many of his traits, including his sharp wit and his commitment to helping others.

But she had far more trouble with her mother, Carrie Kaplan Medalie, who, like her husband, had used education to climb out of the Jewish ghetto. While George Z studied law at Colombia, she majored in the classics at its sister school, Barnard College, where she graduated in 1905, a rare feat for a woman of that era. She taught school for several years, and then the couple had three children:

Alice, the oldest, who died when she was only five; Arthur, the second, who was the preferred child, because he was a boy; and Mom, who was two years younger than Arthur.

By the time Mom was born, the family was rolling in dough, and her mother no longer worked. But although she was home more than her husband, she was emotionally absent, and she lacked warmth, affection, and thoughtfulness. She insisted that everyone, including her own children, call her by her initials "CK," so Mom grew up without anyone named "Mommy," or "Mom," or even "Mother." And in most ways, CK didn't act like a mother. She made rules and routines that didn't suit her daughter, such as serving meals that Mom abhorred and giving her such a small weekly allowance that she could only afford a single candy bar. Moreover, CK didn't try to get to know her daughter. Instead, she passed the time at her stockbroker's office, reading the ticker tape and making small trades, and at lectures, where she hoped to improve her mind. Mom was left with a string of revolving nannies, none of whom were around long enough to form a loving relationship with the little girl.

As an adult, Mom wrote a 20-page, typewritten profile of CK—not for publication—highlighting her mother's eccentricities. Not once does the story display even the smallest hint of affection by Mom for CK, or vice versa. Mom's prose drips with disdain, as she paints a picture of a highly educated woman who was incapable of independent thought; a rigid person allergic to change; a germaphobe who washed the plates of strangers over and over; and a terrible tightwad, who became a hoarder, despite the family's wealth. CK's obsession was fierce. Year after year, she added cardboard boxes and cheap furniture to their designer-decorated apartment, until all 10 rooms overflowed with containers of everything from fur coats to junk that she couldn't bear to get rid of. When Mom and Dad became engaged, she asked CK for several of her scores of pots and pans, but CK said no. She couldn't give up one of her pots, although this time money wasn't the problem, as she offered Mom a credit line at the store of her choice, where she could stock her own kitchen.

Mom was rarely at ease around CK, instead preferring to be home alone, lying in bed, eating chocolates and reading books or movie magazines, or at the movies, when she could wangle her aged grandmother into taking her (CK never went).

Mom grew up without proper nurturing or guidance, so unsurprisingly, she became a rebel. To get what she wanted, she lied to her mother and taunted her.

For instance, CK liked to say that she was "proud to be a Victorian," which meant she avoided sex and hated swear words. So Mom would walk up to her mother and say "fuck." CK's only response was "Oh Gladie dear." No wonder CK could never rein in her headstrong daughter.

Mom's early wild streak and lack of supervision led to some long-term bad habits. George Z often held parties at home, and starting when Mom was young, she'd stay awake until the guests left, and then rush into the living room and drain the remaining liquor from every glass. George Z liked scotch, and by age 11, so did she. She started smoking the following year. No one stopped her.

Mom's parents had married after graduating from college, but they'd never been soulmates. He was dapper; she was dowdy. He loved the high life; she abstained from alcohol and preferred a sober lecture to a night on the town. He was affectionate; she was stiff. Once George Z and CK finished having children, they drifted apart—although they never divorced—and left intimacy behind. He devoted his life to work, charity, parties, and, according to Mom's Uncle Willy, an opera singer whom he kept in a separate apartment.

So Gladys grew up in a loveless household. She was captivated by her largely absent Daddy, but she was stuck with CK, who paid little attention to her daughter's wants and needs. Gladys learned very little about empathy. Instead, she relied on her intelligence and her iron will.

CHAPTER 4
RICH AND POOR

Mom rebelled throughout high school. Although she was fiercely brilliant and adored reading, she often refused to do homework, probably to annoy CK, who revered education. When Mom actually completed her work, the results were sometimes perverse. Once, when an English teacher assigned Hamlet, Mom read Othello. Later, she often claimed that she almost flunked out of high school, but that was unlikely. The school would never have allowed George Medalie's daughter to fail. She slid by, graduating in 1939.

When Mom was a senior, she had a crush on a Stanford boy, so she decided to apply to Stanford. But her grades were less than stellar, so George Z extracted recommendations from two of the most prominent men in the country: ex-President Herbert Hoover, who was then living on the Stanford campus, and George Z's protégé, Thomas E. Dewey. By the time Mom was accepted, she had fallen out of love with the Stanford boy, but her fate was already sealed.

From the beginning, Mom loved Stanford. Far from her parents, she converted the energy from her teenage rebellion into a formidable desire to succeed on her own terms. She didn't look to others to guide or teach her. She applied her exceptional mind to creating unique plans, and then she worked exceedingly hard to achieve success.

In Mom's freshman year, she developed an unusual plan to excel in her classes. She memorized her detailed class notes (her memory was incredible) and then regurgitated her professors' own words, verbatim, onto her exams. She got all A's. According to Dad, she began to think for herself in her sophomore year, and still got all A's. She loaded up on classes, taking as many as 21 units in a quarter (instead of the usual 15), and attended summer school, so she graduated in three years, very near the top of her class.

According to Mom's account—which is not to be totally trusted, as she loved to embellish stories about herself and her family endlessly—in her senior year, she spotted a handsome guy in a chemist's white lab coat, with an athlete's spring to his step, and curly brown hair, which he wore slightly too long. A friend told her his name was Julius Heldman, and that he was a star athlete and a PhD candidate.

Intrigued, Mom asked him to a Sadie Hawkins party, where women were allowed to invite men. Dad accepted only after checking out her grades in the Stanford "bawl-out" sheet. He was impressed.

Mom and Dad had a lot in common. Both were extremely smart and superb students who worked hard. And although they passionately hated all religions, they never denied being Jewish, unlike many who changed their names and their religion to avoid the prejudice against Jews.

Otherwise, their backgrounds were polar opposite. Mom's parents were rich, and Dad's were poor. While she rebelled against her New York City private school education, he sailed through public schools in Hollywood, California. She arrived at Stanford with trunks of clothing and a leopard coat. His own small wardrobe was ordinary. As a teenager, he was a star tennis player whose parents barely scraped together enough money to buy the long, white flannel pants that male players wore in that era. He bicycled all over Los Angeles wearing those flannels. Once, he peddled 15 miles from his Hollywood home to a junior tournament in Santa Monica, where he won four matches, took the title, and returned home at dusk, balancing the trophy and his rackets in the bicycle's basket. When Mom was a teenager, she spent her summers either at camp in Maine or traveling around Europe with her family. Until she met Dad, she had never touched a tennis racket.

Even their personalities were opposite. Mom had inherited her father's quick wit and his love for a good joke. Dad was a bit shy and thoroughly inept at small talk, and he spoke with a scientist's precision. Sometimes he'd go on forever about esoteric chemical properties or obscure mathematical theorems, but he was voraciously interested in the world. He loved music and singing; Mom was a step above tone deaf. Still, he taught her to harmonize on a few popular songs.

Despite so many differences, they were immediately attracted to each other. Dad liked and admired strong women, having grown up in a home where his mother was the strength of the family. Even at age 19, Mom was a force to be reckoned with, and Dad was drawn to that. Early on, she made it clear that she'd never be a stay-at-home wife. She didn't want to be confined. I think another big attraction for Dad was her family's money. They were so rich that George Z once earned $300,000 in one case in the 1920s, a sum currently valued in the tens of millions of dollars. They were so rich that the Depression didn't impact them. Dad rarely told us how much he hated growing up poor, but poverty had a profound and lasting impact on him, and the possibility of enjoying a more comfortable life had to have been tantalizing.

Mom was initially attracted to Dad's good looks, but she soon realized that he had a lot more going for him. Like George Z, Dad had come from a hardscrabble background, yet he had the will and the ability to make something of himself. He was already a star in both tennis and academics. He had pursued both at UCLA, which he entered at age 15. He played Number One on the UCLA tennis team for three years, and he performed so well academically that UCLA nominated him to be a Rhodes Scholar. He came close, barely losing out to Byron "Whizzer" White, an All-American college football player who later became a Justice of the U.S. Supreme Court.

At 17, Dad won the U.S. national tennis title for boys 18 and under (called the "National Juniors"), and he had plenty of talent to go further. But there was no money in tennis back then, and he'd had enough of poverty, so he chose academia over tennis. When Mom and Dad met, he'd hardly touched a racket in three or four years. He'd just scored magnificently on his PhD exams, and he'd been awarded the ultra-prestigious National Research Fellowship, the highest award in the U.S. for a Chemistry grad student. The Fellowship paid $1,800, enough to live on frugally for a year, and it provided Dad the opportunity to spend a year working for the chemistry professor of his choice. Dad was succeeding on his own terms, and Mom admired that.

By their third or fourth date, Julius Heldman and Gladys Medalie were in love. Soon afterwards, he asked her to marry, and she accepted. They set a date: June 15, 1942, the day after they both graduated from Stanford, she with a bachelor's degree in history, he with a PhD in physical chemistry.

The families of the bride and groom converged on Northern California for the wedding, his from Los Angeles, and hers from New York City. Mom's parents flew cross country, in an era when air travel was only for the wealthy. Jet planes were not yet available, so the trip in a DC-3 required over 12 hours, and the plane's noise, vibration, and instability were draining. Mom and Dad picked up George Z and CK at the San Francisco airport. As usual, George Z, although tired, looked dapper in a tailored suit and heavy overcoat, while CK, who never cared a whit about clothes, looked frumpy. Instead of giving his future son-in-law a hearty "Welcome to the family," George Z pulled Dad aside, reached into the pocket of his coat, and extricated a bunch of empty sample scotch bottles that had helped him get through the flight. George Z surreptitiously handed the bottles to

Dad, and his first words to his future son in law were "Would you get rid of these for me?" Later, George Z grilled Dad about his prospects and seemed content to hear that Dad wanted to be a professor.

George Z and CK stayed at San Francisco's upper crust St. Francis Hotel, where the wedding reception would take place. The kind of luxury that was second nature to the Medalies was unknown to Dad's parents, Nathan and Lottie Heldman, who arrived by train the day before the wedding. They had escaped from Poland in 1914, one step ahead of Nathan being drafted into the Russian army, which was brutal to Jews. Nathan was a watchmaker and jeweler who worked slowly but masterfully with his hands, but he struggled financially. For years, the family—Dad was the youngest of three brothers, all born in America—moved often in Los Angeles and Hollywood, living mostly behind jewelry stores. Once, the five of them were stuck in a cold-water, one-room, dirt-floor flat, and Lottie boiled water for their Saturday night baths. Although they were close to going hungry at times, Lottie, the practical one, kept them fed and clothed. The Depression continued to hit the family hard until they were saved in the mid-1930s when Nathan and his middle son Sam got steady jobs making precision timing instruments needed for drilling oil wells.

The wedding was held at Stanford's nondenominational Memorial Church, and at George Z's request, it was officiated by a rabbi. The event was during World War II, when many items were rationed, including butter, meat, tires, and, most importantly, gasoline. Mom organized the reception and accumulated gas rationing stamps for the big day, ensuring that the 100 guests had rides to San Francisco. The reception came off perfectly; caviar and champagne were served. It was the first of Mom's many successful promotions.

Mom and Dad spent the first days of their honeymoon in Yosemite, and then George Z footed the bill for them to fly to New York—Dad's first airplane ride—where they stayed in the enormous apartment where Mom was raised. Dad's eyes were dazzled by their world of muted opulence.

Back from the honeymoon, the newlyweds moved into a cottage in Berkeley, California, which was chosen by Mom but paid for by George Z. Dad pursued his research for the 1942-43 academic year with the professor he had chosen at the University of California at Berkeley. In June 1943, once his studies were over, his draft status became 1-A, which meant he would soon be inducted into the army. While he was waiting for his draft notice, he taught Chemistry at Cal as an "Instructor," the lowest rank for college teachers. When the draft notice arrived, Dad asked the Dean of Chemistry for help, because Dad didn't want to fight. Speaking cryptically, the dean said "We can keep you out of the army if you are willing to sign up for a war project I can't tell you anything about." Its name was the Manhattan Project, and its purpose was the biggest kept secret of the war. Even Vice President Harry Truman would be ignorant of the project until he became President. But Dad figured it out quickly, using his up-to-date knowledge of physics and chemistry, along with his sizable experience in science laboratories. The purpose of the project was to build an atom bomb. Dad was duty bound to keep that information hidden from Mom. We'll never know if he did, because they always refused to discuss the subject. Anyway, Dad agreed to work on the Manhattan Project, and a week before his induction date, his draft board received a telegram stating that, by order of President Roosevelt, Julius Heldman was exempted from military service.

Mom's working career had a wobblier start. While she was still at Stanford, she sought a job with a corporation. She was, after all, near the top of her class, with glowing recommendations from professors. The placement officer asked "Can you type?" When she said "No," she was told she could be a sales girl or a receptionist. She never forgot that rebuff.

During the first year of their marriage, Dad worked extremely long hours—a lifelong habit—and although Mom enjoyed reading day and night, she needed a focus for her extraordinary energy. So she returned to academia, earning a master's degree in medieval history at Cal, finishing her courses and her thesis all in one year. Her husband was still largely absent, so she searched the newspaper for jobs. The San Francisco Chronicle had an ad for a "full professor" at the Williams Institute in Berkeley, a little-known school for students who hadn't done well enough in high school to get into college, but were looking for a second chance. Mom, forever competitive, took the job, because she'd be a professor while Dad was only an instructor. Williams hired her to teach the history of Western civilization (her strength) and calculus and differential equations (her weakness—she never took college math). She brazenly took on the challenge, blithely assigning math problems she couldn't solve, and then crammed as if she were studying for a final. Dad was a math whiz, so in a pinch, she could wait until he came home and explained the concepts to her.

Mom's teaching job made the time pass, but soon she became pregnant.

Carrie was born August 5, 1944, and Mom nursed her newborn even though that was out of vogue. As usual, she followed her own path.

Both parents were flushed with excitement and adored baby Carrie, who luckily was easy going and docile. Those traits came in handy when she was only three weeks old, and the Manhattan Project gave the budding family two days' notice that they were being sent by train to Oak Ridge, Tennessee, one of the major centers for the Manhattan Project.

Dad was needed to troubleshoot a problem with uranium separation, which he solved in less than a month. He was then transferred to another project at Oak Ridge, one that required glass blowing skills, which he had aplenty. At both UCLA and Stanford, chemistry labs were primitive compared to those of today, and Dad had had to design many of his own apparatuses and build them using sophisticated glass blowing techniques. When he discovered that his Oak Ridge co-workers were terrible at glass blowing, he gave them a week-long seminar. He taught them well, and used that experience the following year, when he wrote a glassblowing textbook so highly regarded that it was used in graduate schools across the U.S. for several decades.

As Dad worked endlessly, Mom grew increasingly isolated. Oak Ridge was an ugly and barren town which had ballooned up almost overnight from 3,500 residents to 60,000, due to the Manhattan Project. Their pre-fab house was tiny, and there were no phones, so Mom didn't know when Dad would come home. The meat was rancid, the eggs were powdered, and the butter was reprocessed. Mom said she lost so much weight that her milk dried up. The winter was freezing, so mother and child spent their time indoors, but the coal ran out, and for days at a time Mom was stuck in front of the electric stove, with her feet in the oven. She bolstered her spirits, as she often would throughout her life, by reading omnivorously.

In early 1945, the young family returned to California, where Dad went back to teaching at Cal, as an assistant professor, and Mom became pregnant with me. They realized that their cottage would soon be too small, so once again Mom turned to her father. Before I was born, she chose a house that George Z funded, this one quite large and situated very near the Berkeley Tennis Club, which they joined.

Soon, there were huge changes. Dad had achieved his goal of becoming a professor, but he was deeply disappointed with his paltry salary and with the ugly academic infighting in Cal's Chemistry Department. While he was still a PhD student at Stanford, Shell Oil had offered him a job, and they continued to seek him out, promising lifetime employment and a pension, a security that he craved. He took the job two months before I was born on December 8, 1945.

CHAPTER 5
LAURA SAVED ME

Carrie and me, ages three and two. I cried a lot.

Some women love being pregnant. Mom wasn't one of them, and by the time I came along, she'd been pregnant for 18 of the previous 25 months. Some women love little babies, but Mom wasn't one of those either. She could tolerate them when they were quiet, as Carrie was, but I was born crying. I needed to be held and rocked day and night, or else I howled. I made mincemeat of my parents' sleeping habits.

Mom couldn't handle my crying. Because her hearing was highly sensitive, even small sounds irritated her, so my cries must have ripped right through her. And because she grew up without much love or nurturing, she had little foundation for developing empathy for my illnesses and distress. She was the family chronicler, who loved to recount her own good deeds, such as nursing me. But she never claimed that she comforted me when I was little. She just couldn't.

By the time I was two months old, Mom was crawling the walls. She despised housework, and she clearly couldn't raise two babies by herself, especially when one was a squalling newborn.

Her only fun was piling Carrie and me in our double stroller and pushing us to the Berkeley Tennis Club. On weekends, Mom watched Dad play on the club's courts, and the desire to play tennis began to bubble up in her.

In mid-20th-century America, mothers stayed at home and raised their children. For a few years, Mom tried to fit into that mold, but it was driving her mad.

At age 23, the indomitable Gladys Heldman decided to forge her own path. She would spend most of her time at the Berkeley Tennis Club, learning to play tennis. But to do so, she needed a maid.

Just before I turned three months old, Mom got news that her father was gravely ill, so she bundled up Carrie and me and set out on the train for New York. At the Chicago stopover, she phoned CK and found out that George Z had died. He was only 62. Mom arrived in New York in time for the great man's funeral, held at Temple Emanu-el on 5th Avenue in Manhattan. Over 2,000 people attended, including numerous dignitaries.

In that era, unpleasant truths were often publicly covered up. George Z's New York Times obituary said that he died of acute bronchitis. The American Jewish Committee archives said he died of congestive heart failure. My father, in his later years, finally told us the truth. Yes, George Z's heart was bad, but he had died of drink, succumbing to cirrhosis. Mom had alcoholism in her genes.

After the funeral, Mom harangued CK for money to pay for a maid, and CK consented. Back in Berkeley, changes to our lives came fast and furious. First, Mom stopped nursing me. Then she placed an ad in the newspaper for a maid. It was early 1946, not long after World War II had ended, and black women were pouring out of the South in search of jobs. She hired Laura Haywood, a 27-year-old, attractive black woman from Mississippi whose marriage had broken up and who needed work. Laura was a warm, loving, and industrious caregiver who began working for our family right away.

My life improved immediately. Mom was all sharp shoulders and bony ribs, wary of cuddling. Laura was stocky and soft, and she spent hours holding me against her pillowy breasts. When I was cold, she wrapped me in blankets. When I had colic or asthma, her heart opened up to me, and she tried to make me well. Years later, Laura told me she hadn't minded either my constant crying or my frequent illnesses. "I jes felt so bad for you," she'd say, retaining her black-

Southern accent. When I was one, Dad made a home movie that shows Laura holding me tight, then playing with me, and then beaming when she brings me close to her face. Her love shines through the grainy, black-and-white film.

Laura raised me and gave me the gift of love. Without her, I would have been lost. Laura saved me.

I have Mom to thank for bringing Laura to me. Mom grew up without a constant caretaker, but she made sure that Laura was always there for Carrie and me. Many employers exploit household workers by underpaying them. Not Mom. She always paid Laura well. Laura was proud that she earned enough to support not only herself, but also her daughter and several other relatives in Mississippi.

Laura worked for our family for over 30 years, and every time our family moved, Mom asked Laura to come along. Sure, it was self-serving, because Laura brought Mom freedom. But my life would have been very different without this wonderful woman.

Unfortunately, while Mom gave, she also took away. If Laura made a mistake, Mom screamed at her cruelly. Fortunately, Laura could let the abuse slide right off her, saying "That's jes yo mama." I think Laura was always grateful to have a steady job, and she sometimes even thought of Mom as a mother figure.

But there were more insidious problems. Behind Laura's back, but in front of me, both of my parents would say "Laura's a hard worker, but she's stupid." They also made fun of her handwriting. Laura had been raised amid poverty and prejudice, and because her formal education stopped after the first grade, her handwriting looked like a child's scribble. It's curious that my parents valued education, yet they hired an uneducated woman. It's equally curious that neither thought of helping her learn more. Laura knew her place, which was to work hard and never speak up. She hardly ever mentioned her childhood, her marriage, or in fact anything other than work. She basically shut down. She knew she was just there for the heavy lifting.

Sadly, my feelings for Laura were undermined by my parents' ongoing disdain for her. And it didn't help that Laura was so closed off. Despite all that she had given me as an infant, as I grew up, I thought of her more like an empty shell, a person whom I couldn't know. I forgot how much we had loved each other. I've been able to recollect some of those feelings only by looking at old photos and home movies, and by remembering a few words that she said. What a loss for me.

When Laura started working for us, she was immediately invaluable to Mom, who could then play as much tennis as she wanted. She started by practicing against the Berkeley Tennis Club wall, waiting for Dad to come home from work and hit with her until dark. But she knew she wasn't a naturally gifted athlete, and that it would be an ambitious project to start playing at age 23, so to learn tennis, and for that reason alone, she jettisoned her lifelong aversion to submitting to someone else's authority. She turned to Tom Stow, the Berkeley Tennis Club pro who had helped Don Budge become the first man to win the Grand Slam in 1938. To concentrate on Mom's form, Stow began teaching her in an empty room. He required endless repetitions and perfect execution, and she soaked up everything he taught her. Once she got the hang of it, she graduated to the courts, where they worked diligently for hours, frequently losing all track of time. She applied the spectacular work ethic she'd developed at Stanford to the daunting task of learning the complicated tennis techniques that are ordinarily taught to the very young.

Tennis became Mom's all-encompassing obsession. Soon, she was playing from morning to night, far away from her children and their messy needs.

While Mom was a novice, she had trouble finding practice partners, because tennis etiquette forbade her from asking a better player to have a hit. So Dad jumped into the breach. On the weekends, he played with her often, to help her improve her strokes and as her mixed doubles partner. He was such a good player that everyone wanted to play with him, so Mom got invaluable practice against high quality opponents.

Mom loved the scene at the Berkeley Tennis Club. Dad's pals in academia and at Shell Oil bored her, but she came to life when tennis players were nearby. In the early years after the war, the Berkeley Tennis Club was alive with players of all calibers, from beginners to Tom Brown, who reached the 1946 Wimbledon finals, and Pat Todd, who won the 1947 French Championships (the precursor to the French Open). Soon, my parents' social life revolved around the club, where they played bridge and talked tennis. For the rest of Mom's life, she would love gabbing and writing about tennis, debating strokes, and gossiping about the players who cheated and the ones who choked when the score got close.

Soon, Mom turned over all the household duties to Laura, who watched over Carrie and me, did the marketing, cleaned the house, prepared dinner, and gave us baths. After Dad drove Laura to the bus, Mom and Dad were back in charge, but by then, it was nearly time to put the babies to bed.

Mom loved one aspect of child rearing: teaching Carrie, who was extraordinarily bright. Instead of playing childish games with Carrie or making her giggle, Mom taught her the alphabet, and always stood by her claim that Carrie learned to read before she turned three. And instead of reciting nursery rhymes to Carrie, Mom taught her Greek mythology. She enhanced the myths by bringing them into our household, even naming her two cats Agamemnon and Iphigenia, characters in Greek myths. Years later, Mom would claim that in Berkeley she had taught the myths to both of us, but that wasn't true. At the time, I was an infant, far too young to understand the tales that she wove.

The indomitable Gladys Heldman hated listening to other parents talk about their children, so she relied solely on her own ideas about child rearing. And she basically didn't enjoy children. So she never learned our idiosyncrasies and our needs. Instead, she concocted an upside-down belief system about us: that we didn't need to go through childish developmental phases, because we were already as capable as full-grown adults, and we didn't need her—or any other adult—to care for us. At one level, she actually bought into this bizarre view. At another level, those convictions served her own purposes, because if we didn't need her, then she could justify largely abandoning us from an early age.

One result of her distorted beliefs was that throughout my childhood, Mom would place me—far more often than Carrie—in situations that were way beyond my capacity, and when I ran into trouble, instead of helping me, she'd laugh at me. Her mud tea party was a perfect example. When I was about two, she cooked up a plan for Dad to film a home movie of Carrie and me having a party on the lawn of our Berkeley home. The film starts with a shot of us standing side-by-side, Carrie much taller than I. We look like overgrown dolls, in our matching white dresses, with our normally unruly, curly hair slicked down perfectly for the occasion. Next, we see Laura in her starched, white uniform prepping a child's-size table outdoors on the lawn, complete with a teapot and two cups and saucers. It apparently never occurred to Mom that a two-year-old might not understand the concept that "mud tea" was just for show, not to be drunk. So no one was supervising me. The rich brown liquid must have appeared luscious to me, because while the film is running, I disappear from view. Abruptly, the camera turns and finds me bawling, having drunk some mud tea. Then we see Laura dashing to give me comfort, while further away, Mom is creased with laughter at my foolishness.

CHAPTER 6
SHELL MOVED US

Mom was a maverick who shunned many of the customary rules of marriage in mid-20th-century America. But in one way, she remained traditional. In the late 1940s and the 1950s, Shell made a habit of moving its promising employees, including Dad, to different cities, and amazingly, Mom didn't complain.

His first transfer, from Northern California to the Wilmington refinery in Southern California, came in 1948, when I was two. Mom took the move in stride, and in Long Beach, she located a rental house that was nestled between the Long Beach Bay and the Pacific Ocean. Because the two bodies of water would occasionally rise and meet each other, the house had been built on stilts over the sand. Laura moved with us, which was essential, as Mom remained entranced with tennis. In fact, she played even more in Long Beach than she had in Berkeley, because in addition to practicing all day long, she began entering weekly tournaments held at night. At first, she lost every match in singles and doubles, but in the mixed doubles, she had Dad by her side, and they had better success. She kept plugging, driving 30 miles to Hollywood for coaching. She had started playing tennis at such an advanced age that no one expected her to win anything, but she was stubborn and tough and committed, and she finally began to win a few matches. My sister interviewed Dad in his early 80s for an oral history. Here's his take on Mom's matches in Long Beach:

> "Within a year, she became the second best woman player in Long Beach. Jane Little, an aircraft engineer working for what was then called Douglas, was Number One. She worked on the wing design for the DC series. She was famous throughout tennisdom for never wearing a bra, and was well endowed. Jane was as steady as a rock, and could run for hours. Gladys was well trained, moving her opponent side to side. Jane defeated Gladys in the finals of a number of tournaments in a row. But Gladys's determination kicked in, and she finally prevailed."

In the fall of 1949, soon after Mom's victory over Jane Little, Shell transferred Dad again, this time to Houston, where the weather was often hellishly hot and stifling, and air conditioning was still rare. Yet Mom didn't complain. "She was a good soldier," Dad said. "She was eager about the tennis." They arrived in Houston at night, and she insisted on playing tennis right away, so they headed straight for the center of Houston, to play on the red clay courts at the Municipal Center, where she happily hit tennis balls under the lights.

Mom returned to the courts the following day, and every day for the next four years, except when it rained or when she was traveling to tennis tournaments. She developed lifelong friendships with some of the players, yet rarely did her tennis life intersect with her home life. She hardly ever brought Carrie and me to the courts, and only occasionally would she invite her tennis friends to our home. As a result, our home life was a closely held secret.

CHAPTER 7
THE CULT OF GLADYS

In our family, Mom ran the show. She began promulgating rules when the family lived in California, but once we moved to Texas, when I was four, she expanded her dominance with new edicts, many of them unspoken, which the rest of us were required to obey. By the time we moved to New York City when I was seven, she had turned our family into the Cult of Gladys.

Yes, I really did mean to use the term "cult." And no, we weren't a crazed religious sect. But our family had many of the core characteristics of a cult: an exceedingly strong leader; isolation from the rest of the world; control, coercion, and abuse by the leader; and for the followers, total subservience.

Everyone who met Mom was struck by the strength of her personality, a necessary characteristic of a cult's leader. Yet no one outside the family could have imagined the control she exerted over our secluded family.

Our first two Texas homes were isolated, largely due to Mom's tactics for finding great, affordable residences in rural communities surrounding Houston.

At 27, she'd already acquired shrewd business skills. She focused on renting properties that were up for sale, and she was able to negotiate inexpensive leases because she agreed to move out in a hurry once the properties were sold. But the deals she cut weren't good for me. Our homes never had children nearby with whom I could play.

More than anyone in our family, I suffered from our isolation. Carrie was old enough to go to school, and I wasn't; Dad went to work; and Mom commuted to Houston to play tennis. I sometimes accompanied Laura to the store, but otherwise I remained home and played mostly alone. My loneliness wasn't alleviated even when Carrie came home from school, because she refused to talk to me or play with me.

Our first home in Texas was a 37-acre ranch located in a hamlet called Genoa, deep in the sticks. We had a barn and chickens and horses and a pig named Uncle Willy. Our only neighbor within walking distance was a woman named Miz Mabel, who lived in a dilapidated house with no running water, just an outdoor water pump and an outhouse, which I found fascinating.

But when Miz Mabel offered to let me use her facilities, Mom said no. She didn't want me visiting a woman who had an outhouse. I never saw Miz Mabel again, and there was no one else to visit.

One day, a delegation from the local white Baptist church offered to pick up Carrie and me and take us to Sunday school, which meant we'd get to see other children. When we returned home, Mom asked what we did, and I answered excitedly: "We ate cookies and we got to color a paper plate."

"What did you draw?" she asked.

When I piped up: "the Christ child," Mom stopped cold. Years later, she claimed that she'd responded "I forgot to tell you we're Jewish." I'm sure she didn't have the presence of mind to say that, because she'd been caught unawares. She had mindlessly let us go to Sunday school, somehow not foreseeing that the Baptist church would teach us the Christian religion. Once she heard my words, she put a stop to Sunday school. Never again did I play with any other child while we lived in Genoa.

Our second Texas home, which was also in the country, without visible neighbors, abutted Kemah, a town larger than Genoa, but still quite rural. Once again, Carrie attended school, but I was still too young, which meant I played alone in the driveway or in the house. During our year and a half in Kemah, only one child visited us, a little boy whose mother had asked if he could come over. The boy clearly hated the arrangement. He walked in our front door and made a beeline for the bathroom, which he entered and locked. He refused to open the door until his mother came to pick him up. He was my only "playmate" in Kemah.

So for three years, from the ages of four to nearly seven, when I should have been skipping rope and laughing hysterically with kids my own age, I spent the vast majority of my time alone. My isolation from outsiders was impenetrable.

Fortunately, in those long lonely days, Laura was around, and she hung out with me after she finished her housework. Laura was kind, but not very playful. We enjoyed solitaire and Old Maid, but we didn't run around or play ball. I never learned to have fun playing kids' games, and ever since, having fun has been elusive.

Still, Mom kept more and more outsiders away. During our initial months in Genoa, Dad invited several Shell Oil families with children to our house. But Mom didn't like them, because they didn't talk tennis, and they weren't at the top of the corporate ladder. So she promulgated what I call the "No Shell Visitors" rule. From 1949 until Dad retired from Shell in 1982, Shell people weren't allowed in our home, and Mom never went to dinner with any of Dad's co-workers. With one notable exception. In the mid-1970s, she met and adored the most recent ex-President of Shell USA, an Englishman who lived with his wife in Switzerland and visited Houston occasionally. Throughout Mom's life, she was drawn to charming and powerful men and women who, like her father, had achieved extraordinary success.

Many isolated families can at least turn to their relatives, but not ours. When I was three and we were still living in Southern California, we occasionally visited Dad's parents, Grandpa Nathan and Grandma Lottie. But that stopped when we moved to Texas. For the next 14 years, I never saw either of them, or any other relative on Dad's side of the family. Dad never explained why his relatives were ostracized. Late in life, he admitted that after he'd met privileged people through tennis, he became ashamed of his parents' poverty and lack of sophistication. Although Mom never spoke about Dad's parents, it's clear she felt nothing in common with them, because they weren't rich or highly successful, and they didn't talk tennis.

On Mom's side of the family, the only relative we ever saw was CK, my grandmother. She visited us in Texas just a few times, but once we moved to New York, she came to dinner every few weeks. Those visits were rarely pleasant. She wasn't a warm person, so we didn't get hugs and kisses, but she always handed us a present, usually a small bag of honey candies from the health food store. Then she'd disappear into Mom's room, where Mom would scream at her viciously— so loudly that we could hear her throughout the apartment—until CK loosened her purse strings and agreed to increase her payments for World Tennis, Laura, Mom's Cadillacs, and the family's vacations.

CK wasn't the only person Mom raged at. She also unleashed her fury at Laura, Dad, and me. I was Mom's favorite target, and her onslaughts felt like a storm of pain slamming into me and shaking me to the core. The power of her anger was bad enough, but her unpredictability made it worse. One day, she'd barely raise an eyebrow if I spilled a few drops of coffee. Another day, she might go berserk over the same mistake. That capriciousness left me constantly in fear.

I was also shaken when I heard Mom attacking the others. Those outbursts taught me a lesson that stuck with me throughout my life, that at any moment, someone might erupt.

And I had no recourse. No one, not even Dad, was allowed to stand up to Mom, and I was forbidden to defend myself or contradict her. And throughout her life, I was never allowed to display any anger towards her, or even annoyance.

As a result, for most of my life, I remained petrified of making an error, fearing it would trigger someone's anger. I tried so hard to be perfect, but when I inevitably made even the smallest mistake, I would rapidly spit out "I'm sorry! I'm sorry!" as a talisman against the potential impending doom, although that never worked.

And no one in the family, except Carrie, escaped Mom's wrath. Carrie was probably exempted due to a cornerstone of Mom's personal mythology. She'd frequently declare, "Carrie is just like me, and Julie M is just like her father." That put Carrie on the winning team, and Mom protected the child whom she saw as her mirror image. I never objected to that pronouncement. True, Dad and I were relegated to the losing team, but I was paired with my beloved father, and we were the good guys.

Besides her anger, Mom had another, less obvious tactic for asserting her dominance: the acid edge of her humor, which demeaned the victim. While Mom sprinkled her derision around the household, I definitely got the lion's share of her mockery. She delighted in laughing at me for crying, having short, stocky legs, a constantly stuffed up nose, bad pronunciation, the smallest vocabulary in the family, and the list went on. And when Mom wasn't around, she deputized

Carrie to humiliate me. The outcome of their repeated humiliations was that I spent most of my life feeling stupid, incapable, and forever the underdog, no matter how much I achieved.

Another of Mom's scary traits was her intense anxiety about being late. She planned her day down to the minute, and she'd often say something like "We have to leave in three minutes, at 5:53, to arrive at the restaurant by 6:02." At 5:52, her voice would rise, and her speech would quicken, and she'd become frantic, which sometimes spilled into anger. I learned never to be late, which was useful training for me, and I've never missed a flight or a tennis match.

For me, Mom's hardest trait to pin down was her silence. If I said something, and she didn't respond right away, I feared that she would either erupt or make fun of me. On the other hand, her silence sometimes had no meaning at all. Because I didn't know which way the pendulum would swing, I automatically assumed the worst.

On the other end of the spectrum, Mom drew me in by dispensing extravagant praise. If the dinner I brought her was just right, she'd say "You're the best in the whole world. You're the most wonderful, the most marvelous." Each time, I'd be thrilled, but inevitably, the positive effect of her over-the-top compliments never lasted, because they were so unreal—a part of me always knew I wasn't the best in the whole world—and they were out of proportion to the deed and unconnected to it. Still, I was addicted to that praise like a drug, and I kept wanting more, even though I knew she swung between emotional extremes, and that at any moment calamity could be lurking around the corner.

Dad was the opposite. He was spare with his praise, even understated, and I could trust him. Yet because Dad wasn't volatile, Mom believed he was clueless about emotional matters, and that she was the emotional expert in the family. Sadly, he bought into this skewed notion. If I cried in front of Dad, he'd say "Emotions are your Mom's area. Talk to her." Bad idea. He might have been emotionally reserved, but she was just as likely to dismiss my woes as to humiliate me for being upset. And he never stopped her.

Outsiders never glimpsed the extent of Mom's tyranny. To them, she'd joke: "My husband is ranked Number One in the family, I'm Number Two and the children are both Number Three." That sounded like a benign description of a traditional American family of the 1940s, 1950s, and 1960s, with the man firmly in charge. But that's not what she meant. Mom was talking about tennis rankings.

For everything else, she was unquestionably Number One, and Dad was Number Two. And even though she always acknowledged that Dad was a far superior tennis player, her intense competitiveness drove her to eclipse him in his very own tennis world—not on the courts, but off them—and he helped her do it.

*   *   *   *

At all costs, I had to be capable beyond my years and accomplish miracles. But if I made an error, I felt like a miserable failure. My only option was to try harder and harder and harder.

I became driven, and no one, not even I, knew why, because Mom's behavior at home was our family's dirty secret. Even among ourselves, speaking of her sins was forbidden. Due in part to this conspiracy of silence, I spent most of my life doubting my own experiences.

I lived in a hermetically sealed family unit, ruled by Mom. There was no one to turn to. Except her.

I lived in the Cult of Gladys.

CHAPTER 8
ZOU PUSHED ME

When my sister and I were little, our Mom often told us the Zou Pushed Me story, which goes like this:

A little girl is being bad, and runs away from her Mommy. At the top of the stairs, the Mommy tries to grab her, but the girl falls down the stairs.

The Mommy says "I'm so sorry. Are you OK?"

The girl screws up her face and says "Zou pushed me."

"Where are you hurt?"

With a tiny, gnarled voice, the girl says: "Zou pushed me."

Her Mommy rushes her to the doctor.

In the car the Mommy says "I'm sorry."

"Zou pushed me."

The doctor asks what happened. Almost whispering, the girl says "I faw down."

The doctor gives her a band aid and a lollipop. The Mommy and the girl go home. In the car her Mommy asks "Do you feel better?"

The girl looks straight at her Mommy and says "Zou pushed me."

That's the end of the story, and the point at which our Mom always laughed. She never explained the moral of the story. She expected us to figure it out on our own.

This is the moral I gleaned from the Zou Pushed Me story: "Never tell on Mommy. The outside world must not know."

CHAPTER 9
THE BIRTH OF WORLD TENNIS

Mom began her first tennis publication in 1950, when she was 27 years old and a journalism neophyte, having never worked for a magazine before starting her very own. At the time, no one could possibly have predicted that within a few years she'd create a magazine called *World Tennis*, which, by the end of the decade, would become the largest and most influential tennis magazine in the world.

Her first attempt at journalism was amateurish. Soon after our family arrived in Texas in 1949, Mom and Dad joined the *Houston Tennis Association*, he as president, and she as a volunteer, where she applied her colossal energy to raising money for juniors, teaching clinics, running competitions, and forming alliances with retail stores during "tennis week." By January 1950, the association had so much action that she started a mailer to communicate with the members. In her small, cramped handwriting, she scribbled two pages of information, mimeographed them, and sent them out as *The Houston Tennis Association Bulletin*.

Her next efforts were far more professional. She changed the publication's name to the *Houston Tennis News*, expanded it to four pages, had it printed on glossy paper, and loaded it with articles displaying her love of tennis, her camaraderie with other players, and her special connection with all tennis enthusiasts. But Mom wasn't contemplating a career in journalism. Playing tennis remained her main occupation, and her magazines were a mere sideline.

In early 1951, her horizons expanded, when she met the flamboyant and fabulously wealthy Glenn McCarthy, who had made his money as an oil wildcatter and had built the Shamrock Hotel, the largest in Houston. He had just added a few tennis courts and wanted to lure tennis-playing guests, so Mom proposed a concept worthy of his own outsized vision of life, a competition styled on the Davis Cup (the world team championship for men), pitting Mexican players against Texans, headlined by Dad, to be called the McCarthy Cup. McCarthy fell for the idea, agreed to fund it, and donated a giant trophy. Mom made all the arrangements, and everything was going smoothly until four days before the event was due to begin, when the Mexican association announced that its players would not be permitted to compete in Houston. Upon receiving such devastating news, many a promoter would have canceled the event. Not Mom. No Mexicans? No problem. She called some tennis buddies, with whom she'd shared drinks and dinner, and within 24 hours they jumped on airplanes to save her event. The McCarthy Cup became Texas vs. the United States, which was represented by Gardnar Mulloy, Bill Talbert, Frank Shields, and Sidney Woods, all great players in their 30s and 40s who, except for Mulloy, were past their prime. I can only imagine how much appearance fees McCarthy had to shell out. No matter; the fans had a great show.

Mom produced a slick, 16-page program for the McCarthy Cup, and filled it with page after page of ads that she'd sold. Before the Mexicans pulled out, her program included photos and bios of both teams. Once they withdrew, she removed everything about the Mexican players, leaving the program's reading material a bit thin. Even that didn't matter. Somehow, at age 28, she pulled off one miracle after another, and she gained a Texas-sized success.

The McCarthy Cup was Mom's very first tennis promotion, and in many ways it was the precursor of all that followed. In each one, she drew on the people she had met while playing and writing about tennis, and devised brilliant and often unique ideas to make her events succeed.

After Mom produced the McCarthy Cup program, the journalism bug bit her hard, and she increased her magazine to 16 pages, and began calling it *the roundup*, "The Magazine of Texas Tennis," although it wasn't just about Texas tennis. To fill all those pages, she included a variety of features, such as "Tennis Tidbits," a gossip column about tennis people, and each month she wrote a tennis-based fiction, whose protagonists had names similar to tennis greats, such as "Gardnar Mooloo" instead of Gardnar Mulloy, and "Vector Sexless" (she always loved jokes about sex) instead of Victor Seixas. She also recruited a crew of circuit players to write about tournaments around the world, including the four majors—Australia, France, Wimbledon, and the U.S.—and even tiny events sprinkled here and there, in places like Baden Baden, Cairo, and San Pellegrino. Her little Texas magazine was becoming international in flavor.

The *Houston Tennis News* had been small enough that Mom could publish it and play tournaments without breaking a sweat. But she needed all of her vast energy to produce *the roundup* while simultaneously competing on the circuit. She'd travel to three tournaments in a row, rush home to work furiously day and night for a week to write, edit, and assemble the magazine, and then return to the tour. That left almost no time for anything else, including the family. Given a free moment, she chose tennis over children. In the March 1952 issue of *the roundup*, she wrote: "Julius Heldman is off on another [business] trip around the country and won't see Texas for another month. While he's away, his missus will make hay by playing the clay [court tournaments in the Midwest and South]." In many ways, she lived as if she didn't have children, which was made possible by Laura, who took care of Carrie and me.

The roundup lasted just over two years, falling prey to a casual conversation Mom had with Gardnar Mulloy, the incredibly handsome Floridian, who was 38 in 1952, and ranked Number One in the U.S. in singles. Gar was in many ways unlike other players, in that he had a law degree, reportedly refused to accept expenses at tournaments, carefully watched his diet, and didn't drink or smoke, all unusual for a top-flight player. He also wrote articles for *the roundup*, often ranting against the United States Lawn Tennis Association (the "USLTA"), the sometimes bumbling and often bombastic amateur association.

Gar and Mom were both independent thinkers, and one day they were discussing the terrible state of U.S. tennis magazines since the demise of *American Lawn Tennis*, which closed in 1951 after a 44-year run. Its replacement, *The Racquet*, had anemic tennis coverage, because the magazine's focus was split between tennis, badminton, and squash. Mom and Gar got to talking about producing a really good tennis magazine. She said she'd do the work if Gar would deliver advertisers and write an article every month. When he agreed, Mom was sold. She dropped *the roundup* and began her new magazine, which she called *World Tennis*, to demonstrate the range of the coverage she intended to carry.

Mom launched *World Tennis* in June 1953, when she'd just turned 31. Its first edition was 36 pages, more than double the size of *the roundup*, and much broader in scope than its predecessors. It's astonishing that a young woman had the courage to start such a large venture in the male-dominated world of the early 1950s. Years later, Mom would snicker when she told people that women in the 1950s would often say "Isn't it wonderful that your husband lets you work." Sure, Dad always supported her, but that was part of their deal. From their earliest days together, he understood that she was indomitable, and that she'd need to work on her very own projects.

Mom was convinced she could pull off *World Tennis*, but she was no fool. She knew that her own name meant very little, but Gar's name gave the magazine legitimacy, because of his Number-One ranking, and also just because he was a man. So from the start, she exaggerated his involvement in the magazine, placing his name front and center. The last issue of *the roundup* featured a letter from Gar, in large type, enclosed in a half-page black box, announcing the coming of *World Tennis*, which Mom and Gar curiously called a "non-profit magazine, written by and for the players." The "non-profit" designation was never to be seen again, but the motto "by and for the players" would last for years, as the magazine depended on the contributions of players at all levels.

World Tennis's first home was our family's apartment in Houston, where we had moved from Kemah while Dad waited for yet another a transfer to come through, this one to Shell's headquarters in New York City. Mom had planned to put Maureen Connolly ("Little Mo") on her first cover, because the 18-year-old American wunderkind was already halfway to winning the Grand Slam—winning all four majors in the same year. But just as the magazine was going to press, Mom learned of the death of Bill Tilden, the 1920s tennis superstar. Ever nimble, she scrapped the Little Mo photo and replaced it with a shot of the great Big Bill.

From the start, *World Tennis*, like its predecessor, *the roundup*, was idiosyncratic. Perhaps because Mom had no journalistic training, her head wasn't cluttered with any settled notions of how a magazine should look and what it should contain. And the indomitable Gladys Heldman rarely asked for advice. So she barreled full speed ahead, formulating her own unique creation.

Other tennis publications stuck to writing about tournaments, tennis politics, and instruction. Mom did that and so much more. From the beginning, she maintained a voluminous, worldwide correspondence, which grew exponentially along with the magazine and paid multiple dividends. She printed photos she received from far and wide, and her "Letters to the Editor" column was chock full of vigorous debates about issues in the tennis world. In the 1950s and 1960s, there was virtually no tennis on TV, and the Internet wouldn't arrive for decades, which meant that tennis results were nearly impossible to come by. So Mom made *World Tennis* the journal of record. She obtained results from three main sources: the tournaments themselves, her trusty worldwide correspondents, and the 10 daily newspapers delivered to our family's doorstep every day, mostly from around the U.S., but also from London, Paris, and Melbourne. It was Dad's job to scour them for results and any other juicy tidbits he might find, and then Mom typed them up and sent them to the printer, for placement in the back of the magazine, in the "Results" section, which she called the "six point," for its small type. For women, she included fashion photo spreads. For the older folks, she had a "25 Years Ago" column. And for general interest, there were often lengthy interviews of top players by "The WT Reporter" (Mom).

Starting with *the roundup* and then in *World Tennis's* earliest days, Mom let her imagination fly, making up crossword puzzles and word puzzles with tennis themes. Her fiction in *World Tennis* became even wackier than before, such as "Murgatroyd Hoskins: Mr. Tennis," about a man who gave up his career with a city garbage department to become an umpire.

Readers had always loved Mom's "Tennis Tidbits" column, so in in *World Tennis* she lengthened the column and made it more international, calling it "Around the World." It was packed with intimate details of the tennis world, and many avid readers turned to it first, before scouring the remainder of the magazine cover to cover. Part of its charm was its randomness. Any given paragraph might announce a new tennis center in Morocco, a top player's temper tantrum in Australia, and the transgressions of a tennis association. Where else could a reader discover that "Japan's Prince Akihito was pictured in the English newspapers hitting a two-handed forehand volley"? Where else were the private lives of players laid so bare? Around the World announced:

> *Pregnancies*: "England's Jean Walker-Smith infanticipating" [a word lifted from gossip columns];"
>
> *Celebrity Watching*: "[American heiress and socialite] Barbara Hutton was at the Monte Carlo tournament, looking luscious in mink;"
>
> *Trivia*: "The Wimbledon lockers are built in tiers of four. Hugh Stewart, who is 6' 4", was assigned a bottom one, while Felicissimo Ampon, who is 5' 1", was given one on top and could barely reach it;"
>
> *Rumors of Romance*: "Anita Kanter has been receiving long distance calls from Indianapolis;" and even
>
> *Weight Loss*: "Joan Merciadas has gone on a diet and has lost five pounds so far."

During *World Tennis's* first few issues, Gar kept up his rants against the USLTA, but although the masthead declared that the magazine was "Published and Edited by Gladys M. Heldman and Gardnar Mulloy," most of his supposed involvement was a pretense. He never tried his hand at editing and did very little publishing indeed. Worse, he failed to deliver the ads he'd promised, so Mom had to do that too. In the beginning, the magazine had so few ads that it was a veritable siphon for money, and each month Mom had to turn to CK to make up the deficit. It took about a decade for *World Tennis* to turn a profit, which it eventually did, with a vengeance.

During the first few months of *World Tennis*, *The Racquet* magazine approached Mom with a proposition. It was planning to cease publication and offered to sell Mom and Gar its subscription list for the astronomical price of $10,000. Mom wasn't keen, but Gar insisted. Once again, she turned to CK, who underwrote the purchase, giving *World Tennis* a monopoly of U.S. tennis magazines. But *The Racquet's* exorbitant subscription list turned out to be a dud, because *The Racquet* didn't have many more subscribers than *World Tennis*, and many of them were duplicates. Mom's reaction? She had a drink, kept her chin up, and continued to work.

However, that purchase marked the death knell of Mom's partnership with Gar, although she kept his name on the masthead for over a year, and he continued to write articles for the magazine for a decade.

Mom's ferocious *World Tennis* workload turned her priorities upside down. She was too busy to play tennis, too busy to have a social life, too busy to be with her family. The magazine sucked out every ounce of her energy.

Nonetheless, she remained the family's ruler, and if she lacked the time and energy to follow through on her plans, some things just didn't get done. Before our move to New York City in the summer of 1953, Mom found a smallish apartment at 200 East End Avenue, on Manhattan's tony Upper East Side, across from the mayor's mansion. But when the movers arrived in New York with all our stuff, she was too busy to deal with them, so she uncharacteristically had them dump everything in the middle of the floor, and she left it there. Instead, she moved into CK's 10-room apartment, where Mom had been raised, while CK was summering in Europe. This permitted Mom to ignore the mess at the East End Avenue apartment and concentrate on the magazine. When Dad and the rest of us moved up from Houston, we also settled into CK's place.

When CK returned home, she was shocked to find an apartment overflowing with our family, a handful of visiting tennis players, and all the workings of a magazine. CK rarely stood up to her daughter, but this time she kicked everyone out, which forced Mom to fix up the new apartment. It was way too small to accommodate *World Tennis*, so Mom found an office, a tiny, ex-candy store on East 89th Street, a few blocks from our apartment, and gave the magazine its third home in three months. She hired a secretary, but still there was so much to do that Mom worked incessantly. Visitors to her office were welcomed and handed envelopes to stuff or photos to file, and Carrie and I—ages 9 and 7— quickly learned how to complete those tasks. Because we were accurate, she praised us generously. Since then, I've never minded tackling a clerical task that others might consider drudgery, because I've carried with me her luscious praise from those early days of *World Tennis*. Carrie and I also supported *World Tennis* in other ways. At the busiest time of the month, when the magazine was going to press, we'd bring Mom's meals to her office, first dinner and then breakfast, lunch, and dinner again. Once, she got so stressed out that her stomach was killing her. Someone told her that papaya juice was a magic elixir, so she sent me halfway across town to buy some fresh papaya juice. Although I could barely see over the counter, and I wasn't sure exactly what she needed, I was able to bring home a large container of juice. I don't think it helped much. She never sent me on that errand again.

Although the candy store was cheap and close to home, its benefits were heavily outweighed by its deficits. The street was dark at night, and sometimes dangerous. Once, hooligans stood outside the *World Tennis* office screaming epithets, so Mom called the cops, yet no one came for hours, until a drunken police sergeant showed up and was abusive. Even worse were the fumes wafting upwards from the basement, where a man sold coal and fuel oil. When Mom came home from the store, she smelled awful. Ever the scientist, Dad sniffed carefully and told Mom that the nitrogen bases in liquid fuel oil would deaden her olfactory nerves. She really had to get out of there.

She was saved from her tiny hellhole in 1954, before the end of *World Tennis's* first year. Sidney Wood, a former tennis great—and McCarthy Cup participant— visited her office and was horrified. He owned a building in midtown Manhattan, where he ran a laundry business, and on the spot he offered *World Tennis* a new home. Mom readily accepted, and he rapidly sent around several laundry trucks to move the contents of the candy store into their new home. Mom's life improved immediately.

CHAPTER 10
THE TIGER, THE MANAGER

I'm five, and we're standing outside our house in Kemah, Texas. Daddy says "Let's have a race." I've never raced anyone before, but maybe it'll be fun. He chases me around our house, and I win! Then he races Carrie, and she wins too! We both laugh and scream. Mommy comes outside, and when she finds out what's happening, she says "Now it's my turn to race you." She races both of us and beats us badly. I start to cry, and she laughs at me, saying "Daddy just let you win." I hate losing. And I hate it even more when Mommy laughs at me for losing. Or for crying.

Now that I'm five and three quarters, Mommy takes me to the Kemah Elementary School to start the first grade. They won't let me in, because I have to be six before September 30, but my birthday is December 8. The school says I'll have to wait another year.

Mommy is angry. She doesn't like their rules. She says "We'll show them." Although she taught Carrie to read by the time she was three, she hasn't spent much time teaching me. Until now. She still plays tennis all the time, but at night and on rainy days she teaches me to read and write and add and subtract. I learn quickly. After I memorize the addition and subtraction tables, she says: "Now I'm going to teach you algebra. Five plus four is nine. X plus five is nine. What is X?" I enjoy getting the answers right.

I'm six and three quarters, and the school year is starting again. They have to let me in, because I'm old enough, although I'm really short. But they want me to start in the first grade, and Mommy is fighting them. She says she taught me enough to skip the first grade, so she makes them give me a test. It's really easy. I zip through the book called *See Spot Run* and all their arithmetic problems, and they let me skip the first grade.

After I'm in school for just a few months, our family moves to Houston, where I start a new school. There are lots of kids around, but even though I'm seven, I'm not used to playing with kids, and I don't know what to do, so I just watch them. Close to our apartment, there's a swimming pool, and Mommy signs us up for swimming lessons. After about a month, she enters us in a race. The day of the race, Mommy tells me I can win. "You're the best," she says. But when my race is announced over the loud speaker, there's a big surprise. "Next up is the race for children ages six and seven, across the pool, stops allowed." I never practiced that kind of race. I've only swum up and down the length of the pool. Mommy laughs because "stops allowed" is for babies. There are only three kids in the race, including me, so I know I can win. But when the race is over, the judge says I came in third place. That's wrong! I know I came in second. I opened my eyes under water and saw my hand touch before the other kid's. I cry because they cheated me.

Mommy thinks it's hilarious that I came in third out of three kids and that I cried. She says I cry too much. She tells everyone how funny I was.

In Kemah, we lived in the country, with no sidewalks. In Houston, everything's paved near our apartment. Daddy gets me a bike, and one afternoon he teaches me how to ride it. After an hour or two, he says "OK, you're ready. Go practice by yourself." Over and over, I fall off and get back on. I keep skinning my knees and elbows. Soon, I have giant scabs, which turn red and then yellow. I'm proud of my scabs. They prove that I try hard. I'm a good rider now. Daddy got me started, but I taught myself the rest.

Soon after I learn to ride my bike, we move to New York City, where we stay in CK's giant apartment in a building called the Belnord on West 86th Street. The apartment doesn't have much light. In Texas, I was outside most of the time, in the sunlight. Here, we hardly ever go out. One day I beg Mommy to let me go out to play. She says OK, but only if I first learn to count from one to 10 in both French and German. She writes the numbers and the words on a piece of paper and then leaves for lunch. When she returns, she tests me, and I get them all right, so she lets me play downstairs in the Belnord's concrete courtyard. By myself.

CK's traveling in Europe, so we have the apartment to ourselves. Mommy started *World Tennis* magazine a month before we left Houston, and she works on it day and night. Because noises upsets her, Carrie and I have to tiptoe around.

One day, we forget, and we run down the hall, which makes Mommy angry. "BE QUIET! I'M WORKING!"

Mommy needs us to be out of the apartment, so she sends us to day camp. Five days a week, a big yellow school bus picks us up at the Belnord, and during the long ride to camp, the other kids make fun of us. They all know lots of songs, and we don't, so they tell us we're stupid. I hate being called stupid. I try not to cry, and I try really hard to fit in. I learn their songs, and when Carrie and I come home, we sing and talk like the other kids. Mommy's horrified. "Where did you pick up that awful accent?" Mommy hates New York accents, because they're "low class." I don't know what that means.

At dinner Carrie says "The big kids on the bus make us repeat words we don't know, and then they laugh at us."

"Like 'shit' and 'fuck,'" I pipe in.

Mommy laughs. "It's time you learn. 'Shit' means 'BM.' 'Fuck' means making love. Do you remember I told you about how men and women make babies?"

Boy do I remember. I was just four years old. Daddy was driving our car at night when we were returning home from dinner, and Carrie and I were in the back seat in the dark. Mommy turned around and started talking, but I couldn't see her face. It was scary. She started telling us about making babies. When she got to the part about grownups being naked, I stopped listening. It was too embarrassing. She never explained that stuff again, so I don't know how babies are made.

At camp we play games that are new to us. I try very hard, but I'm small and lousy, and I always come in last. Then I cry, and the New Yorkers call me a sissy.

One night at dinner Carrie and I beg to quit camp. Mommy slaps us down fast. "You have to do something! You'll have to stay at the camp until the end of summer."

Camp's finally over, and CK has returned from Europe and taken her apartment back. We move into our own place on East End Avenue between 89th and 90th Streets.

Right after we move, the U.S. Nationals at Forest Hills begins, and Carrie and I are working in the *World Tennis* booth under the Stadium. Carrie's nine, and I'm seven. Usually it's quiet around the booth, but when a Stadium match finishes, and people rush out of the stands, I scream as loud as I can "*World Tennis*, get your *World Tennis*, 25 cents a copy!". The men next to us yell "Hot franks, cold drinks, cold beer and soda." I buy a Nestlé chocolate bar from them and take a bite. Something's weird. I look at the rest of the chocolate bar. There's half a worm wiggling in it. I'll never eat chocolate again.

In the *World Tennis* booth, we sell magazines and tennis books. Mostly we're in the booth alone. Mommy says "Because you're adorable, people will buy from you. And you don't need any help from adults. You're smarter than most grownups." I'm almost always great at making change, but the only time I make a mistake is when Mommy comes by. A man buys a book for $3.50. He hands me $5, and I give him change of $2.50. Mommy points out my error and laughs at me. "I'm sorry, I'm sorry," I say. Again and again she laughs and tells people about my mistake. Carrie never makes mistakes like that. I hate being stupid.

More than anything I want a bike, so that I can ride it just like I did in Houston. I tell Mommy I'll use the money I earn at the *World Tennis* booth to buy a bicycle.

"It's a waste of money," Mommy says. "You'll grow tired of it right away." She won't help me, but Daddy takes me to FAO Schwarz, the Fifth Avenue toy store, and I use my own money to buy a bike.

Across the street from our apartment, there's a park surrounding the mayor's mansion, with lots of grass and sidewalks, but it does me no good. Every few yards there are signs that say: "No skating. No bicycle riding. No ball games." It might as well say "No Children." Instead, I ride my bike proudly around the streets near our apartment until the snow comes. Mommy won't let me keep my bike in the apartment, so I store it in the bike room in the basement of our apartment building. In the spring I go to pick it up, but it's just a skeleton. Someone stole the seat, the chain, the tires, and the bell. Mommy laughs and says "I told you so."

The first time it snows, Carrie and I see the hillside covered with kids who are illegally sledding. Daddy buys us sleds, and the two of us rush across the street to the hill, before the snow melts. But before we get to slide down the hill, two giant boys grab the sleds out of our hands. At first we stand still, shocked. Then we return to the apartment, empty handed. We'd love to go sledding again, but it's no use. We need an adult to protect us, but no one will do it. That's the end of our sledding.

I hate New York.

Mommy says we can't stay in the city next summer. But at least she won't send us back to the old camp. She says we'll go to a tennis camp run by Mrs. Jean Hoxie in Hamtramck, Michigan, a town surrounded by Detroit. She's taught local kids for years, with lots of success. At Forest Hills, she told Mommy that she wanted to start the very first tennis camp in the United States, and they made a plan. Mrs. Hoxie will rent a house in Detroit, where out-of-town campers will stay. *World Tennis* will give the camp free advertising, and in return, Carrie and I will attend the camp all summer for free.

But I don't want to go there, because I don't like tennis. In Texas, Mommy played tennis all day, every day, and Daddy joined her on the weekends. A few times, they took Carrie and me to the tennis courts so that we could watch. Watching is boring. So we climbed behind the stands and fought until the players yelled at us to stop making noise. Being quiet is boring.

In Texas, Carrie took a few tennis lessons, but I've only played maybe once in my whole life. Now that we're in New York, Mommy says "Pack your bags. Your father and I are going to give you a tennis lesson." I've never packed my bag before, and Mommy doesn't help me, so I forget my shirt. Mommy laughs at me for being stupid. I try to choke back tears. The pro shop doesn't have children's shirts, so Mommy buys me a small men's shirt. It goes down past my knees. She laughs because I look funny. I'm not funny! Mommy and Daddy play with us for a few minutes, but I keep swinging and missing. This isn't fun.

But Mommy says we have to go to tennis camp.

It's June 1954 and Carrie and I are on a plane to Detroit. Carrie tells the stewardess "Sometimes I throw up on an airplane." The stewardess is nice. She shows us how to push the button to call her and where to find the vomit bag.

"How old are you little girls?" the stewardess asks.

"Carrie's nine and I'm eight." I talk for both of us. Carrie has never liked to talk much. She prefers to read.

"You should be traveling with an adult."

"We're OK. We've flown without Mommy and Daddy before."

Mommy says Carrie and I flew alone from Houston to New York when Carrie was four and I was three. Mommy was proud that we didn't need anyone to take care of us on the airplane. Once the plane landed in New York, the stewardess opened the plane's door and unfolded the steps. Then she took Carrie's hand and led her down the steps. CK was waiting at the bottom.

"Where's the other little girl?" CK asked.

Carrie said, "She wet the seat and she won't budge." Mommy laughs every time she tells the story. She tells it a lot. I'm ashamed that I had an accident, but I was only three, and no one took care of me.

On the plane to tennis camp, Carrie reads her book and refuses to play cards with me. "Just play solitaire," she says. So I tickle her and she gets mad. The plane bounces a lot and Carrie throws up twice and misses the bag a little. We don't tell the stewardess. We don't want her to be angry.

This time I don't wet the seat.

After we land in Detroit, the stewardess walks us both down the stairs. They're steep and they wiggle. Mrs. Hoxie meets us at the bottom. She has bright red lipstick, and she gives slobbery kisses. Then she rubs the lipstick marks on our cheeks. Yuck! Carrie says Mrs. Hoxie smells weird, but I can't smell her. Mommy always makes fun of my lousy sense of smell. She says because my nose is always stuffed, I call her "Mobby," and then she laughs. It's not funny. I can't help it. Once, Mommy took me to a doctor in Texas to see if I had allergies. He poked me with lots of needles, and I got a red mark on every spot. He said that meant I was allergic to everything. Mommy said that was impossible, so she decided that I should never go to an allergy doctor again. I still have a stuffed-up nose, and I get sick all the time.

Mrs. Hoxie drives us to her apartment in her big station wagon. We meet her husband, Mr. Jerry Hoxie. He's in charge of the kids at Hamtramck Park. Mrs. Hoxie acts like she's the boss, but he says she doesn't come to the park much.

Mr. Hoxie is big and strong, and he has short white hair that sticks straight up. I tell him he has weird hair, and he laughs. I feel like I'm going to cry. I don't like people laughing at me. But he's just being nice. He explains that it's called a brush cut, and he puts stuff in his hair to make it stand up straight. He lets me touch it.

I wake up in the night wheezing. I don't mean to be sick. My asthma disturbs Mommy, and she hates to be disturbed. I'm not supposed to wake her up. I don't know if I'm allowed to wake up Mr. or Mrs. Hoxie. So I stay in my room.

In the morning, we dress in our white tennis clothes. Mr. Hoxie shakes his head slowly. "White clothes are for tournaments. We don't wear white clothes at the park, and your shoes are too thin. You'll need new clothes and Converse shoes."

We leave for breakfast and pick up a big guy named Gerry Dubie. He has very short hair. It's called a crew cut. I've never met anybody with a crew cut. Mr. Hoxie says Dubie's a really good tennis player, and he works at Hamtramck Park. Mr. Hoxie takes us to Greenfield's, a very, very big cafeteria in downtown Detroit.

We've never been in a cafeteria before. We get in line. Mr. Hoxie orders eggs, and so do I. And I get cereal and orange juice, but I can't eat it all.

"Your eyes are too big for your stomach," he says.

"My eyes aren't that big." Mr. Hoxie says we have to finish all our food. Mommy never makes us eat everything on the plate.

He says "Eat or be eaten. It's the law of the jungle." Dubie finishes his food and ours too.

"Now we go to Hamtramck Park," Mr. Hoxie says.

"Is it far away?" I ask.

"It's about half an hour, but you won't notice it if you listen to the radio." He turns it on, and it plays a song called "Sh-Boom." We like it. When Mommy's in the car, the radio has to be turned off. She says it gets on her nerves.

Hamtramck Park is much smaller than Forest Hills, but it still looks big to me. And it smells so bad that even I can smell it. Mr. Hoxie says that's because it's Wednesday, when the dog pound burns the animals.

Mommy bought us new rackets, but Mr. Hoxie doesn't like them. "Those rackets aren't heavy enough and the handles are too small. Bigger rackets help you hit harder." He gives us each a big Wilson wood racket named after Jack Kramer, who's a famous tennis star. Mr. Hoxie walks us down to the wall and introduces us to a tall woman with short, black hair. Her name is June Stack. "She'll teach you how to play."

Lots of kids are waiting at the wall in four lines—two in front and two in back. June's teaching the forehand line, where everyone starts. Some kids hit very hard, again and again, and move to the next section of the wall. Some hit the ball too high, and it goes over the top of the wall and into the empty ice skating rink. To retrieve their balls, they have to go all the way along the fence to the gate, and then into the rink. Most of the kids miss and go straight to the end of the line. It takes forever to reach the front of the line. When it's my turn, I don't know what to do. I want to do well so June won't laugh at me.

June shows me how to grip the racket. "Hold out your hand like you want to shake hands, and put the palm of your hand against the side of the grip. Then wrap your fingers around it."

The grip's too big. "My hand won't go around it."

"That's OK, you'll grow."

Next she teaches us how to swing. "Watch what the good kids do. Open the door, and then shut the door. That's all you'll need to know." She shows us how.

She hands me a ball. It's gray and bald. "Mommy and Daddy always play with white, fuzzy balls," I say.

"These are wall balls. They're old and dead, and they're easier to use against the wall than live ones because they don't bounce back too fast."

I try to hit the ball in the air. June says no, I have to bounce it first. I do that, but I swing and miss. She bounces it for me. I still miss. She lets me try three more times. I keep missing. She pats my head and sends me to the back of the line. I go through the line many, many times. June says you can't play on the tennis courts until you pass the test on forehands, then backhands, then volleys, then dropshots. On each test you have to hit the ball 20 times in a row above the line, with only one bounce. I can't do it once, but I try so hard that I want to burst. June lets me stand closer to the wall. On about the 20 millionth try I finally hit the ball over the line!

June says "Atta girl, Tiger. Now the trick is hitting two or three in a row." I keep trying, because I want June to like me, and I want to play on the courts. The line gets shorter because kids either quit or they graduate to the courts. Then June stops teaching at the wall.

She walks us to the courts. There are eight courts side-by-side, all full, with kids and grownups waiting to play. It's very noisy and no one tells you to shut up. Mr. Hoxie is in charge of the courts. He tells you who you're going to play, and he sends you to a court when it's free.

It's boring to watch others play, so Mr. Hoxie teaches us how to bounce the ball using the strings of the racket. "That's a good way to learn. Once you can do that for 20 bounces in a row, I'll teach you how to bounce the ball upward on the strings."

For lunch, Mr. Hoxie takes us to the restaurant across the street from the park called Hazen's, although the kids call it the "The Greasy Spoon." There's a machine at each table and on the counter. It's called a juke box. I've never seen one before. An old man at the counter puts in a nickel, and the music sounds really different.

"It's a polka," Mr. Hoxie says. "Polish people like polkas. Most people in Hamtramck are Polish or Ukrainian."

I order a hamburger. I try really hard to finish it, but I can't, so Mr. Hoxie finishes it for me. After lunch, June takes us to her house next to Hamtramck Park. She introduces us to her Busha, which means grandmother in Polish. She says Busha's last name was Stackowski, but her family changed it to Stack when they came to this country. Busha sends Carrie and me to bed for a nap.

"I'm nine," Carrie says. "I don't need a nap."

"You try go sleep," Busha says. She has an accent that's hard to understand. I fall asleep right away, and when Busha wakes me up, Carrie's awake. I don't know if she slept. Busha gives us juice and cookies. Mommy has never done that.

While Mr. Hoxie's driving us to Greenfield's for dinner, he pops something in his mouth.

"What's that?" I ask

"It's medicine for asthma."

"I have asthma too."

"Do you take medicine for your asthma?"

"No. I've never taken medicine for asthma. Mommy says it doesn't help."

In Houston, Mommy told me that her doubles partner, who's a doctor, offered to take my tonsils out for free. He said that would make my asthma better. But I had the operation, and my asthma didn't improve.

Every day we go to Greenfields for breakfast, then to the park. Carrie and I love to listen to the radio, and we learn the songs, especially the commercials. Everyone likes to hear us sing the Ajax commercial. I like the part where they sing "You'll stop paying the elbow tax when you start cleaning with Ajax. So use Ajax, boom boom, the foaming cleanser, boom boom boom boom boom boom. Floats the dirt right down the drain, boom boom boom boom boom boom boom." You have to get the "boom booms" just right.

We play against the wall every day. I work hard to hold up the head of the racket and swing just right, so that I hit the ball. After a few days at the wall, my palm is bright red all over and sore, but I don't tell June, because I don't want to bother her. But she sees it and sends me to Mr. Hoxie.

"Whoa, Tiger, those are some big blisters. Let's fix you up." He makes me hold my hand flat, and he slaps two band aids across my palm. Then he sends me back to the wall. My hand still hurts, but not enough to make me quit. I'm still lousy at the wall. I hate being lousy. I bet everyone makes fun of me behind my back. I have to get better so they won't laugh at me.

I've been trying for two weeks, and finally I hit 20 forehands in a row over the line, all with one bounce. June lets me graduate to the courts to play sets even though I don't know how to hit a backhand. Keeping score is confusing, but I learn. I'm the worst player on the courts. I try with all my might to get better.

Mr. Hoxie mostly has me play little kids. Sometimes he lets me play bigger kids, but they beat me badly. He just pushes me harder. "Come on Tiger, fight!"

Carrie is better at tennis than I am, and she's also smarter. She's always lording it over me, and I can't stand it, but I try not to show it. I don't want her to make me feel awful.

I throw myself into every shot, and I fight hard for every point. Sometimes I cry, sometimes I scream. But I never break a racket. I heard a boy yell "shit" when he missed a shot, but he didn't get in trouble. I saw the same kid throw his wood racket onto the ground, where it broke. Mr. Hoxie got really mad. "Rackets cost money," he said. "You'll have to earn money to buy yourself a new racket." He loans the kid one of the steel rackets from the park. They're lousy rackets, but they're unbreakable. They have steel strings and when you hit the ball, the racket vibrates all the way up your arm, and the strings make a dull, buzzing sound.

Wood rackets have either nylon or gut strings. Some people call gut strings "cat gut," but that's not correct. They're actually made from cow intestines. Mr. Hoxie says gut strings are expensive and a waste of money, because they don't last as long as nylon. Everyone in Hamtramck uses nylon strings.

One day, when there's a giant thunder storm, we beg Mr. H to let us play tennis in the rain, even though moisture ruins wood rackets and all kinds of strings, even nylon. But steel rackets are perfect for the rain, so he hands them out to everyone. He also gives us wall balls. When they hit a puddle, they squirt all over the place. I love getting splashed. We take off our shoes and giggle and get soaked. It's wonderful to run around and have fun, although it rarely happens.

I'm going to play in my first tournament! Mr. Hoxie says the park is holding a tournament for novices, and kids will come from all over Detroit. He enters Carrie and me in the 13-and-unders. I'm sure I'll win the whole thing, even though I'm just eight. Each match gets a can of new balls. When Mr. Hoxie opens the can, it makes a big "pfft" sound and even I can tell that it smells funny. New balls are nice and fuzzy, and they don't fly off my racket as fast as old ones that are bald and gray. But everything flies faster than wall balls.

In the first round I play a girl who is 10. I have to beat her. I run as fast as I can, but I can't reach a lot of her shots. She hits a ball that I thought was going out, but it lands on the line. I yell "Out."

"You're cheating," she says.

"No I'm not! It was out." I know it was in, but I don't want to admit that I cheated. I beat her, but I'm ashamed, and I hate being ashamed. And I don't want to get caught. So I promise myself that I'll never cheat again. In the next round, I lose to a much bigger girl. I hate losing.

I want to win so badly. When I win, Mr. Hoxie and June are proud of their very own Tiger, and no one laughs at me. Sometimes people even congratulate me.

Most of the Hoxie kids live in Hamtramck all year round. Many have names like Joyce Pniewski and Ray Senkowski and Phyllis Saganski. A few Hoxie kids aren't Polish. There's a good player at the park named Gwen who's Colored. Mr. and Mrs. Hoxie treat her the same as everyone else. They're rough on everyone. They just care about winning. The older kids go to Hamtramck High School, where Mr. and Mrs. Hoxie teach. Members of the high school team are called the Hamtramck Hot Shots, but everyone calls them the Hoxie Hot Shots. They have the best high school tennis team in Michigan. The Hoxies started the tennis program so that Hamtramck kids could earn tennis scholarships to college. That's why the Hoxies push the kids to practice hard and win matches.

Mr. Hoxie says: "Other players are afraid to play against Hoxie kids, because we're tough. Hoxie kids don't play for fun. Tennis isn't supposed to be fun. It's about winning."

Mr. Hoxie fills the station wagon with kids, and we go to Kalamazoo to play the Michigan State Closed. All the seats are full, so he tells me to sit on the floor below the dashboard, in front of the passenger seat. He doesn't stop when I tell him I have to go to the bathroom. So I wet my pants, and I tie a sweater around me to hide the spreading stain. He enters Carrie and me in youngest age group, the 13-and-under. The tournament is just for kids from Michigan. Carrie and I aren't from Michigan, but Mr. Hoxie says we are. In the first round I play a girl who's 13. She beats me 6-0, 6-0. Her name is Nancy Foote. I'll never forget her name. Ever. Ever. Ever. I go back to my room in the dorm where all the Hoxie kids are staying. I cry a little.

I see Joyce Pniewski, whose nickname is "Chicken Bones," crying in one of the rooms. She says she lost to a girl in the 18-and-under whom she should have beaten, and she's worried. "Mr. Hoxie always says 'You don't win, you don't eat.' I'm scared he won't let me eat." I tell her I lost too. She says she's sorry.

In Hamtramck we're allowed to go to the corner store. It has candy, popsicles, soda, Bazooka bubble gum, and chocolate. I don't eat chocolate. Not since I ate the worm at Forest Hills. The store also has comic books, which I love, especially Superman. He rescues people who are in trouble, and I want to do that. Mommy and Daddy give us money, but Carrie always loses hers or runs out. I start carrying all the money for both of us. When Mr. Hoxie sees me give Carrie the money for a soda, he starts calling me the Manager.

Carrie and I write home a few times each summer, and sometimes we're allowed to make a long distance collect call home. Daddy comes to visit us once during the summer. Mommy doesn't come. "I'm too busy," she says, "but I still love you."

Daddy's a great tennis player. Mr. Hoxie asks him to play Dubie, who's really good, but Daddy beats him 6-1. Afterwards, Daddy comes with us to Greenfields.

"You have to eat everything on your plate," I tell him. So he does.

After 10 weeks in Hamtramck, Carrie and I go home. We want to show Mommy that we're good players.

"I'm proud of you," she says. "Let's see how good you are." Mommy plays each of us a set. Neither of us wins a single point against her. "And you thought you were good," she says, and she laughs.

CHAPTER 11
GETTING TO BROOKLYN

Last summer in Hamtramck it was easy to play tennis all day, every day, either against the wall or on the courts—except when we ate lunch or went to the candy store. We never had to wait long for a court.

But in New York City, getting a court for practice is a big problem. Once the weather turns cold, we have to play indoors, and New York has very few indoor courts. The indoor club that's closest to our apartment is the Seventh Regiment Armory, on Park Avenue between 66th and 67th Streets, where the U.S. National Indoors is held. I played there once. Its courts are made of polished wood, and they're way too fast for me. I can't get my racket back in time. And its lights are so dim that during the National Indoors a newspaper measured them at seven watts. And the club makes it almost impossible for children to play. We're banned after 4 PM on weekdays and after 9 AM on weekends. It's obviously not for us. But there's hardly anywhere else.

Mommy and Daddy join the Heights Casino club in Brooklyn Heights. It has two courts with high ceilings stacked on top of each other, so if you're scheduled for the upper court, you have to climb up four flights of stairs. Going up, I practice being light on my feet, barely touching the stairs with my toes. Coming down, if I'm alone, I fling myself down the banisters, my legs flying high. The courts are canvas on wood, so they're not too fast, and they have bright lights. But it's still hard to get much court time there, because you can only reserve a court for one hour a day, and you have to call the previous day at exactly 10 AM, when I'm in school. Mommy or Daddy have to phone for us.

During the week, Carrie and I—she's 10 and I'm nine—take the subway after school to Brooklyn, loaded down with books, tennis clothes, and rackets. Our school is near the IRT 86th Street subway stop, where we take the express train, which is wonderfully fast. It barrels past the local stations and arrives at the Borough Hall exit in Brooklyn in under a half hour. Riding the subway takes practice. The cars sway so much that it's hard to keep your balance. Although we sometimes find seats, I usually have to stand, using one hand to hang onto a pole or a strap, and the other hand to hold my rackets tight. I place my bag between my feet so no one will steal it. The metal wheels screech so loudly that it's impossible to talk, so I just stare at the subway map or read the same ads over and over. In Brooklyn, we walk three long blocks to the club, which isn't so bad, except when the snow is piled high.

Some adults worry that it's not safe for Carrie and me to take the subway alone. I tell them I'm not scared. I have my racket for protection. Ha ha. Actually, the only time I get a little afraid is during the trip home in the dark. But no one has ever attacked me.

On weekends, Mommy and Daddy often play tennis with us. When Mommy comes with us, we sail like fancy folks down the East River Drive in her bright red Cadillac convertible, with Daddy driving and Mommy doing the *New York Times* crossword puzzle in ink. Carrie and I have to be silent so that she can concentrate. Mommy's very, very sensitive, like the princess and the pea. She never takes the subway, because she can't stand noise and commotion. And she hates our upstairs neighbor, who keeps Mommy awake at night by frequently flushing the toilet and marching around in heels on bare floors. I don't know why Mommy doesn't yell at the noisy neighbor. Instead, she complains to us, but there's nothing we can do. Mommy also hates bad smells. I remember one time in rural Texas, we were driving around and got hungry, so we stopped at a small roadside restaurant. We'd barely walked in the door when Mommy said the place reeked of lard, which made her feel sick, so we turned around and walked back out. Maybe I was lucky to have a stuffed-up nose, because I couldn't smell a thing. Mommy's sensitive about lots of things. She loves movies, but she stopped going to movie theaters because someone might kick her chair. At least Daddy takes us to the movies. And he doesn't mind the subway, which he rides to work, so if Mommy's too busy to play tennis, the other Heldmans hop on the IRT.

One day, Mommy tells us we're going to play a tournament. Playing tournaments is new to me. I've only played two tournaments in my whole life, both in Michigan last summer.

Mommy says "This tournament is in Brooklyn, but not at the Heights Casino. It will be played at a big armory just like the Seventh Regiment Armory." Oh no. That place is awful. "Your first match is next week. You'll be playing Dottie Knode."

"Who is she?"

"She's my friend, and she's a good player."

"Is she my age?'

"Oh no, she's an adult. This is a women's tournament."

In the second tournament I played last summer, I lost to a girl who was 13. She was much bigger than I am, but I still hated losing to her. Now I'm supposed to play a full-grown adult. The only grownups I've played are Mommy and Daddy, and Mommy beats us without losing a point.

When Mommy drives us to the tournament, she tells me not to worry if I get nervous. "You can always take a little rest by bending down and tying your shoes." I've never done that before.

Dottie and I walk on the court, and although she's kind to me, I'm really scared. She's tall like Mommy and I'm really short. I want to win, but it's too hard. Dottie keeps hitting the ball over the net, without missing. She wins 6-0, 6-1, and I hate it. I try to hold back tears.

When I come off the court, Mommy says "Dottie was nice to you. You didn't earn that game. She gave it to you. She's been ranked Number Five in the world and you're just a little girl. And you were really, really funny. You bent down and tied your shoes twice." She tells other people about how funny I was, tying my shoes.

I'm confused. Mommy's making fun of me for doing exactly what she told me to do. Why does she laugh at me so much?

CHAPTER 12

THE MYTH OF THE NEAR-PERFECT DADDY

Starting in the spring of 1946, Mom delivered me to Laura during the day and handed me off to Dad at night. Every evening when I cried, he wrapped me in a blanket, held me close, and walked me up and down the halls of our large Berkeley home, hoping I'd finally nod off.

Beginning with those nighttime strolls, Dad and I developed a special bond, which endured throughout his life. I adored him because he loved me unequivocally, and because he was kind and paid attention to me. Unlike Mom, he knew what kind of ice cream I liked, he protected me from being burned in the kitchen, and he taught me to sleep sitting up in bed during an asthma attack. He brought home little presents, such as pencils embossed with the Shell company logo. And during the summer when I was six and Carrie was seven, we played outdoors all summer long—hardly talking—waiting eagerly each afternoon to hear Dad honk at the edge of the road to signal his arrival home. We'd run barefoot on the gravel driveway to climb on the hood of his car, and shriek gaily while he drove us to the house at a crawl.

I always loved being alone with Dad. When I was five, Dad was a manager at the Shell Refinery near Houston, where there was a strike. Until the labor dispute was settled, management took over running the plant. To avoid crossing the picket line, Dad rose before dawn, and when I heard him in the kitchen, I bolted out of bed to join him. He made us breakfast, and every day I asked him to explain the strike. No matter how clearly he spoke, the concepts were too hard for a five-year-old, but I still loved to hear him talk. And then came the moment when he had to leave, and the screen door slammed shut. I didn't cry; I simply treasured those moments in the kitchen, with just the two of us.

Years later, once we moved to New York, he still found time for us to be alone. Sometimes we took the bus and the subway to the Heights Casino, and after we played, he'd say "You're a real athlete," a high compliment from him. And I looked forward to our lunches near his office at Shell's headquarters in

Rockefeller Center. We always returned to the same Mexican restaurant, where he ordered for me, remembering exactly what I liked (Mom had no clue), and then we visited his office, where I saw how much the secretaries adored their warm and handsome boss.

For most of my life, I idealized my father, and it's been a struggle to give up the myth of the near-perfect daddy, but now I know that he failed me profoundly. He was a kind and moral man, but he surrendered his principles in deference to Mom. When she aimed her fury at him, he never said "Stop!" He'd just sit at the dinner table, or wherever the torrent was being unleashed, take the abuse, and sigh. Worse, he did nothing to protect either of his children. He was the only person who could have stood up to Mom's rules and her emotional abuse. Our lives would have been so much better had he protected us even once. But he never did.

Fighting back against his wife wasn't in Dad's nature. He was sweet and gentle, like his father Nathan. Dad's mother Lottie was both loving and tough, but sometimes their poverty would get to her. According to Dad's oldest brother Morrie, Lottie would occasionally line up her three young sons in front of Nathan and tell them their father was a failure, that he couldn't make a decent living, and that she ought to divorce him (She never did.). As usual, Nathan hid his feelings and didn't stand up for himself. These powerful images must have impressed Dad mightily: that in his family, his mother ran the show, and his father could neither defend himself nor have any recourse against his wife's abuse. In our home, Dad and Mom recreated the same scenario. It's also no surprise that all three Heldman boys grew up to marry strong women, and two of them (including Mom) ruled their families with an iron hand.

Another reason Dad didn't fight back was that, early in his life, he learned to stuff down his anger, even after suffering a huge setback, such as the one engineered by Perry T. Jones, the tyrant of Southern California tennis. At 17, Dad was already a star tennis player with a killer lefty serve and long, fluid, and accurate groundstrokes. More than anything, he wanted to win the National Juniors. But he was poor, the tournament was in Indiana, and he couldn't afford the trip. Jones controlled the purse strings for Southern California junior players, but he was anti-Semitic (and a racist, a misogynist, and a snob). Still, Dad was too good to ignore, and to Jones's credit, he directed the Southern California Tennis Association to pay $150 for half of Dad's travel back east (UCLA kicked in the rest). He was seeded number five, but won the finals in a five-set, seesaw battle over the highly favored Joe Hunt, also from Southern California. Dad had been down two sets to one, and then ran through the last two sets 6-1, 6-1, threading the needle with passing shots each time Hunt rushed the net. "I was in the zone," Dad said.

Jones wasn't pleased. He preferred the blond-haired Hunt, and the following year, Jones refused to pay Dad's way to the Juniors, effectively preventing him from defending his beloved title. It was a huge slap in Dad's face. Jones got away with impunity because Dad was poor and Jewish, and had nowhere else to turn. Yet Dad always denied being angry at Jones. He said he preferred to focus on the good things Jones had done for him. How could Dad not have been angry? The only answer is that, by the age of 17, he had learned to suppress his anger because he didn't want to make waves.

Still, on the tennis court, Dad was fiercely competitive and occasionally even cantankerous. And he could be tough if he thought someone was taking advantage of him. In 1959, when Dad was 39, he played Barry MacKay, the U.S. Number One, in the quarter-finals of the U.S. National Indoors. When the match reached 4-all in the third set, Dad hit a great passing shot to break Mackay's serve, but Mackay disputed the call. Tennis protocol required Dad to stay put until the controversy was resolved, but he was geared up to win, so he marched to the far baseline, prepared to close out the match, which he did. It was a huge upset.

Off the tennis court, Dad usually tamped down his anger, no matter how great the slight. With two strange exceptions. Several times, when he was driving our family on the highway, he became infuriated when another car cut ours off, and he retaliated by driving recklessly through traffic and returning the favor. And occasionally, when a waiter screwed up an order, he blew up. Perhaps he had buried too much anger over the years, and it had to erupt somewhere. And when it did, Mom was at a loss for what to do, so she cracked a joke and laughed nervously. I wonder what would have happened if Dad had ever exploded at Mom . . . but he never did.

Nor did Dad ever explode while working at Shell. He made his way up the corporate ladder by being smart, working hard, and knowing lots of science. He also made a practice of getting along with everyone, burying his ego, and disavowing his anger.

Julius Heldman, the 1936 National Junior Champ,
walking on court at the Los Angeles Tennis Club to
play Fred Perry, the 1936 Wimbledon champion.
Julius wasn't allowed to practice at the club or be a
member, because he was Jewish.

Dad's first job at Shell was in a small office in San Francisco, which he shared with a few others. Soon they dumped a whopper of a project on his desk. Shell had performed a great deal of expensive research, with the goal of developing a formula for "octane," to gauge the quality of gasoline. Others at Shell had previously worked on the project, but there were two kinds of data—from the laboratory and from road tests—and they didn't correlate, and no one could make sense of the mess. When Dad got started, he knew his chemistry but needed to learn statistics, so he bought statistics textbooks, and crammed until he had absorbed their contents. Then he sat in that little office and crunched numbers endlessly—often through the night—using an old-fashioned adding machine.

Eventually everything fell into place, and he realized he needed to use both sets of data to develop a solution to the problem. He devised a preliminary formula, and then tested it and refined it again and again. It worked. Shell used it internally right away. Then it was taken up—and partially modified—by the industry as a whole. And it has largely stood the test of time. Every time you pump gas in the U.S., the gas dispenser displays a formula for octane. That formula is the direct descendant of Dad's work.

Dad wrote up his discovery in a scientific paper. He had worked alone, but a slew of other names joined his on the paper, due to corporate politics. Dad didn't protest. He said he "understood the pressure everyone was under." To appease the warring factions, he allowed others to share his glory.

Dad eventually became a vice president, a wonderful accomplishment for anyone. But given that Shell at the time wasn't friendly to Jews, and Dad was only the second Jewish person in history to have reached such a lofty perch at the company, his achievement was downright astounding.

Before the Shell board of directors gave Dad the promotion, they must have known that he got along with difficult people. In fact, that may have been a significant factor in their decision. His new boss was so unpleasant that others refused to work for him, yet Dad weathered the storm. Never did he come home fuming about the daily slights he must have endured. He just put aside all of his boss's nastiness—and thrived.

Dad did the same at home, where he took whatever Mom dished out, and did whatever she asked him to do.

Throughout their lives, she turned to him for help, often with tasks normally given to a secretary, not to a PhD in physical chemistry. From the day Mom founded *World Tennis* magazine in 1953 until she sold it 19 years later, Dad was its sole proofreader and the man responsible for scouring newspapers for tennis results. Often he returned home from business trips and then toiled away deep into the night, finishing work for the magazine while gulping handfuls of aspirin to calm the headaches he got from overwork. He didn't dare stop before he was finished, because he knew Mom would be furious. And she refused to get another proofreader, because she said Dad was the best. He never protested or tried to get a replacement. Mom was in charge.

Dad also provided *World Tennis* with an invaluable, homegrown tennis expertise. He corrected errors about tennis, and he wrote photo captions that were unique and enlightening. Under his expert gaze, a straightforward action photo would become a lesson in technique and tactics at the highest level, such as: "Butch Buchholz is hitting the most difficult shot in the game—a wide lunging backhand volley of a ball which is almost past him. It takes a wrist of iron to accomplish it the first time, but all good volleyers eventually learn to hold the racket head forward by sheer wrist power."

Readers ate up Dad's captions. They also loved his longstanding monthly series "Styles of the Great," by "JDH," (for Julius David Heldman), in which he combined his analytical skills, his tennis knowledge, and his photographic memory of great players. The results were highly detailed, carefully written articles, like scientific treatments, except far more readable. Many of his articles have been reprinted in anthologies of great writing about tennis.

All this Dad did for Mom. She didn't reciprocate. She couldn't bear to be subservient. Sure, she nervously cheered him on at tennis tournaments, but she didn't support him in his work or at home. She needed to rule the roost.

I've occasionally wondered why Dad never left the marriage, but it wasn't in the cards. Dad loved Mom, and he was intensely proud of her determination and her successes. Plus they came from an era when marriages were supposed to last forever. And so were jobs. He stayed at Shell for 37 years, even after he received a lucrative offer in the 1960s from another oil company. He was even proud that, in his entire career at Shell, he fired only one person, a man who had done no work for an entire year.

Another reason Dad stayed in the marriage was that he had grown up in poverty, and Mom's family was rich. He made a good salary as a vice president of Shell Oil, but his cumulative earnings amounted to less than the amount she eventually inherited. And he enjoyed being rich.

Dad knew his place, and because of it, the marriage lasted 61 years. Mom and Dad fit together like a complex jigsaw puzzle. They were both brilliant and driven to succeed, but she was the alpha animal, who had to be in charge of everything. His role was to facilitate her dominance.

CHAPTER 13
MONEY, POWER, AND CENTURY

For many years, Mom was so in love with tennis that she'd play almost anywhere, although she was happiest when she had an excellent tennis home base. Her first headquarters was the Berkeley Tennis Club, a tennis mecca that was perfect for her: It was close to home, had a great coach, and boasted an abundant selection of players of all levels. When the family moved to Long Beach, California, she wasn't as lucky. Sure, there was a small club near our house, and it had nighttime tournaments, but it lacked a good coach, and Mom was still learning the game. In Houston, she found a great tennis home at the Houston Municipal Center, with its vibrant tennis community and beautifully maintained red clay courts. She called it the "finest public clay court center in the country."

But once our family moved to New York City in 1953, Mom was overwhelmed by work and no longer had endless hours to linger at the courts. Whenever she could cadge a few minutes to play, she gravitated to Rip's, a public club on an empty lot in Sutton Place, one of the poshest enclaves in the city. Rip's was convenient to our apartment and drew all levels of players, from those who'd competed on the circuit to older guys who hacked and chopped. The players' financial conditions ran the gamut from super rich to living on the edge, yet few players cared about who was rich and who wasn't. Far more important was who could fit into a game of doubles. And most crucially, Rip's was a rare breed, an outdoor tennis club in Manhattan, which was starved for courts.

Dad sometimes joined Mom for a set or two at Rip's. If the courts were full, they'd pickup games with other tennis enthusiasts. One of Rip's regulars was Marvin Levy, a man with limited tennis skills who at 44 was 10 years older than Dad. Because Mom and Dad liked him, they often played with him, flying in the face of normal tennis etiquette, which formed a barrier between the good players and the not-so-good. Their on-court friendship blossomed into evenings on the town, which included Marvin's wife Jane. Marvin, the top salesman at the elite Lehman Brothers investment bank, was making oodles of money. He thought nothing of going to the glamorous 21 Club, greasing the palm of the head waiter with a $100 bill to secure one of the best tables, and then dropping hundreds more on drinks and dinner. In the early 1950s, that was a ton of money. He and Jane loved to drink to excess, tell dirty jokes, and howl at the punchlines, which usually contained a word that was taboo in that era—the more taboo the better. Mom joined in with the drinks and the hilarity. Dad also liked to laugh, but he didn't drink much.

Marvin, a savvy New Yorker, enjoyed teaching Dad about Eastern manners and about living large, and Dad grew to consider Marvin his mentor. Because Dad was a Depression kid, he'd always been careful with money, but Marvin encouraged him to loosen up. When Dad admired Marvin's suits, Marvin urged Dad to have some made at Brooks Brothers, as Marvin did. Each suit cost a hefty $160, so Dad first ordered just one. He was a handsome man, and he looked so impressive in his new suit that he was a big hit. So he bought some more.

It took Dad a while to learn to pry open his wallet, but Mom was an easier sell. She'd grown up awash with money, and she adored many items that smacked of wealth: the leopard coat she brought to Stanford but never wore; the expensive Packard she purchased at Stanford before she'd learned to drive; the large house near the Berkeley Tennis Club that she chose for her small family; the grand piano she purchased, even though no one in the family played piano, using up all of Dad's advance on his glass-blowing book, and the 1950 Cadillac convertible that she'd had to track down. She'd craved that car, but there were none left in Houston, because the Cadillac model had recently undergone a complete redesign, and the cars were flying off the lots. So she phoned all over Texas and located a car hundreds of miles away. She hopped a plane, picked up her dream car, and drove it for six hours to return home. She loved to show off that car.

As a teenager, Mom had enjoyed Manhattan night life, which she'd missed in the intervening years. So when Marvin and Jane took Mom and Dad out on the town and ordered the finest food and drink, Mom was delighted. She ordered fresh Beluga caviar, flown in from Russia, which she savored while knocking down a dry martini. She also enjoyed the close proximity of the very rich and the very elegant. Although she was extremely nearsighted and always wore dark glasses, she absorbed whatever she could at the nightspots. Hands down, Mom preferred tennis players over anyone else, but she also adored the best that money could buy.

Mom's number one priority remained her magazine, and she began to realize that, to sell enough ads to keep *World Tennis* afloat, she'd need to play the part of the affluent owner by emulating the style of Manhattan's rich elite. Her straight, jet-black hair and her bright red fingernails were already pristine; since her teens, she'd visited a beauty salon twice a week. And she had that killer Cadillac convertible, which she upgraded every few years. But she didn't trust her taste in clothing, so she hired a clothing designer, Ronald Amey, who agreed to dress her, but only if she lost enough weight to fit into a size 10. Ever disciplined, Mom instantly lost 10 pounds and never gained it back. From those days onwards, she looked every bit the Manhattan business woman, immaculately dressed and ready to take on the world.

But to sell ads, she needed an entrée into the corridors of power. Tennis was a minor sport in the U.S, and few companies outside the tennis community were willing to commit money to the sport. From the early days of *World Tennis*, she knew she'd flame out if she pitched an advertising agency or even a mid-level executive at a big company. And she knew some doors were shut just because she was a woman. She realized she'd need to reach CEOs, the most powerful men in their companies, so that she could sell them on the game of tennis.

Mom ran into the occasional CEO at Rip's, but she needed to meet more. One day in 1954, Marvin made a proposal that led to a treasure trove of opportunities. He suggested that Mom and Dad apply for membership at the Century Country Club, where he belonged. In New York City, tennis clubs weren't segregated, but in the greater metropolitan area, country clubs definitely were. They either didn't accept Jews (or blacks or Italians), or they were exclusively for Jews. Century, located in Westchester County, was considered the premier Jewish country club, primarily because many of its members were extremely rich and connected with the highly influential Jewish Wall Street merchant bankers. The 1967 book *Our Crowd* chronicled those bankers, most of whom were German Jews—the most elite group of Jews—and described how they immigrated to the U.S., became highly successful, and then created dynasties by intermarrying with other bankers and keeping the companies in their families' hands. Many of those families were members of Century: the Lehmans of Lehman Brothers fame; several Loeb clans, some from Loeb Rhodes and others from Kuhn Loeb & Co.; the Weinbergs of Goldman Sachs; and plenty more. Other Century members had close connections to these banking families, often resulting from intermarriage. For example, if a member of a Jewish family that owned an investment bank married into a Jewish family that owned a successful department store, it was like a merger. The bankers would shop at the store and the store owners would raise money through the bank. Other very rich people who belonged to Century were Edgar Bronfman (a future *World Tennis* advertiser), whose Canadian family owned the liquor company Seagram's; Ben Buttenweiser, both a partner at Kuhn Loeb and a director of many other companies; and Joseph Cullman 3rd, who would become a formidable force in the tennis world. His family had been in the cigar business for generations, and was wealthy, although not super rich, but Joe hit the jackpot in 1935, when he married the fabulously wealthy Sue Lehman, the daughter of Herbert Lehman, a Lehman Brothers partner who eventually became the Governor of New York.

Marvin nominated Dad for membership at Century and then lubricated the process by introducing Mom and Dad to other members. They understood that their station in life was a strike against them. Dad was making a moderate salary as a mid-level manager at Shell Oil, and Mom's magazine was still losing money every month. But they hoped that their tennis could swing the deal. Century was well known for its two excellent golf courses and many top-notch golfers, but despite having seven green-clay tennis courts, the club had very few good players. Mom was far better than any other woman at the club, and Dad was in another stratosphere, as he was one of the best Jewish players ever. If Mom and Dad were accepted, the quality of the club's tennis would improve instantly. Yet despite all the preparation, the interview with the membership committee floundered until Mom was asked who her father was. When she said "George Medalie," everything changed. All New York Jews knew his reputation: the famous, brilliant, rich and impeccable New York Jewish lawyer; the federal prosecutor who put gangsters away; and the ethical man who was devoted to Jewish charities. His name sealed the deal, and our family became members at Century.

Actually, Dad was the member, because in that era the man had the membership, and the wife was his appendage. Yet the difficult truth was that Dad's salary didn't cover all the money they were spending. His co-workers at Shell occasionally asked veiled questions about how he could manage the rent for our Upper East Side apartment. That alone was probably beyond his means, but add onto that Laura's salary and *World Tennis*'s losses, and Mom and Dad couldn't have possibly afforded all those luxuries on their own. Time and again Mom turned to her mother to fund her lifestyle, and when the family joined

Century, it was CK who paid their dues.[1] For years, Mom repeatedly sounded the refrain that "We're the poorest members at Century." I guess that was true, but I wonder how that made Dad feel. Diminished? More likely, he was willing to forego his dignity for the chance to be so close to big money and real power.

Once we joined Century, Mom had a new tennis headquarters, but her criteria for a tennis home base had changed. No longer did she need to be near home—in fact Century was a 40-minute drive from our apartment. Nor did she seek a good coach or opponents who could test her skills. Instead, at Century she focused on mingling with the rich and famous and seeking out potential advertisers for *World Tennis*.

As long as I can remember, wherever the Heldman family went, Mom's needs were paramount, and she made all the decisions. She chose the family's friends, where we went to dinner, how our hair was cut, and pretty much everything else. That same pattern continued at Century. Mom needed Dad, because he was handsome and a great tennis player, but she ran the show. She ordained that they would spend their days at Century socializing near the tennis courts and playing with various members. For lunch, Mom held court in the Century dining room, always filling up a large table with friends. Afterwards Mom would play tennis with her lunch guests, everyone from rank beginners on up. She actually enjoyed playing with lesser players, because it gave her the chance to trounce them 6-0, 6-0, which made her quite happy.

While Mom and Dad schmoozed and played tennis at Century, Carrie and I sat alone for hours on the grassy knoll overlooking the courts, waiting to play for at most an hour with our parents and possibly an occasional set of doubles with other Century members. We were also required to join our parents at their long, boozy (at least for Mom) lunches. I was beyond bored in the all-adult company, yet there was nowhere else to go. The obvious choice would have been for us to hang out with other Century kids, but we never did. They weren't part of our lives.

I have no idea where the Century kids spent their time, other than taking lessons from Sammy Giammalva, Century's great teaching pro. Mom and Dad

---

[1] CK was the trustee for George Z's estate. Mom would eventually inherit half of CK's money, but when Mom and Dad became members at Century, the money was all in CK's name, and Mom couldn't access it without going through her mother.

had helped him when he was a promising junior in Houston, and he became one of the top players in the country. But after he got married, his son became ill, and Sammy had to quit the amateur tour to pay the medical bills. When the teaching pro job at Century opened up, Mom proposed Sammy, and he taught there for years. But Mom never let us take lessons from Sammy, although she never explained why, even though he might've improved our tennis and helped us pass the time. As an added bonus, we might've gotten to know the Century kids who hung around Sammy's court. But Mom had made a decision, which stood as the rule of law.

Besides, Carrie and I were really different from Century kids. We were committed to tournament tennis; they weren't. But the biggest disparity was that their families had enormous privilege and wealth. Many lived in grand country estates, with an apartment in the city and at least one vacation home elsewhere. For the Heldman family's first nine years in Manhattan, although we had a fancy address on New York's Upper East Side, we lived in a small, two-bedroom apartment, in which Carrie and I shared a room. Another factor was that we were city kids, while most of the Century kids lived in the country. Plus for nine months of the year, most of the Century boys were ensconced at the fanciest boarding schools that accepted Jews, even farther from the city. After we'd been members at Century for four years, Carrie and I began attending Dalton, one of the very best private schools in the city that accepted Jews. We got a fabulous education, but even attending Dalton didn't vault us into the kind of privilege that Century kids enjoyed every day of their lives.

But that never bothered me a whit. I never cared about rubbing elbows with the Jewish financial nobility. At heart, I was more of a Hamtramck kid than a member of the privileged elite.

But Mom and Dad seemed to enjoy being near the Jewish oligarchs at Century. While George Medalie's law practice had made him wonderfully rich, a number of Century families were many times wealthier. So wealthy that they had private airplanes, a rarity in the 1950s; so wealthy that they didn't need to show off their possessions. Ben Buttenweiser was worth countless millions, but he played tennis in baggy old shorts. Mom loved her Cadillac, but apparently many Century members were indifferent to the joys of owning fancy cars, and the valets who parked the members' cars handled far more banged up Fords than Rolls Royces.

In the early years of *World Tennis*, Mom struggled to find advertisers, even with the super-rich so close at hand. Companies that sold rackets and strings came on board, but their black and white ads barely paid the light bill. To make real money, a magazine needed to sell four-color ads. Her *modus operandi* for selling them was to meet a CEO of a big company and invite him to lunch at Voisin, the elegant French restaurant in midtown Manhattan where she had a "due bill," a barter arrangement in which the restaurant got free advertising in *World Tennis* and Mom got free lunches in return.

Mom took CEOs to lunch for almost five years before striking gold. During that discouraging dry spell, several of the men propositioned her, and others demeaned her because she was a woman. But the indomitable Gladys Heldman never stopped. Whenever her efforts failed, she headed to Tiffany's to console herself with a gold trinket. After a few years, she owned a lovely assortment of gold cigarette lighters, gold bracelets, and gold necklaces.

During those interminable years, Mom kept slaving away, a one-woman whirlwind who wrote most of the articles, edited the others, kept up a huge correspondence, did the layouts, managed the office, did the paste-ups, and sold ads. When she sold her magazine in 1972, she liked to say that she was "replaced by seven men." That was probably true.

She worked so hard that she had trouble eating. The papaya juice I once brought her didn't do the trick. Instead, she turned to scotch, and before long, she began consuming two neat, double scotches every night before dinner. Although she usually hated euphemisms—she said "croaked" instead of "passed away" or "died"—she referred to herself as "tight" after her nightly scotches, never as "drunk." For her, "drunk" meant slurring, and to avoid that dreaded possibility, she kept close control over when she drank and how much. She saw any deviation from her nightly drinking-and-eating schedule as a calamity, resulting in panic and a potential explosion.

Mom's drinking affected our family profoundly. At our dinner table, she frequently launched into booze-fueled monologues, often venting the rage she otherwise hid. Her rants ranged far and wide, from complaints about pushy tennis promoters, or Century tennis players with bad tennis manners, or our noisy upstairs neighbor. Alcohol also loosened any inhibition she might have against attacking or humiliating Dad or me. And if CK came to dinner, Mom would excoriate her mother for wearing frumpy clothes or try to foist Putty, our cat, onto CK's lap, although CK clearly hated and feared cats, believing that her first-born daughter Alice, who'd died at age 5, had succumbed to "cat fever."

Once Mom had worked herself into a lather, we had to ride out the storm. No interruptions were allowed. Yet within a few hours after dinner, when the scotch had worked its way out of her system, she returned to work, and often toiled into the wee hours of the morning.

The only time Mom exceeded her usual nighttime quota of drinks was at parties, which she adored. The extra alcohol made her looser and funnier, and she enjoyed telling dirty jokes, with their shock value, and put-down jokes, to skewer an absent person, or sometimes even one nearby, if she felt superior to the one she was belittling. She had a reputation as a very funny person.

But the pressure of running *World Tennis* never stopped mounting, and within a few years, Mom added two double vodkas before lunch. Because vodka didn't make her breath smell, she could conduct a meeting during or after lunch. For years, she kept her weight at 115 pounds, yet she consumed eight shots of hard liquor every day. That's a lot of booze.

Despite Mom's careful distinction between "tight" and "drunk," she really did get drunk twice a day. It would be correct to say that she, like her father, had become a high-functioning alcoholic.

In the late 1950s, *World Tennis* was already beloved by tennis players everywhere, yet the magazine kept losing money. Mom sold more and more black and white ads, yet only a paltry few in four color. But she kept plugging, searching for a pitch to give potential advertisers more for their money. She decided on a scheme to offer each company a greater presence in the magazine if its CEO would commit his company to a series of four-color ads. More than once, she sold ads with a promise that every month she'd give a special award in the company's name. The monthly column about women tennis players that I wrote in the late 1960s and early 1970s was a perfect example. Each column honored that month's recipient of the Germaine Monteil trophy, an award invented to get the cosmetics company to place monthly four-color ads.

In early 1959, five and a half years after she started the magazine, Mom finally broke through and sold a series of four-color ads to Pepsi-Cola, which took the inside front cover. It was the first long-term sale she'd made to a company outside the tennis industry, and a Fortune 500 company to boot. From then on, the magazine published a monthly, half-page article, called "Pepsi-Cola Salutes," featuring a different tournament every month.

Mom's sale of ads to Pepsi wasn't connected to Century, but her second major sale, to Joe Cullman, certainly was. In fact, Joe was Mom's all-time biggest catch at Century. When they met at the club in around 1957, he was a fine club golfer, and he'd played tennis in boarding school, but he hadn't touched a racket in years. Mom invited him to play tennis the following day, and she fought hard to beat him as badly as possible. He was a good athlete, so he avoided embarrassment by winning a game or two. From the start, he applauded Mom's competitive spirit, and they began to play frequently. In short order, she introduced him to other tennis enthusiasts. At first he knew nothing about the tennis world, but she schooled him, and he was a quick study, although he could never know as much as the people who'd been immersed in the sport all their lives. But when he was unsure about his tennis knowledge, he turned to Mom.

Mom met Joe at a pivotal time in both of their lives. She was 35 years old, and she'd run *World Tennis* for four years, but it was still losing money, and she yearned to make it profitable. Joe's life had been quite different, but he too was on the verge of a huge success. After he returned from combat in World War II, he entered his father's tobacco business. In 1955, when Joe was 43, his father made a deal with a relatively small cigarette company named Philip Morris, which, as part of the arrangement, gave Joe a job. Two years later, they put him in charge. The company had a number of brands, including Parliament, Benson & Hedges, and Alpine. Its least successful brand was Marlboro, which had been marketed since the 1920s as a women's cigarette, and sported a pink filter tip to mask lipstick stains. The following year, in 1958, Joe made a series of brilliant and bold moves that turned Marlboro around. As he wrote in his memoir, he decided that Marlboro needed to become "a full-flavored filter brand that had a virile image." He turned to Leo Burnett, a Chicago advertising wizard, who created Marlboro advertisements showing rugged wranglers with weathered faces in the great outdoors of Montana or Wyoming, which they called "Marlboro Country." Within a year, Marlboro's market share soared from less than one percent to the fourth best-selling brand, and it kept growing exponentially. By 1983, Marlboro had become the best-selling ***product*** in the world.

During the 1960s, as the success of Philip Morris skyrocketed, Joe Cullman became the spokesman for the tobacco industry, and frequently appeared before Congress, declaring that tobacco didn't cause cancer. Yet starting in the early

1950s, there had been reputable research showing tobacco's culpability, and over the years, the evidence kept mounting. Still, Joe stuck to his mantra, lying to Congress, along with all the other tobacco industry leaders. Mom didn't care. She smoked like a chimney, and Joe's company was a major supporter of tennis.

Mom and Joe grew close, along with their spouses. Mom and Dad still had high flying nights on the town with Marvin and Jane, but now their social schedule included muted dinners at Joe and Sue Cullman's palatial country estate. Mom respected Sue's intelligence and admired the work she'd done during the war, helping break the Japanese code. But Mom wasn't close to Sue. Joe was her kindred spirit; both used their intelligence, their drive, and their business sense to break through into unexplored territory.

Joe Cullman and Gladys Heldman, best friends, revolutionaries, and titans of the tennis world.

In late 1959, as Mom was drawing Joe further and further into the tennis world, Philip Morris began placing monthly four-color ads on the inside back cover of *World Tennis*. The company at first revolved its brands, one month Marlboro, the next Parliament, and then Alpine, but after a few months, it settled almost exclusively on Marlboro. In early 1960, the Marlboro wrangler first appeared in *World Tennis*, in full and living color, smoking a cigarette. A few months later, *World Tennis* began a monthly feature called—no surprise—the "Marlboro Award," honoring major contributors to tennis. Every month for over a decade *World Tennis* published an article presenting the Marlboro Award.

Mom's partnership with Joe continued through most of the 1970s. It started on the tennis courts at Century Country Club, expanded as his company became a major advertiser in *World Tennis*, and then became revolutionary as they brought massive changes to modern pro tennis. Mom was the tennis brain, and Joe provided the money and the power.

Century Country Club is known as an elite enclave of the richest and most powerful Jews in America. No one could ever have predicted its importance to the modern tennis world. It wouldn't have been, without our family. At Century, Mom had fun, she was able to give her magazine a kick start, and most importantly, there she molded a club golfer named Joe Cullman into one of the most influential figures in the history of tennis.

Their tennis partnership was unique and unmatched. By the end of the 1970s, both had been inducted into the International Tennis Hall of Fame, the highest honor in tennis.

It's ironic that both these tennis icons were Jewish. Throughout the history of U.S. tennis, until the open era became thoroughly established, Jews were frequently marginalized, excluded from many important tennis clubs and sometimes treated unfairly at tournaments. Yet Mom and Joe weren't trying to improve tennis just for Jews. They made it better for everyone.

CHAPTER 14
EIGHTH GARDER

I'm 10, and I've just finished my third summer at the Hoxies. I'm proud of my huge Hoxie forehand. I can win with my forehand. I run all over the court trying to avoid hitting any stroke other than my forehand.

The past three summers I practiced all day long, seven days a week. I worked on forehands, backhands, volleys, and dropshots, but not on serves. Mr. Hoxie has a crazy idea about serves. He thinks no one under 12 should serve overhand, because little kids give away too many points with weak serves and double faults. So he's made me serve underhand, which is like hitting a forehand without letting the ball bounce. An underhand serve is reliable, but you can't get any power. Dad says no other coach would have made me serve underhand, and that Mr. Hoxie's nutty idea will slow down my future progress. Mr. H never cares about the future. He wants us to win right now.

Throughout the past summer, I begged Mr. Hoxie to let me serve overhand, but he always refused. "Wait until you win some 11-and-under tournaments, Tiger." Last summer I won three of them. I'm ready to start serving like a big kid.

Dad's going to teach me how to serve. Everyone says he has one of the best lefty serves in men's tennis. He uses so much spin that his serve looks like an egg whirling through the air. He's also accurate, and he places his serve anywhere he wants, sometimes at the receiver's body, sometimes in the corners. Like other great lefty servers, he can swing it so wide in the ad court that he pulls the receiver outside the alley. I hope he'll teach me to serve like that, even though I'm a righty.

As soon as I return from Hamtramck, he starts teaching me. He makes serving look easy, but for me, it's a nightmare. The stroke has way too many moving parts to coordinate.

The left arm has one job—to toss the ball to the precise spot at just the right moment—but it has to be done perfectly, which is hard to do. The right arm has three separate movements: bring the racket up near the head, drop it behind the back, and swing the racket up to smack the ball. It's so hard! Why didn't Mr. Hoxie teach me a proper serve when I was younger?

After two lessons, Dad says "You've made a good start, but you need lots of practice." I need his help, but he's frequently away on business, so I'm often on my own. He says "You'll have to go out every day and hit serves against the wall of the sanitation building." Oh no. I've never minded practicing against the Hamtramck wall. It's fun to be with the other kids, and I enjoy the challenge of reaching a goal. But I hate the yard outside the sanitation building. It's close to home, but that's the only good thing about it. When I practice against the sanitation building wall, I'm usually on my own I can't fix any mistakes I make on my brand-new serve. Plus New York has lots of rain and snow, and when the freezing wind off the East River slices through me, my fingers get numb and I start wheezing. I'm sure tennis players who grow up in warm climates don't suffer like this. And the sanitation building is surrounded by a metal picket fence with bars spread so wide that tennis balls fly right through them. When I mis-hit my serve—which I do all the time— the ball skitters away from me, making me scurry to catch it before it flies onto the East River Drive, gone forever. And as if all of that isn't bad enough, one day I get so distracted by the sanitation-building horribleness that a taxi almost hits me as I cross the street to return home. The driver screeches his brakes, honks, and screams at me. I tell no one. I'm 10. I'm not supposed to be so stupid.

But I'm determined to learn a serve. I'm so eager that I constantly practice my swing, even without a racket or a ball, in our apartment, in the tennis club locker room, and even on the school staircase. In fact everywhere. It drives Carrie nuts. One Saturday afternoon, Dad takes us to the movies, and as we walk down the aisle, I start practicing my swing. Carrie hisses "Stop. You're embarrassing me." I can't help it. I need a good serve. Dad doesn't get embarrassed. He knows how badly I want to improve.

If only I had a nice place to practice, like the Heights Casino. We used to go there more often, but this year our school, Walt Whitman, moved from the Upper East Side to Harlem, where public transit isn't safe, so reaching Brooklyn is much more complicated. That means I have to spend even more time against the sanitation-building wall, which I hate more every day.

Carrie's lucky. She'll finish Walt Whitman in May and start high school in September. Finding the right school should be a piece of cake for her, because she's a genius. We've both skipped a grade, but I'm nowhere near as smart as she is. She's always been the best in her class. When she was seven, she won a spelling bee in Texas for kids up to 12 years old.

In February, Carrie takes the private school entrance exam and scores off the charts. Mom makes all the family decisions, so she tells Carrie to apply to Manhattan's top three all-girl private high schools, Brearley, Chapin, and Dalton. Of course she gets into all of them. Mom chooses Dalton for her. She says Brearley and Chapin have a terrific reputation, but most of the students are gentiles, and Dalton is the best private school in the city that is mostly Jewish. It's not like we're religious or anything. Mom just doesn't want Carrie to be the odd girl out.

So come September, Carrie will be off to Dalton, but I'll be stuck at Walt Whitman, watching it shrink. Once the school moved to Harlem, lots of families jumped ship, leaving my sixth grade class with only three students. You'd think I'd get lots of personal attention, but it hasn't worked out that way. I learned almost nothing during the sixth grade, except of course math, because I do my own math workbooks. I also learned a bunch of Gilbert and Sullivan songs, which are at least fun. And we spent an excessive amount of time at recess in an enclosed, paved yard the size of a matchbook, where there's no room to run or play ball. One day last winter no teachers were around, and we had nothing to do but break up the ice on the ground, so I started smashing the ice with a metal pole until I accidentally slammed it into my eyebrow on the way back up. Blood gushed everywhere, so we called a teacher, who put a band aid on it. When I got home, Laura was worried, so she called Mom, who made fun of me for being so stupid. At least she sent me to Dr. Leader, who stitched up my eyebrow. I really have to get out of Walt Whitman.

But Mom has done nothing to get me out of there, so I start my fourth summer in Hamtramck with the prospect of facing another year trapped in a tiny, dying school, and another year of torture at the sanitation-building wall. I'm frustrated, but complaining isn't allowed. The only place I have some control is on the tennis court. I'll just fight like crazy every time I play and try to block out my disappointment.

During my first week in Hamtramck, I'm playing a set on court six when a kid walks up to the fence and says "Mr. Hoxie says you have to go to the office. Your Mom is on the phone."

I run so fast that I'm panting when I say "Hello."

Mom says "I called Dalton and asked if they have room in the seventh grade. I told them 'My younger daughter is also quite smart.' The admissions officer told me the seventh grade is full, but a spot has just opened up in the eighth, and I'm applying for you."

So now it's my turn to take the entrance exam, which means flying home for just one day. It's worth it if I can leave Walt Whitman. The test is a breeze, and I'm in and out of New York in a flash. Back in Hamtramck, I chew my fingernails, waiting for results. Then a surprise: I'm hitting on the back side of the wall when I hear my name being shouted. It's a man wearing a Western Union uniform, who hands me a telegram that reads: "CONGRATULATIONS EIGHTH GARDER LOVE MOB AND DAD." I race from the wall to the courts, laughing, screaming, and waving the evidence at everyone. Carrie skipped a grade, and now I've skipped two! Finally I've done one thing better than her. But something's niggling at me, so I reread the telegram. I knew it. The telegraph operator made a mistake, misspelling "GRADER." I've learned to catch mistakes while working for *World Tennis*. And there's another problem with the telegram. Mom signed it "Mob." She does that to make fun of my constantly stuffed up nose. She did it in my moment of triumph. Not funny.

Once my excitement passes, reality sinks in. I don't know why Dalton accepted me. I'm not a genius; Carrie is. I haven't read many books. She has. I'm just a regular kid who likes math books, Superman, and Archie. Carrie hardly needs any help with school work. I do. Occasionally I mispronounce words, and Mom insists on repeating my mistakes over and over, laughing each time. Mom never laughs at Carrie.

I'll show them all. Dalton accepted me. The school must believe that I'm smart. Mom and Dad are successful because they're brilliant and they work really hard. I'm not a brain like Carrie, but I know how to try my guts out. I've done it on the tennis court. I can do it at Dalton.

Now that my school problem has been solved, I can buckle down to tennis. I still have my big forehand, and I can still run. But my serve stinks. Over the winter, Dad traveled too much and I practiced too little. Mr. Hoxie sees that I'm struggling, and he makes me work on my serve. Every morning and afternoon he sends me down to Court 8, the last court, with a bucket of balls and a few racket covers to use as targets in the corners of the service box. But I still can't coordinate all the moving parts. My toss roams from too far right to too far left to too far back, and I swing my racket either too soon or too late. It's so frustrating.

Mr. Hoxie is the top guy in Hamtramck. He's in charge of everything, including practice. And in Hamtramck, practice is serious. No screwing around. We fight hard to win. Mr. Hoxie picks who you play. Except today. He's gone from the courts, and he put Gerry Dubie in charge. But Dubie has a mean streak.

Everyone knows I hate playing Carrie, but Dubie makes me play her anyway. "If you don't, you'll be in big trouble."

I bristle and say "I won't do it."

But Dubie pulls rank, so I have to back down. He sends us to Court 3, and I'm so mad that I play horribly. The first time I serve, the bottom falls out. Double-fault. Double-fault. Backhand error. Double-fault. And now it's Carrie's turn to serve. Instead of politely sending her the balls, I move close to the net and smash the balls as hard as I can, trying to hit her. I miss. I'm furious that I missed. I can't take it. NOTHING'S GOING RIGHT. With tears streaming down my face, I run off the court to the candy store, where they have a pay phone. I call home collect. Mom answers, and I tell her what happened. I beg her to let me leave Hamtramck.

She doesn't listen. She doesn't understand why I'm so upset. She doesn't care. "You cannot leave. You'll have to stay and tough it out." She won't help me, because if I were home, I'd be in the way.

I remain in the store for a long time. When the tears have passed, I return to the courts. No one says anything about what happened on Court 3.

Soon after, the tournament season begins. I'm 11 but I'm too old to play the 11-and-unders, because I have a bad birthday. The cutoff date for birthdays is December 31, so even though I won't turn 12 until December, I'll be considered 12 all year long. My new age group is the 13-and-under, and while I'm quite short, I'll be facing some 13 year olds who are full-grown behemoths. I'll also play some 15-and-under tournaments, where you can guarantee they'll all be bigger than I am. That's ok. I'll be ready to face the big kids. I can do it. I'm tough. This summer I'm going to be a champ. I just know it.

Our first tournament is the Kentucky State, where we go every year. Mr. Hoxie usually drives us, but he isn't available. Instead, he deputizes Mr. Sunday, whom we hardly know, to drive six Hoxie kids, including Carrie and me, to Louisville, and to coach us there. Mr. Sunday is funny, so we have a good time on the road, even though the trip takes six hours, and it rains the whole way. The Louisville Boat Club has giant puddles infested with mosquitoes, which use me as a pin cushion. I'm allergic to mosquito bites, so they turn into welts that itch like fury. I can't stop scratching them, and I end up covered in scabs. The Hoxie kids are housed with members of the club, and we're introduced to our hosts, but we have nothing to do while we wait for the rain to lift, so that we can practice on the green clay. But the rain refuses to stop. So Mr. Sunday drops us off at the clubhouse and says "Go have fun." We squeeze into a few chairs and play Hearts with any kid who comes by. In the three years I've played tournaments, I've barely spoken to any of my competitors, but now I'm having a little fun with them.

Finally, we get sunshine, and Carrie and I breeze through our 13-and-under matches. We meet in the singles finals, where she beats me, 6-3, 10-8. At least the second set was close. During the trophy ceremony, I hold my emotions in, despite my grief at losing to her again. Afterwards I rush off to a quiet spot behind the clubhouse and sob until the tears dry up.

Carrie and I are a good doubles team, and we often play together, but our matches are far from pretty. People come from miles around to watch us scream at each other. In Louisville, we're the best doubles team in the 13s, but Mr. Sunday wants to make sure we won't go easy on our final-round opponents. So he makes us a deal. If we beat them 6-0, 6-0, we'll get a big, juicy steak at dinner. If we hit one of them with a ball during a point, we'll earn an ice cream cone. We giggle throughout the match as we keep taking aim at their bodies. I finally hit one of them. We get the cone, but not the steak.

We aren't always that mean.

The rest of the summer, I keep losing to bigger kids. Quarter-finals at the Illinois State 13s. First round at the Western 15-and-under. First round at the National 15s, tears streaming down my face towards the end of the match. I can't stop crying because I'm losing so much. My serve is a mess. One double fault after another. Dad tells me to keep practicing, that it just takes time to adjust to a new stroke. "There's nothing wrong with your swing. You just need thousands and thousands of repetitions, that's all."

Back in New York City, we get ready for Dalton. First, Mom makes her annual excursion with Carrie and me to select our fall and winter clothes for school. We take a taxi to Bonwit Teller on Fifth Avenue, and we head straight for the Juniors section. While we watch, she goes through the racks and chooses our clothes, and then she hands her selections to a salesgirl, who brings them to a changing room. I try on the outfits Mom chose, and she tells me which ones she'll buy. Then we change back into our street clothes, she pays, and we take a taxi home. Efficient. Perfect for her. Not for me. She never asks me what I want or what I like. I've learned not to care.

The first day of school is only two weeks away, but I've barely made a dent in the Dalton summer reading list. It's hard to concentrate on school work during the tennis season, when I fall into bed every night exhausted from a full day on the courts. At home, to my great surprise, I like some of the books Dalton has assigned. I spend my days curled up on the couch, enjoying them. I especially like Sinclair Lewis's *Arrowsmith*. He makes me want to be a doctor. Maybe this school will be OK.

I wonder if I'll be able to make friends at Dalton. All my life, I've wanted to make friends, but I've never been in a situation where friendships were possible.

Before I started school, I was so isolated that I never had any playmates. Once I arrived at the second grade in Kemah, I badly wanted to be friends with Jimmy Boy, who sat next to me. But he wasn't interested in me, and then he got the chickenpox. During his absence, our family moved to Houston, so I never saw him again. But I did get the chickenpox from him, and gave it to Mom's great friend Dick Savitt ("Sav"), the 1951 Wimbledon champ. He was so sick that his mother flew down from New Jersey to take care of him. Mom said adults get chickenpox much worse than kids. When Sav recovered, he and Mom went back to talking and laughing all the time, until I got the measles. He got so worried that he refused to talk to Mom, even on the phone, until I recovered.

After we moved to New York, I still didn't have friends. During the four years I attended Walt Whitman, I made just one friend, but that lasted only a few days, until I invited her to our apartment, and Mom met her. That night Mom mocked my friend's New York accent. Mom never said "Stop being her friend," but I understood that Jeanne wasn't welcome. The friendship ended.

Last year, when I was in the sixth grade at Walt Whitman, I almost made a friend, when a girl from my class invited me to her house. I asked permission from Mom, who told me to find out where the girl lived. Her address was in Harlem. Mom said I couldn't go there. Too dangerous.

And I haven't had any luck making friends with tennis players. Every year, Carrie and I have stayed all summer long at the Hoxies' big house on the Detroit River, but we're the only out-of-towners who remain that long. The others come for just a week or two, not much time to become close buddies.

Throughout the summer, we play tennis with the kids who live in Hamtramck, but I haven't gotten close to any of them. Our backgrounds are like night and day. Mom and Dad are both highly educated, with big-time jobs. And Mom's father made a pile of dough. Carrie and I come to Hamtramck as paying customers (sort of—Mom has a barter arrangement). The parents of the Hamtramck kids are mostly immigrants from Poland or the Ukraine, without much education, and many have jobs in the Chrysler plant. There's nothing wrong with that. We just come from different worlds.

When I'm around Hamtramck players, I hide the fact that my parents belong to a country club. Mr. Hoxie scoffs at country clubbers, saying they just want pretty strokes, and they don't try as hard as the Hoxie kids. How could I explain to the Hoxie kids that I come from privilege, but I'm not like other privileged kids?

So because I'm an out-of-towner and a country clubber I don't quite belong in Hamtramck. But there's an even bigger reason that I haven't made friends there: No one comes to the courts to have fun. In every point of every set, we try to beat each other as badly as possible. In that environment, it's pretty darn hard to cozy up to other kids.

My first day at Dalton isn't too bad. There are 20 kids in my eighth grade class. Just like last summer in tennis, I'm 11 and they're 13. And I'm the shortest. Some of the boys look pretty dorky, but the girls all seem grown up—they have breasts (or "breasties" as Laura, who is shy about body parts, would say) that point straight out, their hair is poofed just right, and they sneak a little makeup, even though it's against the rules. I'm flat as a pancake, with frizzy, curly hair and bushy eyebrows.

I say hello to a few girls, and they're polite, but they have their own friends. Many have been together since kindergarten. They go to each other's apartments after school, but I'm never invited. They're all too old for me, and we don't have much in common. They talk about makeup and boys, and I think about winning and losing. They know how to act at parties; I know how to travel around the country and play tennis tournaments. Carrie and I are the only girls in the school who are athletes. I'm proud of my muscles, and most girls hate strong muscles, because they think muscles make you look like a boy.

It doesn't take long for me to discover that at Dalton, just like everywhere else, it'll be hard for me to make friends.

But I do like some of my teachers, especially my English teacher, Hortense Tyroler Finkle, whom everyone calls Miss T. The first month she teaches us grammar, and we diagram lots of sentences. That feels a lot like math, and I'm right at home. Of course at Walt Whitman I learned math on my own. At Dalton, I have to learn from teachers, and I'm scared that they'll make fun of me the way Mom does.

That almost happens in my first music class. Mr. Aks, our music teacher, taught my classmates last year, so he expects all of us to have some musical literacy. He hands out blank music paper, plays a few notes on the piano, and tells us to write what we hear. Then he asks the students, one at a time, to pass him their papers, and he plays their written notes on the piano. They're all awful, and he laughs at them. I sit at the back of the class, desperately trying to hold back tears, knowing he'll laugh at me too. When he asks for my paper, I say "I never studied music before."

"That's no problem, just give it a try."

"I can't." I mean I REALLY CAN'T. I can't handle ridicule. From anyone. Fortunately he sees my distress and leaves me alone.

The remainder of the class is spent singing. Mr. Aks hands out lyrics, and he teaches us songs from many cultures. He accompanies us on the piano, and we all chime in. I sing loud and on key. It's joyful.

My musical ability helps in French class, where I quickly acquire a good accent, because we speak only French in class. All week long, we listen to a record and memorize a short conversation between two French people discussing such thrilling topics as taking a train or finding a hotel. At the end of the week, we have to stand up in class and recite what they said on the record. Learning French like this really works. I'm beginning to learn a whole new language.

*　　　*　　　*　　　*

The whole year I was 11 was tough. I struggled with my serve. I lost lots of matches. I changed schools. My classmates are nice enough, but I'm not like them. So once again I spend most of my time alone.

Finally it's my 12th birthday. Mom and Dad aren't fans of birthday parties, but they usually get me a present. Rarely, they buy a cake for the family to share. But they've never thrown me a party, and they've never invited anyone else. Today they've made the most minimal plans possible. They've reserved a court at the Heights Casino so that the four Heldmans can play tennis together. That doesn't make me even the teeniest bit happy. But at least I'll get out of the apartment for a little while. Mom and Dad leave early to visit Marvin and Jane Levy. She's very sick, and was recently admitted to a nearby hospital. Marvin's sad, so Mom calls to say they'll use our court time to play tennis with Marvin instead of us. Mom says they'll call later to make new plans. But they don't. Three hours pass, and I'm beyond dejected and boiling. This was supposed to be my day! I can't stay home anymore. As I'm leaving the apartment, I tell Carrie I want to run away from home. I take the elevator to the lobby, hoping to find a doorman to talk to. He's in the street, catching cabs, so I walk two blocks to the stationery store, where the woman owner has always been nice to me. I tell her what's up, and she says "You better go home." I have nowhere else to go.

I open our front door, and Carrie says "Mom called, and you're in big trouble." So Carrie ratted on me. The entire family is against me, and I have nobody else.

Mom phones again, steaming. She says "How could you?" There's nothing I can say. I have to clam up and take the brunt of her wrath. I can't even show her that I'm sad. Or angry.

CHAPTER 15
"I CAN HEAR YOU BREATHING"

Most mornings, it's my job to wake up Mom. Today is Sunday, and it's 8:45 AM, time for me to go to work. I silently open her door, tiptoe to her bedside, and gently shake her, saying "Good morning Mom."

As always, she grumbles "Five more minutes."

I tiptoe out and set the kitchen timer. After the "ding" I do the routine again.

"One more minute." Out I go again.

The third time's the charm. Now I join Dad in the kitchen to make Mom's breakfast. She needs her coffee right away.

I hate being yo-yo'd in and out of her room, but I dare not make a false step, because she could blow up. So I always stick to the routine. Except once, last month, when I rebelled. After she said "One more minute," I didn't tiptoe out. Instead, I stood stock still, watching the clock. I tried to be quiet, but it didn't work. "Leave the room! I can hear you breathing!"

I admit it. My breathing is noisier than most. For two reasons: my nose is always stuffed up, and I often have asthma. So I snuffle and wheeze a lot. Breathing with asthma is like sucking air through thick goop.

Dad says I've had asthma since I was very little. I got it from him. He's had asthma all his life, yet he was a terrific tennis player. Asthma affected his stamina, but he fought through it. His asthma got worse once he met Mom. She smoked, so he began smoking too. He kept it up until one day, when we were living in Kemah, Texas, an ambulance came to our house and carted him off to the hospital, where they put him in an oxygen tent, because he was having trouble breathing. His doctor told him never to smoke again. I'll never smoke.

But Mom still smokes. Two packs a day. Three a day when *World Tennis* is going to press. Sometimes Dad sits up in bed at night, wheezing and coughing while Mom's working and smoking.

I get sick even more often than he does. Winters in New York are brutal, and I'm in bad shape from December through March. We live on the corner of East End Avenue and 90th Street, right off the East River. In the winter, frigid winds whip up 90th Street, stirring up my asthma. My breathing gets worse when we pass the sanitation plant. Dad says it spews sulphur dioxide into the air, which is terrible for asthmatics. He taught me to wrap a thick scarf twice around my head, leaving just my eyes exposed, to keep the freezing, toxic air from irritating my lungs. That helps a little, but I still get wracking coughs. Sometimes I wish we lived somewhere else, somewhere gentler on my asthma, but it isn't in the cards.

Mom hates it when I'm sick. It annoys her and makes her cranky, so I try to hide it from her. But sometimes I cough so much that I can't stop. Once I was in the foyer of our apartment, hacking away and bent over with a really big fit. From deep in her room, Mom screamed "BE QUIET! YOU'RE COUGHING TOO LOUD!" I should have known better. She's very sensitive to noise. I went back to my room.

Very few people understand what it's like to have an asthma attack. More than one of my teachers has pronounced that asthma is psychosomatic, and that I'm making it up. When I'm straining to get air in my lungs, I sure don't feel like I'm making it up.

Even fewer people have reached out to help me. Flo Blanchard was one who tried. When I was 9 and Carrie was 10, Mom and Dad sent us to Miami Beach over Christmas vacation to play in the Orange Bowl tennis tournament, and then they skedaddled to Montego Bay, Jamaica for a vacation without the kids. We stayed with Flo and Mike Blanchard, who are tennis umpires. Mom and Dad knew the Blanchards well, but Carrie and I had never met them before they picked us up at the airport. The first night, they put us to bed at 9 o'clock. Soon I started wheezing, and Flo got scared. She didn't know what to do. "Your Mom didn't tell us you were sick."

I said "I get asthma all the time," but the more I wheezed and coughed, the more frightened Flo got. So she sat with me until I dropped off to sleep. The next morning, she hustled up an international operator to phone Mom.

"Don't worry," Mom said. "She gets sick all the time. She'll be fine."

"Should we get a doctor?" Flo asked.

Mom said "There's nothing a doctor can do."

So the whole week I stayed sick, and Flo was a nervous wreck, because she really wanted to send me to a doctor. But Mom had laid down the law. No doctor.

Every Christmas we return to Miami Beach to play the Orange Bowl, and every year I get sick there, hacking and coughing before, during, and after matches. I still manage to win. I'm a fighter. This year I'm 12, and for some reason, my asthma and coughing are at their worst, and in between points I sometimes double over, coughing loudly and struggling to catch my breath. I win the match, and after I leave the court, I find Mom standing on the lawn with a man who's a friend of a friend or something like that. He has a cane, his hair is pure white, and he walks very, very slowly. Mom says he's a famous lung doctor who in the 1930s helped Alice Marble—a great tennis champion—when she had lung problems. While we're standing around on the lawn, Mom says "Julie M has asthma. Can you help her?"

"Spit on the ground," he says. I wonder why, but he doesn't explain. I spit.

"He asks "Can you find the spit?"

I can't. It's in thick grass.

"Does anyone have a handkerchief she can spit into?" No one does. And then we wait and wait, and finally someone brings a white towel. Then we wait some more, until I cough up some gunk into the towel.

"It looks infected," he says. He suggests penicillin. Dad's allergic to penicillin, and he's afraid I will be too, so he won't let me try it. That's it. The famous doctor offers no other medicines or treatments. I continue playing the tournament, sick as a dog, but I never give up.

When we return to New York, I'm worse. Finally Mom calls our pediatrician, Dr. Sidney Leader. He's plump and sweet. He comes to our apartment, listens to my chest, and gives me an injection of adrenaline. "That should help," he says. "You may feel like your heart is racing, but don't worry, that's what happens with this medicine. You'll feel better soon."

Soon, my heart slams into a rapid thump-thump-thump rhythm, and I go into Mom's room. "I can feel it!"

"Feel what?"

"My heart is thumping big time."

"You're just making it up."

Why doesn't Mom believe me? I'm not making it up, but I'm not allowed to contradict her. I'm still very, very sick, so she makes a new rule. While I'm sick, I can knock on the wall behind my bed, which separates our rooms. The first night, I knock, and she comes in. Ditto the second night. The third night I'm better, but my cough hasn't gone away, and I feel all beat up from this sickness. I knock, and she comes in. "You aren't sick enough anymore, so stop knocking."

How can I know when I'm sick enough to ask for help? I can't be my own doctor. At least Laura and Dad understand how sick I get. If only they could call the doc. Maybe they'd get me help sooner. But Mom's in charge and she gets to decide when I need a doctor. She usually decides to do nothing.

CHAPTER 16

A BREAKTHROUGH SEASON

Summer's here and that means Hamtramck. The routine of working to win. Hour after hour of just tennis. The Hoxies advertise in *World Tennis*, calling themselves a tennis camp. Kids at school hear the word "camp" and ask "what other sports do you play?" None. "What else do you do?" Not much. Maybe one day all summer long we drive around Belle Isle—an island in the middle of the Detroit River. And once every few years we go to the beach. I learned to swim when I was seven, but I've hardly swum since then, and I've forgotten how. Mr. Hoxie says "Tennis players need hard muscles. Swimming makes your muscles smooth, so swimming isn't good for tennis players." And Mr. H doesn't believe in any kind of exercise other than tennis—no running, lifting weights, or stretching.

Just lots of tennis.

And he doesn't impart much stroke technique. He believes in simplicity and repetition. Every day in Hamtramck starts with The Wall, where you must complete four tasks: 20 forehands in a row, 20 backhands in a row, 20 volleys in a row, and finally the combination of 2 drives and a dropshot, repeated 20 times in a row. If you miss in the middle of any of those tasks, you return to the back of that line. So you learn not to miss. When you've completed the Wall, you graduate to the courts, where Mr. Hoxie arranges matches and drills. You play all kinds of players, from young kids who pitty pat, to teenagers who slug the ball, to older men who hack and chop. You take a bucket of balls and practice your serve. You hit a slew of overheads. You practice smothering soft returns by smacking forehands into the corners. And you play at least eight sets a day.

Now that I'm 12, I'm stronger, but I'm still small. Mr. Hoxie says I've grown from being a peanut to a shrimp. My forehand, always my biggest weapon, is harder now.

When I was little, Mr. Hoxie taught me to figure out my opponent's weaknesses. Back then it was easy—most little kids have problems with their backhand and their serves. I learned to spot those weaknesses a mile away and prey on them until the opponent popped up a juicy one. Then I'd line up my forehand and drill it.

Last year I lost to Carrie in the finals of some 13-and-under tournaments. Now she's too old for the 13s, so it should be my turn to win them. Mr. Hoxie is helping me. "Tiger, most kids try to hit every ball as hard as possible, but you like to think on the court. You already know how to beat little kids. Now I'm going to teach you how to play against bigger kids."

I already know which opponents run well side to side. Now he shows me to spot how fast my opponent runs forwards and backwards: "Early in the match, you have to try out your dropshot. If your opponent can't reach it, do it again and again and again. If she reaches it, lob over her head. All that running will slow her down."

He lectures me about how to play when the opponent hits a really good shot deep and wide. "Buy time," he says. "Hit a defensive lob as high as you can so you'll have time to return to the center of the court."

And he explains a whole new tactic. "You've always hit to the opponent's weakness. Now do the opposite! Make the opponent run wide to her strength. That'll open up the court and you'll have wide open spaces to attack her weakness."

And I've added something of my own to the mix. I've developed a topspin forehand, which dips and swerves. I can use it to help all my other ploys.

My serve remains my weakness. Although I'm more accurate, and I hit fewer double faults, I can't hit it very hard. If I play someone who hits hard, I know she'll pummel my serve, and I'll have to start running.

But I back up my serve with my other shots, and soon I catch on, and the wins come. I bag a few 13-and-under tournaments, including the Kentucky State. I win several rounds at the big 15-and-under tournaments (the Westerns and the Nationals). This week I'm playing the Detroit women's singles. My first opponent is very tall, but Mr. Hoxie tells me to ignore her size. "Just find her weakness." I run through that opponent and two more, and now I'm in the finals against Virginia Hesse, a Hoxie Hot Shot who's 19. Since I've been coming to Hamtramck, she's been the best female player at the park, way out of my reach. Mr. Hoxie tells me to forget about the past, and that she's just another opponent. She starts out slamming a big Hoxie forehand winner. I shrug it off. The next point I hit a gentle dropshot, and she can't reach it. So I do it over and over again. When she finally reaches one of them, I lob over her head, according to Mr. H's plan. I beat her in straight sets. That makes me the Detroit women's champ. Not the 13-and-under champ or the 15-and-under champ. I'm the best woman player in the city and I'm only 12. That makes me a very young, very short Hoxie Hot Shot. It's a big breakthrough.

Mr. Hoxie shakes my hand and gives me a big grin. We did it.

In 1954, Carrie and I were the first out-of-town campers to stay with the Hoxies. Now it's 1958, and tons more out-of-towners come to stay, attracted by the Hoxies' advertisements in *World Tennis* and by the success of the Hoxie players. Kids come and go throughout the summer, and sometimes a dozen are staying at the Hoxies' great big house overlooking the Detroit River. But even with all those kids, there's not much time for chortling and running around, only a few minutes before we leave for breakfast and a little more after we come home from dinner. All of our energy is focused on beating the person across the net.

For the very first time, I've made a friend at the Hoxies. Her name is Carol, and she's from Windsor, Ontario, just across the Detroit River. She was here for only one week last year, and she returned just in time to watch my finals against Hesse. After the match, in the station wagon, she says "It looks like your hair is getting in your eyes. I bet that's a problem when you play." Now that I think of it, she's right. "Would you like me to help you do something different with your hair?" I actually never thought about that. Mom makes all those decisions. At the Hoxie house, Carol says "Come in the bathroom, and let's fix you up." So she works on it and I work on it, and we come up with something totally new: two pony tails, one over each ear, or sometimes behind my ears. I really like it! And my hair is out of my eyes. This can be my new look! My very own!

But there's no time for fooling around. The summer's almost over and while Carol goes back home, I prepare for our annual 10-hour drive to Ottawa to play the Canadian National Juniors. Mr. Hoxie's taken me there every year since I was nine. The first year, I was so little he made me sleep on top of the luggage in the back of the station wagon. Short trips in the Hoxie station wagon are always fun, but when I was little, the Ottawa trip was pure torture. Mr. H. wanted to get there in a hurry, so he plowed on with very few stops. It seemed like I always had to pee, so I begged him repeatedly to stop, to no avail. No one else stuck up for me, so by the end of the trip I was always a smelly, sopping mess. And deeply ashamed.

Now that I'm bigger, I've outgrown that misery. But the trip is still very long. All the kids sing, play games, and listen to the radio, and we're still not close to Ottawa. When Mr. Hoxie wheezes and pops pills, we whisper "Is he having a heart attack? Are we going to crash?" Despite our worries, he's always fine. He drives straight to the Rideau Club, where we pile out of the car, roaring with energy after being cooped up so long, and we run around madly and hit the snack bar with a vengeance. We check in at the tournament desk, and I inspect the draws. I'm flabbergasted. Mr. Hoxie has entered me in nine events—the singles, doubles and mixed for the 13, 15, and 18 age groups. Playing in three events is a normal load, six is too tough, but nine is absurd. "You'll be fine, Tiger," Mr. Hoxie says. "It'll be good practice." Yeah, right.

The first day is good—I win four matches. I start the second day with an 18-and-under match against the Canadian Number One, last year's champ. She's 18. I'm 12. She towers over me and looks like an adult. I focus on Mr. Hoxie's advice: I forget about how big she is, and I start figuring her out. I find she has a weak backhand, so I hit there. Her second serve is a lollypop, so I run around my backhand and slam my forehand. I know I'm going to win. I'm Mr. Hoxie's Tiger. Some of our points are very long, but I refuse to lose. In two hours, I beat her 6-4, 5-7, 6-2.

After we shake hands, a dozen people jam around me. "Congratulations." "How tall are you?" "Have you always lived in Hamtramck?" A photographer poses me and my racket and takes a bunch of shots.

I'm tired and hungry and I have a lump in my throat after winning such a big match, but the tournament won't let me rest. "You entered too many events," they say, "so you'll have to go out right away." It's a 15-and-under match. I try, but my tank is empty. I scream when I miss, and I can barely run. There's no place to sit down, so I lean against the back fence, totally drained. Mr. Hoxie walks up to me, and I tell him I can't go on. So he tells me to default. We powwow over lunch and reassess. He says he'll pull me out of all the events except the 13 singles, the 15 doubles (with Carrie), and the 18 singles and mixed.

The next day, in the 13 singles I play Faye Urban, the top 13-year-old Canadian girl. They put us on a court down a steep hill from the clubhouse, far from any other court. Faye has a big forehand, and I can see she's going to be tough. I'm still drained from yesterday, and I start missing shot after shot. I fume. I yell. The crowd smells blood. Many are hanging over the side of the clubhouse, screaming for me to lose. They cheer and stomp when she makes a good shot, when I miss a forehand, when I miss a backhand, and when I double-fault, all of which is against tennis etiquette all over the world. Tears begin to burst out of my eyes. IT'S NOT FAIR!! My serve breaks down and I can barely push it in. Faye takes advantage of my errors, and beats me comfortably. It makes no sense. I beat the 18-year-old and lose to the 13-year-old.

I'm devastated. They hate me and they were cheering for me to lose. I need help. I have to call Mom. I reach her at her office and explain about the horrible crowd and that I lost. She says "That's how it goes. You'll just have to get used to it." That doesn't help me at all. I've read articles in *World Tennis* about full-grown American men who went ballistic when Australian crowds did just what the Canadian crowd did to me today. And Mom sympathized with those men, and never said "They'll just have to get used to it." Why does Mom treat me worse than them? It makes no sense, and it isn't fair.

The day after I lose in the 13s, Mr. Hoxie springs a huge surprise. "Follow me, Tiger," he says, as he walks to the station wagon. In about 10 minutes, we arrive at the Ottawa airport, where he introduces me to a guy who's even bigger than Mr. H., who says: "Tiger, we knew each other in the army. He's loaning us his airplane." It's a tiny single-engine plane, just big enough for the two of us. Mr. H takes the pilot's seat—I never knew he could fly—and I'm the co-pilot. Once we take off over the city, it's crazy exhilarating. I should be more scared, but I feel safe with Mr. Hoxie, so long as he doesn't pop any of his wheezing pills. He screams over the roar, "OK Tiger, here's your chance." He issues me a few instructions, which sound like muffled mumbles, and gives me the thumbs up to fly the plane, which then wobbles all over, hits an air pocket, and drops suddenly. I look over at Mr. H., who smiles. Soon he takes back the controls. I've had fun for an hour. Fun is a rare word in my life. Now it's back to the tournament.

In the finals of the 18 singles, I play Barbara Seewagen, the top American seed (This tournament, like no other, has Canadian seeds and American seeds.) She comes from a tennis family—I've heard of her brother Butch. Once again my opponent is tall and 18, and I'm short and 12. The match is a grinder, with me running everything down. I pull all my rabbits out of the hat—dropshots, lobs, swerving topspin forehands, and flat forehands pounded to the corners. She has three match points and misses a sitter on one of them, but I'm the Tiger. I never stop trying. I barely squeak out a win, 6-1, 4-6, 9-7. At the award ceremony, she's crying. I feel badly for her; I know how it feels to lose. I overhear her telling her father "I'm giving up tennis."

A miracle has happened. The 12-year-old Hoxie Hot Shot has won the Canadian National 18 and Unders. Mr. Hoxie's waiting for me by the edge of the court, this time with a big hug.

Carrie wins the 15 singles, but no one pays much attention to her; everyone's focused on me, the phenom. We phone home, and our parents are excited for us both. Mom tells both of us, "You're the most wonderful, the most terrific."

The next day, my grinning mug, revealing my buck teeth and my very own ponytails, is plastered all over the front page of the *Toronto Globe and Mail*, one of Canada's major newspapers. This is a very big deal.

On Monday, *Sports Illustrated* runs that same picture in "Faces in the Crowd," their column for future stars.

When I return home a few days later, I bounce into the apartment, feeling like a big shot. Mom comes out of her room, looks at me, and says "Your hair is ugly. You'll have to get it cut right away." I want to say "It's not ugly" and "It's **my** hair." But it's no use, I'm not allowed to argue. I say nothing.

Shorn, I play my last tournament of the summer, the women's singles at Century Country Club. Dad says if I win, he'll give me a reward, anything I want. I win easily. I've never been to an amusement park, and there's one nearby, so I ask him to take me there. As we drive up, I change my mind. Maybe this would be fun with a friend, but I don't have any.

Century holds an awards dinner under a huge tent for all the tennis and golf champs. At the end of dinner, after they ask for quiet, the M.C. announces my victory in the women's singles, and hands me an engraved silver cigarette case, as my trophy. Perfect for an asthmatic child. After I return to my family's table, the M.C. springs a surprise: "Friends, we also need a round of applause for Julie's spectacular triumph last month. She won the Canadian National 18-and-under and she's only 12. Please stand up, Julie, so that we can give you a round of applause." I do so, and I can't stop grinning.

While they're still cheering, Mom tugs on my skirt and whispers "Sit down! You're embarrassing us. You've been standing up too long." I didn't know I was standing too long. I didn't know that was bad. I sit down.

There's more excitement. The *New York Times* runs an article about our family, with a picture of the four of us. The article tells about our summers at the Hoxies and about our successes in Canada. Mom's the only one quoted, but a lot of the article is wrong. It says I'm better than Carrie at math. Not true. That I comprehend Stendhal (a French novelist) and I speak French. Nope. Some of the other stuff is true, like Dad being a terrific player and beating some really top stars. Then Mom launches into her usual family rankings shtick: "My husband has the top ranking in the family. I'm Number 2, and Julie and Carrie are tied for third." But after that, she turns weird: "My husband and myself play singles against them every summer when they return from Hamtramck. We try to beat them by big scores. That keeps them in line. Anyway we couldn't stand losing to such little girls." I don't get it. Dad never ever tries to beat us badly. He doesn't need to; we know he's great. And is she trying to be funny, or does she really think about beating us badly all the time?

I settle into the ninth grade. Same old same old. I study hard, but I'm 12, and most of the others are 14, and we have nothing in common. I want to have a life. One day my loneliness finally bubbles over the top, and I enter Mom's room crying. I say "I have no friends!" Mom doesn't say much, and after a while I calm myself down, in time to make her dinner. The next day, I'm elected secretary of my home room. It's no big deal; I'm the only girl willing to do the job. When I tell Mom about my new responsibilities, she laughs and says: "And you said you didn't have any friends!" She laughs about that for days.

*After I won the Canadian 18s, my photo, with my
very own hairdo, appeared on the front page of the
Toronto Globe and Mail.*

*The Heldman family in the NYTimes, soon after I
won the Canadian 18s. I'm shorn, because Mom
hated my hairdo.*

CHAPTER 17
UNSURPASSED

Gladys Heldman was an extraordinary, unsurpassed tennis promoter. Sure, others have profited grandly from tennis promotions, and Mom didn't. But she wasn't in it for the money. Her primary goal was to help tennis players, but she accomplished that by improving the game of tennis. And while she was doing good deeds, she made sure to publicize *World Tennis* magazine.

Mom possessed the right characteristics to become an exceptional tennis promoter: a broad knowledge of the game, an unequalled Rolodex, a massive work ethic, a wellspring of creative marketing ideas, and the willingness to turn on a dime if she needed to. Add to the mix her indomitable character and her innate brilliance, and the results were extraordinary.

Mom succeeded at all her promotions, starting with the 1951 McCarthy Cup in Houston. She waited six years for her next promotion, the Art Larsen benefit which she masterminded in New York City in 1957.

Larsen was a unique character. He had served in World War II, where he saw many of his buddies killed by the enemy, and later, even more were strafed and slain by friendly fire, when American planes mistook them for Nazis. After the war, those memories plagued him, and he had trouble coping. A doctor suggested that he do something healthy, so he took up tennis seriously. As it turned out, he was exceptionally talented, not unlike John McEnroe, who came along 30 years later. Both were lefties, with a supreme ability to move the ball around the court and perform miracles with the flick of a wrist. Larsen didn't have McEnroe's great serve, nor did he possess enormous firepower, but because he was quick, and he played cleverly, he was a threat to any opponent. And although he rarely practiced and never trained—he often prepared for matches by partying through the night, eating hot dogs, and drinking beer—he had incredible natural stamina. He was so talented that his fellow players came out to watch him play, and fans around the world loved his free spirit.

Mom had a close connection to Larsen. They collaborated on a bunch of articles published in *World Tennis*, starting with its first issue in June 1953, which featured "Why I Tap," under his byline. In the article, Larsen, whose nickname was "Tappy," explained how his many tics and other oddities arose out of his war experiences. His most prominent tic was tapping anything stationary, from the dinner table, to doorways, to the net post, to his own baseline as he was about to serve. Each day had its special number, such as a two, which Larsen called a "twosie," when he would tap everything twice. In another idiosyncrasy, he became unhinged if a ball boy threw him the ball without bouncing it just once. And then there was the phantom eagle that sat on his shoulder, whom Larsen would consult during a match.

After Larsen won the 1950 U.S. Nationals at Forest Hills, he was ranked Number One in the U.S., and he remained in the American top 10 for six more years. But in November 1956, the motor scooter he was riding in Northern California was side-swiped by a truck, and he lay in a ditch for hours, bleeding. His injuries were near-fatal: his eyesight was badly damaged, his right side was paralyzed, and he suffered brain damage. The immediate prognosis was uncertain.

Like most top players at that time, Larsen was an amateur, and he lacked the funds to pay either his initial medical bills or his projected long-term needs.

To help Larsen, Mom opened her heart and her wallet. She organized a tennis exhibition in New York City, raised funds through *World Tennis*, and donated her own money. Throughout the years she was involved in tennis, she was always the first to contribute to tennis causes.

Mom was the wizard who made the Larsen benefit hum, but she chose to remain the silent partner. She knew that tennis stars would draw headlines, and she wouldn't, so she asked two celebrated tennis players to head the campaign: Sav and Don Budge, at that time the only man who'd ever won the Grand Slam. Mom, Sav, and Budge had no trouble rounding up players for the exhibition. They picked up the phone, and one player after another jumped at the chance to help Tappy, even though they'd have to pay their own way to New York and play for free. Budge Patty, the debonair and highly ranked American ex-patriot, came the farthest, flying in from Paris, but Sammy Giammalva came from Houston, "Gorgeous Gussy" Moran came from Los Angeles, and former Wimbledon champ Fred Perry came from Florida. Some of the players were amateurs, and others were pros. Before the Larsen benefit, the USLTA had never allowed amateurs and pros to play in the same event, even an exhibition. Mom convinced the association to break down that barrier, for Tappy.

The benefit was played indoors at the Seventh Regiment Armory, the club with dim lights and slick wood courts that I hated so much as a child. The armory agreed to forego charging rent, and other benefactors donated bleachers, so expenses were minimal. Unfortunately, the armory never had much room for fans, and the limited number of seats sold out in record time, so standing room tickets were printed and sold, and still over a thousand people were turned away on the night of the benefit. It was a grand event, and $20,000 was raised for Larsen, including donations mailed to *World Tennis*. The magazine printed the name of every single person who sent money for Larsen.

Thanks to the money that Mom was instrumental in raising, Larsen was able to recover significantly, although he remained blind in one eye and with weakness on his right side. He lived another 56 years, due in large part to all the people who reached out to help their beloved Tappy.

The Seventh Regiment Armory was also the site of Mom's next promotion. For decades, the U.S. National Indoors had been held there, but a few months before the 1959 event was due to take place, the USLTA decided to cancel it, because their volunteer officials were unable to entice top players to compete, and the armory's rental fee of $3,500 was so exorbitant that the tournament never made much money anyway—just $386 in 1957 and $552 in 1958. When Mom heard about the tournament's cancellation, she immediately came to the rescue. No one but the USLTA had ever financed a U.S. national championships, but Mom suggested something entirely new. She offered that *World Tennis* and two anonymous donors would pay the armory's rent and guarantee the event against losses. They'd get their money back only if the tournament made enough money.

Once the USLTA accepted Mom's offer, the National Indoors had a new lease on life.

Mom's first move was to ask Billy Talbert, a former top player and Davis Cup Captain, to help run the tournament. Their biggest priority was to secure the participation of all the American Davis Cup players, especially Alex Olmedo, the star. The USLTA's tightwad officials had initially offered the players very little expense money, which they turned down, and once the players left for the Challenge Round in Australia, the officials gave up. When Mom and Talbert took charge, they phoned and cabled the American players, first asking them how much money they wanted, and then agreeing to pay their price, but only if the tournament made enough money. Mom was again breaking new ground by giving amateur players a stake in the outcome of a tournament.

Mom and Talbert banked on getting Olmedo to compete at the Indoors. He was a Peruvian, yet he represented the U.S. in Davis Cup under Captain Perry T. Jones. In Australia, he led the U.S. to its Davis Cup Challenge Round victory, and then he won the Australian Nationals (the precursor to the Australian Open). Wherever he went, he drew crowds with his charm, athleticism, and easy temperament. Mom and Talbert negotiated hard to get the rising star.

The other big star of the Indoors was Sav, who lived just a short cab ride away. Unlike Olmedo, who at age 22 was in the prime of his career, Sav was 32, and he'd played only part time for years, yet he continued to excel with his punishing serve and his flat, pounding groundstrokes.

Before Mom took over the National Indoors, it had been an anemic event. But with her and Talbert at the helm, it became a hit. Besides Olmedo and Sav, the draw was filled with fine players who produced a string of well-fought matches, which fans flocked to see. The final, between Olmedo and Sav, was a dogfight, with Olmedo edging Sav 12-10 in the fifth. Journalists and tennis insiders called it one of the finest indoor matches ever played.

With so many big tennis names and so much good tennis, the tournament netted $8,000, which wasn't a fortune, but it was far greater than any amount that the National Indoors had garnered in recent memory. The proceeds were shared by the USLTA and the Seventh Regiment Armory club. As always, Mom didn't take a cent.

More importantly, Mom and Talbert had run their first major, national event, and they moved mountains in barely a few months. Mom's creativity led to many groundbreaking concepts, and she also proved that if you bring in the best players, the fans will come pouring in the gates.

For the Larsen benefit, Mom played down the extent of her participation, but for the National Indoors, she trumpeted *World Tennis*'s involvement. The difference was personal publicity versus publicity for the magazine. She was dedicated to the magazine's success, and she had no compunction about publicizing it, but she believed she shouldn't seek personal publicity. Instead, she hoped that others would speak up on her behalf.

CHAPTER 18
THE SEMI-FINALS

I'm 14, and I'm stranded in a bleak dorm in Cincinnati, Ohio with no kids my age, no family, no chaperone, and no coach. I've been left alone for the biggest match of my life, the semis of the National 15-and-Unders. If I win, I'll be in the finals. If I win that, I'll be the champ. They'll rank me Number One in the U.S. I want this bad. Dad was the National Junior champ. I want to be like him. I gotta hold on.

Until last night, all the Hoxie kids were staying together in the dorm, where the tournament housed us. Then the rest of them lost, and Mr. Hoxie decided to take them back to Hamtramck. "They'll just cause trouble here," he said. He looked me in the eye. "You'll be fine on your own. You can do it, kid. You're a Tiger."

Mr. Hoxie knows I'm tough. When I was eleven, I traveled alone on a Greyhound Bus from Louisville, Kentucky to Middletown, Ohio, from one tournament to the next. I stayed silent the whole way, and I held my rackets on my lap, so that no one could take them. I held them so tight that my knuckles got stiff. But I did it.

And Mom's proud that I don't need help. "That's my girl," Mom said. "You're a Heldman." Mom and Dad don't come to my tournaments. That's what Mr. Hoxie's for. "It's not like I sit around eating bonbons," Mom says. "I'm busy, and I'm not one of those hovering tennis mothers who has nothing else to do." Mom has rules. They're unspoken, but I don't dare break them. Don't Talk Back. Don't Ask for Help. Don't Complain. I keep my trap shut.

It's weird to wake up all alone in a dorm room. I check the clock. Damn! I forgot to set the alarm. It's 9:55, five minutes before the cafeteria closes for breakfast. I thrash through the pile of dirty clothes in the corner. I pull out a bra. It has falsies; I'm pretty flat-chested. I find a blue shirt and red-and-green plaid shorts. I've no time for niceties. I shove a pile of coins in my pocket and run down the dull-green hallway, past summer-school girls in brush curlers. They're dancing to Elvis Presley's "All Shook Up."

At the cafeteria, the sweaty, fat cook is locking up. I beg him to let me eat breakfast, but he won't budge.

"There are rules, young lady." I know about rules. "Use the vending machine."

I hate him.

My eyes ache. I won't let him see me cry. "NO!" I bellow. The cook slams the lock shut and walks away.

There's no choice. I have to get something out of the vending machine. Mom forbids junk food, but this is an emergency. I drop in a nickel, push A5, and nothing happens. "NO!" I scream again. I kick the coin-eating monster hard a few times, and a Hostess Twinkie falls to the bottom with a thump. I tear open the wrapper, take a big bite, and chew slowly. It's so sweet! I lick my fingers one by one, down to their webs.

Back in my room I search for my tournament whites. My favorite white shorts are wrinkled. I put them on anyway. Tennis clubs have dumb rules. You must wear white. Shirts must have collars. Skirts must not be too short. You must not pick your nose. I prefer Hamtramck Park. Mr. Hoxie won't let us wear whites in practice because they show their dirt too soon. Colored clothes can be worn a couple of days in a row because they hide stains.

I tuck my two wood tennis rackets under my arm—I always bring a spare in the rare case a string breaks—and I head out to the curb to wait for the tournament transportation. A white Cadillac convertible pulls up. It has huge fins and the top is down.

"Hop in," the driver says.

She has bleach-blonde hair that's teased and sprayed into place. And a deep tan. Like a country clubber. Like she spends all day by the pool. She's wearing tennis whites, but there's no sign of muscles. I bet she doesn't even play tennis.

She gives me a big smile, and introduces herself as Mrs. Dillard. "I was supposed to pick up five kids," she says. I tell her the others are gone.

"Do you mean you were alone here last night?"

I nod, and then I sit quietly. I'm extremely lively when the conversation is about tennis, but I'm lousy at small talk. Mrs. Dillard's nice. She doesn't ask me if I like the weather or other stupid stuff like that.

The clubhouse of the Cincinnati Tennis Club has two stories, and it's covered with ivy. It's surrounded by 10 courts that have green, sandy clay. The court nearest the clubhouse looks great. It's been brushed with a four-foot-wide broom. The nailed-down synthetic lines have been scrubbed clean. A sign on the gate says "Saved for the National Semi-Finals." The court has been manicured for me!

I check in at 11:30 for my 12 o'clock match. You can't be late for matches in a tournament. Fifteen minutes late and you lose. Mrs. Camden, the tournament referee, gives me a can of new balls for practice. I love the smell of new balls. In Hamtramck, we usually play with used ones that are gray and balding. The rough Hamtramck courts chew up balls, shoes, and rackets. Mr. H saves new balls for big occasions.

I always warm up with another Hoxie kid. But they're gone. I wish I could ask an adult for help, but I suck at doing that. I get all tied up, afraid they'll get mad at me. So I won't practice. I try to find a quiet spot. No such luck. I have to sit near country clubbers. One woman tries to chat. She asks how I like Cincinnati. I say "fine," then I turn away.

As I walk onto the court for the match, my shirt won't stay tucked in. My shoulders hunch. I hang my head low. My opponent, Maggie Taylor, looks spiffy. Her pleats are perfect. Her short blonde hair lies flat. I run my fingers through my frizzy hair. Not good. She's a giant, at least six feet tall and heavy. I'm five one and slight.

I may be an almost-midget, but I'm the favorite. Two weeks ago in Louisville I crushed Maggie 6-2, 6-2. I have great wheels, and I pounded her with my big Hoxie forehand. I ran her butt off until she withered in the heat.

I'm seeded sixth, based on last year's rankings, but I'm much better than that. National rankings can be messed up. Two years ago, the ranking committee royally screwed me. They placed me at 24, several spots below a girl I'd beaten four times that summer. I pleaded with Mom and Dad to get my ranking changed, but Mom blew me off.

"It's not important," she said. "If you're not Number One, it doesn't matter."

And now I have an opportunity to be Number One.

To determine who serves first in the match, I spin my Wilson racket and ask "M or W?" The racket's butt has a "W" written on it, which is an "M" upside down. Maggie calls "M" and wins. Bad omen for me. I hate losing at anything. We warm up for three minutes. My game is off. I should have practiced. I should have eaten.

The umpire announces the match. The stands are already half full, with maybe 200 spectators. A big crowd. Most of them are wearing white. Country clubbers always wear white. Mr. Hoxie makes fun of country clubbers. He calls them Fish. Fish have smooth strokes taught by club pros. Fish aren't hungry. They don't know how to fight and win. Today the air is like hot soup. Fish wilt in the heat. A bunch of them hide under a big oak tree.

Maggie's from California. Her California friends are in the stands. So are their mothers. They all came out to root for Maggie. I have no one. I look around for a friendly face and find just one—Mrs. Dillard, who smiles at me.

Maggie plays hit-or-miss tennis. She smacks everything hard. Really, really hard. Occasionally, her shots whiz into the fence on the fly. This week, she's done better than usual. Fewer shots into fences. My plan is to keep the ball in play. Wait for her to miss.

She starts the match with two powerful serves. I barely get my racket on the returns. She wins two more quick points. Ouch.

"Game Miss Taylor," calls the umpire, and we change sides. My head droops to its familiar bent-over position. My shoelace has come undone. I tie it. I berate myself for losing that game. I hope Maggie starts missing soon.

The next game, Bam! Maggie's forehand blisters to my right. Bam! She smacks a powerful backhand. She pounds on my backhand—my weakness. Like a Fish, I plunk it helplessly into the net. 2-0 for Maggie. She keeps charging. 3-0. After each winner her supporters explode, and she smiles at her mom. I look in that direction. I'm on my own.

Nothing's working. Everyone knows I'm fast on my feet. Not today. I feel like I'm in a nightmare, frozen in one spot. More than once I howl, "NOOOO!" Mr. Hoxie never minds my temper; he says it just proves what a Tiger I am. The gallery isn't thrilled. There are stupid sounds of "tsk tsk" and "oh, no." I hurl my racket to the ground, and there's a splintering sound. Oh god. I cracked it. I retrieve my spare. Two kinds of trophies are given in girls' tournaments. One's for winning. I have lots of those. The other kind's for good sportsmanship. Those I never win.

Maggie's up 5-2. So much for my wait-and-see plan. I reverse course and throw her some junk. Topspin then slice. High then low. Soft then hard. I start winning points. I catch up to 5-all. She cranks another winner. Then another. I make two errors and lose the first set 7-5. I refuse to panic. Hoxie players don't panic.

As Maggie's fans cheer loudly, I glare at them. "It's not fair," I snap. "You cheer for her, and you hardly clap for me." The crowd responds with silence. Maggie continues to surge forward early in the second set. As we cross sides, I snarl "Shut up!" at the California supporters.

"Mind your manners!" a spectator yells.

The second set seesaws. She leads, I catch up. Again she leads. Again I'm hot on her tail. The points get longer. That's good for me. She hits a big serve to lead

4-2. She's two games away from the match. I claw away at her power. I make her run. After two long points I draw even at 4-all, to momentary silence from the crowd. Then, "Come on, Maggie!"

I look straight at Maggie's mother, and plead: "How about some cheers over here." I get none. I win the second set 6-4.

"There will be a 10 minute break," the umpire announces. "Play will resume at 1:36."

At the break, players usually head towards the locker room to change clothes and get advice. I have no backup clothes. No coach. I don't know where to go. Mrs. Camden stops me.

"Now, Julie," she says "You really cannot behave that way. You'd better mind your manners. I'll have to phone your parents."

I get all choked up. I can't respond. I find a quiet spot behind the clubhouse where I can see a clock. I slink away alone, where no one can see the tears running down my cheeks. At 1:35 I go on court.

The crying has dulled my fury. I stop fighting the crowd. I run freer and the sweat pours out of me. It smells good. My junk has screwed up Maggie's rhythm. Her shots spray a lot more. A few go near the fences. I sneak in a dropshot. She just looks at it. Her tank is empty. She plants the butt of her racket on the ground and leans over from the waist, onto the top of the racket head. She looks at her supporters. They can't help. She wins some games, but I steam roll through to the end, 6-4.

At the net, I shake Maggie's hand. She tries to be polite, but she looks unhappy. The Californians file silently out of the stands. None of the spectators congratulate me. Forgetting I don't have a change of clothes, I shamble off towards the locker room, but Mrs. Camden stops me. She looks grim.

"Your mother is on the line." I don't know what to do. I feel like smacking my racket into my leg and breaking the bone. I walk to the phone, barely holding back tears.

"What did you do, Julie M?" Mom says. Angry voice. No congratulations. "They said you were very naughty."

Naughty? I'm not a baby, I think, but all I can do is sob.

"They said you were yelling at Maggie's mother."

"It's not fair, Mom. They wouldn't clap for me. They even cheered when I double-faulted."

"Well, what do you expect? You know that's how things go. Sometimes the crowd's for you, sometimes it isn't."

"But Mom. . . ."

"You'd better improve your behavior, Julie M. It's embarrassing for your father and me. I'll call Mr. Hoxie. He'll be angry."

"I'm sorry. I'm sorry."

I enter the locker room. Maggie's on the other side. Her hair's still damp from the shower, but somehow she's remained spiffy. She's wearing a white blouse and pink skirt and chatting with her mother. I duck into a private booth next to a shower stall. I sit on the little bench and turn the water on hard, to cover the sound of my crying.

I hear someone call my name. It's Mrs. Dillard. She tells me I'm going to stay with her family tonight. "I'm going to help you." As we walk out, I hide my face. I don't want to be seen with red, puffy eyes, and I don't want Mrs. Camden to scold me again. Mrs. Dillard drives me to the dorm and helps me stuff my clothes into a suitcase.

Mrs. Dillard's house is nice, although a little too fancy for my tastes. Lots of fluffy cushions and flowery chairs. "My daughters are in college," Mrs. Dillard says "so for tonight you can be my new daughter." I'm mute. "Now, into the shower and wash all over. Don't forget to make your hair nice and clean," she said.

I'm humiliated. She sees my hair is scummy. I pick at a scab on my elbow. It bleeds a little. When I emerge from the shower, Mrs. Dillard is washing and ironing my clothes, humming as she organizes my things. Mom has never done that.

Mrs. Dillard serves Mr. Dillard and me a steak dinner. I'm starving. He wants to talk. He asks how my day has gone. I tell him I won. He digs for more information. I stare at my shoelaces. They're fine. I peek and see Mrs. Dillard bring her finger to her lips to shush him.

I wake up happier. Mrs. Dillard helps with my hair. Mom has never done that either. Mrs. Dillard back combs my hair and puts on some hairspray. I like it.

The doorbell rings, and there's Mr. Hoxie, sweating buckets, his collar sticking to his bull neck. His giant hug crushes me. It feels good.

"Hey, Tiger," he says. "I hear you won a tough match. That's my girl." He looks around at the Dillard house. "Well, look at this place. You sure made out swell."

Mom said he'd be angry, but he isn't. He's here to help.

We arrive at the club plenty early. I'm crisp and clean and ready. Mr. Hoxie finds me a practice partner. On the next court Maggie is warming up my final-round opponent, Mimi Henreid. She's a Californian too. I have a quick fantasy of scratching Maggie's eyes out. I talk tactics with Mr. Hoxie. He says Mimi likes to come to the net, so I should pin her to the baseline with deep, hard shots. "And make her run." He tells me to turn to him if I get worried.

I march onto the court for my final round match. The California crowd yells, "Go Mimi," louder and louder. I'm limp inside. Yesterday took its toll. I vow to block everything out.

Mimi wins the first game. The Californians roar. I look over at Mr. Hoxie. He nods slightly. I win the next point with a spectacular backhand retrieval. I hear a little applause for me—from Mr. Hoxie and Mrs. Dillard. I stick to the plan. I pin Mimi back and send her to the races. In a flash, I lead 4-1. I play like a champ. I can do no wrong. I win 11 games in a row, and close out the match in a rout, 6-1, 6-1.

I did it.

I smile, but I don't leap up and yell "Whoopee!" It's tacky for a girl to show off. So I just stroll to the net and shake Mimi's hand. She says "Well played." I look at the crowd. The Fish are leaving. The Californians look glum. Then I see Mr. Hoxie by the gate and run to him. "Well done Tiger. You were great!" Mrs. Dillard holds me tight and kisses me. I hug her back. Mom doesn't give hugs. She worries about getting bruises.

Mr. Hoxie and I rush to catch the 4:45 flight to Detroit. We head straight for Hamtramck Park. All the Hoxie kids are there. I hope they're not too jealous. We eat the cake Mr. Hoxie bought, and then he puts me on a plane to New York. I take a cab to the apartment, and I enter Mom's room. She pecks me on the cheek.

"You're the best," she says.

Should I say "Thanks," or "No I'm not?"

I want her to ask me how I played, and what happened after the match, and how it feels to win the Nationals. Most of all, I want her to congratulate me. Instead, she says "Now that you can beat me, I'll never play you again." I never realized that she only played me because she knew she would win. Now, she seems most worried that there will be payback for all those years that she beat me as badly as possible.

I feel choked up, but I say nothing. I know the rules.

*   *   *   *

In the next issue of *World Tennis,* the article written by Mary Hardwick about the National 15s makes it seem like my victory was a foregone conclusion:

"By the end of the first day's play all the competitors I talked to were certain that Julie Heldman of New York would be the 1960 Champion. . . . Julie, age 14, not only won but played with the maturity and will to win of a seasoned Wightman Cupper. The new Champion has a decided flair for competition as well as the ability to use the court like a chess board. This is a quality that is rare not only in one so young, but at any level of today's play. 'Julie M.' will surely go far in this game, for apart from her natural and easy movement she is a thinking player."[2]

CHAPTER 19
PLAYING FOREST HILLS

"Julie M!"

I know the drill. Mom shouts for me, and I drop everything and race into her room. She gets mad if I don't come fast enough. For Mom, time travels at warp speed.

"I just got off the phone with the Forest Hills tournament referee. Because you won the National 15-and-unders, and you're a local girl from New York, they're going to give you a chance to play the women's singles at the U.S. Nationals in Forest Hills. The tournament starts next Thursday, and they've made you a wild card, which means you're not guaranteed a spot, but if anyone drops out, you'll take her place in the draw."

"What do I do?" In my entire life I've played only a few women's tournaments, and now I may get to play the biggest one in the whole country. I don't know who to call, what to ask, or where to go. Mom played Forest Hills. She must know the ropes. She'll have to help me. At least I'm familiar with the West Side Tennis Club, where the tournament is held. I've gone there tons of times, starting when I was seven, and Carrie and I sold *World Tennis* magazines under the Stadium.

---

[2] Hardwick, Mary "Julie Heldman Wins National 15s." *World Tennis magazine,* October 1960.

We retired from that job after about three years, and since then I've gone to the tournament as a tourist, wandering the grounds, occasionally watching matches, and at the end of the day chomping at the bit to leave, while Mom talks endlessly to one person after another.

None of that has prepared me for actually playing the tournament.

Mom says "The referee's office told me that we have to call the tournament every day to see if you're in."

Every morning, I wake up eager to find out if I'm in the tournament. Once Mom's had her coffee, I ask her to make the call. After three days, they tell her a spot has opened up. Mom says I'm the youngest player ever to play the tournament. I'm both over-the-top excited and dead-bang scared.

"Who do I play?"

"Billie Jean Moffitt." I know her. I lost to her in doubles at the National 18s. She's from Southern California and just two years older than I am. I wonder if she'll bring a cheering squad, like the other Southern Cal girls I played in the National 15s. I've watched Billie Jean play singles twice, and I know I'm in trouble. She's a net rusher, the opposite of me. She's made for playing on grass. I'm not.

I have no idea when we'll play. Mom says we're supposed to check the *New York Times* every day, which will have the schedule.

Three days in a row, I wake up extra early and open the front door to the apartment to bring in the newspapers and scour the schedule for my name. Today it's there. We're on deck for court 15, but the paper doesn't say what time we're supposed to play. I ask Mom to find out. She calls once, but no one answers. Then she gets stuck on a bunch of calls, and all of a sudden she's going nuts because she might be late for lunch. I'm frantic to find out when I play, but there's nothing I can do about it now. We drive to the club, and I want to check in, but I don't know how. If this were an ordinary event. I could handle the situation. But this is the big time. Plus the women's tournament desk is situated in the women's locker room, and I've never been allowed in there. During the tournament, it's open only to members and competitors. If I try to enter, someone might yell at me. I need Mom, but she says "Later," because of her lunch date. And she's dying to have her first drink of the day. We sit at a table on the Clubhouse terrace, barely 30 feet from the locker room, and everyone and his uncle comes up to chat with Mom. I can't do anything at all until Mom is good and ready. I place my rackets and my bag on a nearby chair, so I'll be ready to jump up when she finishes. As their lunch drags on, I'm so flustered that I cannot eat.

When Mom finally finishes her lunch, we walk straight through the locker room door, and she tells the woman at the tournament desk who I am. The woman gives me a foul look and says "You're late! You were scheduled to play 20 minutes ago."

I want to scream "It's not my fault!" But that would throw the blame on Mom, breaking one of her unspoken rules. I wonder if they'll kick me out of the tournament before I even get to start. I just stand there frozen.

Thankfully, Mom starts talking. "We couldn't find out when Julie M was scheduled to play."

The woman says "All right. We'll forgive you this once. Go change clothes. You'll be on in 15 minutes."

I always try to warm up before my matches. Mom's lunch got in the way of that.

Mom leaves the locker room, so now it's up to me to pull myself together for my first match at Forest Hills. My heart is thumping hard, and my throat aches. I'm on my own, a short, squat kid in a world of grownups.

Way too soon, the woman at the tournament desk calls "Julie Heldman. Billie Jean Moffitt. Report to Court 15."

We walk out to the court together. Mom has found a spot courtside. Dad isn't there; he's at work. A few other spectators wander by.

Billie Jean serves and makes quick work of the first game. We change sides, and I look down as I walk to the back of the court to ask a ball boy for two balls, so that I can serve. All the ball boys and ball girls I've ever had have been short and quite young. When I look up, I realize that the ball kid in front of me is actually a ball man, taller and huskier than Dad. I'm the youngest player in the tournament and absolutely everyone towers over me.

Once the match starts, many points go predictably: She serves, races to the net, volleys, end of point. Or I serve, stay back, and try to hit forehands. When she reaches my backhand, she rushes the net, volleys, end of point. I also win some points and games with my speed, my Hoxie forehand, and my dropshot, and she makes some errors, but she's just too tough. She routines me, 6-4, 6-2.

"Game, set, and match Miss Moffitt." All too soon, my first Forest Hills is over. I hope the next time will go smoother.

CHAPTER 20

ON OUR OWN

For seven summers, I was a Hoxie Hot Shot. Hamtramck was my home base, and Mr. Hoxie drove us to tournaments in his station wagon. Now, in this summer of 1961, I'm too old for the 15-and-unders, and I'm ready to test my skills against older players, in events where the Hoxies never go. Carrie and I are setting out on our own, to compete in tournaments around the South, Midwest, and East.

Mr. Hoxie usually called me Tiger, but sometimes he called me The Manager, because I excelled at taking care of details. Carrie's always preferred to leave the arrangements to me, so when we travel, I hop right into my Manager role. We're friendlier now than before, because she has fewer opportunities to lord it over me, now that I've surpassed her as a tennis player. Still, our relationship isn't easy. We're more like oil and water. She's tall, thin, quiet, and introverted. I'm much shorter and more muscled, and although I lack friends, I'm a chatty extrovert who reaches out to everyone, from doormen to Mom's pals at Century. Before I turned 10, I learned how to make Mom laugh. I'd phone her at the office, pretending to be a French tennis player or a worker with a thick Brooklyn accent, and I loved it when she chuckled and said "Isn't that funny!" But it's maddeningly difficult to make Carrie laugh, and she still rarely talks to me, even when I ask her a question. So when we're together, I often end up stewing.

Our travels begin with the clay court tournaments. I love playing on clay. It's my best surface, because it's similar to Hamtramck's rough cement courts, where I've spent so many hours. On both surfaces, the ball bounces high, so points tend to last longer, giving me time to run down shots and smack forehands. The main difference between the two surfaces is that, on clay, you can slide into the ball. Try that on Hamtramck cement and you'll break your neck.

Our first two tournaments are for women of all ages, and my singles play is in the toilet. But in the Southern Women's doubles, in Winston-Salem, North Carolina, Carrie and I play well, despite putting on a vivid display of sibling rivalry. We're as different on the court as we are off of it. She likes to hit everything hard and flat. I prefer to vary the pace and hit swerving, topspin forehands. Our contrasting styles lead to disputes. But to everyone's surprise, the Southern

Women's Doubles champs are Carrie and Julie Heldman.

During our final two weeks on clay, I have very few victories, because I just can't find my rhythm. So much for clay being my favorite surface. I feel miserable from all this losing. Sure, most of my opponents are a lot taller and older than I am. But that's no excuse. A loser is a nobody. All my life I've needed to be somebody. I have to get some wins.

Next we head east for the grass court season. I doubt I'll do better on grass courts, which are the bane of my existence. I've rarely played on grass, because there are very few grass court clubs in the U.S. And grass courts rarely provide friendly high bounces. In fact, the bounces are so low and erratic that you have to crouch down until your knees and butt almost scrape the turf. The best grass-court players have strong serves and rush the net constantly, to hit the ball before it bounces, to avoid the surface's unpredictability. My serve is my weakness, and while I can volley pretty well, Mr. Hoxie taught us to be allergic to the front part of the court, especially in singles. The upshot is that grass-court play is foreign to me, but I'd better learn. So many important tournaments are played on grass, including the U.S. Girls 18-and-under (the "National Juniors"), the U.S. Nationals at Forest Hills, and Wimbledon, where maybe I'll get to play one day.

The first grass-court tournament for Carrie and me is a women's-only event at the Germantown Cricket Club in North Philadelphia. We're staying with a friendly family, who give us the attic room, where their dog, who just died, used to sleep. Carrie leaves for home at the end of the second day, having won a round and then lost the next. I lose in the first round, which is actually lucky, because the tournament has a consolation event, a whole new tournament just for women who lose in the first round. The more I play, the more I get the hang of the surface, and for the first time this summer I get a groove, and I win a few matches.

There's one weirdness. My legs have lots of itchy bumps. I figure I'm allergic to the grass. I call home on Friday, and Laura says "Your sister has flea bites." Oh no. That's what I have. Tons of them. And they're huge and red. I must be allergic to fleas. I reach Mom, and she says I should tell the tournament that I'm getting asthma from the dust in my room, and I need to move to a motel. Why doesn't she want me to tell the truth? She doesn't say. Why doesn't she tell them herself? Instead, she alienates me from my lovely hosts by making me lie to them.

I'm on my own in the motel, which doesn't bother me, but the bites certainly do. They're so bad that I'm up half the night, trying shock treatments—ice cold water, then scalding hot water, anything to make the itching go away. Nothing works. At 3:15 AM I can't sleep, so I pass the time by counting my bites. I stop at 72. Despite constant scratching, which turns my bites into scabs, I win my first tournament on the summer women's tour. I'm thrilled, even though the competition is just for first round losers.

A few weeks later, I play the Juniors, which is also held in Philadelphia. I've always dreamed of winning this tournament, just the way Dad did in 1936. It was his biggest victory, and it's my only goal in tennis. But I have a long way to go before I feel comfortable on grass, although I'm improving steadily. I reach the quarters, where I play Billie Jean Moffitt, the favorite to win the title. Last year at Forest Hills, she handled me easily, but this year I dig into the match right away, and we split two tough sets. In the third, I'm up 4-3, serving with the wind, poised to win. Instead, she turns the tables, blankets the net, and robs me of any chance to get comfortable. In a flash, she runs off three straight games, and the match is over. I'll have to do better.

CHAPTER 21
GROWING AND MATURING

In September 1961, I leave tennis tournaments behind and return to Dalton, where I begin my senior year. My two worlds—tennis and Dalton—are completely estranged from each other, but they're similar in one way: I have no friends in either world. In the tennis world, the other players and I at least have similarities in our competitiveness and athletic skills. But at Dalton, my classmates and I are separated by a barrier that's impossible to overcome: Our ages. I'm 15, and they're 17 or 18. Plus most of them conform to the mold of Upper East Side Jewish girls, who look like full-grown adults, with clothes and manners that are expected on Park Avenue. Dalton is a magnet for families in the arts, and many parents are actors, writers, or artists. My interests, and the way I walk and talk, show exceedingly clearly that I don't fit into that mold. Still, my classmates treat me well, rather like a younger sister with whom they have little in common. Although they know I'm a tennis player, they don't have a clue about the tournaments I've won or how high I'm ranked. None of them ask, so I largely keep my tennis world to myself.

Last May, Carrie graduated from Dalton. Throughout high school, she remained a superstar student, and this month she starts Radcliffe, the sister school of Harvard. I've spent all my life in her academic shadow, but now that she's gone, I feel freed up to shine. The school has given me a wonderful education. There's remarkably little rote memorization here; the teachers try to instill a love of learning. I'm lucky to have my four favorite teachers this year. Miss T, who teaches English, dresses severely and draws her hair back in a bun, but she's neither rigid nor didactic; she's funny and kind and caring. I did incredibly well in Mr. Hanlon's 10th grade Geometry class, where I was often able to solve proofs all by myself. This year he'll teach us calculus. In Mme Ernst's class, we speak only French, and she keeps the discussions lively, ranging from romance to politics to French culture. And of course I adore our irascible music teacher, Mr. Aks, who has introduced me to a wide range of sounds and words.

My studies have improved in lock step with my tennis. My intense need to win on the court has helped me develop the focus necessary to fight from behind or to close out a match. In the classroom, that same drive has translated into riveted concentration. Dalton doesn't give us grades, but I can tell that in math, French, and science I'm near the top of the class, although I'm not as good in English. For the most recent parent-teacher conference, Miss T wrote "Julie does quite well, considering that she never reads books unless they're required for class."

As autumn slides into winter, I hear my classmates discussing where they'll apply to college. Almost all want to remain on the East Coast, preferably to attend an Ivy League school. I don't want that. I'm seeking a college where I can play tennis outdoors year round and still get an excellent education.

Colleges with quality women's tennis programs are hard to find. The Ivy League schools have either terrible tennis programs or none at all. Plus I hate the cold, and I've heard that Ivy League students are snooty, like Carrie, and I hate that. Only a few colleges offer women's tennis scholarships. The best tennis school is Rollins College, in Florida, but its academic reputation isn't stellar. The same is true for the "tennis colleges" in Texas and Arizona. None of them appeal to me. But Stanford does. It has a terrific academic reputation, and even though it lacks women's tennis scholarships and a women's tennis team, several quality women players attend Stanford, and I hope they'll practice with me.

But I really know nothing about Stanford, except that my parents went there 20 years ago. Dad helps me by introducing me to his mentor at Shell, a Stanford alum who interviews me on behalf of Stanford. He tells Dad that he'll put in a good word for me, but he doesn't think I'll need his help, with my school and tennis successes.

I'll also need to do well on the SATs. Carrie scored off the charts, even though she was sick with mononucleosis when she took them. Our teachers give us a little SAT prep, mostly on math problems and vocabulary, but I don't search for additional ways to improve my scores, the way Carrie did. Still, my scores are very high, and Stanford ought to accept me.

All the Dalton seniors tense up in April, hoping for fat envelopes from colleges, signifying acceptance, and dreading thin envelopes, meaning rejection. Stanford sends me a fat envelope, and I'm set.

Once my classmates' futures are fixed, most lose interest in their studies and barely crack a book during the last few months of our senior year. But I'm becoming more and more fascinated with my classes. After I turned 16 in December, I began changing rapidly. I've grown a few inches, and I've become more curious about the world. In every single class, I take a leap of maturity.

Shortly before graduation, during our weekly all-school meeting, Mme. Ernst announces the annual winner of the French Award, given to the outstanding French student in the 12th grade. Carrie won it last year, and to my surprise, I win it now. Mme. Ernst presents me with a large, engraved medal, and I'm thrilled. I show it to Mom and Dad, but they aren't that interested. They obviously don't understand that Carrie has always made me feel stupid, and how important it is for me to match one of her academic achievements,

With graduation around the corner, everyone signs my yearbook, and most say "We must keep in touch!!" but I know that's not true. After five years at Dalton, I don't know where any of my classmates live or what they like to do.

Mom sent us to Dalton because of its impeccable reputation, but she isn't interested in how we're taught or what we learn. She finds the twice-yearly parent-teacher conferences boring and useless. She's even detested my class plays. When I was 13, I was excited to take on the role of the buffoon Sir Toby Belch in our all-girl production of Shakespeare's *Twelfth Night*. Mom sat through the play, but afterwards she barely mentioned my performance, because she was preoccupied with laughing at a girl in my class who lisped. Mom tried to excuse herself by saying that another parent—Bert Lahr, the Scarecrow from the movie *The Wizard of Oz*—was laughing too. Both of them were cruel.

Today, June 8, 1962, is my graduation, and Mom grudgingly makes an appearance, looking unhappy. But I love our graduation ceremony. Like the school itself, the event is well thought out, personalized, and fulfilling. I'm overjoyed that I had the opportunity to grow up and learn in such a warm and caring environment.

After graduation, I focus on tennis. At the Hoxie's, I always had weeks of practice before I started playing tournaments. Not this year. I'll jump right into playing tournaments, which is risky. Mr. Hoxie and Dad always rammed into my head that practice is the life blood of a tennis player. I'll just have to take my chances.

I'll be traveling alone, because Carrie's fully immersed in helping Mom save the U.S. Nationals at Forest Hills from its near demise, a huge undertaking. They spend countless hours arranging for players to get to New York and organizing housing, special events, and parties. Carrie's plate is full.

Like last year, I'll play clay court tournaments in June and July and then move to grass court tournaments in August and September. Traveling on my own at age 16 isn't too bad. The world of tournament tennis is predictable, and I know it well. Every morning I go to the courts, practice, have lunch, and play matches. The tournament puts me up in the home of a club member, where I shower, have meals, and sleep. My biggest challenge is getting from one tournament to the next, but players with cars usually let me hitch a ride.

My increased maturity in the classroom is surfacing on the courts. I start out on a tear, winning five singles titles in four weeks, relying on both skill and guts. At the most important clay court tournament in the U.S., the National Clay Courts, I reach the semis, but Donna Floyd, a long-term U.S. top-tenner, crushes me. She played in Europe this spring, and she's improved so much that it feels like she's toying with me. One day I hope to play in Europe too.

In August, I play three grass court events for 18-and-under girls: Wilmington, Delaware; the Intersectional Team Competition; and the Juniors in Philadelphia. I'm still determined to follow in Dad's footsteps at the Juniors. I'll turn 17 in December, so I have only one more year to match his victory. I think I'm good enough this year to reach the finals, but I'm not yet ready to win it, because Vicki Palmer's in the way. She's 17, but she already won the Juniors last year, over the favored Billie Jean, by hitting so hard and flat that many of her shots were unreturnable. I don't know how I could stand up to her.

In the Wilmington semis, I meet Janie Albert, a Californian whose father, Frankie Albert, was a famous quarterback at Stanford and for the San Francisco Giants. As we walk on court, I feel cocky. I figure she can't be that good, because I've never seen her or heard of her. And she sure as hell doesn't scare me; her looks are more prom queen than star athlete. I'm more of a jock. Sure, I sleep every night in brush curlers and tease my hair every morning, but while she always appears polished and smooth, I slump and bounce and weave, ready to do battle. I know how to fight and win.

Once the match starts, I realize Janie's a fine athlete. Our first set is close, but it goes her way, and then she runs away with the second, startling me and punching dents in my confidence. Her natural grass court style causes me fits. Her strong serve propels her forward, where she uses her excellent volleying skills to thump on my backhand, my weaker groundstroke. She often takes my serve on the rise, scampers to the net, and takes over the point before I can settle down.

My loss to Janie feels calamitous. Worse, we meet again in the semis of the Juniors, and although I'm now familiar with her style, she thumps me again, in a match that's even more one-sided than the one in Wilmington.

Those two losses have awakened in me a fear that I'll never be able to achieve my dream to win the Juniors. Two girls are now obstructing my path to glory, Janie and of course Vicki Palmer, who wins the Juniors for the second time by beating Janie in the finals. They're both better than I am on grass, and if I play my normal style, I'll lose. I'll have to get creative. I have a year to figure out how to take charge of my own fate and achieve my goal.

CHAPTER 22
THE FABULOUS 1962 NATIONALS

Until the end of the 1960s, the USLTA was in charge of competitive tennis in the USA. It made the rules, sanctioned the tournaments, and issued rankings. But the association was run by volunteers, and although many of them worked hard, some bungled their tasks.

Even before Mom started *World Tennis*, she wrote about the mistakes made by the USLTA. In 1961, she wrote an editorial decrying the absence of overseas players on the U.S. summer circuit and at the Nationals. Although the players were amateurs, they needed enough money to survive, and the American tournaments consistently refused to pay them much, while European tournaments were far more generous with under-the-table cash. So while the USLTA forced Americans to play on home soil, most foreigners stayed away. Mom wrote that Wimbledon was the finest tournament in the world because its draws had all the best players from every country. She suggested that the path to greatness for U.S. tournaments would be to copy Wimbledon and load the draws with overseas players.

The response to Mom's editorial was a resounding silence. But she kept trying. She had heard rumors that Perry T. Jones wanted to move the Nationals from New York to Los Angeles, and she wanted to pre-empt his campaign. She came up with a startlingly creative plan, to charter an airplane to import 80 players from Europe. The $18,000 cost of the charter was enormous, and the money had to be found. At first, she turned to the USLTA, but it declined, crying poverty. With no other reasonable alternative, she put together a consortium of 10 people (including herself). Each one agreed to make a tax-deductible contribution of $1,800. The donors' money would be returned if the 1962 Nationals earned at least $18,000 more than in 1961. All sides agreed, and a deal was struck between the donors, the USLTA, and the West Side Tennis Club. For the first time, a group unaffiliated with the USLTA would be responsible for a large portion of the finances of the U.S. Nationals.

Mom was the first donor to sign on, and then she hit the telephone. Her first two calls were to close friends Joe Cullman and Marvin Levy, and both agreed to help. Other donors included Mitchell Cox of Pepsi-Cola, the first regular, non-tennis, four-color advertiser in *World Tennis*; Frank Hunter, a tennis star in the 1920s turned executive of 21 Brands, a liquor company; and Alastair Martin of the Eastern Tennis Patrons, a patrician of enormous wealth who would become President of the USLTA in 1969 and 1970. No one but Mom had such a stellar Rolodex.

Determined to help the U.S. Nationals succeed, Mom used every arrow in her quiver. She wrote one editorial after another, hyping the event. She printed large announcements, asking fans either to house overseas players or to contribute money for their hotel stays (One of the 10 donors was the president of the hotel chain, and he gave the players reduced rates). She even printed free advertisements for the tournament. Mom always loved parties, so she planned special events and other festivities, including her own annual soiree.

And most importantly, Mom concentrated on bringing the best players to Forest Hills. Rod Laver was one of the first to sign up for a seat on the plane. He'd won the first three majors in 1962, and victory in New York would make him the second man—after Don Budge—to win the Grand Slam. Mom contacted national associations around the world, informing them that there would be room on the plane for terrific players. She knew that every quality player whom she snagged would bring a greater likelihood of the tournament's success. With a plane full of excellent players, she calculated that even if the tournament had two days of rain, there'd be so many good matches that the tournament would be highly profitable.

A letter was even sent to the Soviet Union, whose players had never ventured beyond the Iron Curtain. Although the Soviet Federation declined seats on the chartered plane, it sent a team via Aeroflot, the Russian airline, to compete in the U.S. for the first time ever.

There was excitement aplenty.

Mom was always savvy about courting the press, and in 1962 she turned to them to help make the tournament succeed. During the spring, she appeared at the Lawn Tennis Writers luncheon in New York City, to bring the writers up to date and get them revved up for the main event. After she finished, Walter Hoag, the president of the West Side Tennis Club, got up to speak. He startled everyone and brought a hush to the crowd when he said that as far as he was concerned, the club wasn't committed to returning the $18,000 to the donors, no matter how great the profits might be. Fortunately, the press largely ignored Hoag, and his remarks were soon negated by Ed Turville, the new and forward-thinking USLTA

President. Turville promised unequivocally that the donors would be paid back, even if the money had to come out of the USLTA's share of the profits.

Importing 80 terrific players was all-consuming, but Mom still needed to run *World Tennis*. To do it all, she often worked through the night. During the summer, Carrie came on board, having finished her first year at Radcliffe. Both worked feverishly to make sure 80 overseas players were taken care of. Carrie said she'd never seen anyone work as hard as Mom. Mom said Carrie did the work of three people.

I too had a role in the 1962 Nationals. The Soviet contingency consisted of three men players, one woman player, and three male officials, who kept tabs on their charges. The woman, Anna Dmitrieva, needed a practice partner, so Mom offered my services, and I got to spend the day speaking French with her and practicing on grass. At lunch, during a rare moment when the players were out of earshot from their minders, I learned a geopolitical lesson. In the U.S., we used the words "Soviet" and "Russian" interchangeably, but Tomas Leius of Estonia and Alex Metreveli of Georgia hated being called Russian. They craved independence from the Russian Bear.

When the chartered plane landed in New York, everyone, including Mom, was thrilled, although she was disappointed that there were five empty seats, all of which had been promised to the Italians. Several of them claimed illness, but the others were just no-shows who failed to give any excuse. Mom couldn't help calculating how much money had been lost with the Italians' thoughtlessness.

Once the tournament started, every match brought excitement. The fans were entertained by new faces from Scandinavia to the Middle East, from Scandinavia to South Africa, and from Australia to South America. The players were thrilled to be playing in front of large crowds. Even in early rounds, the stadium was packed, for the first time since anyone could remember. The tournament was a huge success, attracting the best crowds since the late 1920s, during the glory years of American stars Big Bill Tilden, Little Bill Johnston, Helen Wills, and Helen Jacobs.

In 1962, despite the much improved competition, the top players still dominated the final rounds; Laver won his Grand Slam, and Margaret Smith won the women's singles over American Darlene Hard. But the tournament write-ups were far more glowing than usual, because everyone realized that Mom had pulled off a unique tour de force.

After the tournament, Mom published pages of glowing Letters to the Editor from overseas players, their hosts, and regular fans who'd been bowled over by their experience at Forest Hills. She also printed numerous photos of players who'd come to this country for the first time, with captions written, as usual, by Dad, whose descriptions of their styles of play enlightened *World Tennis*'s readers.

The event had been magical.

Soon after the final ball was struck at the 1962 U.S. Nationals, Mom and the other nine donors were repaid out of the tournament's healthy profits. Those were the only funds Mom received from the event. To put it all in context, her innovative concepts and her hard work were the cornerstone of the tournament's achievement. Those contributions would have been exceptional had they come from a business woman or businessman driven by a profit motive. But Mom did it all for free. And of course she also dug into her own pocket to cover the cost of her party and to help pay for the players' hotel.

Mom wasn't involved in the 1963 U.S. Nationals, and I don't know why. Perhaps the club wanted the headstrong Jewish woman out of the way. Perhaps the USLTA wanted to run the event themselves. Maybe she'd had enough. For whatever reason, no one would ever replicate either her idea of chartering a plane to bring in 80 players, or the fabulous 1962 Nationals.

CHAPTER 23
A FRESHMAN

It's September 1962, and I'm flying cross country to start my life as a 16-year-old Stanford freshman. No longer will I live in Manhattan, go to comfy Dalton, or take the subway to Brooklyn to play tennis. No longer will I live with my parents. I'll start life on my own.

I've been assigned to Roble Hall, built in 1918, the same dorm Mom lived in when she was a freshman. Like every other girl on my corridor, I have a single room. I love my very own room.

Once I put away my clothes, I open the door to my new world, a hallway that's teeming with girls like me who're excited to start their new lives. We wander down to dinner in Roble's giant dining hall, where three meals a day are served to the dorm's 300 students. During tennis tournaments, I've occasionally been housed in dorms, so I'm not surprised that the gray-brown pieces of meat on our plates (instantly dubbed "mystery meat") are barely edible.

After our meal, six girls from our corridor pile into a small room, and we talk for hours about who we are and what we want in life. No one seems to care that I'm two years younger than most of them. This is the first time I've ever felt enough kinship with a group of girls to sit around and shoot the breeze. I'm so thrilled to feel like I belong.

At Stanford, I want girlfriends, with whom I can share my secrets, and boys whom I can date. I'll also need to concentrate on studying and playing tennis. I'll be busy.

Orientation begins with endless lectures in giant auditoriums about what to expect at Stanford. I take an immediate dislike to impersonal lecture halls, which are so different from Dalton, where my largest class had 20 girls. After the incoming freshmen have been stuffed with useless information, we stand in interminable lines to sign up for classes. For years, I've fantasized about becoming a doctor, and I take my first step in that direction by signing up for several pre-med classes.

I really want to fit in, so I stay up at night yakking, and I buy season tickets to Stanford football, where I sit in the student section and cheer when I'm told to do so. And for the first time in my life, I go shopping for clothes by myself. The popular girls on my corridor wear conservative A-line skirts and blouses with round collars, all in pastel colors. I decide to copy them.

But few of my efforts to fit in work out. I hate being told when to cheer at football games, so I stop going altogether. My midnight yak fests leave me in constant sleep debt, so I retreat earlier into my room to rest and decompress. It's hard to change a lifelong habit of aloneness.

I also need more time to study. Two of my classes, calculus and chemistry, are really tough. At Dalton, I was a whiz at concrete math problems, but college math requires abstract thinking, and I discover that's not my forte. Give me a defined space, such as a tennis court, and I thrive. Take away the lines, and I'm lost. And in chemistry, I'm constantly a step or two behind. Most of my classmates already took chemistry in high school, while Dalton never offered the class.

Still, I'm keeping up moderately well in my classes, but the tennis situation is far worse than I'd expected. The two upper-class women I'd hoped to practice with are no longer on campus. The main tennis center, where the men's team practices, is several miles across campus, and I don't have a car. The "women's courts" are close to my dorm, but they're usually empty, so finding a practice partner is challenging. I try to play a few times a week by walking to the courts and waiting around for someone to show up, a setup that's far from optimal. But I've spent every winter since I was eight trekking to Brooklyn to practice just a few hours a week. I'll get by.

Before I came to Stanford, I knew it offered very little to women tennis players. Still, I'd hoped that the university would provide some assistance. I become momentarily optimistic when I receive a phone call from a Mrs. Guthrie, who works in the women's P.E. department. She says she's here to provide support for women tennis players. But it turns out her help is limited to driving us to two tennis tournaments next spring. That's all Stanford has to offer.

But my desire to win the Juniors hasn't diminished. I've heard a rumor that Vicki Palmer won't defend her title next summer, and if that's true, Janie Albert will be my biggest rival, so I work on a two-part plan to beat her. The first part is to restore my confidence. Every night, once I turn out the lights, I'll spend a few minutes convincing myself that I can beat her. The second part of my plan gives me a road map. Last summer, Janie beat me by constantly rushing the net, a typical grass-court tactic. I can't let her do that again. To keep her away from the net, I develop a "Janie Strategy," a hybrid of grass and clay-court tactics. In the clay-court aspect of the tactics, I'll hit high and deep to her backhand, pinning her to the baseline and making her reach up uncomfortably. We'll both be in the back of the court, where I'm better than she is. In the grass-court aspect of my tactics, I'll smack my forehand early and hard, to dominate the points. The combination should turn the odds in my favor. Every night I'll review my tactics, so that they'll become second nature. I'll be ready.

Day by day at Stanford I change and mature, but I'm still not meeting boys. I have no idea how some girls attract hordes of boys. When I see guys walking around Stanford, I'm baffled. Having spent so little time around boys, I know very little about them. They seem like a foreign species to me.

Mom has never been helpful about how I should behave around boys. She thinks that, to be attractive to boys, I should sit, stand, walk, and bat my eyelashes in absurd ways. I've always refused to comply. My refusal is a rare and unspoken act of rebellion against her, one of the few ways I stand up for myself.

But I have no one else to turn to for advice about how to act around boys. I have no choice but to be my normal self and see what happens. I show up at mixers and start conversations with a few guys. No one's pounding down my door, but from time to time I go out on a date. I even have my first kiss, while Johnny Mathis is crooning love songs on the record player. It's nice, but bells don't ring. I wonder how I'll meet someone I could love.

In my quest to find a boy, I have to look my best. But I'm gaining weight. Every morning, I weigh myself on the scales in the communal bathroom at the end of the hall, and the numbers have been creeping up. So far, I've gained just two pounds, but I dare not put on any more. I'm deeply afraid of becoming fat. I get that from Mom, who controls her weight by standing on the scales 5-10 times a day. And as long as I can remember, she's made fun of my legs, because they're chunkier than Carrie's or hers. I'm sure everyone must think I have unattractive legs, and I don't want them to get any thicker. To lose the weight I've gained, I make a plan. I've never liked getting up for breakfast, so instead, I'll skip it and buy a candy bar at the student union on the way to class. After a few weeks of doing that, I still haven't lost weight, so I start skipping lunch also. Soon, when I look in the mirror, I see a lovely, sleek new me.

I'm not the most diligent student—I'm trying too hard to grow up!—but I take exams seriously. As the quarter moves along, I have loads of midterms, which I'm not used to, because Dalton didn't emphasize exams as much as Stanford does.

And I spend a week cramming for finals. When they're finished, I'm exhausted.

My first night back home, I fall into my old routine, bringing Mom her drinks, cooking her dinner, and spending the rest of the night alone. I enjoy sneaking Mom's carton of Häagen-Dazs coffee ice cream into my room, but when she suddenly appears at my door, I shove the container behind my bed and stand up rapidly, to hide the evidence. And then I faint. When I regain consciousness, I'm on the floor, and my head is jerking, as if I were having a fit. Mom is horrified and scared, and the next morning, she drops her usual reluctance to call the doctor, and sends me to Dr. Leader. He's not worried. "Your blood pressure is quite low. Have you been getting enough sleep?"

"Not much during finals week."

"Have you been eating well?"

"Not too bad." I don't tell him about my candy bar diet.

"Did you know you've grown two inches since I saw you last? That kind of growth spurt takes a lot out of you, so you have to try extra hard to eat and sleep well."

So that's why I was gaining weight! I resolve to eat more regularly, so I won't pass out again.

Over the holidays, I get my grades: a few A's, a few B's, and a disappointing C in chemistry. I can't wait to return to campus, to do better.

And I do. Second quarter chemistry requires lots of concrete math skills, my forte. I even slam dunk the final, getting every problem right, but the professor makes an error grading my paper, and gives me a "B." I knock on his door to contest the mistake, but when he opens it, I burst into tears, terrified that he might get angry at me. But fear doesn't stop me from fighting for what is rightly mine. So I dry my eyes and show the professor his mistake. He changes my grade to an A.

Notwithstanding my perfect score in Chemistry, my grades aren't fabulous. Some of my classes are exceedingly difficult, and I'm not that disciplined about studying. Plus I keep trying to develop a social life. As a result, for the first time in my life, I lower my expectations, and I don't expect stellar grades.

But I still have high hopes for the Juniors. I practice as often as I can, and every single night, I focus on my Janie Strategy.

At the end of April 1963, Mrs. Guthrie drives us to the annual tennis tournament held in the Ojai Valley, a few hours north of Los Angeles. From the moment we arrive, there are constant rain storms, and my first match keeps getting pushed back, until on the third day, the tournament is so far behind that I'm scheduled to play at 5:45 AM. That's inhuman. But Mrs. Guthrie really helps out, promising to get up early and to wake me up only once the rains have stopped. And I'm the happiest kid around when I open my eyes up at 7:00 and see that rain is still coming down. When the skies finally clear, I win the tournament for Stanford, and Mrs. Guthrie drives us back to campus. She isn't a tennis coach, and she can't help me with my game, but she's a kind woman, and I'm grateful for that.

As summer looms closer, my thoughts of winning the Juniors in August become nearly constant. From Stanford, I sign up for the summer tournaments, as always, first on clay and then on grass.

CHAPTER 24
THE JUNIORS

After my last final, I fly to New York. On Saturday, the family drives out to Century for some tennis, but I'm too exhausted to move my butt off the chair. At first, I blame my fatigue on cramming for exams, but after three more days of debilitating fatigue, I realize something worse must be happening. I beg Mom to let me visit Dr. Leader, and she agrees. Because he's a pediatrician, he easily recognizes the symptoms of the mumps, a childhood disease, even though I don't have the illness's signature chipmunk cheeks. He says the mumps are usually pretty mild when you're a young kid, but they get rougher as you age. I'm not old; I'm 17. But the illness has me whipped. His prescription is simple: rest. So I crawl under the sheets, hoping to recover quickly, but no such luck. After a week, I'm still exhausted, and I vow to stay in bed to wait the illness out.

During my long days in bed, I fluctuate between sleeping, resting, and boredom. I'm often stuck watching crummy daytime TV. There isn't much else to do. There's rarely anyone to talk to. Mom pops her head in the door occasionally, but not for long. Dad is mostly out of town on business trips. At least Laura brings me toast with butter and honey, her lifelong remedy for illnesses. Meantime, worries churn in my head. I turn 18 at the end of this year, so this is my last shot at winning the Juniors. I really must win it.

But first I have to get well.

After two weeks in bed, fatigue still shadows my every move. The mumps have clearly deep sixed the early part of my season, and I'll have to skip all my beloved clay court events and go straight to the grass. I'm itching to get going, desperate to practice and play matches.

Finally, I'm well enough to practice. I start gently, to avoid any setbacks. When I can play for a full hour, I figure I'm ready. I take the train to Philadelphia for my first tournament of the summer.

Out on court 6, it's sunny and humid and really, really hot, a typical Philadelphia July day, yet I'm shivering and losing to someone Mr. Hoxie would call "a Fish." A patsy. My forehand is usually my bread-and-butter shot, but it won't go in, and my backhand is a mess. I'm feeling slow and weird, but I refuse to lose this match. So I start going for broke, hitting harder to shorten the points. The tide turns. I run away with the last two sets, 2-6, 6-1, 6-1. But to win the match, I had to use up all my reserves. As I walk to the net to shake hands, I feel my energy crashing.

I trudge to the tournament desk to report the score. Before I say anything, I find a seat and slump down. Someone asks if I'm sick.

"Maybe."

"Do you have anyone to help you?"

"Nope. It's just me."

"You really ought to get checked out. Why don't you see the tournament doctor? He's inside the clubhouse, across the hall from the locker room."

Slogging down the hall leaves me sapped. The doctor sits me down, lays a hand on my forehead and looks concerned. "Open your mouth and put this thermometer under your tongue." A minute later he checks the results. "You have a temperature of 103." He starts grilling me to find out what's wrong.

I tell him "I just got over the mumps."

He says "Young lady, you need more rest."

I reluctantly decide to pull out of the tournament, return home, and recover in my own bed. I've been staying in a dorm this week, so I return there to pack, but I'm fried. I start by placing my suitcase on the bed, but that exhausts me, so I lie down for a while. I look around the barren room, which is devoid of color or personality. Never mind, I need to pack. I walk to the closet to pull out shoes, but before I place them in the bag, I have to lie down again. After 10 minutes, my suitcase has just a puny spattering of clothes. I need help. But asking for help can be agony. It was trained out of me young. I always assume that no one wants to help me, and that if I do ask for help, I'll be perceived as an annoyance. Lying in this grim room, hardly able to fill my suitcase, I realize I have no choice. I open the door to scan the hallway, and I spot one of the tennis moms. It's Mrs. Taylor, mother of Maggie, whom I played in the semis of the 15s. During that match, I was rude to Mrs. Taylor, and ever since, I've been ashamed to say hello, petrified she'll tell me to go to hell. Today, I have no choice.

"Mrs. Taylor, will you please help me? I need to finish packing my bag, but I'm sick, and I can't get it done."

"Oh, poor dear. Of course I'll help. You just lie down, and I'll get you all fixed up."

This is too good to be true. She's gentle and efficient, all in one package. In rapid succession, she finishes my packing, calls me a cab, walks me to the dorm's entrance, and wishes me well. I say "Thank you." I wish I'd said something like "You're an angel," or "I'm forever grateful" for all of her kindness and generosity.

Dad's office is near Penn Station, where the train is bound, so before I embark, I call him collect and ask him to pick me up. On the curb outside the station, he greets me with a big hug, grabs my bag, and catches us a cab. I'm thrilled he's collecting me, because I'm too exhausted to get home by myself, as I usually do. The next day, I visit Dr. Leader, who doesn't know why I got such a high fever. "Maybe it's the aftermath of the mumps, or maybe the heat or the exertion, but probably a combination of all of them. Time is all you need." But I'm almost out of time, with the Juniors starting in just a few weeks. Still, I catch all the rest I can get, this time just a few days. Then I leap back into tournament play.

The next event is a women's tournament, held at the Merion Cricket Club, a posh enclave on Philadelphia's exclusive Main Line. "Exclusive" means membership is not bestowed on every Tom, Dick, or Harry. To join, you have to know a bunch of members and you have to be blessed by the membership committee. To be even a guest, you have to be a WASP (White Anglo Saxon Protestant), which obviously excludes all Jews (including me) and blacks. So for 51 weeks a year, I'm persona non grata. That's true for most of the Eastern grass court clubs.

The cards are stacked against this Jewish girl from New York. The Juniors are played on grass, but finding grass-court practice is difficult, because most clubs with grass courts are "exclusive."

Yeah, but no one tries harder than I do.

At least the grass court clubs let me play their tournaments.

In the early '50s Althea Gibson, the only black woman to reach the top of the game, had a much tougher time. When she was coming up, the prejudice was so grim that many of the best white women players shunned her socially and refused to play doubles with her. Mom hated those players' ugly prejudice, and she was happy to befriend Althea. Grateful, Althea chose Mom as her doubles partner several times, even though Mom was ranked much lower than "Big Al." Mom told us that the grass court clubs were the most prejudiced. She said one tournament shut its doors permanently rather than invite Althea. She showed them all. She became a big star, winning the women's singles at Wimbledon and Forest Hills in both 1957 and 1958.

On Monday at midday, I check in at the Merion tournament desk, where in return for my entry fee I get an envelope filled with goodies: my player's badge, the name and address of my host and hostess for the week, the rules of the club, and other important papers. A fellow player says "Shall we have lunch in the club dining room?"

"I didn't bring much cash."

"No problem. Your packet contains lunch tickets. Check it out." I do just that, but there are no lunch tickets. So I return to the tournament desk and ask, "Is there a mistake? I can't find my lunch tickets."

The tournament staff fusses around a bit, and one woman disappears into a back room. When she returns, she says "Sorry, but there weren't supposed to be any lunch tickets in your packet."

"What?"

"The committee chairman says lunch tickets are only for those who live far away, and you live in New York."

"You mean I'm supposed to take a two-hour train ride to New York City every day to eat lunch, and then another two-hour train back to play my match?"

"Sorry, those are the rules."

Shocked, I try to understand the rationale. Maybe they mean that players who live far away need more financial help. But some Californians, like Maggie Taylor, are well off. Her father runs a major oil company, and I assume he makes big bucks, yet Maggie gets lunch tickets. I ask around. I'm the only Jewish player, and it looks like I'm the only player without lunch tickets. Why is this happening? Because I'm Jewish? Because I have an influential—Jewish—mother? I have no idea what to do, so I call Mom, who basically says "Don't rock the boat." That means I should pay for my own meals and say nothing. So I shut my mouth. And seethe.

Tuesday, I rise and shine and play my first round singles match, which is a disaster. I lose to someone I should beat easily. Why did I lose? The aftermath of the mumps? Not enough practice? My fury at the tournament committee? None of that matters. The only thing that matters is the Juniors. I'll have to buckle down and practice harder—on grass. Maybe I should stay at Merion all week and play on their courts. What, and grin and bear their prejudice? Unh unh. I'm out of here.

I return to New York and try to scare up any practice I can find. At first, I'm stuck with clay court practice, but that's not what I need. Finally, I call a woman whose tennis is only so-so, but she has one major attribute—she belongs to the West Side Tennis Club in Forest Hills, the home of the U.S. Nationals. It's barely an hour away from our New York apartment, and it has scads of grass courts. For the next few days, I practice on grass.

I need the West Side Club's grass courts, so I try to block out the fact that the club is also prejudiced. Until a few years ago, it didn't admit blacks or Jews. In 1959, there was a huge scandal, when the son of Ralph Bunche, a black man who'd been the Ambassador to the United Nations and who'd won the Nobel Peace Prize, was turned down for membership. Although the club rapidly reversed its position, and admitted the young Mr. Bunche, a firestorm of fury was unleashed. For several years, protesters marched in front of the Clubhouse during the Nationals, decrying the club's prejudiced ways. The club claims that it has changed, and now accepts blacks and Jews. Mom says they've admitted only a token few.

On Monday, Mom drives me to the next tournament, the Eastern Grass Courts, in South Orange, New Jersey—also an hour from home—which the players call "Orange." We have fun together flying down the highway in her Cadillac convertible, with the top down and the wind in our faces, as I make her laugh. She loves hanging out with the players at Orange and gathering news for *World Tennis*, so she commutes there daily. That means I can get plenty of grass court practice. Lady luck is finally winking at me.

I register, and my player's packet is filled with luscious lunch tickets. I win my first match on Tuesday, but I'm still not playing so hot, and I crash and burn in the next round to Carole Caldwell, a U.S. top tenner. Even though her ranking is much higher than mine, and even though I have so many strikes against me, I really hate losing. At least I put up a good fight in the second set.

The three tournaments I've played so far this summer were for women of all ages, but now it's time to compete against girls my own age in the Intersectional Team event in Germantown, Pennsylvania. I'm playing on the Eastern team, which consists of players mostly from the greater New York area, where there aren't enough courts and there's too much rain and snow. That adds up to not much practice. As a result, few Eastern girls climb high in the rankings, and our team isn't expected to win. Sure enough, although I win my singles match, our team loses in the first round.

That's it. No more tournaments before the Juniors. At least I don't have to pack up and travel. The Juniors will be held a short car ride away, at the Philadelphia Cricket Club. Before the tournament starts, I'll practice for a few days and get lots of sleep.

At the Juniors, I'll have no coach and no family. Mom and Dad have scheduled a vacation in Jamaica during the tournament, a real slap in my face. It would have been easy for them to come watch me when I'm playing so close to home. Between the aftermath of the mumps and my lack of match play, I could really use some help, but I tell myself it doesn't matter. I've been dreaming about this moment for over a year. This is my turn to shine. I won't let worries—or anything else—get in the way of me winning the Juniors.

On Sunday, I check in with the tournament committee, who tell me I'll be housed with the Ludlow family. Boy did I get lucky. Mrs. Ludlow takes care of me, and the whole family adopts me as one of their own. Their young children have been reading about voodoo dolls, so the family decides that for each round I play, we'll make a doll that represents my opponent, stick pins in the doll to cast a spell, and place it in a small brown paper bag. I figure, *What the Hell*. It's ridiculous, but the family is so nice.

Bam, bam, bam I win three rounds in a row with relative ease. But then the draw turns tougher. After I lose the first set to Wendy Overton, a fine Florida player, I regroup and run away with the match, 6-0 in the third. The quarter-finals brings Jean Danilovich, a Californian who's steady as a rock. We've played several times on clay, where she gets everything back, and our matches have been endless. But the Juniors is on grass, and I'm better than she is on this surface, so for the second match in a row, I lose the first set and go on to win.

I've reached the semis. That means I have two matches to go. My parents are leaving tonight, so I call home to report in for the last time.

Over the years, Mom has seen me play a few tournaments, but never when it really counted. Sure, she watched my matches at the Orange Bowl in Miami Beach. She likes going there because the whole family stays in a fancy hotel that has its own swimming pool and courts. And during the 10 days of the U.S. Nationals at Forest Hills, she practically lives onsite, and she's been really good about watching my matches there, but so far, they haven't been crucial to my ranking, because I've been out of my league, and she hasn't had much to cheer about.

But neither of my parents has seen my big victories, when I won the Canadian National 18s title when I was 12, or the National 15s when I was 14. This week is the most important tournament of my life, and Mom and Dad have made other plans.

So it's a shock when I call home and Mom says "Carrie and I are coming to Philadelphia tomorrow to watch you play."

Flustered, I say: "How about your vacation?"

"Dad is flying out tonight, and I'll meet him there when your tournament is over."

I'm completely thrilled. They're coming to help me.

The next day, Mom and Carrie arrive in time for lunch at the club. As always, Mom's frantic for her drinks, but once she has her vodkas and her roast beef sandwich, she mellows out. After lunch, Carrie warms me up. Mrs. Ludlow has washed and ironed my best tennis outfit, and I've touched up my tennis shoes with white polish. I'm looking mighty spiffy, I must say.

My semi-final opponent, Kathy Harter, is one of the best California players. She has all the attributes of a fine grass court player—she serves and volleys and instinctively covers the net. She's about 5 feet 9, but she seems taller, because she holds herself perfectly erect. I played her a few weeks ago, and squeaked out a three-set win. Today, from the very beginning, every point is tightly contested. I stay back, and she surges forward. I smack forehands and loft lobs, and she hits smashes. After two and a half hours, it all comes down to a few points. She breaks my serve to lead 6-5 in the third. At 30-all, she's two points away from the match. This is way too close to shattering my dream. She serves to my backhand, and I swing as hard as I can. She lets it go, thinking it'll go out, but up puffs a cloud of white smoke. The ball has landed on the baseline. It's 30-40. Another serve, and once more she tests my backhand. I hit another winner, and now it's 6-all. In this one game I've surpassed my weekly quota of backhand winners. She looks distressed, and misses a few shots. Clearly, my clutch backhand winners have deflated her. So I put my foot on the accelerator, and the match is mine. I'm in the finals of the Juniors. Against Janie Albert. One more match to go.

After shaking hands, I head towards Mom. She doesn't look well.

"That was too hard to watch. I couldn't go through that again. I have to leave now. I'm heading back to New York right away so that I can catch a late flight to Jamaica."

Nary a "Well done." Not even a "Good luck tomorrow." Mostly "I gotta get out of here."

I feel like I've been body slammed. I thought she came to help me.

I look at Carrie. She says "I'm staying. I'll be happy to warm you up before the finals." Huge pillows of relief. The sister who constantly belittled me is now coming through.

Mrs. Ludlow is next to us. "We'd be thrilled to have Carrie stay with us too." Heavenly delight.

Mom is leaving. I won't let that shake me. Tomorrow is my big day. I'll start getting ready now.

Today is finals day, crunch time. As Janie and I stride onto the court for the finals, the announcer tells the crowd a little bit about us. Behind my baseline are two TV commentators. I look closely and realize that one of them is Maureen Connolly Brinker, one of the greatest players of all time. She was a superstar in her teens, winning the Grand Slam in 1953, when she was 18.

I've never played on TV before. It doesn't matter. I'm determined.

I'm ready for the worst, aware that Janie will try to smother the net and take advantage of my weaknesses. Instead, I turn on my "Janie strategy," which has become part of my marrow. I hit ball after ball high and deep to her backhand. When I get a short ball, I whack the hell out of my forehand or I dropshot, just the way Mr. Hoxie taught me. I get really lucky. Janie's's off her game and makes error after error. I take the first set 6-3. The second set starts the same way, and I'm up 5-2, coasting. One more game and the trophy is mine. Out of the blue, her game improves. At 5-4, I have four match points, but Janie claws back to 5-all. I hear the announcers talking loudly, saying "Janie is such a fighter. She's making a big comeback." Why are they cheering for her? I throw them some filthy looks and mumble a few choice words. If they're so excited for Janie, at least they could talk softer. But I make my own comeback, powering some forehands that lead to my victory. That's it. It's over. I've thought about this match so often, yet it's gone by in a flash.

"Game, set, and match, Miss Julie Heldman, 6-3, 7-5." Carrie rushes up to me for a hug. So do the Ludlows. I fleetingly think about my parents. On vacation. Not here.

I'm really happy, and I can't suppress a huge smile. Janie remains poised and lovely. I don't know how she does it. I'd be close to tears.

There's a TV interview after the match. "Did you know you're the first New York girl to win the National 18s since 1939?"

I look down and around and mumble "No, I didn't."

"I bet your parents are proud of you."

"I guess so."

That night Carrie and I celebrate with our surrogate family, and we phone our parents in Jamaica. Mom says "You're the greatest, the most wonderful." I'm giddy with the praise. But she's not here.

I did it. I won the Juniors. My head is swirling with emotion. But there's not much time to take it all in, because tomorrow we leave for the next tournament.

It's Monday morning, and our bags are packed. Carrie and I take the train to Boston, where we're playing the Women's National Doubles at the Longwood Cricket Club. Our first stop is her apartment in Harvard Square, to drop off our luggage. When we open the front door, we're assaulted with a blast of heat and the stench of food rotting in the sink. She shows me my bed, a mattress on the floor that's covered with crumpled up sheets that are gray with filth. Dust balls populate the corners. Suddenly, fatigue grabs me, and I slump down. During the Juniors, I was brimming with energy, which has just been sucked out of me. I can't imagine playing one more match. But my sister came to the Juniors to help me, and I owe it to her to play by her side. So we tuck our rackets under our arms, put a change of clothes in a small bag, and head off to Longwood to check in. We enter the clubhouse and run into waves of people milling around, waiting to practice or play a match. Once again exhaustion clips me at the knees. I find a corner to collapse in, while Carrie checks us in. She says our first match is Wednesday, so I can rest for a few days. As we get up to leave, Margaret Smith, the 21-year old Aussie who just won Wimbledon, walks over. "Congratulations, Julie. Good job winning the Juniors." She's currently ranked Number One in the world, and she's just been kind to me. I'm so thrilled I can barely say "Thank you."

Back at Carrie's apartment, the exhaustion continues. I try to figure out why. Maybe I never really got over the wreckage of the mumps, and I was playing on fumes. Another possibility is that, having finally won the Juniors, I feel adrift, without a goal. And of course, I have to face the fact that my parents abandoned me when I needed them the most. And being in Carrie's apartment makes everything worse. What I do know is that I can't go on. I can't play the doubles. I can't stay in this apartment. I have to go home. So I zip up my bags and leave for the train station, letting down the person who stood by me when it really counted.

Back home, I crawl under the covers once again, but I don't seem to be getting better. I leave my room only long enough to play a match at Forest Hills, but I certainly don't shine. My heart isn't in the tennis.

I prepare to return to Stanford. I had hoped to arrive on campus as the conquering hero, but instead I feel hollow. I've achieved my life's goal, but my parents didn't throw a party, or even a simple dinner, to celebrate my victory. I have a major, major letdown.

At Stanford, I'm too tired to play tennis or to go out and have fun. I sign up for another bunch of tough pre-med classes, including organic chemistry, but it's a bear. Tons of memorization is required, and I'm too spent to concentrate. I get further and further behind, so I drop the class. With that decision, my dream of becoming a doctor flies out the window. This quarter I can get by taking fewer units because I have a cushion. I did really well on the French SAT achievement test, and as a result, Stanford gave me 11 units of French, nearly a complete quarter. Last year, I had a vague wish to take advantage of my French skills by going to Stanford in France, but that was clearly impossible while I was pre-med and preparing for the Juniors. But now I'm freed up to do whatever I want. Everything's up for grabs.

CHAPTER 25
STANFORD IN FRANCE AND BEYOND

I've always wanted to be like Dad. He won the National Juniors, and now I've done it too. A few years later, he quit the tennis tour. He wanted security, so he set his sights on becoming a university professor.

Now that I've achieved my biggest goal, I don't know whether to keep competing or be like Dad and change my life entirely. I've been thrashing around for new directions, without luck. At Stanford, I still play tennis, because that's what I do, but no longer with the passion that brought me the Juniors title. I take interesting classes, I make a few friends, and I go out on dates. But I need something else.

So I decide to go to Stanford in France.

*   *   *   *

It's September 1964, and tonight I'm joining my Stanford-in-France group to fly from New York's Kennedy Airport to Paris's Orly, my first trip unconnected to tennis and my longest trip ever. Most of my classmates look giddy with anticipation. I sure am. We're 80 students who'll spend six months living, studying, and eating together in one building in Tours, France. We'll have classes four days a week, and during the other three days, we'll be free to explore Europe.

Once we board our flight, I fall into my usual airplane routine. I stash my tennis rackets overhead, shove my carry-on bag under my feet, and settle into a window seat—so that I can snooze with my head propped up by the glass. Normally, I curl up and close my eyes immediately, to shut out the world. On this flight, I eagerly chat deep into the night with my Stanford-in-France seat mates, before I catch a few hours of sleep.

At Orly, we gather our luggage, and then we endure a two-hour bus ride to our new headquarters along the Loire River. The time change and lack of sleep are hitting me big time, and I desperately need to rest, but first I have to move into my room with my roommate Lucy.

Before our flight, I'd only talked to Lucy once, last spring at our group's "meet-

and-greet" picnic on the Stanford campus. After just a few minutes, Lucy and I agreed on a whim to share a room in Tours.

In our tiny room, I tell Lucy that I want to unpack quickly, so that I can grab a bite and then crash. I recklessly toss my possessions into one side of our tiny closet, fill up my miniscule drawer, and then sit on my bed, waiting for her. But she continues at a clunky pace, meticulously finding the perfect spot for every item of her clothing. I begin to fret. Didn't she hear me? Or doesn't she care? While she works, we chat, and I quickly discover that we have very little in common. She's Miss Conformist, muted and proper; I want to be noticed, so I laugh and make jokes and wear bright-colored clothes. She disdains all sports; tennis has been an essential part of my life. She's a staunch conservative; the political science class I took last quarter turned me into a rabid liberal. Each new subject brings disagreement. We're still moving into our room, yet it already feels oppressive.

What a relief when Lucy finally finishes, and we walk down to the basement dining room to eat at one of its large, communal tables. Joining us is Robert, the Resident Associate ("RA"), a 23-year-old Stanford grad who's here with his new bride. Part of his job is to explain the French culture and help us deal with problems.

Because this is our first meal in France, he doles out some basic wisdom about French table manners. In the States, we're taught that's it's impolite to leave your hands on the table between bites. French culture requires the opposite, that hands must always be visible. Robert tells us "The French assume that hidden hands mean that there's hanky-panky under the table. They have sex on their minds." We Americans have sex on our minds too, but apparently the French talk about it more openly than we do.

The kitchen serves us what they call steak, although it doesn't resemble any steak I've ever seen. Most Americans like their beef thick, juicy, and well done. French steaks are as thin as pancakes, and they're cooked "barely acquainted with the pan," as the French say. When you cut into the meat, the insides are bloody. The flavor's very different from American steak, but I could get used to it.

Robert tells us that Stanford-in-France food can be quirky. Generally, it's not terrible, but occasionally it's so odd that it's a deal breaker, like when the kitchen serves seared calves' brains, a French delicacy, which are also "barely acquainted with the pan." Most Americans are repulsed and refuse to eat the dish, because it looks far too much like human brains. But Stanford has no control over the kitchen. When Stanford made its deal with the French government, the French ordained that meals served to Stanford students had to be the same as meals served to students at the University of Tours. That edict has had unintended consequences. French meals are almost always small, and because most American boys have grown up consuming huge volumes of milk and meat, they lose weight over here. Yet for some reason, many Stanford girls gain weight in France from snacking on the patisserie (French pastry) that they buy in shops. I'll have to watch what I eat.

On our second day in France, the group takes a field trip to Mont Saint-Michel, an historic landmark off the coast of Normandy. We leave after breakfast, which includes strong French coffee, and soon most of us are begging for a pit stop. The driver lets us off outside a bar, and we all run inside, requesting "la salle de bain," the term taught in American schools that literally means "the room with the bath." The owner looks at us quizzically and throws up his hands, exclaiming that his bar doesn't have a bath. We hit an impasse, until someone comes up with the word "toilet." His establishment doesn't have one of those either, but he sends us out back, where there are two tiny structures, one for men, the other for women, each covering a hole in the ground that emits a fearful stench and is surrounded by flies. That's too disgusting for me. I return to the bus and cross my legs until we find a proper toilet.

I never knew that French culture is so different from American. I suppose I expected to find the United States with a French accent. Robert explains that, even though 19 years have passed since the end of World War II, France and much of Western Europe are still recovering, and they're barely beginning to gain some of the affluence that the U.S. has enjoyed since the early 1950s.

The following Monday, our classes begin. Stanford professors will teach us English and music, and professors from the University of Tours will provide immersion classes in French for eight hours a week. I'm in the top French group, because of my French SAT scores, but I haven't studied French in two years, and I'm rusty. At the beginning of our first class, in which only French is spoken, our professor reads aloud an 18th century romantic French poem, which uses stilted language that I can't stand. We have to write down what we hear, accents and all. That's called dictée. The French language has tons of accents, and we have to get every one of them right. But when the professor returns my dictée, it's covered with red marks, each one signifying a mistake. He also gives numerical grades, using a scale from 1-10. He gives me a 2, a failing grade. My eyes flood with tears; this is the worst I've ever done at any school I've ever attended. I suppose I could switch to an easier French class, but that would be admitting failure, which I refuse to do. I need to improve, but I don't know how, so I ask the professor for advice. He says "Read lots of poetry and just keep trying." I can't force myself to read the dull and irritating poems he teaches (even though they're actually famous), but instead I lay my hands on anything I can find in French, from comic books to political tomes.

I frequently retreat to my room to decompress and study French. All my life, my room has been my refuge. But when Lucy's in the room, I often leave. There's a growing chasm between us, and I don't know how to narrow it.

Even when I'm alone in the room, I feel lost without the music I listen to in the States. At home, in cars, and in my Stanford dorm, I've always tuned in to Top 40, Motown, and even Country and Western stations. And early this year, I got caught up in the Beatles explosion. Give me a catchy tune, a beat, and fun lyrics, and I'm happy. But in Tours, the only rock n roll I find is on Radio Luxembourg, which plays sappy, lollipop tunes. Sometimes I tune into a French station that plays the great French singers—who doesn't love Edith Piaf?—but their artistry can't plug the hole in me that my own music usually fills.

Seeking enrichment, I decide to explore Tours. After breakfast on a Friday morning, I step brightly onto the street. First, because I'm out of gum, I look for a candy store. No such luck, so I enter a Tabac (tobacco store) where the clerk, like other members of the French working class, wears a blue smock. In my best conversational French, I explain what I want, but she shoots me a filthy glare, points her index finger upwards, and then wags it back and forth, saying "tsk, tsk," a gesture that represents scolding in the States. Does she mean I broke some hidden rule? My heart sinks, so I leave quickly. On the street, I run into a Stanford student. When I ask him about the wagging finger, he chuckles and says "That's her French way of saying 'No, we don't have any gum.'" That makes sense in the abstract, but in the here and now, she was unpleasant and rude. I wish I'd fought back, but I didn't know what to say.

I forge ahead, down the street, forcing myself to be chipper. But in store after store the blue-clad clerks are frosty. Change of plan. I'll give the stores a miss and seek something beautiful. The city of Tours is known as the gateway to the chateaux (castles) of the Loire Valley, which were built by the French nobility centuries ago. Some of the chateaux are gems. I wander the streets of Tours, hoping to find a few urban gems, but all I find is an industrial city, pretty much devoid of beauty. And there's not much to do in Tours, a city of 100,000. Paris is where the action is.

Before I began walking around Tours, I was already struggling. After I return to our building, I fall into a deep sadness. All my life, I've tried to be cheerful around people, to turn on a smile. Now, even at meals, I can't perk up. While my classmates are reveling in our experience, I sit mostly mute and glum. Often, kind students try to pull me into conversations, and I'm grateful. But after a few minutes, I fall back into despair.

I'd probably feel better if I could play tennis, but although I brought my gear to France, I never expected tennis to be a big part of my life here. Maybe I should reconsider. I'd probably feel better if I could run and sweat and compete. Ever since I started playing tennis, I've needed to win, because winning makes me feel like somebody. I miss that feeling.

I'm not just missing playing tennis. I'm also missing talking tennis. When I was growing up, my parents and the Hoxies both discussed nothing but tennis. Never politics, or art, or music. Rarely was there a word about literature, except when Mom showed off the unusual words she learned while reading. Tennis was my idiom, and I understood its intricacies.

In Tours, I hardly ever hear or say a word about tennis. I'm 18, and I've already been ranked in the Top 10 of U.S. women for the last two years, but I don't talk about that, because that would be bragging. Mr. Hoxie taught us never to brag. Mom and Dad both showed by example that bragging is forbidden. And besides, Mom has never liked me to get much praise.

But today, I'm on a bus for a field trip, and I've had news from the tennis world that's so exciting that I can't help crowing about it. I tell everyone around me: "Manolo Santana, who's a great Spanish tennis champion, has invited me to stay with his family in Madrid over winter break and then play a tournament in Valencia." Robert the RA is sitting nearby, and I expect him to give me a hooray! Instead, he says: "Is tennis all you ever talk about?" That's not fair! And untrue! How could he say that? I turn away to hide my tears.

When we return from our bus trip, I retire to my room and come to the wretched conclusion that I've sunk into an impenetrable gloom, unlike any I've ever felt before. It crosses my mind that this could be culture shock, due to the behavior of the French people, but I know it's more. There's also my fear of getting a bad grade in French class, the barrenness of Tours, and the total absence of tennis. And the topper is my relationship with Lucy. I can't stop fixating on her, silently blaming her for almost everything, even when I know she's not at fault. I want her to understand me. But that doesn't seem possible.

I need to switch roommates. I used to think I could turn to Robert for help, but after his remark on the bus, I realize he's more like the enemy. There's one more place to go. I approach the Stanford-in-France house mother and request a new roommate for the second quarter, beginning in January. She says there's nothing she can do, that roommate changes have to go through Robert the RA. I don't even bother to ask him.

I need help. I book a phone call to my parents, which is challenging, as there are only two phones for the 80 students, and the French telephone system is ridiculously erratic. Reaching someone—either crosstown or across the world— is a crap shoot. I wait for hours and hours, and then I get lucky. The call goes through, and Mom answers. I tell her that I can't cope. I hold my breath, hoping she won't make fun of me.

"I'll contact the French Tennis Federation and arrange for you to practice with the top French women in Paris." That feels better.

"You'll need a car. We'll wire you the money and you should go out and buy one right away." I never thought of that. I'm really grateful.

"Tomorrow morning you can eat your thick French coffee with a fork and knife." Her humor can be peculiar, but at least this time she's actually trying to help me, and she's figured out exactly what I need. If only she would do that more often.

I start by researching cars, but I know next to nothing about them, because I grew up in New York City, where few people drive, and I didn't get a license until six months ago, in California. I don't know one automobile from another, but I decide to buy a French car, hoping that the infamous French bureaucracy will look more kindly on that decision. The choices are a Citroen and a Peugeot. Because the former has a strange looking suspension that I don't understand, I choose a Peugeot, but even so, the red tape is Kafkaesque. I battle two French agencies, both declaring that the other must give its approval first. Eventually, I blow up at a clerk, who informs me that in France, women get further by using their feminine wiles. Despite my American ways, I eventually break through and get my car registered. Once I get the keys to my very own car, I have freedom!

Every Friday morning I hit the road to Paris, where for a few hours in the late afternoon I play tennis indoors, on red clay, with French women tennis players. They're nice enough, but they don't take me into their lives. That's OK. Isolation defined my childhood, and aloneness remains my norm. I happily amble solo through Paris's cobbled alleys and along its wide boulevards, where buildings sparkle after having being cleaned for the first time since the war. I spend hours trolling museums. My favorite is the Jeu de Paume, because who wouldn't adore impressionist paintings, with their brave and irreverent uses of color? I also love the Rodin Museum, a hidden gem where the great sculptor's works are lovingly displayed both inside the house where he once lived and outside in his luscious garden.

For each trip to Paris, I delve into my travel bible, France on $5 a Day, to find a new, inexpensive hotel. I usually end up either on the Left Bank or in the red light district. The beds are lumpy, the rooms are universally dusty and shabby—I sometimes wonder if they ever clean the bedspreads—and the bathtub and toilet are always down the hall. That's not the end of the world; my freshman dorm had the same configuration, although its amenities were much cleaner. In my Paris hotel rooms, I splash water on my face in the sink, but I save the bidet for soaking the red clay out of my tennis socks.

Traveling in France on the cheap is pretty darn funky, but that doesn't bother me. One of Mom's many pronouncements was: "I love luxury, but your father doesn't care. He could live happily in a shack. And you're just like him." Whether or not that's true, I've learned to survive with whatever is available to me, without seeking more.

As much as I love my weekends in Paris, nothing beats the Stanford-in-France field trips, which I treasure. My traveling in the U.S. focused almost exclusively on tennis. In Europe, we've journeyed around France and to Italy and Spain, and we've visited museums like the Louvre, the Prado, the Vatican, and the Uffizi. We even took in the Paris Opera, where I enjoyed opera (a little) for the first time, and I loved the newly unveiled Chagall ceiling. My only disappointment on field trips was the unending succession of cathedrals in Spain, each filled with vast amounts of gold stolen centuries ago from South America.

Winter break brings my visit to Manolo Santana in Madrid. I first met him when he stayed at my parents' apartment in New York City a few years ago. When we were introduced, he announced that he was engaged to a woman named Maria Fernanda, and he pointed to her framed photo, which he'd placed by his bedside. A few nights later, he was invited to a night club. Before he left the apartment, he turned the frame face down, where it remained for the rest of his stay.

In Madrid, I'm met by Manolo and Maria Fernanda, who are now married. Manolo gives me a tour of the city, starting with his tennis club. He was born into poverty and learned tennis the hard way, while he was earning pennies as a ball boy at the club. He has extreme buck teeth, because he never had money for braces. After being around him for just a short while, I forget about his teeth, because I'm captivated by his humor and his sparkling eyes. On the tennis court, those eyes are a window into his determination. When he's coasting, his eyes look normal. When he's digging in and fighting, they narrow to a slit. This once impoverished ball boy is now one of the best players in the world, having twice won the French Championships, the premier tournament in Europe.

Manolo is proud of his apartment and his car, which he's earned through tennis, although he's still officially an amateur. He has two sources of income: the tennis tournaments that pay him generously under the table, and his job with Philip Morris. Mom's friend Joe Cullman, the company's Chairman of the Board, has given jobs to a small group of top men players, enabling them to maintain their amateur status. As far as I can tell, their corporate duties are to play tennis with the boss, make a few appearances, and smile brightly for the cameras.

After a few days in Madrid, Manolo, Maria Fernanda, and I drive to Valencia for a tournament. On the way, we stop at a renowned restaurant that specializes in blood sausage, whose dominant ingredient is, in fact, pig's blood. I'm squeamish, but Manolo encourages me to try it. It tastes strange. The next morning, my first in the Valencia hotel, my stomach and head feel rotten, and I ask for a doctor, who comes to my room. He's stiff and shy, and he doesn't come near me. Instead, he hands me a thermometer and tells me to place it under my armpit, which I do while he looks away. Apparently I have a fever, but that's all the information I can glean from this strange fellow. He gives me some packets with powder, which I take while spending a few days in bed. This enforced rest interferes with my tournament preparation, but I'm ranked a lot higher than any other woman in the tournament, so once I'm well, I fly through most of my matches, except for a one-set lapse in the finals.

The Spanish are big on celebrations, and tonight there will be a banquet to bestow the trophies and to count down to the beginning of the New Year. One of the Spanish women players decides to improve my appearance. First, she finds me a dress, and then she sends me to a hairdresser, who teases my hair unmercifully and then does my makeup. When he's finished, I look in the mirror, where I see a Spanish belle of the ball. My hair is piled at least three inches high, and my eyes, which are heavily made up, look huge. I look stylized but gorgeous.

Shortly before midnight, we're each handed a cup containing 12 grapes, a Spanish New Year's custom. Once midnight sounds, we're told to consume one grape at each strike of the clock, for good luck. I start out well, but by the 12th chime, I still have quite a few in my mouth. But I've had a fine time at the party, and that's plenty good for me.

Back in Tours, I receive an invitation from Teddy Tinling, the great tennis dress designer, to come to London for a fitting. My tennis clothes, like those of most Americans, are pretty simple. I wear Fred Perry white, pleated skirts—which are a bitch to iron—and thick, white, cotton shirts with collars. Teddy's tennis dresses are completely different. Each one is unique, designed to enhance the player's personal characteristics. Receiving a Tinling dress is a special event, and a fitting by Teddy is a rite of passage for top-level, international tennis players. And best of all, I won't have to pay a cent. He makes his money selling designer tennis dresses to rich women. I'll be one of his fashion plates.

I schedule a flight for Friday morning, January 29. I usually drive to Paris alone, but this time some kids ask to hitch a ride. I explain that I'm going only as far as the Orly airport, but that's all right with them. From Orly, they'll snag a commuter train into the city. I have an early flight, so we load up the car before breakfast. The Peugeot fits only five people, but they ask if an extra person can come. I agree, and we stuff four people in the backseat, which is supposed to hold only three. It's freezing out, and we're all wearing thick winter coats, so they're sandwiched in pretty tight. After an hour of driving along the winding, two-lane highway that's lined with trees, the steering gets weird. I make a few small adjustments, and then a voice from the backseat says "I think the road is covered in black ice," a term I've never heard before. I keep trying to wrestle the car under control, but suddenly it does an unintentional U-turn, and the passenger side of the car slams into a tree by the side of the road. Sarah, the girl sitting by the door that was smashed, is hurt badly. Something is protruding from her collar bone. It must be broken. I have no idea what to do. Seeking help, one of the guys flags down a car, while the rest of us stand around Sarah, shivering in the cold. Within a half hour, an ambulance arrives, and the police give us a ride to the next town, where I try to phone Teddy. No luck. We wait and wait, trying to figure out what to do. The others choose to return to Tours, but I decide to continue on to London on a later flight. Dazed and shaking, I make the arrangements. When I land at Heathrow, it's hard to concentrate. I change some money and try to phone Teddy, but the pay phone stymies me, with its "pip pip pip" sound. Fortunately a kindly soul shows me how to shove the money in. I reach Teddy and explain what happened. He tells me to take a cab to the hotel and he'll meet me there. Experiencing London for the first time should be a pleasure: clambering into a London cab, riding on the left side of the road, ogling the famous sites, and deciphering the strange-looking English money. But today I'm not a typical, first-time tourist. These are extreme circumstances, and I'm just trying to hold myself together. When the cabbie reaches the hotel, I hand him all my money, and ask him to take what he needs. He cheerfully complies.

Soon, Teddy and I convene, and I'm shocked by his outrageous appearance. He's six feet six, gangly, and bald, and although he's in his 50s, his clothes are outlandish and mod—a style meant for young men. His first words to me are: "I'm amazed to see you the very day you nearly killed someone." Oy.

He's brilliant, with a vast recall of tennis history, albeit with his own inimitable slant. He hates any woman player who doesn't wear his dresses, but he adores many of those who do. He's also an incurable gossip, and he gleefully drops juicy tidbits about his favorite stars, beginning with Suzanne Lenglen, the great French champion of the 1920s, for whom he frequently umpired on the Riviera while he was still in his teens. The American Gussy Moran made him famous in 1949 by playing on Wimbledon's Centre Court while wearing the "shocking" lace panties he had designed. Her outfit created such a stir that photographers twisted themselves in knots to snap her undies. One of those photos made the cover of *Life* magazine. He's still designing outfits for tennis greats, including the graceful Brazilian Maria Bueno, who continues to collect trophies at the world's biggest tournaments.

Teddy is interested in more than tennis: "This is a very special night. Winston Churchill died last Sunday, and thousands of people are standing in line to pay their respects. First we'll have dinner and then we'll go see the body of the great man." After we eat, we stand in a slow moving line outdoors, in the piercing London cold, which navigates up my legs until they're numb. As Teddy talks about how Churchill saved England, I hit the wall. The extreme weather and the aftereffects of the accident have done me in. My mind constantly replays the

Peugeot's moment of impact against the tree. My whole body is shaking. I try to soldier on, hoping to push through, but I finally tell Teddy I can't continue.

The next day, he does my fitting, chattering away about my small waist and bust, and then he asks me about my studies. He speaks fluent French, so we discuss French poetry. I tell him that I'm not a fan of stylized 18th Century French romantic poetry, but I love the 19th Century poem by Charles Baudelaire that starts: "La Nature est un temple où de vivants piliers/Laissent parfois sortir de confuses paroles." ("Nature is a temple where living pillars sometimes emit confusing words.") Teddy asks "What do you like about it?" I explain that I enjoy the symbolism throughout the poem and I also get a kick out of knowing that the author was an opium addict. Teddy is momentarily silent, which is rare for him. "I've never met a world-class tennis player who recites French poetry." For the remainder of the day, we discuss living in France and why American players struggle on European clay.

On Sunday I return to Tours. The kids who were in my car at the time of the accident tell me that Sarah's still in the hospital with a broken collar bone, but the prognosis is good. They're all angry at me. One guy says "You should have stayed with Sarah." He's right. I was responsible. I screwed up. And another guy gives me a driving lecture: "Even though you were driving on ice, you could have regained control. You should have turned into the swerve." I wish I'd known that before. They all suggest that I visit Sarah in the hospital, which I do. I don't know what to say, so I mumble a little and ask her how she is. After a few minutes, I mutter "I'll see you soon," but I don't. I've sure made a mess of this accident.

I'm trying my hardest, but I've only been driving for a few months, and I've just turned 19.

My car is totaled, so I begin the process of dealing with the insurance company and ordering a replacement car, all in French. Peugeot promises me a new car within a month. I don't relish struggling with the red tape.

Without a car, I don't know how I'll survive, but out of nowhere, I get a phone call from a man named Monsieur LeMonde, who wants to visit me and discuss playing tennis in Tours. I wait for him by the entrance to our building, and I'm amused to see a short, plump, middle-aged Frenchman with a wide smile and a twinkle in his eye. I adore him instantly. "Our group rents an indoor court every Wednesday night, and we'd love you to join us." Fabulous.

M. LeMonde picks me up on Wednesday at seven, and we drive to an undistinguished building. We enter, and on the right is a large window opening onto a red-clay court, which means we can watch others play. The court is currently empty, as the entire group is waiting for us at the dinner table, on the left. I walk around the table, shaking hands with everyone and saying "bonsoir" ("good evening"), according to French custom. Dinner is wonderful, far better than the Stanford-in-France bill of fare, and so is the wine, which I imbibe liberally. Then we play tennis. It's a novelty for me to play while I'm looped.

I can't get enough of M. LeMonde and his friends. How lucky I am to be taken into their lives, even for just two hours a week. French people are notoriously wary of foreigners, especially Americans, but not my Wednesday-night group. We're all tennis players, nationalities be damned. For most of my life, tennis has been paramount. These people are teaching me a life lesson. For them, food, drink, and conversation are as important as tennis.

I particularly like a tall, good-looking guy named Claude, who looks to be in his mid-20s. He asks me to play a set with him, so we walk into the tennis court together. There, we have a moment of privacy, and he nuzzles me and kisses me deeply. The feeling is warm and sweet and loving, and I want more. Soon, we're frequently disappearing behind closed doors, and my heart pounds when I see him. One Wednesday night, he asks if I'm ready to make love with him, but I freeze up, because I've never had sex, and I hardly know him. For several weeks in a row, I call M. LeMonde with an excuse about why I won't be coming that night. Then Claude shows up at the Stanford-in-France building to see if I'm OK, but I act distant. I feel like a creep behaving that way, but I'm too scared to take the next step.

Soon, I realize that I miss M. LeMonde and the rest of the group. So once again, I sit in the Stanford-in-France lobby on Wednesdays at 6:45, waiting eagerly for him to pick me up. One day, while he's driving me to the court, he asks me to represent our Tours club against a club in another city. I say "Of course." Two weeks later, as we're driving to the event, he asks me to teach him a really bad swear word in English. I say "Shit." He practices: "Sheet." I correct him: "No, it's shit." He keeps trying. His match is scheduled first, so I watch for a while. His opponent makes an error and says "Zut, alors," which means "Darn it, then." When M. LeMonde misses an easy forehand, I hear him loud and clear: "Sheet, alors." He and I exchange smiles. I'm up next. Apparently, he hasn't told the other club that he's brought a ringer. I'm so much better than my opponent, that she hardly wins a point. Mr. Hoxie always drilled it into our heads never to give away a single point. I never have. I expect the other team to be angry, but they're fine. They're curious to find out who I am, and we chat over a tasty dinner, complete with wine, of course.

My six months at Stanford in France are ending. I've studied hard, and that's paid off. I'm getting a B in Music, but A's in all my other classes, including French. Even my dictées have become stellar. The administration holds a festive dinner in the communal dining room, where wine is served, which I imbibe liberally, celebrating my good grades and the end of six months in Tours, and hoping I'll never again suffer from a prolonged bout of the blues. At the end of dinner, I have a buzz, and then a few of us cross the street to a bar, where I continue drinking, first champagne and then brandy.

I wake up with my first full-blown hangover, which sucks, because today I'm leaving Tours and driving my replacement Peugeot south to tennis tournaments on the Riviera. Experts on hangovers come out of the woodwork. Several tell me "The champagne is the problem. You should never mix it with other drinks." I privately wonder if the culprit was the brandy, which I tried last night for the first time. Its smell reminded me far too much of Mom's vile scotch. In truth, I need a hangover remedy, not admonitions of what to avoid. I walk to the pharmacy, which recommends a yellow liquid that's supposed to heal the liver. I buy it, but it's disgusting. Finally, I seek advice from the Stanford-in-France house mother, who offers me an Alka Seltzer, which she swears by. After a few swigs, I'm instantly better.

CHAPTER 26

"WHY ARE YOU SO NAIRVOOS?"

Soon after the miracle Alka Seltzer cure, I'm perky enough to pack up the Peugeot and drive to the Riviera, where I'll play tournaments in Cannes, Nice, and Monte Carlo. They're offering me a miniscule amount of expenses, so yet again, I need an inexpensive hotel. The Aussie and South African players, who struggle far from home on tight budgets, point me to a dirt-cheap, mom-and-pop establishment. My room is just as dark and dusty as the Paris hotels I've stayed in over the last six months, but at least this one has a toilet in the room, a great luxury.

I've been looking forward to the sunny Riviera, but apparently the good weather has gone into hiding, and every morning, when I part the curtains, I find that the skies remain overcast. The temperature never heats up, and even the tournament organizers and the hotel owners can be frosty. After six months of intensive French classes, I speak French really well, but the behavior of most French people still gives me fits. Only rarely can I break through the barriers they erect.

I know I didn't play enough last winter, so now I try to practice as much as possible, hoping to win some matches, but my game is way too rusty, and my timing is off. Consequently, I make far too many errors, even on my big Hoxie forehand. Plus I've had minimal experience playing matches on red clay—just one tournament, in Spain, over winter break—and every damn thing about playing here makes the court slower than anywhere else: the balls, the clay itself, and even the heavy and cold conditions. This leads inevitably to long points, because it's hard to hit winners. So patience is primary, and errors are the enemy. I'll need to develop a new style just for European red clay, where I'll focus on maneuvering the opponent, setting up for just the right moment to attack. But I'm not there yet, and I keep losing early, much to my distaste.

At the end of my Riviera swing, I've hardly won any matches. The next three tournaments are in Southern Italy, where it's always warm and sunny, and I'm itching to get on the road. But it's a long drive, and I need passengers who'll join me in the Peugeot. Donald Dell, a top American player who recently graduated from law school, signs on, and so does Vicky "Bird Legs" Berner (she's big on top, with spindly legs), a Canadian player whom I've known since we were 10.

Our first tournament is in Reggio di Calabria, at the tip of the toe of Italy's boot, across from Sicily. The trip is 840 miles, most of them across the spine of mountains barely inland from the sea. It's my car, so I take the wheel, but the road is very narrow, with lots of blind switch backs, and the Peugeot is often so close to the edge of the road that when I look out, all I see is the Mediterranean, hundreds of feet below. And there aren't any guard rails. Between the terrifying road and my residual memories of the accident, I'm rigid with fear. When I can't take it any longer, I pull over and say "I can't go on." Donald replaces me as chauffeur, yet I'm still so scared that I sit in back and stare at the floor.

At about 8 PM, after we've been driving for seven hours, we realize we won't reach Reggio di Calabria tonight, and we need to stop. Almost immediately, a sign flashing "Albergho" (hotel) miraculously appears, but no lights are on. We knock on the door, the lights turn on, and a woman brightly greets us with a cheerful "Buonasera, signore e signori!" ("Good evening, ladies and gentlemen!") What a wonderfully warm welcome! How unlike France! We've arrived after hours, but they eagerly rustle up a feast while we bring a few belongings to our rooms. I'm used to stained carpets and bed spreads in French hotels, but here my marble floor is spotless, a glorious difference. I sleep soundly and then eat a hearty breakfast, but just before we leave, the owners present us with the bill, which is outrageously high. Donald isn't fazed. "Prices in Italy are cheap, so let's not worry. It's still not that expensive." But I feel betrayed. The owners were so warm and welcoming! Suddenly, I remember the advice dispensed by Robert the RA when we were on a field trip in Rome: "In Italy, every bill you receive is the beginning of a negotiation. Double check everything, because most bills have errors, and they're always in favor of the Italians."

I refuse to be cheated. I may be only 19, but I tell Donald, "Let me handle this." I turn to the owners and, using the international one-half sign, which looks like the U.S. sign for "time out," I dredge up one of my few Italian words, "mezzo," which means "half." It's my clumsy way of telling them to cut the bill in half. Unflustered, the owners agree to my demand. That was too easy. Maybe I should have asked for more. But I didn't, so we pay, and off we go.

After six more hours on the road, we arrive in Reggio di Calabria, which is another shock, because it feels like we've been transported into a previous century. All the Italian women are tiny, and they're wearing black, head to toe.

This week is going to be weird, because I definitely won't fit in. I wear a bright yellow-and-orange coat that ends a few inches above my knees, a length that's in vogue in the U.S. and the rest of Europe, but certainly not in Reggio, where I'll be viewed as a brazen Westerner, who is assaulting the locals' sensibilities. And I'm not going to like the Reggio men, who love taunting foreign women by whistling and shouting at them, and trying to pinch them.

Once we check into the nice—and very clean—hotel, Vicky and I are keen to practice, so we change into our tennis gear in our rooms, because the club doesn't have a locker room. To reach the courts, we have to traverse a short tunnel, a breeding ground for Italian men intent on pinching. I cover my very short tennis skirt with my not-a-whole-lot-longer coat, and then we lurk for a few minutes outside the tunnel, waiting for the locals to pass. When the coast is clear, we run like hell, and we have a good practice, followed by a dash back to the hotel. I decide not to leave the hotel grounds again unless I really have to, and I head out to the swimming pool. When I was in Rome, I bought a best seller called *The Italians*, by Luigi Barzini, because it's supposed to be fun, and it explains what makes the Italians tick. Now that I'm stuck at the hotel, I decide to give it a try.

Thumbing through the chapters, I light on a page about flattery, and I'm instantly riveted. In the 17th century, an older Spanish bishop, accompanied by a young, lowly, Italian priest, had the unpleasant task of pleasing a vile French cardinal. When they arrived for their first audience with the cardinal, they found him holding court while sitting on a toilet-throne. The bishop left in disgust at the cardinal's crude language and habits, but the lowly priest remained. To humiliate the priest, the cardinal rose from his toilet-throne and presented the young man with his naked butt. Unflustered, the priest ran to him, crying adoringly "o culo de angelo," ("oh, the ass of an angel") and kissed the cardinal's bottom. The cardinal was immediately captivated by the younger man's presence of mind, and soon, the lowly priest became the cardinal's closest confidant, and eventually one of the most powerful men in Europe.

The moral of the story: Some Italians succeed by using a combination of charm and pragmatism, and by kissing ass.

I read the section again and laugh out loud. Lying on the chaise lounge next to mine is Ingrid Lofdahl, a Swedish tennis player wearing a teeny bikini. Like many Northern Europeans, she's always on the lookout to catch every ray of sun.

She asks "What's so funny?" I read her the story, and we cackle together.

We start talking. Her English is terrific, and we both love gossip and lots of laughs. Our conversation wanders to love interests. She can't stop talking about Arthur Ashe, the black American tennis player whom she adores. I must have looked quizzical. I don't know any mixed race couples. "You Americans have so much prejudice. In Sweden, we don't care about the color of someone's skin." I bristle at the "you Americans" part. I despise all generalizations, and besides, I hate to be thought of as a "typical" anything. But her budding romance is refreshing, and so is her complete lack of prejudice. And she claims that her whole country is that way. I have a lot to learn.

After a few hours in the sun, we join several other players for dinner at the hotel. I'm proud of my ability to speak French, but I feel like a piker around Ingrid, who speaks nine languages, and if there are people at the dinner table from various countries, she can converse with each in his or her own language, i.e. Spanish to one, English to another, German to a third, etc. It's spectacular. Besides, she's funny and bawdy, with the startling ability to make puns in other languages. For instance, at dinner, Ingrid calls a Spanish player "ridiculo," a fabricated word combining the Spanish words for "ridiculous" ("ridiculoso") and "ass" ("culo"). The Spaniards smile brightly. No one else gets it, but the conversation quickly moves along.

After we eat, Ingrid and I venture onto Reggio's main drag, fending off whistles and catcalls. Ingrid says "Let's go to the train station. I bet we can find some magazines there." She buys *Life* magazine, the largest they have. Ingrid is statuesque and striking, with long, straight, sandy-colored hair and a wonderful body. At five feet nine, with broad shoulders, she towers over all the locals. The men sitting at the sidewalk cafes are chomping at the bit to touch her, but she doesn't let them get close. She rolls up her magazine, holds it high, and threatens to hit them with it. She makes them all back down. What a woman!

After three weeks of practice on French clay, my tennis has improved. I'm also playing better because my spirits are brighter after spending a lot of time with Ingrid, who loves to laugh. And the drama of Italy energizes me. Every day there's a new twist. Robert the RA was right about Italians skewing bills, but who knew that the cheating game would spill over into the tennis world? In most countries, the tournament draw is made in the open. In Italy, officials go behind closed doors and rig the draw in favor of Italian players. Even after the draw is made public, Italian players sometimes object. When that happens, the draw is torn up, and the charade begins all over again. This could never happen in the States. Or in England or France. And the cheating game comes out in the open on the court, where line calls are negotiable, if you're willing to expend the effort. To me, life in Italy is a huge, difficult, enjoyable game.

In the first round at Reggio, I beat Rosa Maria Reyes Darmon, a Mexican player who married an Algerian who plays for France. Tennis is a very international sport. I breeze past the semis, and then I win the finals by default. I have won my first European tournament.

After I receive the trophy, Ingrid and I drive to Naples for the next tournament. Unlike Reggio, Naples isn't completely mired in another era. Still, the men of Naples feel it's their duty to harass foreign women, which they do mostly on scooters and motor cycles, and occasionally on foot. Our 20-minute walk from the hotel to the courts is along a broad boulevard, and I learn to cross the street to avoid any confrontation. If that doesn't work, I raise my rackets, threatening any man who comes near me.

My draw in Naples is quite tough. In the semis, I play Helga Niessen, a 6-foot tall, thin German, who seems arrogant, because she rarely speaks, not even to say "Hello." She's gangly, and when she bends down for a low ball, it looks like her long bones point in different directions. I win in three tough sets. In the finals, I'm up against the Australian Madonna Schacht, who defaulted to me in Reggio. I wonder if she was sick, so I decide to tire her out by mixing up deep shots with dropshots, so that she has to run and run and run. My strategy is successful, and I close out the third set 6-0.

So, much to my surprise, before I even get to Rome, I've bagged two trophies.

The drive from Naples to Rome is pain free, but finding the Foro Italico, where the Italian Championships are played, is extraordinarily difficult. Driving in Rome, surrounded by thousands of Fiat 500s—the smallest cars you ever saw—is chaos. The Italians are skilled drivers, and rarely have accidents, which seems implausible, as they're constantly accelerating and braking, to fill the tiniest openings in traffic. Ingrid and I get endlessly lost. Our map shows Rome's tourist attractions, but it leaves out many details, such as which streets are one-way, so we keep coming to a dead halt, and then making endless loops to return to where we just were.

After a few crazy-making hours negotiating Rome, we finally spot the giant statues of nude male athletes that rise above the Foro Italico tennis stadium.

Benito Mussolini, Italy's fascist dictator, loved tributes to male bodies. He's long gone, but his statues remain, as a symbol of the tournament's importance. Many in the tennis world consider the Italian Championships the fifth most important tournament in the world.

I've been in the car so long that I desperately need to pee, so I frantically find a parking spot, and then we make a beeline towards the entrance. A tennis official tells me where to go: "The locker room is at the bottom of the stairs, directly in front of you." I dash down the steps and find two doors, side-by-side, with similar signs, "Spogliatoio Uomini" and "Spogliatoio Donne." I'm completely at a loss. Neither Reggio nor Naples had a locker room, so I don't know the Italian words for "Women's Locker Room." I try to puzzle out the words on the doors. "Uomini" looks like it might be pronounced something like "Women-y." I open that door and see a bunch of naked men. Mussolini would have been impressed with the bodies I saw. I'm just embarrassed.

We check in at the tournament desk and sign up for a practice court, where we get the travel kinks out of our muscles. The tournament has a nice feel, partly because the grounds are intimate. It has only six red clay courts plus the stadium. Plus there's an outdoor restaurant overlooking the courts, and an indoor bar where several of the older English journalists pass the time. All the English journalists are fine writers, especially David Gray of *The Guardian* and Rex Bellamy of *The Times*. *Ingrid* and I buy their newspapers every morning, to see how they've crafted their stories. And also, I have to admit, I want to see if they mention my name.

Teddy Tinling is also here. He's made me several gorgeous dresses, although they're a bit too small at the waist. I guess he lost concentration during the fitting when I started spouting French poetry.

After Ingrid and I practice, we check into a small, inexpensive—but clean!—hotel nearby, and then meet up for dinner with Teddy, David Gray, and Virginia Wade, a young English player, at a restaurant in the Piazza Navona. Teddy holds court, always with a touch of exuberance and exaggeration. The food is tasty, and the conversation is lively, although I'm sometimes distracted by the dazzling Bellini statues. Nowhere but Rome.

In the second round, I draw Lea Pericoli, the Italian Number One. Last year, she beat Karen Hantze Susman, the Californian who won Wimbledon three years ago, in 1962, when she was 19. Karen is way better than Lea on fast courts, but she never got the hang of Rome's slow courts. More significantly, the *World Tennis* write-up of that match described a typical Italian scene in which everyone in Rome was conspiring against Karen. Line calls. Scheduling. The crowds. Karen said they "should be ashamed." But of course they weren't.

I expect similar treatment against Lea. I walk on court wearing a Tinling dress, ready for a war of attrition. Lea walks beside me, also sporting a Tinling outfit, apparently also ready for a night on the town, with her teased hair covered with a broad bandana and her face perfectly made up. I guess she's planning to charm the linesmen, the umpire, and the crowd.

As we choose who will serve first, she's disarmingly friendly. But three points into the match, a linesman on her side of the court yells "out," although my forehand clearly clipped the line. I approach the net, spewing fury, determined not to be cheated.

Demurely, Lea walks towards me. "Ma Giulia, why are you so nairvoos?"

I reply, "I'm not nervous. My shot was good." They won't give me the point, but I have drawn a line in the sand. From then on, we're in a battle. Her style is to hit lots of high balls, so I do the same, waiting for one to land short enough for me to smack my Hoxie forehand into a corner. The umpire and linesmen are determined to get the best of me, but I don't let them. Even the ground crews are in on the fix. At one stage, they water a court next to where I'm playing, so that I get a little wet. Never do they moisten Lea. After more than two hours in the hot sun, it's 4-all in the third set, 40-30 for Lea, and I'm tired and drenched with sweat, not far from reaching my absolute limit. I thump a forehand deep, the linesman yells "out," and the umpire announces that Pericoli leads 5-4. Before I cross over, I hear the booming voice of Texan Cliff Richey, who yells from the stands: "Julie, that ball wasn't out. It was good." His voice acts on me like a jolt of adrenaline. I will not let Lea and the rest of them beat me. I suddenly improve, and my concentration amps up. I even aim to hit the ball far enough from the lines, so that I won't be cheated again. I win three straight games and take the match.

Exhausted and depleted, I return to the locker room. As the shower pours down on me, I hear my name being called to play doubles. Unbelievable. Tournaments never, ever call someone to play doubles so soon after a long, grueling match. I guess the Italians are pissed off at me for beating Lea, and now they want me to lose my doubles. I change clothes and ask for more time, due to the circumstances. Reluctantly, they give me an extra hour, which is of course ludicrous, given the situation. I go out and stink up the court, because I'm spent.

I've reached the quarters in Rome! But there's no time to luxuriate in my victory, because now I'll face Helga Schultze, a seasoned German. I walk on court wondering if I can recover from my match against Lea, and happily discover that the experience has actually energized me, because just being in Rome is so exciting, and it's enormously satisfying to overcome both my opponent and the officials. I'm also proud that, at the end, I fought through exhaustion. Helga's been on the tour for years, and I heard that she's out of shape, so I run her buns off, the way Mr. Hoxie taught me. Side to side and up and back, I'm determined to tire her out. It works, and I win 6-1 in the third.

Now I'm in the semis against Nancy Richey, who's ranked Number One in the United States. It was her brother Cliff, whose voice helped raise me from the dead against Lea. They're both great players, gritty competitors, and devoted to each other. But they're very different. Off the court, Cliff is more outgoing and voluble, and on the court he's willing to attack the net and take risks. Nancy's more buttoned up and serious, harder to get to know, and she usually stays in her safety zone, in the back of the court, where she pounds her punishing groundstrokes into the corners. I played Nancy in Puerto Rico three years ago, when she was 19 and I was 16, and she annihilated me 6-0, 6-0. I still haven't gotten over that shellacking. I've never done well against her.

Nancy's style is tailor-made for playing on Rome's clay courts, which give her time to wind up and hit hard. Against Lea and Helga, I won by mixing in high balls with hard groundstrokes and drop shots. I try that for a few games against Nancy, and she eats up that style. So I switch styles, and I hit harder. The result is worse. I flame out in under an hour.

But I have a lot to be proud of. The Italian Championships is one of the most important tournaments in the world, and I reached the semis. I phone home, and Mom says "You're the best, the most wonderful, the most marvelous!" That feels great for a few minutes, but her praise fades too rapidly, because it doesn't feel real.

The next big event is the French Championships, played at Roland Garros, in the Bois de Boulogne near the outskirts of Paris. At the tournament desk, the officials are typically French, just a little frosty and not very helpful. Already I miss the crazy Italians, who are so full of life. Roland Garros is a huge tournament, but it's so discouraging. The weather is mostly awful. The locker rooms and the players' restaurant are ancient and rundown. The joy I felt in sunny Italy drains away. Although I'm the 11th seed, I exit in the second round. Off the court, I have a few bright moments: when I'm interviewed in French on French TV, and later, when I'm standing around chatting, and the adorable M. LeMonde taps me on the shoulder from behind, having brought Claude and another friend from Tours to watch me play. I feel sorry that I didn't show them my best stuff.

After Paris, I drive to Bristol, England, where I'll play the first of three grass-court tournaments leading up to mighty Wimbledon. Along the way, I cross the English Channel on a ferry, and then I adjust to driving on the left side of the road. It's a long day.

In theory, to play well on grass, I should convert to rushing the net. But that's not my natural style, so I stay back and play lousy in the pre-Wimbledon tournaments.

Mom flies in for Wimbledon, to visit the tournament chairman, not to hang out with me, even though it's my first Wimbledon. She's thrilled about the VIP treatment she'll receive. The All England Club, where Wimbledon is played, is very hoity toity. The tournament's official title is "The Championships." How snooty is that? The Club has two types of members, and only a few of each: regular English members, who play there all year round, and honorary members, who are the ex-Wimbledon champs. During the event, members can eat and watch matches from the ultra-exclusive Members' Enclosure. Mom has been invited to spend the day there, to dine and chat with the tournament chairman, and to rub elbows with some of the greatest players of all time.

She sets aside one evening to have dinner with me at a modest restaurant near my hotel. I tell her that portions in England are notoriously small, so I order a double steak, and she orders a double scotch. Neither is big enough. She drains her usual two drinks, but she's too embarrassed to order a third double scotch (why is she embarrassed?), so she begs me to do it for her.

The Championships begin on Monday, when the Gentlemen's Singles rule the courts. The Ladies' Singles begins on Tuesday, and I'm scheduled for the second match on Court 5, to play a Dutch woman I've never heard of, and I've heard of almost everyone. I'm hoping this means my match will be a piece of cake. Play starts at 2 PM, so I expect to start between 3 and 4, but at Wimbledon you have to plan to arrive really early, in case you run into traffic or the previous match gets cancelled. So I practice at 10 AM at the Queen's Club and reach Wimbledon at 1 o'clock. England is famous for its rain, and today is no exception. Sporadically throughout the day there are downpours, and the moment the rains begin, the ground crews rush out and cover the courts with tarps. Once the rain stops, they pull the tarps off.

With Mom encamped in the Members' Enclosure, I'm totally on my own, so I wait for clear skies either in the noisy and crowded players' tea room—where the food is gross—or in the changing room I've been assigned to. England has a stratified class system, and so does Wimbledon, with its three women's changing rooms. The top one is for seeded players and club members, the middle one is for established players, and the one in the basement, where I've been assigned, is for the lowest ranked players and newbies. Each changing room has its own unique towels, which we must bring on court, so spectators and players can identify which echelon we belong to. The basement changing room is dim and gloomy, with amenities that suck. There are no showers, just baths, which we have to clean before we bathe. The toilet paper has the consistency of wax paper. There's no central heating, so to avoid frostbite while waiting for the skies to clear, I pile on towels and sit in front of a tiny heater, wishing I were in Italy.

When the English skies are cloudless, there's enough light to play matches until 9:30 PM. But today, the clouds have been socked in, so when I finally walk on court at 8 PM, 10 hours after my morning practice session, the light is dim. And when we begin our warmup, I get a nasty shock. It's my first time on a Wimbledon court, and no one told me, not even Mom, that they're lightning fast, harder and slicker than any other grass courts I've ever played on. Mom played Wimbledon once, in 1954, and she must have known. But she hasn't helped me at all.

At the start of the match, nothing goes well. In the third game, I approach the umpire and question a call, but he looks straight ahead and won't even acknowledge my presence. I say "Excuse me," but there's no response. I prefer being cheated in Rome. At least there I was dealing with a human being. Worse, I can barely see my opponent's racket in the waning light, and with such fast courts, I'm late getting my racket back in time. I lose the first set in a heartbeat. But I have lots of experience fighting from behind, so I caution myself to double down on my concentration, shorten my strokes, and bend lower. It works, and I win by the unusual score of 2-6, 6-0, 6-0. Our three sets last under an hour. After the match, Mom congratulates me, and makes a lame joke about watching me from the Members' Enclosure. That's all she says about the match.

After Mom returns home, I'm still in the tournament, and I have a decent draw. I win two more matches, reaching the Round of 16 in my first Wimbledon. There I draw Christine Truman, the British darling who won the French Championships six years ago when she was 18, and whom the British call "Our Christine." She's rosy cheeked, six-feet tall, strong, and not particularly fast, but she has a whale of a forehand. I lost to her handily at the Queen's Club warm-up tournament, so my expectations aren't high, but I'm not about to give up.

Throughout the year, the English are somewhat fond of tennis, but during the Wimbledon fortnight, tennis consumes their lives. Wimbledon is the only tournament in the world where its matches are shown wall-to-wall on the TV, even during England's frequent downpours, when the BBC replays great matches. Unlike my beloved Italians, the English are generally mild-mannered. They don't cheat, and they're polite when they queue for buses or for standing room on Wimbledon's Centre Court. English crowds have a reputation for being fair, but they drop all pretenses of impartiality when one of the players is English. In my first set against Christine, I play from the back of the court, but I'm seeing the ball well, and I'm able to move her around at will. Each one of my good shots is met with silence. At the start of the second set, Christine hits a huge forehand winner, and the crowd erupts for the first time. The more they cheer, the better she plays. This isn't a fair fight, and I lose to the English darling.

I've had enough of England's weather, and way too much of Wimbledon's umpires, changing rooms, and food. Get me out of here.

To protect the American circuit, the USLTA forbids U.S. players from competing in overseas tournaments after Wimbledon. So once I lose to Our Christine, I swing into action to return to the States. I book a flight to New York, and I arrange to have the Peugeot shipped there. Then I scare up some cardboard boxes, fill them with all the papers and souvenirs I've accumulated in Europe, including my Italian trophies, and dump everything in the Peugeot. I'm going home.

In New York, I barely unpack my bags before I have to fill them up again, to fly to Milwaukee, to play the Westerns on American green clay. It ain't Rome. Or Paris. Or London. There's no sightseeing, a complete absence of the joy of unraveling the uniqueness of another culture. I'm back to the monotony of seeing just the home where I'm staying and the club. But there's an upside to playing in the U.S., where I can look forward to a comfy bed and a warm shower.

After a month of rainstorms and the penetrating English cold weather, the heavy heat and humidity of the Midwest are a welcome change. And the tennis is different. For a start, U.S. tennis balls are livelier than European balls, and they pop faster off the strings, so you can go for more winners. And green clay has a harder foundation than European red clay, so the balls bounce higher. Most players use a similar style on all surfaces. I try to adapt to the conditions, but I'm having trouble making the switch to green clay. In Milwaukee, I need to dig deep into my grab bag of tricks. I survive four separate three-set-matches, a few against players I would normally beat more handily. I reach the semis, where I lose to Carole Caldwell Graebner, one of my nemeses. She beats me every time, dammit.

The next tournament is the National Clay Courts in River Forest, Illinois, the most important clay court event in the U.S. All of a sudden, something clicks, and I remember how I played in Rome, mixing up hard and soft, high and low, short and long, plus I use my spins to create short angles. I reach the semis with relative ease. Graebner was the top seeded player in my part of the draw, but she was surprised by Rosie Casals, so maybe I'll have a chance. Rosie's still a junior, and she's quite short, but she has unparalleled talent and she's rising rapidly through the rankings, so this match certainly isn't a gimme. I use my Roman tactics, expecting to throw her off, but she matches me shot for shot, except she's more aggressive than the players I met in Italy, and she often counters my lobs with smashes. The match is so even that it comes down to just a few points, which I win, and the match is mine, 11-9, 7-5.

"It had been a great fight between two of the most potentially brilliant players in the game today. One wins with her brain and the other with her natural ball sense and feel. "[3]

In the finals—I'm in the finals of the National Clay Courts!—I play Nancy Richey, whom I lost to in Rome. There, I tried to outhit her. I'm not gonna make the same mistake again. I'll have to keep her guessing, and when the right moment crops up, I'll hit the hell out of my forehand or sneak in a dropshot. Nancy keeps slugging the balls to the corners, which I run down, while I keep trying to break up her rhythm and the pace. I win the first set 7-5. My concentration wanes, and in a blink of an eye she steals the second set 6-3. At the start of the third set, I pick

---

[3] Mary Hardwick, World Tennis, September 1965

up where I left off at the end of the first set, smacking forehands. At a changeover, the tournament makes an announcement. We've been on the court so long that the men's final, between Nancy's brother Cliff and Dennis Ralston, which had been scheduled to follow ours, will start right away. The tournament has decided to play the matches side by side. This is nuts. With two umpires—and two PA systems—it's pandemonium. When an umpire announces "Advantage Richey," the crowd must wonder "Which Richey?" Yet Nancy and I keep fighting. We get to 5-all in the third, then 6-all. My hand is cramping. I try to ignore it. My leg starts cramping too. I make more errors. At 7-all, Nancy breaks my serve. She keeps pounding the ball and I keep fighting, but my body is letting me down. I have a point for 8-all, but that's my last hurrah. She closes me out, 5-7, 6-3, 9-7. I came so close.

"The title round match between Nancy Richey and Julie Heldman was the best ever seen at River Forest since the war. . . . This was a match between two opposite personalities, styles of play and approaches to tennis. Nancy relies on mechanical perfection, but Julie . . . possessed the versatile and imaginative mind. For two hours and twenty-six minutes they battled.

"So after the most exciting of fights in which we had seen more intelligence than in many a year, Nancy won her third championship. She must be heartily congratulated on her steadfastness against such an array of mental brilliance."[4]

When I left for Stanford in France, I wasn't sure if tennis would be in my future, but I soon discovered that living without tennis left me empty. Once I mixed tennis with travel, I began to have real fun, and I played better. Now that I've enjoyed successful runs in Rome, Wimbledon, and River Forest, I've begun to believe that tennis can have a lasting place in my life.

---

[4] Mary Hardwick, World Tennis, September 1965

CHAPTER 27

PROUD TO BE GLADYS HELDMAN'S DAUGHTER

Wherever I play tournaments, strangers approach me and ask, "Are you Gladys Heldman's daughter?"

When I say "Yes," they lovingly describe Mom's good deeds and praise *World Tennis* effusively. For many people, the magazine is their lifeline to the tennis world.

Mom has subscribers all over the globe, but some live in countries such as Hungary, Czechoslovakia, and Indonesia, which prohibit sending money to the U.S., so they can't easily pay Mom for their subscriptions. Mom appoints agents in those countries, who sell subscriptions and then try to figure out how to pay the magazine. Instead of cash, the Indonesian agent sends intricate wood carvings of imaginary beasts, which hang from our apartment's walls. The Hungarian agent sends exquisite stamps for my collection. And agents from other countries approach me in Rome or Paris, or at Wimbledon, bearing envelopes stuffed with U.S. dollars, which they press into my hands. They've come from far away to pay off their debts.

Players and fans alike tell me how much they hang on every word printed in *World Tennis*: "The moment the magazine arrives, I read it cover to cover, including all the results. I love to imagine what it would be like to play in Monte Carlo or Johannesburg, or even Indianapolis."

And everyone who writes Mom a letter holds her in awe: "I love corresponding with Gladys. She replies so quickly, it's as if I get an answer before my letter to her even arrives."

And many tell me: "Your Mom has helped so many tennis players around the world. You must be proud of her." Of course I'm proud of Mom. She's the lone woman in the male-dominated tennis world. She's a brilliant dynamo. She fights for what's right. And she usually wins.

But Mom's stature in the tennis world, along with her generosity and kindness to others, leaves me feeling confused and upset. She's not a warm and fuzzy mom. Far from it. But at least I can admire and respect her unique and fantastic accomplishments. Those deeds don't take the place of good mothering, but at least they make me swell with pride.

CHAPTER 28
HANDSOME AS A GREEK GOD

It's November 1965, and I live in a Stanford house called Guthrie. It was a sorority until 1944, when all sororities were banned from campus. That's when Guthrie became a "row house," a cozier alternative to large and impersonal dorms.

It's Thursday night, and I'm lying on Guthrie's spacious, second-floor landing, hoping for a miracle. Most nights, clusters of the 25 residents congregate there to work and chat. It seems we're all torn in two directions—we got to Stanford because we're good students, young women preparing to excel at a career. But we're also defined by our social lives. Most of us feel society tugging at our priorities, whispering to us insistently to "hurry, hurry, hurry, grab a guy to marry." To find that guy, we need a Saturday night date.

Saturday night looms close. The girls without steady boyfriends are waiting for the phone call that will transform their lives. I'm a senior, just a few quarters away from graduation, and tonight I don't even have the prospect of a date.

There's one phone line for the 25 Guthrie girls. It rings.

"Julie! It's for you." I scramble over girls in robes and curlers, over fat textbooks covered in scribbles, and I catapult up a flight of steps to the phone.

"Hello."

"Hi Julie, we haven't officially met, but I've enjoyed being around you at a few SAE parties. My name is Mike Hoffert." I used to date someone in the SAE fraternity, and his fraternity brothers seemed cool, and I'm pretty desperate, so I jump at the chance to go out with this guy. After hanging up, I make a beeline for the SAE page in the yearbook. Holy shit! I hit the jackpot! Mike is blonde and gorgeous. I start yelling, "Look who I'm going out with!" Soon there's a gaggle of girls swooning at his photo.

Saturday I dress conservatively for my big date—a short, pink skirt and a flowered top, with a pretty French scarf for that extra little touch. My bouffant hair is teased to perfection, and my eyeliner emphasizes my large eyes. Mike picks me up in his ancient Volvo, and I'm bowled over by his powerful physical presence. He's tall, with broad shoulders, a thick chest, and a narrow waist. I bet if he were wearing shorts, I'd see muscled legs. I ask him if he's an athlete. "I grew up on Southern California beaches, and I've surfed most of my life." No wonder his body is just about perfect. His curly, naturally platinum-blonde hair highlights his knockout looks. He's even cuter in person than in the yearbook photo. You can tell by his clothes that he's a guy's guy: He's wearing a plaid shirt and chinos, the uniform for young California men. Off we go to an SAE party, where we laugh, drink beer, and dance to a live band that plays nonstop rock 'n roll, including "Louie, Louie," "Wooly Booly," and "Help Me Rhonda." A cheer rises when they play "I Can't Get No Satisfaction," every guy's anthem about wanting sex and not getting it.

When Mike drops me in front of Guthrie, he asks me out for next Saturday.

This whole week, I've had trouble studying, because Mike's constantly on my mind. When he picks me up, he confesses he's having the same problem. I've never been in love. I've never had a serious boyfriend. But something is happening here.

We start going out every Saturday and some Fridays, too. Mostly we hang out with SAE boys and Guthrie girls. It's always pretty predictable. Except tonight. We're visiting the off-campus house where my sister is living with Lars Kampmann, the son of a Danish shipping magnate. Lars is smart, and he was well educated at a high-quality boarding school back east. Carrie's brilliant. She spent a year and a half at Radcliffe, and her comprehension of literature is stratospheric. She's also far out. She's living with a guy. No one at conservative old Stanford does that. And her clothing selection is wild. When I was in Tours, other Stanford-in-France students began receiving letters from Stateside friends describing a girl, who, every morning just before 10, walked towards the Stanford Quad wearing something completely unique and utterly outrageous. It was my sister. She'd stay up all night, preparing for her morning promenade, with the goal of shocking the whole campus. Sometimes instead of a dress, she wore a slip. No one else does that. Another time, she painted one leg gold and the other silver. Again, she's the only one doing that. Once, when she wore a branch in her teased hair, a frat boy approached her and asked "Why are you wearing a branch?" In her soft, high voice, she said, "Because I'm a tree."

Mike and I open the door to Lars's small house, and it's like entering a foreign country. No teased hair or crew cuts, no A-skirts or chinos, no contests to chug beer. Instead, lots of shaggy hair and all different kinds of clothes, from bright colors to baggy jeans. The record player is blasting weird, unfamiliar music. Adrienne, a butch-looking fireplug of a woman in her 30s, is reading aloud with a flat, Chicago accent from Henry Miller's *Tropic of Cancer*, a book that was banned in the U.S. until last year, due to its dirty words and descriptions of people taking drugs. Mom swears like a trooper, but nothing like this! Words that **no one** says out loud. Someone taps me on the arm and passes me a teeny cigarette. I don't smoke, so I try to refuse, but Mike explains that the little ciggy is actually a marijuana "joint," and unlike cigarettes, joints won't harm you. He shows me what to do: purse your lips, suck in the smoke deeply, and hold your breath as long as possible. I like it a little and Mike loves it, so at the end of the night, Mike says "Let's go back there tomorrow."

I begin to like smoking pot, and I learn the lingo—pot, grass, weed, dope, all words for marijuana. A roach is the miniscule tail end of a joint. A lid is an ounce of pot that you can buy in a baggy. Pot is illegal. You can go to jail for smoking it. But we feel safe in Lars's home, with a community of like-minded souls.

We spend more and more time at Lars's house. One Saturday, Lars says "We're going to drop acid tonight. Do you want to join us?"

I whisper to Mike, "Does he mean they'll be taking LSD?" Mike nods. He's keen, but I'm nervous. I don't know anyone who's taken LSD, and I've heard things can go very wrong. I ask if anyone will remain sober, just in case, but I get mumbles instead of answers. Momentum carries me along and I say "yes." When we arrive at 8 PM, there are just a few of us, but that doesn't stop Lars. "We might as well get started." After the first ritual of placing the paper saturated with LSD in my mouth, I feel . . . nothing. Forty-five minutes go by. Then my jaws clench and reality changes colors and time scurries and then stops. I slide in and out of reality. I swing from being fascinated to being scared. I prefer being in control. I look around. Too many people. When did they get here? Someone shouts "Pile on!" and everyone jumps on the bed and hugs each other. I'm near the bottom of the pile, where it's hard to breathe, but I feel comforted by all the warm bodies. A woman is painting, and the colors are so vivid, so intensely beautiful, that I want to paint, but then my mind trots off again. Music is blasting, but I can't concentrate on the songs. I have no idea what time it is. Slowly, I regain control. The sun is coming up. Only a few people remain. Mike fires up his trusty Volvo and takes me back to Guthrie.

Mike says that LSD has changed his life. Not mine. I hate the jaw clenching and feeling so disrupted and agitated, although I do love the intense joy I got from colors. On the other hand I really like smoking pot. Pot yes, acid no.

Lars, a senior drama major with the striking bone structure and good looks of a leading man, is directing a play called *Lysistrada*, an ancient Greek classic about women withholding sex from their husbands until they stop fighting the Peloponnesian War. Since Mike first walked into Lars's house, Lars has been blown away by Mike's beauty. Even though Mike has no acting experience, Lars offers to cast him as the gorgeous god Narcissus. Mike accepts, and rehearsals start right away.

Narcissus was stunning but self-obsessed. Not Mike. He hates that people define him by his beauty. He wants to learn and grow, and become a man of substance.

Before Mike met Lars, he was already plenty busy studying, waiting tables, and attending fraternity events. Now he's added *Lysistrada* rehearsals and the psychedelic nights at Lars's house. He's clearly in over his head, and he worries that his grades will suffer.

Still, he wants to spend more and more time with me. He starts hinting about sex, and I don't know what to say or do. The inevitable happens. After a jazz concert on campus, he says "Let's stop by my apartment for a minute." We walk inside, and he kisses me and says "Will you make love with me? I know it will be your first time, but I have some experience, and I'll be gentle." I panic. I want to, but I'm scared. It's such a big step. So he takes me back to Guthrie.

Ten years ago, it was taboo for a coed to have sex with her boyfriend (If she did, she certainly didn't talk about it.) College was for getting an "M.R.S. degree." Women were supposed to start raising a family immediately after marriage. Now it's the mid-1960s, and that's beginning to change, especially since the birth control pill became available, but it's hard to know what the rules are. Most girls still want to get married right away. Most girls still don't talk about sex. Most girls assume that sex with their boyfriend will lead to marriage. Mom talks about sex often, but mostly leading up to the punchline of a dirty joke. No guidance there.

This is momentous. I ask a few Guthrie buddies for their advice, but they say it's up to me. I know I love Mike. I know I could be with him forever. Tonight I'm ready, but there's a glitch. We enter his apartment, but his roommate is home, studying. So we retreat to Mike's dear Volvo, where I have sex for the first time. Aargh. Not very romantic.

My first love. What does that mean? I know very little about him. Southern California surfer. Beautiful face. Beautiful body. Everyone thinks he's drop dead gorgeous. And that makes him more desirable—I have someone whom others covet.

Almost instantly, my flood gates open. I hunger for him. We start going to motels on the weekend. I hide when he checks in, because motels don't give rooms to a man and a woman unless they're married.

My parents are renting a villa in Acapulco over winter break, and they invite us. We accept and decide to drive down through Mexico in the big Chevy convertible that Mom made me buy when I returned from Europe, because she wasn't fond of the Peugeot. Mexico's driving customs take some getting used to. Even on the major thoroughfares, cars don't use their lights at night, which is particularly tricky when large animals lie flat on the highway at night, soaking up the day's heat. We've also heard that Mexican police harass Americans with big cars. They'll stop you for no good reason and throw you in jail unless you pay them a bribe. Fortunately, nothing disastrous happens along the way. In fact, it's an idyllic trip, and each day we eat spicier food and each night we fall into each other's arms in a new motel.

Acapulco is less enjoyable, because we don't share a room there. Anyway, trips with my parents are never fun. They're about presenting myself at meals and to play tennis. Still, this trip is far better than most, because Mike is here, and we can enjoy driving around Acapulco Bay and frolicking in the swimming pool. Mike swims like a dolphin, and he holds me up so that I don't sink.

We've been together only two months, but it feels like we're meant for each other. Mike must feel the same, because back at Stanford, he gives me his fraternity pin, an event that is considered one step short of getting engaged. The Guthrie girls sing to me at dinner to celebrate the momentous occasion. I'm over the moon. I think about him day and night. I know he's mine.

I've never obsessed about getting married, but history is weighing on me. My parents went to Stanford and got married the day after graduation. I'll graduate in four months. I've grown up in a competitive household, and I feel driven to match what my parents did.

But poor Mike is on overload. Some Saturday nights he says he needs to study instead of going out, because he's becoming increasingly worried about his grades. I ignore his concerns, because all I want is sex. Anyway, I don't worry about my own grades, because studying comes easier to me.

It's February 28, and Mike and I have been together four months. Tonight there's an SAE party. The phone rings at Guthrie, and I pick it up. "Hi Julie. It's Mike. I have to talk."

"Come on over."

His face is all hang dog. He stammers. "I'm sorry, but I can't do this anymore."

"Do what?"

"I'm going to have to break off our relationship."

"What? I don't understand. You gave me your pin. We've been so close."

"I'm sorry, but it's just not working."

I'm dizzy, at a loss for words. I compose myself and ask "Is there another girl?"

Big pause. He looks down, silently.

Then he looks up and says "Yes, there is."

I thought he loved me. I thought he'd ask me to marry him. How could he do this without any warning?

I walk around in a giant daze, at first too distraught to cry. I'm a total failure. I've lost my true love, and it's all my fault. I shouldn't have pushed him so hard to spend more time with me. I call my parents. No help. I call my sister. No help. I visit Lars's house, and I don't even feel like smoking pot.

After my initial shock and dismay, tears come pouring out. I wake up crying. I avoid being around people, for fear I'll flood with tears. At least after a good cry I feel spent, an improvement over the rest of the day.

Last year, in Stanford in France, I was deeply sad for a long time, but the pain of losing my first love, of being dumped, is so much worse. I'm spiraling down into a bottomless blackness, feeling rejected and abandoned.

Relief finally comes, but in painful and disturbing ways. For the first time, voices inside my head urge me to end my life. At least that would relieve my sorrow. Out of shame, I tell no one.

I have to get away from Stanford, where too many familiar places remind me of Mike and prompt the voices in my head. I'm just finishing the second quarter of my senior year, and I need only one more quarter to graduate, but that will have to wait. So, although once again I haven't had much tennis practice, I decide to take off spring quarter and play tournaments in Europe, many of which I played last year. I'll start in Italy, which should cheer me up. But in the short term, I'll have my hands full, writing a flurry of letters to tournaments in Reggio di Calabria, Naples, Rome, and Paris, buying airplane tickets, getting the right kind of clothes, and arranging a thousand other details, all while I'm studying for finals—and while my heart is broken.

But the competitor in me forces my adrenaline to flow, and I manage to pass all my classes.

CHAPTER 29
HOISTING A CUP

On the plane to Rome, I have too many empty hours to fill. Mostly I concoct schemes to get Mike back, which I mull over endlessly. But I know it's useless, because he's taken. I'm escaping to Europe to play tournaments I don't care about, but anything is better than being on the same continent as Mike and his new girlfriend.

I somersault back into the rhythm of competition. Planes, cars, checking in to hotels and tournaments, organizing practices, showering, planning meals, playing matches, showering again, getting sleep. Last year I really enjoyed traveling abroad, embracing new cultures, and joking around with new friends. This year, I'm consumed by an internal, persistent voice that says "I want to die," and "I want to kill myself." I never actually make plans to harm myself, but the voices suck up all my energy. I can't tell anyone about the hell I'm inhabiting. They'd be sure I'm crazy. And maybe they'd be right.

When I arrive at my first tournament in Naples, I leave my room only to eat and play tennis. At the courts, I try to look cheerful, and I feel like a failure if anyone catches a glimpse of my pain and asks "What's wrong?"

I say "Nothing. I'm fine."

Despite my grim inner life, I shock myself by playing pretty well. Just like last year, I win Naples and Reggio di Calabria, the tournaments leading up to Rome. I still enjoy the crazy scene in Italy, with all its honking, pinching, and cheating, but despite bagging the two titles, my heart isn't in the tennis.

In Rome, my second round match is against Silvana Lazzarino, the Italian

Number Two, who, just like Lea Pericoli, runs everything down, turning every point into a never ending battle. Last year, my extended, emotional match against Pericoli gave me an emotional boost. This year, even though I beat Lazzarino, the match uses up all of my intestinal fortitude, so that in the following round, against Helga Niessen, my tightly wound psyche unravels. I beat her in both Reggio and Naples, but in Rome, I can't hold it together, and instead of being amused by the Italians' colorful antics, I explode in fury, and then crash and burn. The score, 6-3, 6-2, is ugly, and I'm embarrassed. One English journalist calls me "volatile." Yep.

After my loss, I dawdle in the locker room, and then I stroll towards the terrace restaurant overlooking the courts. While I'm standing in line for a table, Carole Graebner, whom I've still never beaten, walks up to me. She's attractive, stocky, and pleasant off the court. On court, she's well mannered, but fiercely determined. She's friends with Billie Jean Moffitt King—they're both Southern California girls—and although they're only two years older than I, they've spent years ensconced at the very top of the U.S. women's rankings, way above me.

"Hi Julie. Bad luck today. How are you feeling?"

We chat for a moment, and she asks "Do you plan to keep playing in Italy?"

I say "Yes," but I think *Well, yes, I do plan to stick around. There's no boyfriend to go back to.*

Then she says "We may have really good news for you, but I'll let you know tomorrow." OK, that's weird. The next day she approaches me again, and asks "How would you like to play Number Two singles for the United States in the Federation Cup? It starts next week In Turin. Nancy Richey was supposed to play singles for us, but she had to drop out. And I can't play singles, because I just found out that I'm pregnant. So will you help us? We really need you."

The Federation Cup is the women's world team championships, the most important women's team event in existence. This is a huge opportunity for me, even though it was delivered in a truly bizarre way. I'm being approached not by a team captain or a nominating committee, but by a player, who seems to be running the show.

In a heartbeat, I realize that it doesn't matter who's asking me to play for my country.

"I accept."

Why did they choose me? I'm currently ranked No. 8 in the U.S., a spot that's usually too low to be picked for a national team. But as Carole and I talk, I realize that all factors point towards choosing me. At the most basic level, there's the geography of the matter. I'm in Rome, which is 430 miles from Turin. To arrive in time, any other top American woman would have to fly at least 4,000 miles, and suffer lots of jet lag. More importantly, the Federation Cup will be played on European clay, and since last year, I've had more experience on that surface than any other American woman. And last year I had great runs in Rome and at the U.S. Clay Courts on green clay, a similar surface.

I know so little about the Federation Cup that I have to quiz Carole about its format. She tells me that it started three years ago, and it's an elimination event, completed in one week. Each participating country fields a team of two singles players and a doubles pair, and to advance, a country must win two of the three matches. Now that our team is set, Billie Jean and I will play Number One and Number Two singles, and Billie and Carole will play the doubles. I've never represented the U.S. before, although last year the USLTA named Janie Albert and me to the U.S. Wightman Cup team, but just as practice partners. In Turin, I'll take a huge leap in responsibility. Instead of watching from the sidelines, I'll be a key participant. Each day, I'll be first up, and if I lose, the United States team will be on the verge of elimination. The good news is that most countries have only one highly ranked player, and I'll be playing against the second best, so my task shouldn't be horrendous, especially as I'm considered such a hardened veteran of European clay courts.

The next day, Carole and I travel to Turin, where we meet up with Billie Jean and Roz Greenwood, who'll be our Fed Cup captain. Roz is nice, but she sure isn't qualified to be the captain of a national team, because she's never played or coached at this level. The USLTA, in its greater wisdom, chose her because she's logged in countless volunteer hours as the tournament director for the National Juniors, which of course has no bearing on the Fed Cup. Roz's first official act is to give us our team jackets, with "USA" embossed in big letters on the back. Her next official act is to find us a practice court and tennis balls. She's excellent at organizing the details.

Billie Jean's and Carole's lives are both changing. Billie Jean got married last fall, and Carole got hitched the year before. Her husband Clark, who's also a top flight player, is in Turin with us. Billie Jean has traveled around the U.S. and to Australia to play tennis, but she's never played on European clay. Carole has, but just a little bit. So while their experience in top level competition will be beneficial to me, I can provide some useful tips about playing in Italy on red clay.

Both are really kind to me. Our team is tightly knit, and we eat together, laugh together, and practice together. I love to use my small Italian vocabulary whenever I can—at dinner, with tournament staff, and in the hotel. Our second day in Turin, Billie asks me to help her get Vitamin C. She had tried, but the pharmacist didn't understand her. I don't know the words in Italian, but I brashly say "let's give it a try." When we walk in the door, I take a shot at pronouncing the English words with an Italian twist: "veet-ah--meen-ah chay, pair fah-vor-ay," ("Vitamin C, please.").

"Quanti vuoi?" ("How many do you want?") Bingo! It worked.

I ask Billie, and she says "one hundred," so I respond "Chen-toe."

Billie pays, and we walk out elated, cheering my victory and Billie's treasure of vitamin C.

The 1966 Federation Cup is being hosted by the Turin Press Sporting Club, a charming locale with over 20 red-clay courts and a small stadium that holds just a few hundred fans. Europeans like ceremony, so at the start of each day's play, we don our jackets over our tennis dresses, line up behind a uniformed girl carrying the Stars and Stripes, and march onto the court. After us come our opponents, wearing their jackets and following their own flag. Playing for the U.S. agrees with me. I love being part of a team and being supported by teammates. Every time the score is called, I'm reminded of the importance of the occasion. In a normal tournament, if I win a game, the umpire announces "Game Miss Heldman." In Turin, they announce the score twice, first in Italian, "Gioco Stati Uniti," and then in English, "Game USA."

The first and second rounds, against Sweden and France, are a piece of cake for me. The following round, the semis, is harder. We draw Great Britain, led by their Number One player, Ann Jones, who is one of the best in the world on red clay. She's won lots of tournaments on this surface, including the biggest one, the French Championships. As usual, Number Two plays first—that's me!—and if I win, that'll take some pressure off Billie Jean. So you can bet your bahoola (as Billie Jean says) that she'll be cheering me on. But this isn't going to be easy. My opponent is Winnie Shaw, a 19-year-old Scot who's a step above my previous opponents in Turin. I've never played her, but they say she's a fighter, and although I've done well so far, nothing's a sure thing in such an important event, where everyone's nerves are amped up, making matches less predictable.

My start is less than brilliant, because I'm half a step slow. When I'm alone in my room, the voices of self-destruction won't quit, and they sap my energy. To recover lost ground, I grit my teeth and concentrate ferociously on applying the style I've developed for European clay. I start by mixing spins, location and pace, which confuses and unsettles Winnie. First set to me. Then I lose my edge and get angry. Volatile. Ugh. Second set to Winnie.

During the 15-minute break after the second set, I give myself a sensible lecture: "I have to settle down. I'm playing for my country." Once the third set begins, I notice that Winnie is missing forehands on big points. During Federation Cup matches, the captain sits on the court, and only she can talk to the player, but Billie and Carole clearly don't trust Roz to give me the best advice, so they keep jumping out of the stands to pass her notes, with brilliant suggestions like "Tell Julie to hit deep to Winnie's forehand," and "Hit everything to Winnie's forehand." All that pounding on Winnie's forehand does the trick. I win 6-4, 5-7, 6-3.

The next match showcases Billie Jean and Ann Jones, whose differing styles reflect their personalities. Off the court, Billie Jean is outgoing and effervescent, and on the court she exudes passion, determination, and showmanship. Frequently, when she hits a winning shot, she holds a pose at the end of her follow through, as if she were waiting for the cameras to click. Her normal style is to rush the net to smack volleys with a flourish, a tactic far more suited to other surfaces. By contrast, Ann is calm, steady, and determined, both on and off the court. During matches, she mostly stays behind the baseline, playing error free, daring her opponent to miss. Today, Billie complies. Her tennis alternates between flashy brilliance and ugly misses. Ann weathers Billie's storms, and wins handily, 6-1, 6-4. That means the U.S. and Great Britain are even at one match apiece, and it all comes down to the doubles. Into the breach jumps Carole, our pregnant teammate, who helps Billie regain her bearings. In the beginning, they struggle and lose a set, but they're both fighters and terrific doubles players, and they win 6-0 in the third. We've beaten Great Britain. Walking off the court, Billie Jean and Carole both thank me for my victory. "We wouldn't have won without you." Damn that feels good. I'm not used to having other players supporting me, but I love it.

For the finals of the Federation Cup, the organizers play a recording of the Star Spangled Banner while we march into the club's small stadium.

Our opponents, the West Germans, who had a huge upset win over Australia in the semis, follow us in, also to the sound of their anthem. I've never felt this much pressure. I've been playing for my country all week, but today is the most important day. The winning team will be the champion of the world. That's both thrilling and scary.

Once again, I play first, and my opponent is—big surprise!—the blonde and very tall Helga Niessen, who seems to pop up in so many places, including in Rome, where I just lost to her. And where I really stunk. I hardly know her, but my back gets up when I see her, because she never talks to me. Plus I grew up in New York City in the early 1950s, with the TV constantly showing films of Nazi horrors. It's not Helga's fault that she looks like some of the Nazi women shown on my TV screen. When I play her, I lose concentration from time to time, thinking of those films. I vow not to do that today. The Fed Cup is too important.

Helga has improved dramatically since last year. Back then, she hugged the baseline, and I beat her several times by using my unique strategic mix. This year she's committed to dashing forward, where she sometimes wins quick points at the net just by sticking out her very long arms. To extend the point and to tire Helga out, I frequently lob over her head, hoping to push her away from the net and make her run back to the baseline. Today, she has the upper hand. Although I've tried my hardest, I'm down 6-4, 5-3, and she's on the verge of winning. If ever I needed a miracle, this is it. Out of nowhere, my miracle appears. Helga, inches from the finish line, runs out of gas and starts swinging wildly to finish the points fast. I win four games in a row, so that we're a set apiece.

We stop for the 15-minute break. Usually, I take a shower during the break, and that's where the Germans are headed. I'm sweaty and sticky, and Roz keeps urging me to shower and change. But I'm wary to do that. The stadium is really far from the locker room, and I don't want to risk being late for the third set. In Italy, you never know whether they're going to enforce a rule or let it slide. If I'm late, and the Italian umpire defaults me, the U.S. would lose my precious point. And the Italians aren't the only problem. The tournament referee, Herr Kleinschroth, is German, and I don't want to give him an opportunity to rule in favor of his country women. Five minutes pass. My sweat dries and then cakes. Still no Helga. 10 minutes pass, and my muscles tighten up. Then 15 minutes. Where's the German team? They're due back *now*. Where are the umpire and the referee? I'm furious. The Germans should be defaulted. Finally, after a 24-minute break—the longest I've ever heard of—the whole German team shows up.

When we walk on court again, my breathing is shallow, and I'm rigid with nerves. I'm clearly too tense to play my normal game. Luckily, my topspin forehand has remained reliable, and for some reason, I can still run, so I decide I'll only hit forehands. If Helga hits to my backhand, I'll run around it. I find that I can hit forehands with exaggerated topspin so that the ball goes over the net and then dips precipitously. Thank heavens Helga appears to be even more nervous than I am. Her face as usual shows no emotion, but her body is a dead giveaway. She's so stiff that she can hardly bend. We keep playing the same point: She comes to the net, I hit a dipping forehand, and she misses. Again and again. I run away with the third set 6-1. Triumph!

Billie Jean follows me on court, along with her West German opponent Edda Buding. Edda isn't in Ann Jones's class, so Billie Jean is highly favored. Her clay court prowess is improving daily, and in fact she's doing great, considering it's her first week on red clay. Still, Billie struggles during the first two sets, and then she comes alive in the third, which she wins 6-1. We're ahead two matches to none, which means we've already clinched the title, but although it's a dead rubber, the organizers still make Billie and Carole play the doubles. They win decisively, and now we can celebrate by hoisting the Federation Cup high and grinning like we won't quit. WE ARE THE WORLD CHAMPS! I have won for my country. I have proved myself in a whole new way.

Carole, Billie Jean, and me, World Champs!

CHAPTER 30
QUITTING

Tennis at the top means there's always another tournament coming up soon. Translated for me, that means even though we won the world team title in Turin, there's not much time to celebrate. I have to get ready for Paris.

Even before I reach Paris, my joy in winning the Fed Cup fades, and despair takes over, lodging in my brain and in my heart.

After Turin, our mighty American trio (plus Roz) splits up. Roz returns stateside. Billie Jean heads to England for grass court tournaments leading up to next month's Wimbledon. Carole, Clark, and I fly to Paris, but when we land, we go our separate ways. Carole and Clark join other Americans in a modern, American-style hotel which has the creature comforts they're used to—room service, air conditioning, and an efficient phone system. I head out alone to the Left Bank, to a hotel which has none of the above, but which brings me more satisfaction than air conditioning. Here, I get to soak in Parisian ambiance, particularly the ubiquitous sidewalk cafes filled with interesting looking people. Normally, I'd enjoy the sight of Parisian lovers strolling arm-in-arm, but not now. That brings up too many difficult memories.

Before I play my first match, I get more good news. I receive an official cable from the USLTA, asking me to play for the U.S. on our Wightman Cup team. The competition, which is against Great Britain, will take place on the grounds of the All England Club in a few weeks, just before the start of Wimbledon. Once again we'll be up against Ann Jones and Winnie Shaw. Plus they'll also have Virginia Wade, who's most at home on the Wimbledon grass. I accept, of course. They need me. I did so well in Turin.

My Paris draw is really good. I slide into the second week with a bye and wins over two women who aren't highly ranked. After the second win, I celebrate by taking myself to a Moroccan restaurant near my hotel. I try couscous for the first time. Delicious.

At 3 AM Wednesday, the couscous rebels. I'm jolted awake with fever, intestinal cramps, and diarrhea. Food poisoning. My match against Edda Buding is scheduled for noon, but I'm too sick to play. My years of traveling have taught me to be prepared, so I pull out the aspirin and Kaopectate bottles from my medicine kit, set my alarm for 9 AM, and fall back asleep. Once I'm jolted awake, I call the tournament referee and ask him to postpone my match until tomorrow. He readily agrees, and I fall back asleep. I'm feeling all beat up, and I don't know if a one-day postponement will be enough. I can't eat. I can't practice. All I can do is rest.

Thursday morning I check in at the tournament desk and head towards the cavernous, musty, and dim locker room, to suit up. Women's locker rooms in the U.S. tend to be sumptuous, with bright lights, plenty of individual showers, and tiny changing cubicles where players remove their clothes in private. Almost all women's locker rooms in Europe are sparse, and they lack privacy, so players think nothing of disrobing publicly and parading around in the buff. It takes a little getting used to, but after many months of playing in Europe, I strip without a second thought. I change into my favorite Tinling dress, and before I walk out to practice, I scrutinize my appearance in the tall mirror. Well this is a bonus! The illness has melted pounds off me, and Mom would be pleased that my legs look less chunky.

Edda Buding has been on the tour for almost a decade. Her father coached her at the tennis center he built near Marseille, and she's a very good player, without being great. She's famous for sashaying her butt in front of tournament officials and linesmen to distract them from their appointed duty. It's amazing how many line calls go in her favor at the business end of a match. I've never played her, but I'm not afraid of her, even if I'm sick. As a kid, I often played matches while I was hacking away with asthma and bronchitis, and I did fine. Being sick seems to focus my concentration. And once the match begins, I discover that my hand-eye coordination is superb, what players call "seeing the ball big." I smack the ball all around the court, making her run and run and run. Not even her winks to the linesmen can save her. I win 7-5, 6-1, and I'm in the quarter-finals of the French.

After the match, I'm tuckered out and struggling to recover. I hope I'll feel better after a good night's sleep.

No such luck. I'm still exhausted. Margaret Smith whomps me. 6-2. 6-2. Ouch.

The next tournaments are on grass in England, so I hightail it out of Paris to get grass practice.

London is gray, and I feel like crap. I'm triply afflicted, with the aftermath of my illness, my pervasive sadness about the breakup, and the voices of doom that still afflict me. At Queen's, the week before Wightman Cup, I play lousy and flame out in the first round.

But I'm excited about playing Wightman Cup. I get to represent the USA again, and I'll get a whole week of practice on Wimbledon's grass with terrific players. We'll be coached by Margaret Osborne DuPont, one of the greatest players of all time, and by Margaret Varner, her doubles partner, who was also a fine player. And because Billie Jean will be on the team, I have high hopes that there'll be wonderful camaraderie, as there was in Turin. The team is staying near Piccadilly Circus at the Westbury Hotel, which has all the modern amenities. Billie Jean is my roommate, and she's upbeat but serious. She feels at home on grass, and she practices long and hard, laser focused on winning the Wightman Cup and taking the Wimbledon singles for the first time.

I wish I were playing better in practice. I'm happy that I haven't regained the weight I lost in Paris, but also worried, because I remain worn out. But I figure everything will work out well, because the Margarets must know that I came through when it counted in Turin. But they say very little to me, just a few remarks about my weight and that I look a little under the weather.

It's Wednesday night, and with the matches scheduled for Friday and Saturday, the Margarets take the team to dinner at a restaurant near the hotel that specializes in roast beef. The eight of us sit at a round table, and after we finish eating, Margaret DuPont says "Now we're going to announce the team." The top two are a slam dunk: "Billie Jean and Nancy Richey." I figure they'll choose me at Number Three, because in Turin I beat Winnie Shaw, who'll surely play Number Three for Great Britain. Sitting up straight, DuPont calls out: "Mary Ann Eisel." What? That makes no sense. She's a really good player, but she lost to Winnie twice in the last three weeks. This is nuts. The Margarets don't look at me. They don't speak to me. They don't say "We're sorry Julie." For an instant, all I register is shock. Then I feel brutal rejection. After they finish announcing the doubles teams—without me, which is no surprise, as I'm not a doubles specialist—I feel blinded by emotional pain, and tears burst forth uncontrollably. I can't let any of them see me cry, so I wordlessly get up from the table and walk out into the drizzling London night, not knowing where to go. I can't return to the table and be seen crying, and I can't wander around aimlessly in the rain. So I take the short walk back to our hotel, sobbing loudly. As I walk, I continue to disintegrate. I feel like something has to end. Maybe that something is me.

I make a transatlantic call to Mom, and I tell her what the Margarets did. She's sympathetic, and she reminds me of what happened to Sav In 1951. Months after he won the Wimbledon singles, he was selected for the U.S. Davis Cup team, but in a huge controversy, the captain chose a player who was well past his prime instead of Sav. Of course he was furious. Mom's told me that story quite a few times, and I know she means well, but it doesn't help me cope with my ridiculously extreme torment.

Something inside me has snapped so intensely that it scares me. The problem must be pressure. There's too much pressure playing tennis. If I just stop playing tennis, I'll be able to cope better. I have to quit playing tennis forever.

CHAPTER 31
COLD TURKEY

I didn't know that quitting tennis would be so hard. I didn't know that summer days without tennis would be so long. I started playing tennis in 1954 when I was eight, and since then it's dominated my summers. But now it's 1966, and I've quit tennis cold turkey. Except "cold" doesn't describe this New York City summer. We're mired in a 100 degree heat wave, and I don't even bother going out, not to the movies, nor to the Museum of Modern Art, Century Country Club, or even the corner store. I just wait for my sorrow to subside.

I spend untold hours pining after Mike and scribbling drafts of a letter to him. I rip up the draft that says "I want you back." I settle on "How are you?" He replies sweetly, but he makes it clear that he isn't my boyfriend anymore.

Finally, it's fall quarter at Stanford, and I'm back on my old familiar stomping grounds. If I pass all my classes, I'll graduate in December, one quarter late, having skipped spring quarter twice. But even though the campus has hardly changed, and even though once again I have a room at Guthrie, I feel alienated from everything and everybody. Many of my friends are long gone. My classes are boring. I can barely push myself to study. I dread every page of my textbooks. And I still haven't recovered from the distressing aftermath of my breakup with Mike.

I visit Lars and my sister, as Mike and I always did, and we smoke pot and listen to music. That's better. For years, Carrie has wanted to change her name.

When she was 12, she called herself Ralph. Now everyone calls her Trixie, including our parents and me.

Trixie's not the only one changing. The country is coming alive with protests and demonstrations. The Civil Rights movement proved that a core group of committed citizens can bring about legal and practical changes, even in the face of violent opposition. And now protests against the Vietnam War are increasing, and the Black Power movement is gathering strength.

Other young Americans are rebelling in an entirely new way. They're following Timothy Leary's advice to "Turn on, tune in, drop out" by taking psychedelic drugs and becoming hippies. Lars and Trixie are doing just that. Because Lars has a magnetic personality, and because their house is always overflowing with dope, they attract members of the growing counter culture. One day, while I'm visiting, Trixie pulls me into another room and whispers that the guy who just walked in the front door is Neal Cassady, whom Jack Kerouac wrote about in *On the Road*. True to Kerouac's descriptions, Cassady talks non-stop, and leaves once he gets high.

Seeking familiarity and comfort, I start spending more time with Lars and Trixie, although we're so very different. I'm not a hippie, and I don't feel that much in common with their friends or other figures from the counter culture.

Meanwhile, Lars and Trixie are being drawn further into that world. For quite a while, they've driven into San Francisco on the weekends to hear music at the Fillmore Auditorium. Tired of paying money to watch other musicians play, and most of all craving excitement, they've started their own band, the Anonymous Artists of America, also known as the Triple A or AAA. It's a psychedelic band, which I guess means playing rock 'n roll while high on acid and/or mescaline or pot, and experimenting with mind-bending sounds. Lars is financing the band, using a chunk of the $20,000 he inherited last year to buy all of the band's instruments and equipment. But money is still a problem, because none of the band's musicians has a paying job. So to save funds while they're learning their trade, the band is taking another counter-culture step, to live communally. Next month, Lars and Trixie will leave their small house near Stanford and move with the rest of the band to a much bigger house on Skyline Boulevard, the road that hugs the backbone of the Santa Cruz Mountains along the Bay Area. Their new neighborhood is already a landmark in the hippie movement, because Ken Kesey, the author of *One Flew Over the Cuckoo's Nest*, and an early hippie, used to congregate nearby with his pals, the "Merry Pranksters."

At first, the AAA will subsist on Lars's dwindling inheritance and on the small salaries of a few friends who live in the commune. The band also has a sugar daddy in Richard Alpert, Leary's partner in psychedelic experiments at Harvard. Alpert has known Lars and Trixie for several years, and when he heard about the band, he gave them 100,000 micrograms of LSD—about 400-500 large hits—and bought them a ground-breaking electronic music synthesizer.

So the AAA will be on the cutting edge of music, drugs, and communal living. But their music is still pretty awful. Only one band member, their lead guitarist, has musical experience that translates into playing in a psychedelic band. Lars is charismatic and theatrically trained, so he's the lead singer, but he struggles to stay on pitch. The rest, including Trixie, are just learning their instruments.

Lars and most of the other band members—although not Trixie—have pledged to take LSD every day. Lars says acid helps you learn and will speed up the time needed to become competent musicians. I doubt it. Tennis has taught me that there are no shortcuts to intensive practice.

Today is October 31, 1966, a big day for the band. They're performing at Ken Kesey's "Acid Test Graduation" in San Francisco. He's had 16 Acid Test events in the last two years, all featuring loud music and proselytizing the joys of taking LSD. He's full of pranks, such as serving the crowd Kool-Aid covertly laced with LSD. That sounds despicable to me.

I drive into the city for the Acid Test Graduation, where I meet up with a special out-of-town visitor, Dad. He's here on business and wants to get a first-hand look at Trixie's world. Wearing his usual well fitted gray business suit, he walks into a roomful of people wearing the brightest colors you could imagine. He looks dumbfounded, although being Dad, he doesn't make a fuss. He says "There really are a lot of attractive young women here." I think he likes their long hair and their obvious sexuality.

The Grateful Dead has played at most of Kesey's Acid Tests, but they're not available tonight, so through friendship and an accident of fate, the AAA will headline tonight's Graduation. I came to support the band, even though I'm nervous about my grades, and I need to study. I'd hoped to enjoy the music, but I don't, and soon after the band begins to play, I want to flee. So I leave early and return to Guthrie, where I sit down with my books, but that doesn't work either, because I can't focus. I don't know how I'll get through the quarter.

Over the next few days, my panic rises, and I come to a difficult decision, which I announce to Lars and Trixie: "I'm going to drop out, because I'm miserable and barely functioning, and I'm worried that I'll fail."

Lars gives me a lecture: "You can't quit. You'll just have to suck it up for one more month, until you finish your finals. If you quit now, you'll regret it for the rest of your life."

He makes sense. I don't quit, and I try to buckle down, but my heart isn't in it. My least favorite class is Psychology 101. At the beginning of the quarter, I read a few pages of the textbook, but I've hardly opened a psych book since then. Before the final, I vow to stay up all night reading, but I pack it in at 2 AM. Terror strikes when I read the questions on the final, and I draw a blank. I have a B average. I've never been close to failing a class. But this is very, very bad.

Back at Guthrie, I wait for my results, petrified. At least the news will come quickly, because professors have to expedite the grades of graduating seniors. Two days after the final, the letter comes. I passed. Blessed relief. I'm done. Julie Heldman, Bachelor of Arts.

Now that I've finished Stanford, I feel even more lost, with nowhere to go. Once again, I turn to Lars and Trixie, and I ask them if I can move in with their group and join the band as a singer. I have a good voice, and surely, with a little help, I could learn their songs and harmonies. They agree, so I pack up my car and haul everything up to the house on Skyline. The first day I devote myself to cleaning my room and scrubbing the toilet. The second day there's nothing to do except help with dinner. Ditto the whole first week. Many members of the band spend endless hours stoned, and they rarely practice. No one seems interested in adding me as a singer. I have no one to talk to, so I sit around like a blob.

To make a few bucks, the band rents out the Skyline house for a Stanford fraternity party and promises to provide a disc jockey, so one of the band members takes on the task. I ask what I can do, and he hands me a pile of slides and tells me to do a light show.

"How do I do that?"

"You'll figure it out." I give it a try but I'm completely lame. I hate being lame. At an intermission, one of the frat guys, the ex-boyfriend of an old Guthrie pal, comes up for a chat. Starved for companionship, I give him a tour of the house, and we walk into Lars's giant closet, where he has tons of bright clothes and stage costumes. Lars enters the room, sees us there, and starts screaming at us, "Get out of my closet NOW!" Clearly I made a stupid mistake by showing the closet to an outsider, but Lars's anger is impossibly painful, because it forces me to relive one of the ongoing nightmares of my childhood, when Mom raged at me.

I clearly don't belong here. I'm bored, I want to be active, and I don't want to stay stoned all the time. And now the final straw. Lars, the giver of sage advice, my voice of reason, has ripped me a new one. Tomorrow I'll leave the house on Skyline and go home to New York City.

In my parents' apartment, I try to plan my future. At the top of my wish list is snagging a job at *Sports Illustrated*. I'd be happy with an entry-level job doing research, so that I could work my way up to becoming a writer. But I'm stymied, unable to make a simple phone call to get an interview. As long as I can remember, I've had trouble with the telephone, particularly if I need to ask someone for help, or if I'm unsure about how to handle a situation. In either case, I tend to freeze up, fearful that I'll screw up or that I'll be attacked and unable to defend myself. Whenever I think about phoning *Sports Illustrated*, I get tied up in knots, so I do nothing for two months, and I wallow in boredom.

One day, Mom enters my room out of the blue and says Joe Cullman has gotten me a job at Wells Rich Greene, a Madison Avenue advertising agency. I have no interest in that job, and I certainly never asked for it, but I accept. At least I'll have somewhere to go and something to do.

It's Monday morning, the first day of my first indoor job. I dress nicely and show up early. The office manager greets me warmly and shows me around. I don't need to interview for the job, because Joe's company, Philip Morris, is one of the agency's biggest clients, and he picked up the phone, called Mary Wells, the agency's founding president, and asked her for a favor. Just like that, I got a job. Still, the office manager asks me about my background and my skills, and I tell her I was a tennis player, but I can also type a little, and that for many years I've done proofreading for *World Tennis*. So she decides then and there that I'll have two jobs. I'll be one of two secretaries supporting the 14-person creative department, which consists of art directors and copy writers, and I'll also do the agency's proofreading. My salary will be $100 a week.

Most days, I sit at my desk without much to do. Occasionally I type a letter or make a phone call on behalf of my creative bosses. I share the job with a young woman named Betty, who sits next to me, but we have little in common, so we rarely talk. The hours pass slowly. I envy the guys who deliver lunch, white aprons, dirty t-shirts, and all, because they at least get to spend time outdoors. I ache for sunshine and fresh air.

I know my bosses produce great work, because I've seen it in magazines and on TV. Their ads for Benson and Hedges, a Philip Morris brand, and for Alka Seltzer, are hilarious and memorable. They've also produced quality work for Braniff, Pan Am, and IBM. But I rarely see them working, and I sometimes wonder what they actually do all day long, until one day I see four or five of them pile into a small office, and I hear one of them shout, "Who's rolling the joint?"

My bosses apparently have a blast all day, every day, but my happiness is confined to the weekends. Through Lars and Trixie I've met a group of Yale art students who live in a large house in New Haven, Connecticut, and every Friday night I rent a car and visit them, returning to Manhattan early Monday morning. The group is vibrant and interesting, but the real attraction is a tall, shaggy haired, musty smelling guy named Tom, who rents a room over their garage. He's the opposite of my family and my upbringing—he's not interested in education, not driven, not an athlete, and not looking for a good job. He smokes pot all day and occasionally works a little at tooling leather to make purses for other hippies. But he's wonderfully warm and loving, and he clearly wants me, although our connection isn't exclusive. He loves most women. There's never a hint of pressure being with him. Neither of us is possessive; it's all in the moment.

I try to hide my fling with Tom from the others, so I stay in a room in the main house and sneak up to his room around 11 PM. There I walk into his arms, and we crawl under the covers, and I discover pleasure for its own sake. He plies me with whatever drug he's scored that day, mainly pot and hashish, but never the really hard stuff like heroin or cocaine, although once we smoke opium, which is fabulous, but I instantly decide never to try it again, for fear that I might like it too much and get hooked.

The excursions I take with my New Haven "family" open my eyes to new worlds. Many a Saturday we pile into their Volkswagen bus and do something completely different. Once, we go to an art exhibit featuring work by one of the guys in the group. He had twisted and intertwined multi-colored neon lights in a mind-boggling way. Another time, we attend an Indonesian dance recital. The women dancers wear extraordinary gold-embroidered costumes, and their dances range from subtle finger gestures to sinuous, full-body movements. After the dance, we're served an Indonesian rijsttafel feast, consisting of several rice concoctions and dozens of exotic side dishes. All new to me. One Saturday, we drive to Maine, where I have my first totally positive experience dropping acid. Maine is amazingly gorgeous, and at every twist and turn of the road the ocean crashes into the land in new ways, resulting in breathtaking varieties of green and blue, dazzled by the changing light. Maine would have been fabulous without the drug. But adding LSD to the mix makes everything spectacularly surreal. I am eternally grateful that LSD has opened my eyes to such extremes of beauty.

My family's vacations have always been at tennis destinations, which I've never enjoyed. At Dalton and at Stanford in France, I enjoyed field trips, but otherwise tennis dominated my life, and as Mr. Hoxie always said, "tennis isn't meant to be fun." Now, every day with my New Haven family opens my eyes to fascination and joy.

And because I'm eager for new sensations, I'm enjoying New York City for the first time. Every weekday at five o'clock, I leave work, and I relish: Museums! Movies! Shopping! People watching!

I've enjoyed popular music ever since I learned the words to "Blue Suede Shoes" and "Sh-Boom." In college, I loved to dance, anytime, anywhere, and to sing along with the radio. And now, since the beginning of the hippie revolution, music has become more interesting. The first time I heard The Beach Boys' "Good Vibrations," I got thrills and shudders. Now, with my $100 a week salary and no rent to pay, I have spare money to buy albums. I've loved the Beatles since I first heard their infectious beat and harmonies in 1964. This week they've released *Sergeant Pepper's Lonely Hearts Club Band*, an album that is less rock 'n roll and more an anthem of our times, and I rush out to buy it as soon as it hits the stores. I play it over and over, and it's taken a special place in my heart. I know what they mean when they sing "I get by with a little help from my friends." I figure every sentient being must love that album. As I settle into my desk this morning, I ask Betty, "Have you heard the new Beatles album?"

"Yes I have. It really stinks." Whoa. Is she clueless! I have to get out of here.

The more mind-expanding experiences and fun I have in Connecticut and New York, the less I can abide the boredom of my job. And it's definitely a dead-end position for me. The only way up is to become a copywriter or an art director, or even an account exec, and I'm not cut out to be any of those.

Tonight, Tom has promised me something entirely different. At first, he's pretty secretive, but then he hands me a few dark items that look like buttons and says "This is peyote. It may change your life." Ha! That's what people said about LSD, and that wasn't true for me. But *what the hell*. I give it a shot. After a short while, I become calm, the calmest of my whole life. Then it feels like I'm sitting quietly in the desert, at total peace. I'm now clear. All my life I've been volatile and often sad, but now I know something better exists. I've experienced peace for the first time, and peace is what I want. The drug remains active in my body for 12 hours, so there are some remnants in my system when I knock on the office manager's office.

"I want to thank you for giving me this job, but I have to quit." Hallelujah.

Joe Cullman got me this job, and when I quit after three months, he isn't pleased. He'll get over it.

The best news is that my Connecticut family has decided to drive the Volkswagen van across Canada and down the West Coast to San Francisco. In this summer of 1967, scads of people are heading to San Francisco for the "Summer of Love." Now that I've quit my job, I ask if I can come along, and they agree. On the first day of our trip, we aim for an early start, but it's too big a task, and we don't leave New Haven until 5 PM, so we have no idea where we'll spend the night. We just drive and drive until we're exhausted, and then we pull over and drag our sleeping bags onto a rock. It's miserable on the rock, but worse, we discover too late that we're a few feet from stagnant water that's teeming with mosquitoes, which find me exceedingly tasty. I'm up before dawn, thrilled at our 6 AM start.

The first part of the ride across Canada is spent skirting myriad small lakes. Then we hit an endless Northern version of the Great Plains, which we speed through until we reach Banff, which blissfully compares to Maine in its gorgeousness. There, we spend a long day hiking in the mountains and enjoying the vistas of Lake Louise from high above. But we're behind schedule, so we load the van before sundown, determined to reach the States tomorrow. It's my turn to drive, so I maneuver through the blinding sunset, and then while the others sleep, I drive into the night across the Canadian Rockies, which are stunning even in the dark.

During the long ride, I review my options. What do I want in life? To be a hippie and take lots of drugs? Definitely not. Taking psychedelic drugs can be wonderful, but I've decided I don't want to do it often. I want a more active life. Besides, I haven't had a bath in a week, and I feel grimy. Lots of hippies—although certainly not all—bathe infrequently. That's not for me. Should I try harder to get a job in New York at *Sports Illustrated*? I'm not sure. What else? I don't know. Maybe I'll postpone the decision by visiting Linda Vail van der Meer, a former tennis player who's now married to Dennis van der Meer, a transplanted South African who's the head pro at the Berkeley Tennis Club. When Linda competed on the tennis tour she often stayed at my parents' apartment, and she's always been nice to me, even when I beat her in a tennis tournament when I was a young squirt.

At sunrise, I pilot our van for the descent into Vancouver, and then another driver takes over. We cruise rapidly down the coast, stopping only to pick strawberries at a farm in Oregon.

When we arrive in the Bay Area, I call Linda and ask her if I can visit for a while, and she says "Sure!" The group drops me at the Berkeley Tennis Club, and with a huge round of hugs, we go our separate ways.

Linda invites me to lunch at the club snack bar. We gossip about mutual tennis friends, and I feel at home. She knows I haven't touched a racket in a year. After a while, she gently asks if I ever want to play tennis again. "I don't think so. It's never been fun, and there's too much pressure."

I remember those terrible days last year when I was wracked with sadness and voices of self-destruction. Now I look back and think, "I could have died," even though I never got close to ending it all. But my emotional life was like a living death. And now I feel like I'm being reborn.

"No problem. But if you change your mind, we can hit and giggle for just a few minutes, and you can quit as soon as it stops being fun."

A few days later I give it a try. I'm out of shape and puffing hard, so after a few minutes I hold up my hand and quit.

The next day we hit the courts again. Five minutes is enough for me. Reveling in the freedom of not pushing myself, I stop. I feel a smile creeping across my face.

Every afternoon, Linda and I attend to homemaking duties. We buy steaks and corn and salad, and when Dennis returns home at the end of the day, our happy family shares dinner. We love to play with Dennis's pet cheetah Dropshot, whom Dennis brought from South Africa. That cat sure purrs loudly. Maybe that's because I'm used to our cat Putty, who weighs 10 pounds, while Dropshot weighs 85. To help Dropshot get exercise, Dennis sometimes attaches her lead to his car, so that she can lope behind.

Linda and I start playing for longer stretches every day, and other members of the club begin to ask me for a game. Soon, I'm spending hours daily on the court and my skin turns brown. I make friends with the black women behind the lunch counter, who tease me about how dark I'm becoming and invite me to become one of them. Dennis asks if I'd like to help him teach kids in his summer camp. Sounds good. I absorb his teaching methods, which I begin to incorporate into my own strokes. I discover that it's easier to learn something when you're teaching it. Then Dennis gives me a few individual lessons on my two weaknesses, my serve and my backhand. He's very clear, and he makes the lessons fun, which leads to instant improvement. All my life I've used a Wilson Jack Kramer wood racket, but Wilson has come out with a tournament-quality steel racket called the T2000, which works great if you're fast on your feet and you have good hand-eye coordination. I fit the bill, and the racket helps me hit harder. I continue to have fun playing without pressure, and I begin to beat some of the men players at the club, whom I thought were beyond my reach. A new idea is creeping into my head. What if I play the two season-ending tournaments in September? They're really convenient. The Pacific Southwest is in Los Angeles, followed by the Pacific Coast, held at our very own Berkeley Tennis Club.

I'll play tournaments just for fun. What a concept!

In L.A., I beat Darlene Hard, a former U.S. Number One, and I'm feeling mighty pleased about my form. In the next round, I lose to Rosie Casals, with respectable scores. The loss doesn't faze me, because I'm enjoying myself. I return to Berkeley where, in the second round, I draw Billie Jean King. Last year, when we roomed together in London, she won the Ladies' Singles at Wimbledon for the first time, and this year she repeated that triumph. All year long, she's dominated women's tennis, losing only three matches. She's the star of this tournament.

Our match is due to start towards the end of the day. As the shadows descend, the announcer tells the whole club "Ladies and gentlemen, now's the match you've all been waiting for. On the stadium court Billie Jean King will be playing against . . . just a moment. I'll find that name. Yes, here it is. Her opponent will be Julie Heldman."

Very welcoming.

I've never beaten Billie Jean, but so what? I take my new racket, my retooled strokes, and my new attitude onto the playing field and go out fighting. We struggle and run all over the court. Billie wins the first set 8-6, and I win the second 8-6. I guess her year wore her down, because I win the third set 6-3. I'm high as a kite. I can't believe it. I've gone up against the best and come out on top.

Tonight there's a barbeque party at Dennis and Linda's, and I still can't settle down. And then sleep eludes me. What does all of this mean? That I could go back on tour and play with joy? This is too damned exciting.

I wake up groggy, and I struggle to pull my act together. Linda warms me up for my match against Carole Graebner, my old Fed Cup teammate and nemesis. I start out playing as well as yesterday, but her determined and consistent play wears me down, and she beats me yet again.

But that's OK. I'm starting a new life.

CHAPTER 32

FIBBING ABOUT THE FAMILY

In 1967, just before I boarded the hippie van for California, and before I had an inkling that I might return to the tennis world, Mom asked me to write a monthly column in *World Tennis*, to celebrate a woman tennis player on the international circuit. The player would receive the Germaine Monteil trophy, an award fabricated by Mom to entice the makeup company to advertise in the magazine.

I accepted, because I knew so many players, and because Mom made me feel good about my writing: "Your letters home are great, because they're filled with personality. Write like that, and your column will be terrific." With that kind of encouragement, I accepted, of course. As a kid, I'd done menial work for the magazine. Now I'd be one of its featured writers.

Every month, I interviewed a top woman player, asking detailed questions about her wins and losses and how she played the game. Then I tried really hard to make the article fun, informative, and accurate.

Accuracy was important to Mom and Dad. Since the magazine's earliest days, they avoided errors, not just in the Six-Point section (the results), but also in tournament write-ups and personality pieces. If mistakes crept in, Dad, the proofreader, was the first line of defense. If he failed to catch a mistake, Mom's ardent readers would fire off letters to the editor setting the record straight. But errors were infrequent.

Yet from Mom's earliest publications, when she wrote about the family, she jettisoned accuracy. At first, she used us as fodder for light-hearted humor. In

1950, when I was four, she inserted a joke about me in her first magazine, the *Houston Tennis News*, referring to me as the fiancée of a rising Texas junior named Sammy Giammalva, who was 16. She repeated the gag every month for three straight years, as Sammy became a top-flight player and the magazine evolved into *the roundup* and then *World Tennis*. As late as March 1954, she printed a photo of Carrie and me (age eight) in *World Tennis*, with this caption: "Carrie Heldman . . . and her young sister, Sammy Giammalva's attractive fiancée." I'd characterize that running joke as silly, with a touch of weird.

In the October 1953 issue, when *World Tennis* was four months old, Mom wrote and published an article called "I Hate Tennis" by "Carrie Heldman, Age 9." The fictional Carrie complained that "Whenever we ask if we can play tennis, our mother shakes her head and says 'Too expensive.'"(Untrue. We weren't interested in tennis.)

The final sentences were about me: "[Mom] jokingly asked Julie, my sister, 'Are you going to be a tennis bum like your mommy when you grow up?'

'Oh, no,' replied Julie sarcastically, 'I'm going to stay home and play with my children.'" Of course, at age seven I hadn't yet mastered sarcasm and I had no plans to have children.

The article combined jokes about the family with confessions to Mom's readers that she was obsessed with tennis and didn't pay much attention to the children. Interestingly, she never made a similar confession to us, in person. Sure, a few times she told me "I'm a terrible mother," but I always knew that she was just hoping for me to contradict her. I never did. I stayed silent and let it pass.

Over the years, Mom's fibs about the family continued to grow in scope, even when she was interviewed for a newspaper or a magazine. In 1964, *Sports Illustrated* wrote an article about her, entitled "Busiest Voice in a Busy, Busy Clan," in which Mom told several doozies: One was about Carrie changing her strokes. Mom said: "Carrie's strokes were pretty unorthodox—not that we make too much of orthodoxy—but she suddenly got the idea that she wanted classical strokes, and she asked if she could go to California to study with my old coach, Tom Stow."

Boy was that wrong. Here's what actually happened: Mom unilaterally decided that Carrie's strokes were awkward, and that she'd have to be retaught by Mom's old coach, Tom Stow. So she arranged for Carrie to fly alone to California and to stay with Stow and his family for a month. Carrie wasn't thrilled with the idea, but she did as she was told.

I don't know why Mom told such a whopper. Perhaps to cover up that she'd pushed Carrie into doing something against her will? But she sure chose a strange place—*Sports Illustrated*—to assuage her guilt.

In the same article, Mom altered several other family stories. She said Dad, a math whiz, refused to help her with math problems when she was an untrained professor of mathematics (Untrue. Dad always helped her.); that Carrie and I rode horses bareback in Texas (untrue); and that Carrie and I named the family pig "Uncle Willy" after a family member we'd never met (Untrue; Mom had named the pig, but when the real Uncle Willy showed up, she blamed us for it.). The fabrications in *Sports Illustrated* weren't significant, but they do show how easily fibs about the family flowed from her.

All of Mom's early fiction about the family was chump change compared to the article she wrote about me in 1968, during a month when I was far away, and I couldn't deliver my column. So Mom bestowed on me the Germaine Monteil award, and wrote an article that should have been characterized as fiction, because in one-and-a-half pages, she committed 24 errors. I doubt that *World Tennis* had printed a grand total of 24 errors over the five preceding years.

Most of her errors came from stories she invented about my life. For instance, she described what I did in my spare time as a child in New York: "listening to records, telling jokes to Carrie, reading books, watching TV, and phoning her friends." That was true for a fantasy child, not for me. I rarely listened to records, Carrie and I barely spoke, I didn't read books for fun, and I had no friends to phone. But I did watch lots of TV.

She wrote that when I was little, I was a "mixture of the business-oriented with the emotional," because, according to her, I cried every night at bedtime, until she bribed me with a dollar to stop. It's true that I cried frequently, because I was an unhappy child, but money never fixed that problem.

Describing my breakup with my college boyfriend, her sentences were studded with falsehoods: "[W]ith tears in her eyes, [Julie said] 'I am returning his letters—but I am keeping the jewelry.'" There were no letters or jewelry. She must have lifted that quote from the movie magazines she read as a teenager.

Over and over, her article veered far from the truth. Why would a normally accurate editor of a quality national magazine print an article that was so wrong? I bet she excused herself by claiming she was just joking, which gave her free rein. And she certainly knew I'd never protest. I was reared in the Cult of Gladys, where complaints about Mom were forbidden. And most disturbing, Mom had rarely ever asked about my life and really didn't know me. Stumped about how to portray me, she manufactured a fictional "Julie," accuracy be damned.

I hated what Mom wrote about me. I wanted a mother who could notice me and celebrate my essence. I never got that.

CHAPTER 33
OPENING UP

In the summer of 1967, while I was driving across Canada in a Volkswagen bus with a bunch of hippies, the tennis world was a boiling, political mess, struggling through its transition from a sport that had always been dominated by amateurs to one that would in the future be the domain of the pros. Pressure was building to open up tournaments—especially the four major championships—to both pros and amateurs. At the time, I was focused on nurturing my wounded psyche, and I didn't much care how the rules would work out. But tennis politics would soon enter the lives of all top-level tennis players, including mine.

Tennis has been around since 1874, when its inventor, Major Walter Winfield, marketed the game, calling it Spharistike, a Greek word that no one could pronounce. Soon, everyone called the sport "lawn tennis," because it was played on grass. Winfield sold his product to the leisure class, and for a very long time, lawn tennis remained a sport for the well-to-do, who didn't need to earn a living from the game. Starting in the 19th century, competitors in tennis tournaments, like participants in all Olympic sports, had to be amateurs, and tennis rules prohibited competitors from making any money from the sport.

The transition from amateur to "open tennis"—where amateurs and pros play against each other—was a long, drawn out process that began as early as the 1920s and lasted until 1968, even though the system had been badly broken for decades. The best players trained hard and often, which required money, and few were independently wealthy. Tournaments made money selling tickets, and inevitably, popular players began to demand compensation for appearing in those events. Although there were rules limiting the amount of expenses an amateur player could accept, the men who controlled the game—tournament promoters, members of national associations, and the International Lawn Tennis Federation (the "ILTF")—regularly ignored those rules, and the money that changed hands "under the table" was sometimes exorbitant. Mom told me one outrageous example that occurred in the mid-1960s. The United States Lawn Tennis Association ("USLTA") badly wanted the top two Australian amateurs, Roy Emerson and Fred Stolle, to play the U.S. Eastern grass court circuit, but their regular fee for playing tournaments was far higher than the legal amateur per diem. So the USLTA concocted a plan to pay the players richly through subterfuge. Every week of the circuit, the tournaments provided both men legal expenses plus a new, cashable, round-trip airplane ticket between New York and Melbourne. Obviously, the USLTA was breaking its own amateur rules to secure star players. No wonder some pundits referred to top tennis players as "shamateurs," but using that word made the players seem at fault, when in fact the system itself was the culprit.

By the 1950s, there was no rational purpose for maintaining the amateur system. Yet it hung around, in part because national associations wanted to exercise control over their players. Under the amateur system, if players broke a rule, their national associations could ban them from representing their country in Davis Cup, which was highly prestigious, and from competing in the four major championships. The associations had their players over a barrel, and they largely did as they were told.

During the 1950s, Jack Kramer, a former great player, promoted an all-pro tour, which consisted mostly of head-to-head matches pitting the leading pro player—who was usually Pancho Gonzales—against the previous year's top amateur player, whom Kramer had wooed with a large, one-year guarantee. The tennis was fantastic, but the format wasn't compelling, because the matches were played over several months, in a new city every night, and rarely was the outcome of any individual match compelling. Unlike the pro tour, amateur tournaments used elimination draws that grabbed spectators' interests, because if a player lost, he or she was out of the tournament. Also, amateur tournaments were more manageable, because all matches were played in one location, and the entire event usually lasted just one week. The amateurs had almost all of the best tournaments, which were popular with both fans and players.

Kramer recognized the weaknesses of the pro-tour structure, and he became a vocal supporter of open tennis. When the ILTF staged a vote in 1960 in Paris to determine the future of open tennis, he campaigned hard for its success. The countries that held the four majors, Great Britain, France, Australia, and the United States, controlled a large number of votes and backed open tennis, but the proposition lost, five votes shy of the required two-thirds supermajority.

Several commentators claimed that Kramer's eagerness for open tennis had backfired, due to his unrealistic demands. According to *World Tennis* magazine:

> [Kramer] stated that the major open events would have to conform to his schedule. When pressed on this question, he confessed that if the dates of Wimbledon did not conform he would change them. He announced also that if the tournaments wanted to have his "boys" participate, that he, as their representative, would have to be consulted about the seedings and that each tournament would have to offer a purse of at least $10,000.

Telling Wimbledon to change its schedule was regarded as sacrilege. Trying to strong arm other tournament organizers was seen as just plain stupid, because they jealously guarded their domains. Kramer hurt his cause rather than helping it.

Other pundits claimed the open tennis referendum was defeated because several delegates were less than diligent about voting: at the moment of truth, one was in the men's room, another was on the phone planning a social event, and yet another just plain screwed up, voting "No" when he meant "Yes." However, the opposition was far greater than commentators were willing to admit, as many smaller countries who wanted to protect their own amateur events voted against the referendum.

Whatever the exact reasons, open tennis was voted down, and unbelievably, it wouldn't be put to the test again for another seven years. In the interim, the issue went into hiding, and even lost ground, as the U.S. and Australian associations even turned against it.

In the summer of 1967, the ILTF once again voted on open tennis. England, the U.S., and Australia supported the proposal, but the French abstained, and the Italians voted against it, along with all the Communist countries, resulting in a decisive loss for open tennis. But new forces would soon turn the tables.

The first major move was made by the All England Club, where Wimbledon is held. In the summer of 1967, the club for the first time held an all-pro event on its hallowed lawns, testing out the English public's interest in the pros. The event was an enormous hit, which strengthened the club's resolve to open its draws in the future to both pros and amateurs.

Another factor was the emergence in 1967 of several promoters of pro tennis, who embarked on spending sprees, eventually signing many of the world's best men players to pro contracts. A maverick named Dave Dixon, fueled by oilman Lamar Hunt's money, began negotiating with many of the best amateur men players in the world, including John Newcombe, the 1967 Wimbledon champ. By early 1968, the Dixon-Hunt group had signed eight top amateurs to pro contracts. Because several of them had movie-star looks, they were dubbed the "Handsome Eight," although some weren't exactly heartthrobs. Another promoter, George MacCall, focused instead on re-signing such all-time great pros as Rod Laver, Ken Rosewall, and Pancho Gonzales. He also signed Emerson and Stolle, who would henceforth play for prize money instead of airline tickets. And in April 1968, MacCall added four women to his troop, Billie Jean King, Ann Jones, Francoise Durr, and Rosie Casals, making them the only women contract pros in the world.

With so many stars signing pro contracts, organizers of amateur tournaments worried that their events would be stripped of drawing cards, and some voiced their readiness to open their draws to the pros.

But by far the largest event leading towards the adoption of open tennis was the decision by the British Lawn Tennis Association ("LTA") to go it alone. In October 1967, in a momentous, lopsided vote, the LTA declared that Wimbledon, the most prestigious championships in the world, would be open to all players, and it abolished the distinction between amateurs and pros. Mom wrote: "*World Tennis* considers the resolution the most forward step ever taken by a ruling tennis body. It took both wisdom and courage."

The LTA vote threw the rest of the tennis world into chaos.

In response, the ILTF arranged an emergency meeting for March 30, 1968, when all member countries would vote on three main issues: Would the ILTF approve open tennis in any form at all? If so, how many open tournaments would be permitted? And would the ILTF approve Britain's decision to eliminate the categories of "amateurs" and "professionals," or retain those distinctions?

In advance of the ILTF meeting, the tennis associations of many countries had to tackle their own internal struggles. In the U.S., a number of reactionaries were determined to block open tennis, believing that money would adversely transform the game and that national associations—and not professional promoters—should run the game. A few determined pioneers, led by Bob Kelleher, the USLTA president, steered the ship forward. Before the USLTA annual meeting, he did a whistle-stop campaign, traveling from state to state, buttonholing individual delegates, explaining the need for open tennis, and cutting off opposition before it bubbled up into disaster. He won a resounding victory.

Nonetheless, at the March 30 ILTF meeting, many countries remained firmly against both open tennis and pro promoters. As a result, the votes were a mixed bag. The delegates approved open tennis only for Wimbledon, the three other majors, and just a few additional tournaments. And not only did they vote down Britain's attempt to remove the untenable categories of "amateur" and "pro," they added two more categories, "contract pros" (players who accepted money and had contracts with promoters) and "registered pros" (players who accepted money but played under the auspices of their national associations).

Finally, the delegates ruled that each country would be allowed to choose the categories it would apply to its own players, which brought massive confusion, as Britain initially chose only one category, "players," the U.S. initially chose two, "amateurs" and "contract pros," and many other countries, including France, chose three, "amateurs," "contract pros," and "registered players." One result of the confusion was flat-out crazy. Many registered players could legally receive prize money in some countries while retaining their amateur status when playing in others. It would take several years of struggle to sort out the mess created by these distinctions.

The ILTF clearly gave the contract pros the worst deal. Without explanation, the ILTF excluded them from representing their countries and from being ranked by their national associations. Billie Jean King and Rosie Casals took the brunt of the blow. In 1968, Billie Jean won the singles at Wimbledon and Billie and Rosie won the doubles, yet the USLTA wouldn't allow them to play for the U.S. in Wightman Cup or Fed Cup, and refused to include them in U.S. rankings. It's hard to understand why contract pros got such a raw deal. Perhaps ILTF delegates still feared what Jack Kramer had threatened in 1960, that professional promoters would get too much power.

The transition to open tennis, which began in April 1968, had a rocky start. Few amateur players were willing to play for prize money because the rules were ridiculous and prize money was initially puny. Instead, those "amateurs" continued to collect substantial guarantees. But once the system matured and prize money mushroomed, open tennis became the foundation for the upcoming tennis boom.

CHAPTER 34

MY MANTRA IS A LIE

I quit playing tennis "forever" after the 1966 Wimbledon because, for the second year running, I'd been laid low by despair, which had gotten worse, descending into suicidal thoughts and inconsolable tears. The events that precipitated my distress were breaking up with my first serious boyfriend and not being chosen to play on the Wightman Cup team. At the time, I understood that my emotional reactions were extreme, and that the two setbacks, by themselves, shouldn't have led me to the brink. I concluded that the culprit was the high level of pressure I felt on the tennis tour, and that I had to stop competing.

Since then, I've had plenty of time to mull over what happened, and I'm now certain that my 1966 collapse was caused by something deeper than the pressures of top-level competition. The actual culprit was my entire relationship to tennis. And my lack of fun.

Before I ever picked up a racket, I knew that both my parents' were dedicated to the sport, and that they took it seriously. Dad was proud of his tennis accomplishments and loved to show off his game, and Mom was unwavering in her desire to improve and win.

Remarkably, Mom found a camp for Carrie and me that was even more serious about tennis than the Heldman family. Mr. Hoxie focused on winning, and for seven summers, I listened to him hammer home these aphorisms:

"If you don't win, you don't eat."
(A threat he almost never acted on.)

"Only country clubbers play tennis for fun."

"Tennis is about winning, not about having fun."
(He really meant that.)

Despite the severity of Mr. Hoxie's words, I thrived under his tutelage. My early childhood had left me isolated, attacked, humiliated, and devoid of confidence. I felt like a nobody. But under Mr. Hoxie, I learned to crunch forehands and play points intelligently, which brought me a smattering of confidence. I became proud of my ability to fight, to push myself physically, and to persevere even when I was exhausted. Tennis has taught me self-reliance and the ability to think on my feet, which has helped me in every other aspect of my life.

But from the moment I set foot on a tennis court, my childhood demons played a role. To combat my ingrained horror and fear of being a nobody, I fought ferociously. I'd sink my teeth into a match and never give up. Mr. H loved my grit and called me "Tiger." My sister said competing against me on the tennis court was frightening, because my face would tighten into a fiercely determined grimace. And the pressure to win—and not to lose--never ceased.

Our parents did virtually nothing to mitigate the stress engendered by the Hoxies. During my seven summers in Hamtramck, Dad visited once each July, but Mom showed up for a grand total of just one day in all those years. She blamed her absence on her demanding schedule and on her concern that someone might call her a "tennis mother" who pushed her children to win. That was never a real risk. She rarely helped us navigate the rough waters of competition. Still, because I had nowhere else to turn, I'd call her after losing a match. Usually, she'd repeat one of her stock expressions, such as "I don't love you less when you lose," which felt pretty meaningless and confusing, or "winning doesn't matter." Winning certainly mattered to me. I'd had enough of feeling like the runt of the litter. Besides, I don't think Mom really believed that winning didn't matter. When I was 12, I begged her to help me fight the unfair ranking I'd received in the National 15s. She refused, saying "If you're not Number One, it doesn't matter." Although she never repeated that remark, I realized that winning actually did matter to her, and my losses hurt even more (if that was possible).

Yet despite Mom's fixation on the number-one ranking, she never seemed particularly happy when I achieved that goal. When I won the Canadian National 18s at age 12, the first thing she said to me when I returned to our apartment was "Your hair is ugly. You'll have to get it cut right away." And when I won the U.S. National 15s, which would automatically give me the Number One ranking, she said "Now that you can beat me, I'll never play you again." And after she witnessed me squeak out an extremely tight semi-final in the National 18s, she didn't hug me or say "Congratulations!" She was so nervous that her voice rose and tightened, and she said: "That was too hard to watch. I couldn't go through that again." She left without seeing me win the title and gain the Number One ranking in the 18s.

At a minimum, hers weren't words of support. They were crazy, inexplicable, mixed messages. I hated losing, but if I won, and Mom undermined me, I still felt rotten. The upshot was that I was damned if I won and damned if I lost. I was trapped, straddling a razor's edge.

Competition became damaging to me, yet I received very little guidance to help me on my way.

Mom knew everyone in the tennis world, and she was friendly with some of the greatest players of all time, such as Don Budge, Pancho Gonzales, Lew Hoad, Rod Laver, and Pancho Segura. But she never asked any of them to help Carrie or me with our budding tennis careers. And although Mom loved schmoozing with the players and their wives, she didn't include me in their conversations, so I felt unnoticed and unimportant. As always, her excuse was that she didn't want to seem wrapped up in her children's lives. Again, that was never a risk.

Mom's reluctance to ask famous players to help us was understandable for players she didn't know intimately. But she was also reticent to ask Dick Savitt or Sammy Giammalva for help, even though they were Mom's close friends, whom we saw nearly every weekend at the Century Country Club. Sammy was the club pro, and Mom had plenty of opportunities to arrange for us to take lessons from him, but that never happened, which is a shame. Once, she did ask Savitt to evaluate my game, when I was about 13, and I'd already been playing tennis for six years. We hit for maybe 10 minutes, with him checking out first my groundstrokes and then my net game. Afterwards, he told Mom I had terrific reflexes, but I needed to change my forehand! That was beyond strange. Any tennis aficionado could see that my backhand and serve were my weaknesses. My forehand was definitely a bit unorthodox, but it was my best stroke, my money shot, which eventually brought me lots of success. Although I was furious about his suggestion, I knew I wasn't allowed to protest, so I remained silent, but I chose to ignore his advice. So even the one time Mom asked a great champion to help me, it didn't work out.

Because the tennis stars I met never reached out to me, and because, throughout my childhood, Mom laughed at me and made me feel stupid and inferior, and because my parents never instilled in me the possibility that I could become a tennis star in my own right, I grew up thinking that big-time success at tennis would be out of my reach. Some successful tennis players dream from childhood of winning Wimbledon or being ranked Number One. That never occurred to me. Nor did I dream of beating top stars or winning important tournaments (other than the National Juniors). I'd look no further than the next match or the next tournament.

Instead, I fought fiercely, point by point, pouring insane amounts of energy and determination into winning—or not losing. But no matter how many matches I won, no matter how far I climbed up the rankings, no matter how self-reliant I became, I could never kick the feeling that I wasn't good enough.

Sometimes the bar was set too high. During my last year in the National 15s, I was left completely alone the night before the semi-finals, and during the match, I came unglued and yelled at the crowd. When I spoke to Mom on the phone after the match, she wasn't the least bit sympathetic. She said I was embarrassing her. In other words, it was my fault for being unable to act like an adult when I was just 14 and having to endure a high level of stress without help.

At the 1966 Wightman Cup, the bar was once again set too high. For months, I'd grappled with my insistent and crippling demons, all by myself, an impossible task. When disaster struck, and I phoned home from London, Mom actually tried to help, but she didn't know me well enough to understand what I was going through, and she lacked the requisite empathy to help me stem my deterioration. Seeking sanity, I quit playing tennis.

*   *   *   *

I crashed in 1966 because tennis ripped me apart, and I needed to learn how to have fun. During the last year and a half, I've broadened my horizons and enriched my world. Now that I've gravitated back to tennis, I've discovered that competition doesn't have to be dangerous to my wellbeing.

Now it's time to figure out what to do with the next phase of my life. When I traveled in Europe, I got an itch to see the world, which I still have, but traveling is an expensive passion. Tennis can help me afford my journeys. Tournaments will give me airfare, room and board, and the princely sum of maybe 100 or 150 bucks a week. I won't get rich, but I'll have an interesting life.

To keep my old demons at bay, I'll tell myself over and over that winning doesn't matter. I know that's a lie, and that I care too much. But I plan to repeat it to myself anyway. That lie will be my mantra.

I'll start my 1968 campaign in March, on the Caribbean circuit, where I'll compete in amateur tournaments in Barranquilla, Colombia; Caracas, Venezuela; and Mexico City. I won't get much money, but I hope to have a good time.

That's a few months away, and in the meantime I'm 22 years old, and I want to strike out on my own. Since the hippie VW bus dropped me off last summer at the Berkeley Tennis Club, and the Van der Meers took me in, they've provided me a loving home. We've been very happy, so when I tell Dennis and Linda that I want to get my own apartment, he asks "Why? You don't have to leave."

I reply, "I know, but I've never had a place of my own. It's time." I need the freedom to find a boyfriend or to smoke pot and play whatever music I choose, or just to stretch out alone.

I find a small, furnished apartment near Shattuck Avenue, three blocks from the university, close to the action. A few years ago, while Stanford was still a sleepy backwater of conservatism, Berkeley was a hotbed of unrest, beginning in 1964 with the Free Speech Movement. Since then, it's been the site of protests by the Anti-War and Black Power Movements, and the University is alive with excitement. Shattuck caters to a changing world. Clothing stores display outfits with bright colors, psychedelic patterns, and even African prints. Music stores can barely keep up with the vibrant San Francisco music scene, which is easily accessible, a short ride across the Bay Bridge. Torben Ulrich, the long-haired, 39-year-old Danish tennis player who plays jazz saxophone on the side, is spending the winter in Berkeley, absorbing the changing youth culture, immersing himself in the emerging sounds, and growing his beard until he can braid it. He looks nothing like other top men tennis players, who are quite conservative. He also practices tennis in idiosyncratic ways, such as hitting a ball against the wall in the dark. One night, Torben invites me to a concert at the Fillmore Auditorium in San Francisco. As we return, crossing the Bay Bridge around midnight, we can't access a decent radio station that plays rock 'n roll or jazz. All we find is Chinese opera, with its strange, high-and-whining noises played on instruments I've never heard before. The sounds grate on me, but I'd rather learn from the new experience than turn the station off. And then the station's signal fades into the night.

Across the U.S., Top 40 AM radio rules the airwaves, but not in the San Francisco area, where FM stations play music by artists like Cream, The Doors, Jimi Hendrix, and Janis Joplin. Traditionally, all DJs have been male, but now there's a woman DJ whom I adore. She calls herself "The Night Bird," and when she comes on at midnight, she plays song after song that I want to hear. Not everyone loves her. On other stations, I've heard guys complain that they don't like her because women's voices are less pleasant than men's. What nonsense! The world is changing. It's time to get on board.

During my days, I practice tennis and wander around Berkeley. At night, I kick back in my apartment, but I rarely smoke pot and I don't find a single boyfriend. My only visitor is a black cat with a white chest and white paws, whom I call Spats Tuxedo. I never know when he'll come around. Clearly our relationship isn't monogamous, because he looks well fed, but I try to spoil him anyway. He's not mine. I'm not his. I take whatever pleasure he can give me.

CHAPTER 35

THE WORLD IS TOPSY-TURVY

March 1968 rolls around, and I fly into Barranquilla, a city on the Caribbean known for its resorts, although the parts I've seen look pretty seedy. The airport is tiny and ill kempt, and the air is so hot and clammy that my shoes stick to the tarmac. On the drive from the airport to the hotel, I see vacant fields filled with garbage. Children with bloated bellies line the road, begging for money. My driver zips past them and turns into a wilting resort, my abode for the week.

I've always had two personalities. My private persona, the product of a lonely and sickly childhood, requires huge swaths of quiet time for me to charge my batteries. My public personality, the one Mom enjoys, is bubbly and funny, with my engine's throttle cranked up high. Once I check into the Barranquilla hotel, I kick into high gear, ready to restart my life. I don a dress with a striking African print and go in search of familiar faces. At the pool, I find a bunch of players sitting around, dressed conservatively in plain colors and quiet prints. Boring. No hippies here. They're drinking beer and Coca Cola without ice, and one warns me that the water is contaminated, so we have to watch what we eat, to avoid getting sick. I ask the others if they saw the children with malnutrition along the side of the road. No one seems interested. Instead, the Aussie men boast about how much beer they can drink. Others discuss the state of the tennis courts and the quality of the umpires. I try again: "Has anyone found a good radio station here?" I draw blank stares. I guess no one's interested in music. I am. It's my joy.

I'm having trouble connecting with these players. We're too different. Sure, we have tennis in common, but in some ways, their connection to tennis is stronger, because most of them played every day when they were growing up, while I played full time only during the summer, and the rest was catch as catch can. Yet my tennis experiences were more varied than most. I grew up in a family where the youngest and most demanding child was the world's largest tennis magazine. Our family's dinner table conversations have always zoomed across the spectrum of the tennis world, covering everything from the styles of great players to Mom's innovative marketing concepts. Surely those experiences are unique in the tennis world.

Another difference between me and other women tennis players is my privileged education. From the eighth grade through college, I attended great schools, all paid for by the education trust that my grandfather left for me. Top men players have an opportunity to get a college education in the U.S., where men's tennis scholarships are abundant. But women's tennis scholarships are nearly nonexistent, so I'm one of the few women players with an undergraduate degree.

A privileged education gives some people airs. I have plenty of faults, among them my volatility on the tennis court and my utter failure at keeping up correspondence—but being snooty isn't one of them. My privileged education helped form me, but I remember all too well when I was little and I had no one to talk to except Laura or the doorman in our apartment building. They lacked high fallutin' words, but their kindness was far more important to me than their education.

I wish I had more in common with my fellow competitors. I wish they'd love the music I cherish or they'd talk about more of the things I'm interested in.

Instead, I often retreat to my room, where I have an assortment of paperback novels and of course my cassette player. In Berkeley and New York City, I amassed a fine collection of records, which are too big to stuff in a suitcase, so I copied most of them onto tiny audio cassettes, perfect for going on the road. I'll never have to be without my music. The cassette player also has a radio, so I fiddle with the dial and find some compelling Latin rhythms, a new experience for me.

After my first practice in Barranquilla, a Colombian journalist who's read my articles in *World Tennis* asks me to write a daily column about the tournament for her Bogota newspaper, *El Espectador*. She'll translate my articles into Spanish and they'll publish both versions, side by side. I'll write just a few paragraphs a day. I'm honored, and it sounds like fun.

What's not fun is being bounced out of the tournament in the first round by Francoise ("Frankie") Durr, the world Number Three and last year's French champ. She's a wonderful character who was born in Algeria but lives in France, and makes a striking presence with her thick red hair, her thick French accent, and her propensity to swear in the local language (and also in her own). It's hard to decipher her game, with her weird grips, her highly bent wrist on her backhand, and her amazing speed around the court, which she uses especially well to dart forward to finish the point.

After my quick loss to Frankie, I spend my remaining days in Barranquilla playing doubles, practicing, and writing. True to my aim to get out in the world, most nights I eat dinner with my fellow players. But once the meal is over, I revert to hibernation mode, sampling tunes on my cassette player. On Friday night, I attend the tournament party, complete with a live band that plays music with lush, Latin rhythms, and I get up and dance. Torben is here, and he too looks like he's taken by the singer and the beat. Other than the South American players, he and I seem to be the only two grooving on the band.

When it's time to leave Barranquilla, I realize I've had one big victory: my intestinal tract is intact. Next, the players travel together to Caracas. Rumor has it that flying into its airport is treacherous, and that planes occasionally crash during the descent. We hold our breath as our aircraft lumbers up the side of a mountain, clears the top, drops like a stone, and then levels out to land at the airport. The players communally exhale.

The tournament sends drivers to pick us up. Ours is chatty, and he wants us to know that although the city is dangerous, we'll be safe with him. He shows us his guns—one in his door and the other in the glove compartment—which he handles fondly. I don't feel that safe. Guns scare me. I feel a whole lot better when he drops us off at our hotel.

My first match is scheduled for Tuesday afternoon, once I return from an excursion organized by the tournament. We'll take the "Teleferico" tram to the top of the Avila Mountain, which is renowned for its extraordinary views of Caracas and the Caribbean. Before I returned to the tennis tour, I decided not to bring any pot with me. I don't want to get busted by an airport customs agent. But I am carrying a tiny stash of hashish, under a half inch square, which I hide in the bottom of my bobby-pin bag, for special moments. This feels like one of those moments, so I chew a miniscule amount, which helps me enjoy the outing. Unfortunately, the stuff doesn't leave my system fast enough, and when my match is called at 2 PM, I'm still a little high. I figure, *What the hell,*" and telling no one about my screw up, I march on court as if I were feeling normal. To my astonishment, I actually play pretty well, and win quickly. But I've learned a lesson. Never again will I dip into my bobby-pin bag on the day of a match.

In the next round, I face Frankie Durr again, and this time I'm on the ball, winning the match with the loss of only two games. I don't know why I was able to play so much better this time. Maybe it was the change of altitude; Barranquilla is at sea level, and Caracas is at 2,500 feet. Or maybe I was helped by Caracas's faster courts. More likely, my game is sharper after a week's practice with other top players, and Frankie had a bad day. In the finals, I face Ann Jones, who is ranked Number Two in the world. She's a tough player who rarely misses. I watched her squelch Billie Jean King in Fed Cup in 1966. I repeat my mantra, "winning doesn't matter," which helps keep me calm. For two and a half hours, I stick with her, matching her steadiness and throwing in the occasional dropshot while waiting to pounce. I get ever so close, but she squeaks out a win, 6-4, 11-9. I'm pleased with the way I played this week. It feels like I'm returning to the form I had last fall in Berkeley.

After Caracas, we fly into Mexico City, a thriving metropolis with so much to offer. The courts are located in Chapultepec Park, a giant, verdant area towards the outskirts of town, filled with interesting activities, including the Natural History Museum, which I visit. Downtown is vibrant, studded with buildings that are adorned with multi-colored paintings or designs. In the U.S., we think all Mexican restaurants serve tacos and burritos, but Mexico City restaurants have far more interesting kinds of cuisine, from regional Mexican specialties to fare from many other countries. But you do have to be careful not to eat something that could harm you.

The altitude, which at 7,300 feet is almost a mile higher than Caracas, makes it hard to play tennis. Sometimes it's tough even catching my breath. The thin air makes the balls bounce higher and fly faster than at sea level, leading to shorter points. Shots that would normally be simple lobs soar out of bounds. To adjust, I take my racket back lightning fast, and I rely on my trusty topspin forehand. I play Frankie for the third week in a row, this time in the semis, and I win again. I'm due to play Ann once more in the finals, but she defaults. She'd eaten shrimp. Bad choice.

My new attitude—along with my new steel racket and my improved serve and backhand—is reaping rewards. I'm having a good time, and since last September, I've had one win over the world Number One (Billie Jean King) and two over the world Number Three (Frankie Durr), and I got as close as spit to upturning the world Number Two (Ann Jones). I don't know what to think about these developments, as I've never thought of myself as one of the best players in the world.

After the Caribbean tournaments, I return to New York City, where there's an invitational tournament at Madison Square Garden, the mecca of New York sports. Fans go to the Garden to see the stars. Whoever thought they'd come to see me? In the first round, I draw the short, bouncy, and ultra-talented Rosie Casals, who, during my time away from the game, reached the world's Top 10 in singles and became a doubles superstar, winning Wimbledon and Forest Hills with Billie Jean King. After three weeks on tour, I've gained enough control to jerk her around the court, waiting for the best moment to crush my Hoxie forehand. I close the match out in three sets, giving me another scalp for my collection. In the next round, I start out well against Nancy Richey, but my plan of attack is sabotaged when I start getting cramps early in the match. They begin in my legs, and then move to my hands and even to my abdomen. That's never happened to me before. Something's wrong. After I lose, I make an appointment with Dr. Leader. He says I have a bladder infection, and prescribes antibiotics. He says the problem should clear up quickly. I know nothing about bladder infections, and I'm embarrassed to ask anyone else. I figure I'll be fine. I have to be, because Mom wangled an invitation for me to play in the South African Championships, and I'll have to leave in a few days. The tournament has provided me with airfare to Johannesburg, which is halfway around the world.

My journey to Johannesburg starts with a nine-hour overnight flight to Rome, where I have a 10-hour layover. I'm traveling alone, and I rarely strike up conversations with strangers, so I'm not sure what to do. I take a bus into the city Rome and look around a little, but I'm tired and at a loss, so I return to the airport, where I try to fill the hours by reading a page turner and a few articles about South Africa. Everyone knows that apartheid is a scourge, but I accepted this trip because I want to see for myself. When I board my flight and realize we won't land in Johannesburg for another 11 hours, I come close to despairing. But I remind myself this is just another airplane trip. As always, I stuff my rackets in the overhead compartment and my carry-on bag with my cassette player and my books under the seat in front of me, and soon I pass out for a few hours. When I finally arrive, I'm as wilted as the Barranquilla resort, but fortunately, the expatriate American family that's housing me during the tournament is at the gate, waiting to take me home. They drive me through an upscale, wooded neighborhood to a two-story house behind a security gate. After a meal, I shower and then disappear under the covers, thankful the interminable trip is over.

In the morning, I join my Johannesburg family at a heaping breakfast of eggs, bacon, sausages, bread, and fruit, served by their two friendly servants, both black Africans who live in a shack behind the main house. My host is an executive at Coca-Cola South Africa, and he's proud of the luxury his family enjoys. It's immediately apparent that much of my host's good fortune is due to apartheid. The family can afford servants because their salary is so very small. My host clearly feels no shame in the exploitation, and he justifies the situation by saying that unemployment is high and the servants are happy to have jobs, even though it means they rarely see their own families, who live far away. I feel a rising lump of anger in my throat. After we finish our meal, my host, who is unfailingly friendly and kind to me, proudly shows me JoBurg, sure that I'll really like it, which I don't, because injustice is rife. On the streets, all the cars belong to whites. Black Africans travel by foot, with their possessions balanced on their heads. The good stores and restaurants are for whites only. Even at the tournament, blacks aren't allowed to be spectators. I hadn't planned to be viscerally impacted, but apartheid is an assault. The whites control all the power and the money, and the blacks have so very little.

My host justifies his situation by saying "The United States is just as bad," and recounts some horrifying incidents in our country's racist past. I decide not to argue, because I'm staying in his house, but also because I don't know enough facts to compare the two countries. And I want to believe that the Civil Rights Movement is beginning to improve the plight of black Americans.

The day the tournament begins, we learn that calamity has struck in the States. Dr. Martin Luther King has been murdered in Memphis, Tennessee. He has touched me and so many other Americans with his bravery, his speeches, and his inspiring leadership. How ironic to hear the news of his death while I'm in this country, which badly needs someone like him to bring about change. South African newspapers and TV play down the importance of his assassination, surely because the whites in this country fear that African blacks will rise up one day. To get more news, we turn to the English reporters, who snatch London newspapers fresh off of airplanes. As the days go by, the reports are increasingly scary. Riots mushroom across the U.S., impacting over 100 cities. To South African whites, their fears must seem to be coming true. I wonder if my family is OK, but I can't reach them. What a disaster. It feels like the world is topsy-turvy.

It's hard to play a sport when my country is in turmoil and a great leader has been killed. Still, I must honor my commitment to the tournament organizers, who paid for my ticket. The tennis is difficult, in part due to the 5,700 feet altitude (lower than Mexico City, but still tricky), the wind, and the different tennis balls. Or maybe just because I'm unhappy here. I win a few matches, and then I start cramping again, so I visit a doctor. Once more, I'm diagnosed with a bladder infection, and the doctor prescribes a different medicine, which wreaks havoc on my system, making me feel much worse. After I lose in the quarters, I realize I have to get out of here, even though that means more endless flights. I try to phone my parents, but I can't get through, so I just go ahead and book a flight to London, where I'll transfer to another flight to New York. I send my parents a cable saying I'm coming home, and off I go. At Heathrow, I call Mom, and say "I'm sick." She promises to help. When she meets me at JFK—for the first time since I was 10—she's not particularly interested in my condition. Instead, she can't stop chuckling. She says she'd called the airlines and told them "My baby is sick," so they brought a bassinet to the gate. She keeps repeating the story and laughing. Instead of helping me.

I visit Dr. Leader, who tells me to "stop taking the medicine they gave you in South Africa, and I'll put you back on the antibiotics I gave you in the first place. You'll be fine."

After a week, I feel renewed, and Dr. Leader says I'm good to go, so I hop a flight to Rome, where I'll play the tournament at my beloved Foro Italico. But in less than a week my symptoms return. I see another doctor and take more meds. I'm really upset. I just can't shake this illness, and I'm exhausted from the tennis, the medicine, and the long flights. As a result, I can't play worth a damn.

CHAPTER 36

THE FIRST FRENCH OPEN

The United States isn't the only country in turmoil. All over Western Europe, strikes abound. Italy has a postal strike. In London, it's the Underground workers. And in France, members of the student national union are occupying their universities. Out of solidarity with the students, over 10 million French workers walk out in massive general strikes. Charles de Gaulle, the French President, responds by cracking down on the protesters, igniting anger throughout the country. This isn't just a political problem. In two weeks, the very first French Open will begin. The current turmoil could possibly lead to a revolution, and who knows what will happen to this seminal tennis event and to all of its competitors, including me?

After Rome, I enter a small women's tournament in Reggio di Emilia, in the north of Italy, near Bologna. Most of the competitors are Anglo Saxons, from South Africa, Australia, and England. I'm the only American. Most Europeans speak at least two or three languages, but that's not true for people from English-speaking countries, including my fellow players, who are decidedly monolingual. How they get around in Europe is beyond me. Because I speak two languages, English and French, plus a smattering of Italian, I become the leader of the pack.

Every day we wonder what will happen in Paris, and we scour the *International Herald Tribune* for news, which is patchy and sometimes conflicting. As our tournament finishes—with me as its winner!—the other players nominate me to call the referee's office at the French Open. I get through right away, which is astonishing, considering the mess France is in. The referee said, "Everything's fine. The tournament will go on as scheduled." That sounds like some sort of alternate reality, as the newspapers are universally pessimistic. The next day, the *International Herald Tribune* reports that de Gaulle has ordered French troops to surround Paris. I call again. This time the referee's story has changed. "All the Paris airports are closed, so you'll have to fly to Brussels, and we'll pick you up there." In other words, the situation is becoming grave. Our little group meets, and I assume several will drop out of Roland Garros, but I'm wrong. Everyone decides to carry on, despite massive difficulties.

Monday morning, May 26, we take an early train to Milan, where our first stop is the Alitalia office downtown. There, all of us change our destination from Paris to Brussels. Changing tickets is time consuming, especially for the Aussies. It's cheaper for them to buy all their tickets at once at the beginning of the year, and they all carry a two-inch-thick sheaf of tickets, which makes changes complicated. Once we're done, we still have a couple of hours to kill before our flight, so I suggest an excursion to the magnificent Milan Cathedral, which is nearby. Off we troop, and we admire the outside of the great building, but the guards won't let most of us inside, because our skirts are too short. The U.S. is in turmoil, and so is France, which we're trying to reach. And all these guys care about is the length of our skirts. As Ingrid would say, this is "ridiculo."

When we land at the Brussels airport in mid-afternoon, no one's there to greet us. So we fan out in search of other players, and I nearly trip over a few guys who are spread out on the floor next to mounds of tennis rackets. They tell us they're also waiting to be rescued, but they've been there for hours and haven't heard a thing. We settle in close to them, and bit by bit, other competitors dribble in, until we have a room full of exhausted looking players, many stretched out on the floor, some playing cards, others chatting; a lucky few are napping. About five hours after our arrival in Brussels, a French Open representative shows up and informs us that they've hired a bus to take us to Paris. As we ride through the Belgian and French countryside, nothing looks out of the ordinary, but once we enter Paris, we all go quiet, because everything around us is dark and the streets are empty, so unlike the City of Light. The tournament representative walks up the aisle, explaining what will happen next. Because there's no gasoline in Paris, and the driver has to return to Brussels tonight, he won't be able to deliver us to the hotels where we have reservations. Instead, he'll drop all of us off in the Porte D'Auteuil area, which is the population center nearest Roland Garros, where the French Open is played.

When we reach the Porte D'Auteuil, the bus stops at every flea-bitten hotel, and the tournament representative hops out to ask how many rooms are available. The third stop is at 10:30 PM, and when they ask for volunteers, I raise my hand. So does Carol Sherriff, a young Aussie who's been playing in Europe as long as I have. Just like that we get to share a double bed for the night. The hotel's elevator is broken, so we haul our heavy luggage up four flights, and call it a night.

We wake up to brilliant sunshine highlighting millions of dust particles floating in the air. The room feels just like all the other dusty, cheap hotel rooms I stayed in during my time at Stanford in France.

After breakfast, we pack our tennis bags, tuck our rackets under an arm, and hike the one mile to Roland Garros. The streets are eerily quiet. There are few cars and fewer pedestrians. Most stores are shut. I assume everyone is scared. I am. One of the few cars stops right by us. The driver asks in French if we need a lift. I look at Carol, who looks uncomfortable. Me too. The courts are only a half mile away. "Non merci," I say.

That night, Carol moves out to the players' hotel, which is modern and has more amenities. It's on the Right Bank, much farther away from Roland Garros, but the tournament will provide transportation.

I've decided to stay in my fourth-floor walkup. It's barely tolerable, but I'm too tired to pack up everything and move. Besides, if Paris gasoline dries up even more, the others will be stuck in the middle of town, and I can always walk to the courts. Plus I need lots of rest, while I try to recover from the effects of my lengthy illness and the antibiotics. But one night I can't contain my curiosity about the events on the Left Bank, the center of Paris's tumult. I take the Métro to the Odéon stop, and with trepidation I head up the stairs into the jet-black night. On my right I can barely make out waves of Gendarmes (Paris Police), who are wearing their traditional black capes, which are actually vicious weapons, because they are lined with lead. On my left are thousands of protestors, gearing up for conflict. I don't see any guns, but I get the picture. I retreat rapidly down into the Métro to get the hell out of there. No more curiosity about riots. I'll stick to tennis.

In the midst of all this drama, the first French Open is beginning.

Until two months ago, no one knew whether this tournament would be called the French Championships (for amateurs only) or the French Open (for both amateurs and pros), because the future of open tennis was still unsure. Now, by the accident of the calendar, Roland Garros has become the first major event that's open to the pros. The French tournament has traditionally drawn all the great European players, who consider it the most important tournament of the year, plus many non-Europeans who flock to the shrine of clay court tennis. This year, the draws are thinner than usual, for two reasons. Some players are staying away out of fear for their safety, while others are avoiding the French stinginess with under-the-table guarantees, fleeing instead to the more generous German Championships, played simultaneously in Hamburg.

At Roland Garros, the men's and women's draws are littered with the letters "w/o," which stands for "walkover," meaning that a player entered but didn't show up to play. In some cases, three or four players bunched together on the draw are absent, giving a lucky few a free ride into the third round. It's rare to see those letters in the draws of a major. In fact, this is the first time anyone can remember such a massive no-show.

Some of the missing are excellent players. The top Italian men and women, ever pragmatic, aren't here. The U.S. Davis Cup team has stayed away, although the highly ranked Cliff Richey has made the journey, finishing with a 200-mile cab ride from Luxemburg. Also missing are the Handsome Eight group of contract pros, many of whom are playing in Hamburg. The absence in Paris of so many top players would have been disastrous without George MacCall's group of contract pros, especially Laver, Rosewall, and Gonzalez, long-time pros who are returning triumphantly to Roland Garros after having been excluded for years because they openly accepted money. And MacCall's four women—King, Jones, Durr, and Casals—are the top four women's seeds. At the ILTF meeting in March, the French Federation was wary of contract pros, but now they need each other. The French are desperate for drawing cards, MacCall needs money, and his players need match play. The result: the French Federation has capitulated to the very promoters whom they feared. In return for committing all of his players to the championships, MacCall will receive half of the first $120,000 in ticket sales.

Despite player absences and the political situation in Paris, the first French Open is a rousing success, with amateurs competing against pros, and this year, for the first time, there's prize money, available to all. The sunshine and warm weather have held up, the tennis is fantastic, and because many Paris businesses are still shut down, every day the crowds grow. Delighted fans pour into the stadium. The French Federation is thrilled, as the take at the gate has already surpassed anything in history, and it grows daily.

I start my Roland Garros campaign by racing through the first two rounds with the loss of just a few games. My third round opponent is none other than Frankie Durr. Had I been seeded, I wouldn't have drawn her so early in the tournament. But seedings are based on last year's rankings, and I played only two tournaments last year, not enough to garner a ranking. And my two wins over her this year count for naught. In Paris, Frankie starts like a house afire, and my tennis isn't exactly stellar. By the time I get up to speed in the second set, the match is pretty much over. Disappointing.

After showering, I walk out of the clubhouse, ready to grab a bite at a nearby bistro, when a Rumanian player named Nikki Spear walks up to me and asks me out on a date. I've never met him before. In fact, I've never even heard of him. But he's moderately handsome and nattily dressed, with a well-fitted blue blazer and a tie, and he's a good enough player to be admitted to the French Open, so I figure, *What the hell*, and I accept. Two hours later, at the end of dinner, I realize that my favorite things about him are that he asked me out and he comes from a country I've never seen and know little about. So of course I fall for him. I can't help it. I guess I've been lonely.

I have a few good days hanging around the tournament, but then disaster strikes. I'm sitting under a hair dryer, chatting with my old pal Ingrid Lofdahl, enjoying the makeover the tournament is providing to all the women competitors, when out of nowhere I start feeling cruddy, and I need to pee, so I go to the ladies room. I get scared when I realize I'm peeing blood. I need help right away. The tournament doctors are notoriously awful, and finding another doctor in Paris seems highly unlikely, as the city is still somewhere between iffy and totally shut down. Fortunately, someone connected to the tournament suggests that I visit the American hospital, which turns out to be a godsend. They reassure me that I still only have a bladder infection, albeit aggravated, and they give me meds and tell me to leave Paris as quickly as possible, to get proper medical care. The next tournaments are in England, and Teddy Tinling, who's in Paris, says he has a fine doctor in London whom I can see. But I can't get out of Paris. I can't even phone London for an appointment, because international calls are kaput. I'll just have to wait.

For three days, I badger everyone for information about Paris airports, but news is scanty. Finally, I hear of a small airport in the countryside that's accepting reservations on flights to London. I'm one of the first players—hell, one of the first passengers—to get out of Paris. And it's the anniversary of D-Day, surely a good sign. But when I land in London, I'm confronted with blaring headlines in the afternoon papers: Bobby Kennedy has been shot. Killed. This is unthinkable. Unbelievable. 1968 has brought one shock after another.

I came back on tour to have fun. These recent weeks have been riveting, but not fun.

CHAPTER 37
I KEEP ON TRUCKIN'

Teddy Tinling's doctor is very English, a bit distant, well educated, and sensible. After he listens carefully to my saga, he makes a two-phase plan. Phase one: Knock out the illness. Phase two: Stop it from coming back. For the first two weeks, I'll take a fairly high dose of antibiotics and avoid physical activity, which will severely restrict my preparation for Wimbledon. After that, I'll keep taking the meds, but at a lower dose, for six more months. Oy. They suck me dry.

During the past two months of illness, I've learned that bladder infections are quite common, and usually fixable with a week of antibiotics. No one has figured out why mine is so resistant. Competitive tennis must take a lot out of my body. And each time the illness has returned, it's gotten worse, and now, even though there's finally a good plan, I'm paranoid that the infection will once again reappear. My constant worrying annoys Ingrid. We're sharing a flat in London, and she can't stand it when I rabbit on about my health, so she says "You're fine. It's not that bad," which drives me wild, because that's what Mom used to say when she wouldn't call the doctor.

After a lifetime of having my illnesses ignored, I'm convinced that no one will believe that I'm sick, because everyone will think I'm making it up.

Even now that I'm 22, I carry the residue of those early experiences with illness, and any sickness leaves me bouncing up and down on an emotional seesaw. When I'm first sick, I don't complain. I suck it up because I believe no one wants to hear. I crave a doctor's help, but I'm scared to bother anyone until I'm sure I'm "sick enough." Once a doctor confirms that I'm ill, I become a puddle of neediness. I want someone, anyone, to hold my hand and say "I understand."

Amidst my medical angst, Nikki comes around, which is an exciting distraction. In record time, I become fixated on him. I want him more than he wants me. This isn't healthy.

Most days, while Ingrid and Nikki are out practicing, I sit alone in the London flat, trying to recover my strength. To keep busy, I buy all the London papers, to read the English tennis writers, and there I learn that Nancy Richey (a seasoned veteran, who has had to retain her amateur status under the crazy new rules) and Ken Rosewall (a contract pro) have won the first French Open. But my hours drag on endlessly, and I can't listen to the cassette player all day. So I visit Carnaby Street, to ogle the outrageously dressed shoppers who brighten the London streets with an artist's palette of colors. There, I spend an hour spiffing up my wardrobe. Most of the Carnaby Street stores carry cheaply made garments, but I spot two very short, very colorful dresses that look more durable. They cheer me up. I grin when I realize that neither garment would ever get past the guards at the Milan Cathedral or the maître d' at any conservative London restaurant.

Finally, after two weeks of indolence, I start to practice, and I feel well enough to play the doubles in the Queen's Club tournament, where my form is pretty scratchy. The weather is foul, with lots of thunderstorms, which means practice moves indoors, where it's hard to get much court time. The wooden courts at Queen's are dimly lit and too damned fast. But Wimbledon players need practice, so we make do at Queen's.

The Queen's clubhouse is cavernous, dim, and cold, yet the entire tennis world congregates here before Wimbledon. Looking around, I see some of the best players in the universe, along with assorted reporters and self-styled cognoscenti. I'm standing in line for the traditional Queen's lukewarm tea and English biscuits when I see Teddy Tinling and David Gray across the room, hailing me to join them. Looking serious, they try to convince me to take time off to recuperate, at least until I stop taking antibiotics. That might make sense for someone else, but I can't wait six months. I'd climb the walls. All I want is to travel and see the world, and I can't do that without playing tennis. So I thank these kind friends, but I tell them I'm gonna keep on truckin', using my racket to get a free ride. I promise to schedule plenty of time to rest.

My first match at the first Open Wimbledon is set for Tuesday, June 25, which is Ladies Day. I show up early, even though my body isn't match fit. Fortunately, my match is postponed due to rain showers throughout the day. Ditto the next day. And the day after. Rain is common at Wimbledon, but this year's constant downpours are breaking records. By Friday, the rain delays have clearly become more harmful to me than helpful. I need practice, and I'm not getting much. I need matches, and I'm getting none at all. I spend every afternoon cooped up in a Wimbledon changing room or in the overcrowded and dim players' tea room, forlornly scanning gray skies, until the referee shuts down competition for the day, springing us free.

Saturday morning I wake up to sunshine and the certainty that I'll play a match, albeit four days late. I feel giddy and almost light headed as I march on court. I win in under an hour, which turns out to be a bad thing. No one had warned me about the obscure rule that if you complete fewer than 20 games, the tournament can make you play a second singles match the same day. I'm barely fit enough to play one match in a day, no less two, so I beg the referee for a postponement, but he won't budge. "Those are the rules, young lady." Three hours later, I'm back on court, playing Faye Urban of Canada, whose short blonde hair and pert looks haven't changed much since she beat me in the 13-and-unders in Ottawa. I've played her several times since then, and each time, I've vividly relived the massive assault I felt as the Canadian crowd screamed for my 12-year-old self to lose, even cheering my double faults. I'm currently ranked a bunch higher than Faye is, but that ancient match is deeply imbedded in my psyche, and I'm petrified that she'll beat me again. And she damn near does. The first two sets are a titanic battle that lasts nearly two hours. In the third set, it's hot and I'm exhausted but madly determined, and I push through fatigue, winning 5-7, 7-5, 6-2. I don't feel too terrible right afterwards, but once I bathe and leave for dinner, I begin to ache. The next morning I'm much worse. It's the middle Sunday of Wimbledon, a day without matches, but one day won't help much. Come Monday, I play Maria Bueno, a three-time Wimbledon singles champion and the most stylish of players. My tank is empty, and I'm sore and weak, unable to put up much of a fight.

But I'm still in the mixed doubles with Torben, which is a unique experience, because he looks at life through a different prism than other players. He speaks elliptically, with a lilting, Danish accent, and if I manage to understand him, I often learn something new. When I came off the court from beating Billie Jean in Berkeley last fall, he was there, and I expected glowing praise. That's not his style. He carefully explained that I had won the last few games because I'd waited for Billie Jean to miss. To improve, I'd need to become more assertive when closing out a match. This was news to me.

I also learn a lot playing mixed with him at Wimbledon. In our first round, he teaches me where to stand and how the two of us should rush the net side-by-side. In our second match, we win the coin toss and Torben decides we'll serve first. Almost always, the man serves first in mixed doubles, but Torben hands me the balls, a wordless way to say "Your serve." This is weird, but *What the hell*, he's in charge. Unfortunately, my body is still wracked from my Saturday two-match marathon, and I make a hash of my service game, which we lose. The opponents win their serve, so according to the rules, it's now Torben's turn to serve, but he gets playful and decides to teach me a lesson. Once again, he hands me the balls, saying "You'll do better this time." The crowd knows it's not my turn, and several spectators titter nervously. No one but Torben toys with Wimbledon's inflexible rules and rigid umpires. The umpire sputters "Mr. Ulrich. That won't do. It's your turn to serve." Torben takes back the balls with a twinkle in his eye and steps up to the line.

With Torben fully in charge of our team, we win four matches. He has taught me how to maximize my contribution to the team, when to stay back, when to come in, and when to duck for him to hit a smash. I even occasionally serve and volley with panache. We reach the quarters, where we lose to Fred Stolle and Ann Jones, a well-established and highly seeded team. We had a good run.

After Wimbledon, there are several tournaments on the Continent that sound beguiling. The procedure for entering most tournaments is to send a polite letter. For the after-Wimbledon Continental tournaments, no correspondence is required. I just look around the players' tea room, which is filled with tournament organizers who've bribed the tea room guards to gain entry. Some of the tournaments are open to pros and amateurs, but most of the competitors have remained amateurs, preferring the security of under-the-table guarantees versus the risk of losing early and making less in prize money. In the tea room, the Continental promoters offer the sweetest deals to women players who are pretty and flirtatious, and to a few who are top-ranked. I'm not ranked in the top five in the world, and I'm not a natural beauty, so I take what's left over. In one exciting afternoon, I sign up for five tournaments in Sweden, Switzerland, and Germany.

My body's need to heal has shrunk my life. I travel to interesting places on the Continent, but I do little other than eat, rest, practice, and compete. Almost no socializing. Hardly any sightseeing. Still, this is far better than being home alone. But during the tournament in Gstaad, Switzerland, Torben entices me to accompany him to hear the Indian philosopher Krishnamurti, who'll be speaking in a giant tent a few miles out of town. We go, but soon I'm distracted and fidgety. And unenlightened. I thrive on concrete examples, and the philosopher's ethereal words slide past my literal mind. Fortuitously, the area surrounding Gstaad is intensely beautiful, as gorgeous as Maine or Banff when I was on acid, so the trip is worth it.

I reach the finals of the singles in the first four Continental tournaments, winning three—sort of. I win two outright, and in Baastad, Sweden, rain washes out the finals, so we flip a coin, and I guess right, giving me a third title. In Munich, I win my fourth cup, surprising myself by beating Helga Niessen in the finals. She's a tough cookie, so it's a good win.

I have two losses on the Continent, the first in the finals of Gstaad, where South African Annette Duplooy uses her deadly accurate groundstrokes to administer a painful drubbing, 6-0, 6-1. My other loss is in Hamburg, a cold and wet Northern European city, which is the last and most important tournament of the lot. I reach the semis against Judy Tegart, this year's Wimbledon runner-up to Billie Jean King. Judy's an irrepressibly cheerful Aussie who teaches me what it's like to face a serve-and-volleyer who's on her game. She attacks relentlessly, so I counterpunch. She serves to my backhand, so I throw up lobs. I'm up 3-0 in the third. She squeaks out the match 7-5 in third. And that ends my European summer.

I've won some trophies on the Continent, but I'm disappointed. Without enough distractions, without enough joy, I revert to old, unsound ways. I dwell on my two losses. I repeat "winning doesn't matter," but I can't completely repress my rabid need for victory.

It's time to go home. I have to get ready for Forest Hills, which is only a few weeks away.

I fly into New York, rest for two days, and look in my own mirror. Oh no. My face looks pasty and my skin's a mess. I've made it worse by frequent picking. I stop looking in the mirror.

I soon discover that my decision not to take prize money has brought me an unexpected bonus. I receive a call from Bob Malaga, the captain of the U.S. Olympic tennis team.

"Would you like to represent the United States in the Olympics?"

Without hesitation, I yell "Yes!"

Tennis hasn't been included in the Olympics since 1928, but Mexico, this year's host country, wanted to showcase tennis. The Olympics permit the host country to hold demonstration sports, which are stepping stones for sports to be included in the future as full-fledged Olympic sports. So Mexico has chosen tennis as a demonstration sport. Medals will be awarded, but they won't be official Olympic medals.

Most top American tennis players are passing up the Olympics. The American pros are ineligible, because the Olympics are restricted to amateurs. But the U.S. Davis Cup team, composed of amateurs, has also refused to participate. And others are sticking up their noses at the event, saying a Demonstration Sport is equivalent to a lowly exhibition. I'm going because I figure anything called the Olympics is worth participating in. Plus I love Mexico. Malaga tells me that the men chosen for the team are Jim McManus, Jim Osborne and Herb Fitzgibbon, all ranked outside the U.S. Top Ten. The women are ranked higher: Peaches Bartkowicz is the U.S. Number 4 and Val Ziegenfuss is the U.S. Number 11. I, on the other hand, have been chosen despite my current lack of a ranking, due to my results this year and because I was previously a three-time U.S. top-tenner.

I've hardly seen Peaches in years. I knew her when she was a little tyke, growing up in a house on the edge of Hamtramck Park, where I played for seven summers. At just six years old, she hit 1,750 balls in a row without missing against the Hamtramck wall, which started a brilliant junior career. Before she turned 19, she garnered a record 17 national age-group titles. And now she's become one of America's finest women players. Peaches and Val won the U.S. National Junior doubles three years in a row, and they'll be partners here, where they'll be favored to win the gold. There are no other American women, which means no one to play doubles with me. I guess I'll just play singles.

After the excitement of Malaga's call, I fly to Boston to play the grass-court tournament at the Longwood Cricket Club, which has traditionally held the National Doubles the week before Forest Hills. No more. Now that Forest Hills will be called the U.S. National Open, Longwood has been given the newly created title of U.S. National Amateur Championships. The name is a sham. True, some participants remain strict amateurs. But many foreign participants have been taking prize money for months. They've been admitted to our National Amateurs due to a quirk in the ILTF's new rules, which are an unenforceable train wreck.

I reach the third round, where I lose to Margaret Court, formerly Margaret Smith, previously the world Number One. She played for prize money at this year's Wimbledon, and an English journalist reported that so far in August, she's raked in about $3,000 in prize money and guarantees, far above the limits set for amateurs, yet she's being treated as an amateur this week. I don't begrudge her making money. But she's really a pro, and masquerading as an amateur lacks integrity.

While I was on the Continent after Wimbledon, the headlines were largely tame, but throughout 1968, the news has been volcanic, and since I've returned to the States, the world has heated up again. The nightly news broadcasts have been filled with unrelenting violence and unrest. From Vietnam come scenes of war and devastation. From outside the Chicago Democratic Convention, there's been violence in the streets, fomented by the Chicago police and numerous agitators. From Czechoslovakia, grainy films display a disappointing end to dreams of independence. Earlier this year, the country ousted its pro-USSR leader and instituted many freedoms, resulting in six months of glorious hope, known as the Prague Spring. This week, the Soviets invaded in the middle of the night with 2,000 tanks and 200,000 troops, permanently squelching the rebellion. The dramas of 1968 won't quit.

Fortunately, Forest Hills is free of strife, unless you count tennis politics. But I get a lousy draw, facing Court in the second round, in the stadium. I've competed in this tournament seven times, and I've come no closer to playing in the stadium than when I sold *World Tennis* magazines under the stands when I was little. I have no illusions that I'll beat Margaret, but I start out well. In tennis parlance, I'm seeing the ball big, and everything feels easy. She's long-legged and very fast, but I move her out of her comfort zone by hitting deep and then short and wide. When she rushes the net, I pass her. I win the first set, but when I stop to wonder "What am I doing here?" I lose my feel. Simultaneously, she starts running faster. She wins 4-6, 6-2, 6-1. My parents watch the match from the covered Marquee, where *World Tennis* has bought a box for years. After the match, Mom is effusive: "Do you realize what you just did? Taking a set off of Margaret Court is a rare accomplishment for any player." That feels good. But one set isn't enough. I wanted to win, and I don't know how to tell Mom what I have in my heart, because I can't trust what she'll say.

Between Forest Hills and the Olympics, I play three more tournaments, culminating in the Pacific Southwest in Los Angeles, which has been around forever, but this time it's an open tournament, with prize money. For years, players who previously turned pro had been permanently banned from re-entering the amateur ranks. With the advent of open tennis, brigades of geriatric former stars have emerged from retirement to test themselves against the current generation of competitors. In my first two rounds, I beat Dodo Cheney, age 52 (!), and Darlene Hard, age 32, the former U.S. Number One. Then I run into a freight train named Ann Jones—damn, she's playing well—and I lose badly. Earlier in the year, I stretched her to the limit. I'm finally feeling tip-top again, but I haven't yet returned to my best form.

Once again this chaotic 1968 delivers shocking events, which could conceivably impact my trip to Mexico. Two weeks before the Olympics, terrible news of student-sparked unrest leaks out of Mexico, despite the government's attempt to keep it quiet. The student riots in France led to very little bloodshed. In Mexico City, during a few frenzied hours, troops gunned down students and other civilians in a square, killing somewhere between 30 and 300—the actual number remains hushed up. I guess the government's use of excessive force means the Olympics will be free of disruption. But violence can't be good.

A few days before the Games are to begin, we fly into Guadalajara. The official Opening Ceremony and most of the Games will take place in Mexico City, but Guadalajara will host several soccer matches and the tennis. Our opening ceremony in the Guadalajara soccer stadium is decidedly low key. A few words are spoken, then we walk around behind our flag, and the event is over. One of the tennis teams skips the Guadalajara ceremony in favor of marching in the stadium in Mexico City. That doesn't work out well. They have to wait around for four and a half hours, and once it's all over, they sit on a train all night to reach Guadalajara.

Captain Bob Malaga is famous for his bald head and his ever-present cigar. He's also renowned as a promoter who has brought Davis Cup and Wightman Cup ties to Cleveland. He's a good player, but he's never competed on a national team, so none of us look to him for tactical advice. But he makes a fine matchmaker, suggesting that Herb Fitzgibbon and I play mixed doubles together. I hardly know Herb, but I need a partner, and beggars can't be choosers, so we agree to play. Then I get even better news. Rosie Reyes Darmon asks me to play women's doubles. She's not American. In fact, she's Mexican-French, but that's not a problem. The event has decided that competitors from different countries can play doubles together. My plate is full.

Before the tournament begins, Torben Ulrich and I hear about a dance to be held at a nearby civic hall, which we decide to attend. It turns out to be a fascinating peek at an older culture. Inside a square, concrete building, young people wearing colorful, traditional garb congregate, the men against one wall and the women against the other. The event begins when Mariachi musicians strike up their horns and guitars. The men are expected to take the initiative, by walking across the great divide towards the women, but they move at a snail's pace. Finally, a few brave souls make eye contact, cross the floor, and ask a woman to dance. At the end of an hour, only a few have dared to begin dancing. This could drag on for hours, and we have matches to play tomorrow. So even though we're curious about the outcome, we call it a night.

By the first day of play, many of us are suffering from Montezuma's revenge, the dreaded Mexican runs. Unlike the rest of us, the West Germans came prepared with diarrhea medicine, but they're not sharing. While most of us suffer, Helga Niessen relaxes poolside, working on her tan.

Because I'm entered in three events, I play several matches daily, which would have laid me flat last summer, but now I'm well enough to run around for hours without much fatigue. I win my first two singles matches routinely, and I'm delighted by my two partners.

It turns out that Herb is a fantastic player. His serve and forehand are as good as they get. He hasn't played much mixed doubles before, but he's very smart, and he comes up with a plan. Normal mixed doubles tactics are to hit everything to the woman. He kicks that up a giant notch by pummeling women opponents with fireballs, scaring them, and forcing them back from the net, which gives us the opportunity to rush forward and take over the point. When Herb discovers that I'm steady as a rock and I play mixed well (Thank you, Torben.), he too is flabbergasted. We start winning matches.

I've twice been ranked Number Two in the U.S. in women's doubles, but I'm actually just a good doubles player, not a great one. Rosie, on the other hand, is a wonderfully accomplished doubles player. Ten years ago, two teeny Mexican women, Rosie and her partner Yola Ramirez, were the sensation of the Continent, winning many doubles titles, including the Italian and French Championships. Rosie's only a hair's breadth over five feet, so she doesn't have a big serve (nor do I). But she's accurate and understands the geometry of the game, when to hit a short slice or a long first volley. And she has a well of sweetness, so playing by her side is a true pleasure. As an extra bonus, we have a surprise victory over Peaches and Val in the semis.

At the end of this Olympic event, I'm quite proud. Although I thought I'd only get to play singles, I do well in all three events. I'm not thrilled with losing in the semis of the singles to Niessen, but Herb and I win the mixed and Rosie and I reach the doubles finals, losing to the Germans. At the awards ceremony, I get three medals, a gold, a silver, and a bronze. Ours are Mexican coins, not traditional Olympic medals, but for me they're important because I won them at the Olympics.

After Guadalajara, we play an exhibition tournament in Mexico City and I finally get to savor some Olympic ambience. Athletes are everywhere. So are tickets to any event we want to attend. I'm drawn to boxing, because it's a one-on-one sport like tennis, and both sports are physically taxing. Unlike boxing, tennis players don't aim to harm opponents, but we do try to beat them down. Tennis is unique in the player's aloneness against the adversary—coaching isn't permitted in tournaments--which makes it enormously challenging. Even boxers are permitted more help. Their corners continuously shout advice, and every three minutes they give the fighter their undivided attention. At the boxing arena, I see the second fight of George Foreman, the 19-year-old American heavyweight, who is huge, strong, and talented, and he wins decisively. I've seen very little boxing, but my eye has been trained by watching years of tennis. Foreman reminds me of young tennis players with special promise, who ought to soar to the top.

In Mexico City, we meet other athletes at meals or just walking around. Official news is spotty, so we look to other contestants for reports. I ask one about all the fancy track suits and shoes everyone is wearing. All my life I've worn crappy Converse shoes, which have never fitted well. And they fall apart. On Hamtramck Park's rough cement, after just a few weeks, the shoe's tip would rip open and develop an ever-growing flap to trip on. Soon I'd need a new pair. For the first time ever, a company is giving away high quality gear at the Olympics. I go in search of booty and locate an Adidas tent, where I come away with shoes that support my feet. Wow.

Once again, 1968 bites back. Politics intrude in our lives, this time via two American Olympic athletes. After Tommie Smith wins the 200-meter dash, he and John Carlos, who came in third, each raise a black-gloved fist during the medal ceremony, to show their solidarity with the Black Power Movement and other groups that support the downtrodden. They're rapidly expelled from the Games. Compared to other protests this year, theirs is mild. Basically they've been canned because they're black. The International Olympic Committee and the U.S. Olympic Committee are all a bunch of racist jerks.

After the Olympics, I have one last tournament to play, the South American

Championships in Buenos Aires. I've competed in 21 tournaments so far this year, and my enthusiasm for traveling is waning. But I can't pass up this opportunity. I have one major problem. I play with Wilson T-2000 rackets, which use very new technology. I always bring five rackets, in case I break a frame or a string. In Mexico, I was grateful for the backups, because I broke two frames and busted a string in another. That leaves me with two rackets, and the strings of one are beginning to fray. That dumps me in deep trouble, because if I break a string in both rackets, I'm done for the year. Players with wood rackets can easily find replacements or get theirs restrung. I can't. The T-2000s are unavailable south of the border, and they require special stringing machines that are nearly impossible to come by. Guys in my situation would have an easy decision. Because they run through strings really fast, they'd give up and go straight home. My decision is harder, because I don't break strings often. Still, I want to go to Argentina so badly that I decide to pamper my two remaining rackets and take the ridiculous risk.

Buenos Aires doesn't disappoint. It's loaded with impressive edifices, and it's also an attractive and cosmopolitan compendium of places to go and things to do. The tournament houses me in a boutique hotel, where everyone is friendly, and its walls are adorned with antique pen and ink etchings, which feels comfy. Buenos Aires is loaded with immigrants of many stripes, and the city has numerous fine restaurants. But Argentines are proud of their beef, so we go only to Argentine restaurants, where beef is featured in every course except dessert.

The tournament provides transportation, and when I arrive in Buenos Aires, a young man named Oscar attaches himself to me as my driver for the rest of the tournament. He takes me everywhere at top speed. On a Sunday morning, he gives me a lesson in Argentine culture. We're barreling along an empty, broad boulevard when the light turns red. He barely slows, darts his gaze left and right, and then speeds across the intersection.

"Aren't you worried you'll get a ticket?" I ask.

"No one stops at red lights in Argentina. If you do, the car behind you might ram into you."

"Why?"

"It's not considered manly to stop at a red light."

On the Argentine red clay, my wounded rackets limp along, and I reach the semis of the singles, where once again I lose decisively to Ann Jones. I haven't had a win over a player in the world's top 10 singles rankings (although I sure gave Judy Tegart fits) since the advent of the infection and the medicines. But in the mixed doubles, Herb and I are unbeatable. We have to fight our way through a difficult draw, especially in the semis, where we meet Jones and Stolle, whom Torben and I lost to at Wimbledon. They run away with the first set, so Herb and I devise some necessary strategies. Every time Stolle serves to me, I hoist a high lob over Ann's head, and run like hell forward to steal the net position from the favored pair. It's a successful ploy. And Herb plays spectacularly, serving big and terrorizing Ann with his powerful forehand. That makes all the difference. In the finals, we play an Argentinian woman and a Brazilian man. The Argentinian crowd always backs their own, so I assume they'll be out for our blood. To diffuse a potentially explosive situation, I'm on my best behavior. I even try to act demure. Yes, me. It turns out not to matter. Herb is wonderfully dominant, and we don't give them a chance. We win the South American Championships. This is the most excitement I've had in months. It's even more thrilling than the Olympics, because here we've beaten some of the best players in the world.

As I'm making plans to fly home, a tournament organizer asks me to play the Chilean Nationals, which starts on Monday. I ought to stop, but the chance to see another country is too much to pass up. I fly there, see little, but win some hardware. The whole way home, in my final flight of the season, from Santiago, Chile to New York City, I hold onto the singles trophy, a gorgeous, intricately sculpted bronze statue of a condor, the Chilean national bird.

CHAPTER 38
A SEASON OF WOOING AND WINNING

The 1968 season was as volatile as my temperament. I played great tennis for a while, and some experts ranked me as high as 10 in the world, and I loved the travel. But I've struggled with illness for months, which has left my skin pale and broken out. When I settle back into New York, my hippy sister recommends *Let's Eat Right To Keep Fit*," a health food book by Adelle Davis. I force feed myself chicken livers and eggs, and vegetables and juices, to build up my immune system. Instantly my skin heals and I regain my energy. I decide to take up yoga, although I can't find a nearby studio, so I learn from a book. I practice twice a day and meditate. I join a gym. What a joy to feel completely healthy again, to call on my body and have it answer enthusiastically.

In December 1968, I find a tennis club in a cavernous armory on 34th Street and Park Avenue. Like the dreaded 7th Regiment Armory, the lights are dim and the polished wood floor is lightning fast. But here, the owner and the players are welcoming, and I quickly find practice partners. Within days, I meet Suad Rizvanbegovic, an almost handsome Yugoslav teaching pro with bushy dark hair and curly sideburns. He approaches me and declares "You shit. All women tennis players shit. I beat Maria Bueno 6-0. I beat you 6-0 too."

I don't take kindly to trash talk. So I bet Suad 20 bucks he can't do it. I need to win only one game. I can do that. We stride onto the front court and face off, watched by a few regulars. He's so cocky that he lets me serve first. The points seesaw for 10 minutes, until I get a game point and I blast my Hoxie forehand for a winner. I saunter to the net and stick out my hand for the money. While he hesitates, I gather my rackets and walk off the court. He runs after me.

"Where's my 20?" He forks it over.

"You not so bad. I make you great player."

"What do you know? I never heard of you."

"You too timid tennis player. You must charge net, play like man. You must be fit like man. I teach you how." He's weak on grammar, strong on tennis sense.

I'm intrigued. We start training the next day. I pay him by the hour. We do drills, Suad running me side to side interminably. Then forward and back, pushing me past exhaustion through sore muscles and blisters, and he keeps egging me on. He finds out that I'm a fighter, and like Mr. Hoxie, he believes in me. I blossom and improve rapidly.

Now that Suad and I have found each other, I play with more abandon. At the Hoxies, I learned to be a ground stroker, relying primarily on my forehand, but Dennis Van der Meer helped me improve my serve and my backhand. Mr. Hoxie made us all learn to volley, to be serviceable in doubles, but he wasn't keen on us coming to the net in singles. We came forward to retrieve drop shots, but then we'd back pedal immediately. He did everything but place a "Do Not Enter" sign at midcourt. With Suad's help, I'm breaking down that barrier. Point after point he forces me to charge forward, and he teaches me to play an attacking game. Lots of women, like Billie Jean King, Margaret Court, Virginia Wade, and Rosie Casals, are net rushers, but he still likes to call that style "like man."

Playing well is essential to my well-being, but my 1966 emotional collapse taught me that single-minded devotion to tennis is dangerous for me. When I returned to tennis, I vowed to fill my life with distractions, to soften my otherwise desperate need to win.

As a youngster, I hated New York City. Its cold winters left me frequently sick, and there was nowhere to play and no one to play with. Now that I'm an adult, and I'm healthy, fit, and with a more positive outlook, the city entrances me.

With friends, I attend the Joffrey Ballet and the Broadway hit *Hair*. But nothing beats sneaking out alone to the movies in the afternoon, where I drool over Robert Redford in *Butch Cassidy and the Sundance Kid* and I sit in the front row to see *2001: A Space Odyssey*. And I still can't get enough of the Museum of Modern Art, which I visit every few days.

Through tennis, I finally have friends. I've watched Peaches Bartkowicz since she was tiny, but our three-year age difference felt huge when we were younger, and we rarely spoke. Now she's staying with Marilyn Aschner, a fine player from Long Island. The three of us form a happy unit, practicing together and afterwards having long talks. I learn from Peaches that she too has suffered from the extreme pressure at the Hoxies, although Peaches's situation was far different from mine. Peaches was so good so young that Mrs. Hoxie took advantage of the little girl by traveling with her to faraway places, showing her off, and using her to make Mrs. Hoxie famous, often in blatant disregard for Peaches's health and needs.

With my new happiness and aggression, I mow down all the women and a bunch of men at the armory. There's no guarantee that my good play will carry over into world-class women's tournament. There's only one way to find out: I'll have to test myself in the trenches.

It's March 1969, and I'm playing my first tournament of the year in Curaçao. It's boiling hot and there's not much shade, but I don't mind. Suad made me fit, loose, and ready. On successive days I beat Margaret Court, the former world Number One, 7-5 in the third in the semis, and Nancy Richey, the American Number One, 10-8 in the third in the finals. As I fight, there's a bounce in my step. I'm confident. Gone is the pressure that had dragged me down, that had made me quit tennis "forever." I'm enjoying myself on the tennis court, and the crowd senses it and goes nuts. After a big win, the old Julie would have stayed quietly in her room. I don't want to do that anymore. I go in search of a place to celebrate, and I find a group of players stuffed in a small hotel room, downing a few beers. I settle in and join in the fun. I'm a different person.

The next day my picture is plastered all over the front page and the sports pages of the Curacao newspaper. The article is in Dutch, so I understand nothing. A few days later, I get a call from Mom, sounding shocked. "Did you see the Curaçao newspaper?" One of her correspondents had sent her the articles and had written a rough translation. Apparently it was quite complimentary. They're touting me as the future star to watch.

The tournament covers my hotel, and pays me $150 for expenses. That's it. Pro tennis hasn't yet taken hold in the Caribbean.

Two weeks later I return to Barranquilla, where we still stay at the wilting resort, a haven from the abject poverty outside its walls. And once again I write a daily column for *El Espectador*, which is published alongside a Spanish translation. Unlike last year, when I was just starting back on tour and finding my bearings, this year I'm playing like a house afire. The crowds can't get enough of me, the young woman who's writing for them in their newspaper, playing great, and bubbling over with happiness. Their joy fills me up, and I gut out three-set matches against Virginia Wade, last year's winner of the first U.S. Open, and then against Peaches in the final. It's kinda fun having two Hamtramck players in the finals of a big tournament. But it's too bad that I hardly get to savor my victory, because once Peaches and I receive our trophies, we rush off the stadium court into a waiting car—without showering—to speed to the airport so that we can catch the last flight out tonight. Neither of us is willing to wait until tomorrow, when the only flight out is on a Colombian airline that had two crashes last year. Once again, I get $150.

My Colombian journalist friend sends me a copy of *El Espectador* from the day after the finals. The newspaper went ape shit. Photos of me were plastered all over the front page, and an editorial extolled me as an ambassador for all that is good about the United States. Damn that feels good.

I return to New York, where I take a week off from tournament play. I work with Suad on my serve, so I'll get more cheap points, and I won't have to run down so many shots. My serve is still my weakness. I silently swear at Mr. Hoxie for making me serve underhand all those years.

Onto Fort Lauderdale for the next tournament, at the Lighthouse Point Club. Barranquilla makes a delayed attack on my intestinal track, and I struggle with the runs. In the quarters I play a local 14-year-old girl named Chris Evert who is touted as a future star. She can't handle my attacking game, and I routine her, 6-4, 6-1. My belly is still rebelling, but Lady Luck is with me. I'm rooming with Judy Tegart (nicknamed the "Old Fruit"), and this week we're staying on our host's houseboat, which is anchored behind their house. Just before the semis, when I'm scheduled to play Margaret Court, Judy welcomes a visitor who's an English doctor. He hears about my ailing gut and gives me a prescription for Kaopectate with opium. I have no choice. I either take the drug or I default. So I take a slug and walk on court. I start playing in my normal, determined way, but then I become blissfully oblivious to the outcome, and without a care in the world, I play stylish tennis and float past Margaret, to win 6-2 5-7 6-2. Gotta stay away from that opium. It feels too good. In the finals I decimate Virginia Wade, 6-1 6-4. My work with Suad keeps paying dividends.

$150 again.

Onto San Juan, Puerto Rico. I lose to Court in the finals in blazing midday sun. It has to be over 120 degrees. It's two close sets, a good match, but she has my number today. Win or lose, I make $150.

Five weeks, three titles and a finals. Against the best in the world.

Mom usually downplays my accomplishments. She's never run my photo on the cover of *World Tennis*, even though she's bestowed that honor on women who are ranked 10 or 20 spots below me. I think she's so concerned about looking like a "tennis mother" that she tends to underplay my success. I don't think she'll ever put me on the cover. But this month she doesn't diminish my results. She prints a full-page photo of me inside the magazine, with a caption saying I'm ranked Number One in the world for the months of March and April 1969. I guess that's true.

I take another week off in New York, and then I fly to Monte Carlo. The style Suad and I refined—serving and volleying, advancing quickly to the net on all points, pinning my opponent into defense—works on fast courts with fast balls. But in Europe, slower balls are used, and the red clay courts absorb power and weigh the balls down, slowing everything dramatically. Clay court experts aren't fazed by my blitzkrieg attack. They keep running and sliding and getting everything back. In Monte Carlo, I have a tough time getting to the semis, where I lose badly to Ann Jones. It's true that she's one of the very best on clay, but it's also true that I don't give her much competition.

This isn't going well, and I hate losing, so I decide to change my game and play the boring—but winning—clay court tactics that I've used since I played Lea Pericoli four years ago in Rome. That means long, looping rallies from the baseline, often high to the opponent's backhand, patiently waiting, lulling the opponent into boredom or annoyance. I'll bide my time until a ball lands short, and then I'll pounce, either belting a forehand, dinking a dropshot, or, now that I'm more confident at the net, I can add a third option, advancing forward boldly.

I arrive in Rome for the Italian Open, where the fifth most important tournament of the year offers prize money. Finally! All the best women players in the world except Margaret Court and Nancy Richey are playing at the Foro Italico. I don't care who's on the other side of the net. I feel like I can beat them all.

In the Caribbean tournaments, I really enjoyed having the spectators on my side. But to win in Rome, I'll need to use a style that's sure to bore the Italian crowds. If I have to be boring to win, so be it.

In the quarters I play Lesley Turner, an Aussie with unsurpassed footwork who won the French in 1963 and 1965. But she's newly in love with another Aussie player, Bill Bowrey, and she seems to have lost her edge, so I'm looking for ways to dominate. I'm seeing the ball well and moving it around the court easily. After we split sets, my confidence surges, and I pull out all the stops. On one point, I improvise a forehand, hitting it with so much spin that after the bounce, the ball takes a sharp, low, right turn for a clean winner. That shot seems to break her spirit, and I'm home free. In the semis, I meet Ann Jones, whom I've never beaten—even though I've gotten close—because she stubbornly refuses to miss. In her previous round, she took hours to beat Lea Pericoli, with one rally lasting an unheard of 236 strokes! But I won't fall into that trap, because I plan to dominate the tactics. I repeatedly lob high to her backhand, and although she wins the first set, she slows down and gets frustrated and starts popping up short balls, and wham! I get her. And then the crowd unwittingly helps me. At a delicate junction in our second set, the spectators surge out of the stadium, seeking any men's match they can find. They noisily blow past our court, causing a wild disruption. Ann snaps. I don't. I win the second set.

We take the usual 10-minute break after the second set. As I walk towards the locker room, I get a wonderful surprise. John Newcombe, the great Australian who won Wimbledon two years ago, approaches me out of the blue with these words of wisdom: "You can win this match, you know. Just believe in yourself and you can do it." No one has ever extended a hand to me like that. He's helping me believe. I crush Ann in the third set, 6-1.

In the finals, I'll play Kerry Melville, an Aussie about my age, whose style is to pummel every shot. In the semis, she whomped Billie Jean King 6-3, 6-0, and she's having a banner year. The men's and women's finals are both scheduled for Sunday, but it rains all day, so we're rescheduled for Monday morning, but our match is set for Court 6, not in the stadium. That shows how much the Italians love women's tennis. I ignore the slight, put my head down, and continue with my boring tactics. In front of a handful of spectators, I tough out the match in straight sets. In *The Guardian*, David Gray calls the match "dour," yet he concurs with my tactics: "Those of us who have always predicted Julie would become a great clay court player patted ourselves on our backs. It is pleasant when the crystal ball shows a clear image occasionally and in Rome—where in 1965 she was a semi-finalist at age 19—she had played as toughly and cleverly as we could have hoped."

My prize money for winning the Italian Open is all of $800, which the tournament pays me in $20 bills. I've never won so much before. I bolt my hotel room door and spread out the bills on the bedspread, lining them up first by where they were printed, then by date and serial number.

There's no time to luxuriate in my triumph. Once I finish frolicking with my hard earned bucks, I leave for the British Hard Court Championships in Bournemouth, on the south coast of England. When I check in at the tournament desk, they hand me two telegrams. One's from Suad: "CONGRATULATIONS.

YOU NO MORE SHOT." I guess he couldn't get the telegraph operator to write "shit." The other is from Peaches and Marilyn: "CONGRATULATIONS, CHAMP." What good friends.

After winning the Italian Open, I was exhilarated!

The term "hard courts," as applied to the courts in Bournemouth, is both a misnomer and a bad joke. They're actually an abomination of gravel on top of beaten-down clay. The combination makes them extra slippery and loaded with bad bounces. Yet somehow, after several mighty struggles, I reach the finals, where I go down in flames to Margaret Court.

Onto the Hurlingham Club, located in the outskirts of London. I win my second round match and head towards the Tube, my hair still damp from the shower. I'm wearing a bright yellow miniskirt and a flowered top. A handsome, dark-haired man with cute bushy eyebrows, barely two inches taller than I but holding himself confidently, walks up to me and says "You're fantastic!" A good beginning. "You're just like Barbra Streisand in *Funny Girl*."

"Thank you, but what's '*Funny Girl*?'"

"It's a great movie. Barbra Streisand's the star. She's funny, she's sad, she sings beautifully." He breaks into song: "I'm the greatest star, the best by far, but no one knows it."

"Yep, sounds like me."

"Why don't you come with me to see the movie right now?"

"How about, 'Hello, my name is . . . Fill in the blank.'"

"Hello, my name is Larry Hodgson, and I adore you." The man's on a roll. So I accept, and we take a cab to Piccadilly for the film. At the intermission there are tears in my eyes. Afterwards we go to his favorite pub for a pint of lager and bangers and mash. And we talk and laugh. He tells me that he works for the BBC World Service. That he was born in Newcastle upon Tyne. That he read English history at Cambridge. We have another pint.

I'm smitten, but there are faraway tournaments to play.

Within days I leave for Athens for the Federation Cup. When I check in to my room, I find a dozen roses from Larry. He calls daily, and I'm falling for him hard. The U.S. has a strong team—Nancy Richey, Peaches, and I. Billie Jean and Rosie aren't eligible because of the crazy rules prohibiting contract pros from representing their country. Donna Fales, a terrific player in her own right, is the captain. It's such a joy to have a captain who's smart, experienced, and caring. I'm playing Number One for the U.S. It's a big honor. One of the teams protests, because Nancy is ranked Number One in the U.S., and I'm Number Two, even though there's no rule requiring that players be positioned according to their ranking. Nancy stifles the noise, saying that I've played better than she has so far this year, so I deserve the Number One spot. That's class.

The Australians look stronger on paper, with Court and Melville playing singles, and the Old Fruit is on board as a doubles specialist. I win all my matches leading up to the final round, where I play Margaret Court in extreme heat. I use my slowdown tactics to keep her on court for two hours, but I go down 6-1, 8-6. I'm unhappy about the loss, but Donna tells me not to worry. "You really tired Margaret out." Nancy beats Kerry, so it's up to Nancy and Peaches in the doubles. Margaret and the Old Fruit are daunting at the net. Both have great reflexes and fabulous volleys and overheads. Nancy and Peaches are also great doubles players, but unorthodox. Peaches is a kick. She hits three winners and shows nothing but a poker face. But if she misses, she hangs her head and mutters audibly "I hate this game. I'm gonna quit." Like all Hamtramck kids, she has an aversion for the net, but she doesn't let opposing net rushers dominate. She gives them fits with her flat ground strokes that she slaps low and hard over the net. Nancy's a baseliner by nature, but she's also a doubles star, having won the U.S., Wimbledon, and Australian doubles championships in the last few years. Playing with Peaches gives Nancy the opportunity to roam the net and pick off anything the opponents pop up. Captain Donna, sitting on the court, spots Margaret beginning to droop, so she tells Nancy and Peaches to concentrate all their shots on Margaret, going high with lobs then low with dinks, making her bend and reach, bend and reach. The tactic works, because Margaret is whipped, and our team wins 6-4, 6-4. For the second time, I'm a member of the world champion Fed Cup team. It's thrilling.

Next, we go from boiling and sunny Athens to overcast Paris for the French Open. Last year, the tournament was beyond extraordinary, with the strikes and the empty streets and the crowds. This year, I'm staying in a nicer hotel, where they actually seem to clean the rooms with regularity. Again my room is decorated with Larry's roses, and he calls daily. But I detest the French Open. You have to battle traffic, the inefficiencies of the French, the aging locker rooms, and the grim facilities. Between practicing and struggling to get by, I hardly have time to enjoy a meal in Paris. Larry makes a surprise visit to watch my quarter-finals, which I lose to Nancy Richey in two long sets. At dinner over steak and pommes frites, he tells me again that he loves me. He also tells me he's been married for four years to a Spanish woman he met while on assignment in Spain. She's Catholic, and a divorce is tricky. I'm speechless.

I head back to England for the grass court events leading up to Wimbledon, and my tennis is awful. I'm preoccupied with Larry, and I've forgotten how to play on slippery, low-bouncing grass. I'm still hanging in the backcourt, playing clay court tennis. I lose in the third round at Beckenham to Denise Carter. I'm ranked higher than she is, and I'm supposed to beat her. She's a friend, but the loss rankles. Early the next week at the Queen's Club in London, in the week before Wimbledon, I get thumped again early. I shower and dress, and then I sip disgusting lukewarm tea in the giant public room at Queen's, which is cold and austere. I hear a familiar voice: "You shit. Why you play like that?"

"Suad! What the hell're you doing here?"

"You forget how to play? You better than those fucking girls."

"I know. I don't know how to win anymore."

"You go. Put on sweats. We train."

I didn't ask him to come to London. I didn't pay him to come. He realized that I need him, so he hopped a plane.

Out we head to a back court, where he runs me through his "attack" drills. No matter the drizzle. No matter my disappointment over my losses. We have only a few days to prepare for Wimbledon.

In the second round at Wimbledon, I play Denise Carter again. I will not play from the back of the court. I will go forward and I will win. On the first point, Denise serves to my backhand. I lean my right shoulder in, slice the ball into the corner, and charge the net. Again and again I take over the play. Denise never knows what's hitting her. I clobber her 6-2, 6-3.

Suad, Larry, and I go to dinner at Larry's favorite Italian restaurant in Soho. I hold Larry's hand, but we talk tennis. With Suad there, I'm living, breathing tennis. I get better by the day. Peaches and I, the old Hamtramck pair, are playing doubles together at Wimbledon. On Saturday, we meet Billie Jean King and Rosie Casals in the quarters on Court One, the second biggest stadium at Wimbledon. We're huge underdogs—Billie and Rosie won here the last two years—and we have nothing to lose. As always, Peaches roams the baseline, muttering epithets when she misses. I'm floating on a cloud, in love and enjoying life. I've practiced my volleys with Suad, and my control has returned, so I pick my spots, short and wide, then deep, to keep the opponents guessing. When I win my serve, I grin. Even Peaches smiles. We cheer each other on and the crowd joins in. We break serve twice in the third set, and Peaches serves for the match, but we can't close it out. Billie holds serve, and now it's my turn to finish the deal. Peaches and I look at each other, smiles plastered across our faces, knowing that I'm playing so well that we'll win. The audience is screaming their heads off for us, and when we win the final point on a deft volley from my racket, they erupt. Peaches and I hug and head for the net to accept our opponents' congratulations.

Since the dawn of television in Britain, the BBC has shown wire-to-wire live Wimbledon. At the end of each day, they replay their favorite match as "Match of the Day." And on the first Saturday night, they play their "Match of the Week." Today, our doubles match has been chosen as both Match of the Day and Match of the Week, not only for our good play, but also for our joy and enthusiasm. Peaches and I become instant celebrities. After the match, I bathe, and we drive into town and eat dinner, and then we saunter into Piccadilly Circus. Peaches steps off the curb while the light's still red, and a policeman approaches her. I think "Great, how to ruin a perfect day," but that's not the case. He just wants her autograph.

Sunday there's no play at Wimbledon, so Larry and I go out alone. He tells me he has big news, but refuses to divulge his secret until after my quarter final match tomorrow against Margaret Court. I grill him relentlessly, but he refuses to say more. The next day the tournament puts me back on Court One, which has instantly become my favorite. Larry and Suad watch me win the first set against Margaret. I charge and charge, hitting backhand volleys crosscourt for winners, as I had against Billie and Rosie. The crowd's beyond enthusiastic for me. Then Margaret starts reading my volleys, and I have no Plan B. I lose in three sets.

At dinner Larry orders a lager, takes a sip and says "I'm being sent to Vietnam." I can't speak. I see body bags, flame throwers on the nightly news. Tears stream down my face. I don't speak for the whole meal. I need my sleep, but that night it eludes me.

The following day, I let Peaches down. We lose easily in doubles. I can't think about tennis. Larry's married. I love him. He may die.

But I keep competing and traveling. I'm playing so well I can write my own ticket.

I fly back to New York for two weeks of rest to prepare for the Maccabiah Games in Israel. It's akin to the Olympic Games, but it's just for Jews. It's held in Israel every four years, in the year following the Olympics. The head of the U.S. delegation wanted to be sure I was Jewish, so he asked "What Jewish groups do you belong to—a synagogue, a Jewish community center, maybe a Hillel?"

"Sorry, none of the above," I respond. They let me play anyway. I'm just too good to let go.

He tries another angle: "Are you prepared to pay for your own expenses?"

"No, I'm not." But I've agreed to play an exhibition at the Concord Hotel in the Catskills (the "Jewish Alps") to raise funds for our trip. We're supposed to play outdoors on a court surrounded by stands, but we're rained out, so we move indoors and play in front of only a few dozen people. Afterwards, I take a sauna, followed by a cold shower, and then I lie down on a chaise longue, wearing only a towel. The woman on the chair next to me looks to be in her 60s. She has bleached hair that's teased high and she's naked except for pearls and a towel.

She asks "So what are you doing here?"

"I'm playing a tennis exhibition."

"You could have fun here. They have lots of good looking waiters and bellboys."

"I have a boyfriend."

"Is he here?"

"No, he's far away."

"Is he Jewish?"

"No, actually, he's not."

"Oh my god! Does your muthah know?"

That night, we're glued to the TV, like everyone else around the world. We watch Neil Armstrong take his first steps on the moon.

Larry calls. His trip to Vietnam has been postponed. A weight drops off my shoulders. I don't know why he told me during Wimbledon. Why didn't he wait?

Several days later, I fly to Tel Aviv on a commercial flight that's mostly filled with regular travelers, but it also contains dozens of Jewish athletes from a variety of sports. I'm sitting next to Albie Axelrod, a highly accomplished fencer who's now in his 40s, yet still competing at a high level. Another champion fencer, Carl Borack, comes by to talk with Albie, and we discover that we have so much in common that we can't stop yapping. Quickly we discover we've both experimented with psychedelic drugs. The hippie revolution has spread from the Haight Ashbury section of San Francisco into the highest echelons of sports.

In Israel, the athletes settle into giant dormitory rooms, each holding a dozen competitors, like mini kibbutzim. Marilyn Aschner is on the U.S. team, and we're assigned to the same dorm room. We're also hard workers, so we set a tough schedule of twice-daily practice sessions in the 100-degree, desert sun. Sarah, the woman who runs the tennis club where we practice, welcomes us like family. I've never felt such acceptance and warmth, and she makes us feel at home in Israel. We're all Jews here. But we're also accosted by a few rabid Zionists, who tell us "You have to move here. If you don't live in Israel you're not a real Jew." I let their remarks pass.

The U.S. Maccabiah committee organizes a bus trip to Jerusalem, to show us the Wailing Wall. The ancient city is full of contrasts. We drive through the modern-looking Israeli section, and then we enter the Arab section, which looks medieval. The Wailing Wall is another surprise. Because my parents have never been observant, I had no idea that Jews come from near and far to pray at the wall, where they insert tiny pieces of paper scribbled with prayers.

I'm one of the headliners of the Games, along with Mark Spitz, the American Olympic swimmer who is far more famous than I. Still, the newspapers beg me for interviews. I'm ranked much higher than any other tennis player in the Games, so to no one's surprise, I win three gold medals, for the singles, doubles, and mixed. In the singles, I lose a total of five games. A reporter asks how I do it. I say it's because I eat lox, bagels and cream cheese. *Sports Illustrated* prints the quote.

My decision to compete in Israel was last minute. Previously, I'd planned a leisurely summer, with no events between Wimbledon and the Wightman Cup in Cleveland, a month later. But I squeezed in the Maccabiah Games, because it's a unique opportunity to meet other Jewish athletes and crow to the world that I'm Jewish. Now Cleveland beckons, and I have to leave the Maccabiah Games before the final ceremony. A driver takes me to the airport, and we pass through several security check points, because the Israelis have remained on high alert since the Arabs attacked Israel in the Yom Kippur War, barely two years ago. At the second check point, the guard looks at me closely, and tells my driver in Hebrew that I need to produce every bit of identification that I have. After days of practicing in the desert sun, I'm brown as a berry, and I wonder if he thinks I'm an Arab. When the guard stills seems to be unsure, I produce my rackets, and only then does he relent and let us get under way.

I arrive in Cleveland to compete in the Wightman Cup for the first time. We practice for four days, and then I open the matches against Virginia Wade. It's a great fight, and I squeak through at 8-6 in the third set. After the match, we shower and then speak for a moment. Looking dejected, she says that she hasn't played as well since winning the U.S. Open last year. I tell her not to worry, she's a fine player. It'll come back. I win my other singles, and then the doubles with Peaches. We win the Cup, and I'm named the MVP. One excitement after another.

And I don't slow down. At Wimbledon, a Soviet tennis official invited Peaches and me to play in Moscow. We both accepted instantly. The Iron Curtain is shut tight to almost all Americans, but because of our tennis, we'll have this special opportunity. But the schedule is outrageously tight. The Wightman Cup ends on Sunday, and I fly back to New York on Monday, the very day that the Moscow tournament starts. We're supposed to fly out that night, but at the last minute, we're told that the Aeroflot flight from New York to Moscow won't leave until Tuesday. I explain my schedule to a friend who's a doctor, and he gives me sleeping pills, so that I can sleep on the flight.

We arrive in Moscow on Wednesday, two days after the tournament began. Peaches and I have a suite in a large hotel that masquerades as any other gray, Stalin-era building. Our TV and radio don't work, so I figure they're bugged. I yell "Fuck the Russians" into all of them. I know the phone works—Larry finds me.

Most of Moscow is gray. Even the food's gray, served in giant communal rooms. At the tennis club, women players from communist countries are assigned to one locker room, and all the other women players are assigned to a separate locker room. On our second day in Moscow, an English player complains to us as she's changing clothes in our locker room: "There's no fruit or vegetables, and I'm getting constipated." The next day fruit shows up in our locker room. I'm sure someone was listening.

The Russians have some neat tricks up their sleeves. In the semis, I draw a Czech named Maria Neumannova, whom I've never seen before. Before the match, everything goes wrong. We encounter interminable delays at breakfast and on the bus ride to the tournament. When I finally arrive, the tournament director berates me for being late and says there's no time for me to practice. Clearly, the Russians want me to lose. I start the match cold, facing the weirdest damned strokes I've ever seen, and in record time I'm down 5-2. Then my tennis brain zones in, and I breeze through, 7-5, 6-1.

Peaches gets through the other half, and we play each other in the finals. As we head down a giant ramp into the stadium, we're accompanied by blasting martial music, so I boogie to it, which makes the audience laugh. I win the first set, and I have high hopes of running through the second, so that we can go sightseeing for the first time, but Peaches doesn't comply. She leads 4-2 in the second, and I give it my all in the following game, but when she hits a hard forehand to go ahead 5-2, I can't hold my frustration in. I yell "Sonofabitch!" and look up at the crowd. I realize that I'm eyeball to eyeball with the American Ambassador. Oops. I'd better behave. Peaches wins the second set, but I take the third, and they give me the winner's trophy plus an engraved camera. I ask one of the Russian players what the plaque on the camera says. "It's the 'Award for Spirit,'" she says. "Bob Hewitt [an Aussie famous for his bad temper] won it last year after he got angry, dropped his shorts, and mooned the crowd."

Peaches and I get almost no sightseeing done in Moscow, but the next day we fly to Leningrad, and spend several happy hours at the magnificent Hermitage Museum. Back in Moscow, Peaches will set out by train for Poland, and I'll return to New York. The night before we go our separate ways, as we're settling into the dormitory where we're housed for the night, all of a sudden, she blanches and says "I just realized that I forgot to cash my travelers' checks. I don't have cash, and now it's too late. I don't know what to do."

I tell her, "I'm going straight home. You can take my cash."

The next morning, when I check in at the Moscow airport, I'm told: "Your suitcase weighs too much. You'll have to pay a penalty."

"Ok, tell me how much, and I'll pay."

"You'll have to go to the other counter, which is down there."

It turns out that "down there" is a 10-minute walk with me carting my very heavy bag. I approach the counter and say "They sent me here to pay a penalty."

They check my paperwork, and tell me to pay either 200 Rubles or $200, a ridiculously huge amount, but I say nothing, although I know I'm being fleeced.

Peaches has my cash, so I say "I'll pay you in travelers' checks."

"You can't use travelers' checks here. You'll have to go to the next building to cash them and then come back."

That does it. I blow sky high: "This is completely ridiculous. I was brought here by your government, and my suitcase contains trophies and gifts from them. I will not pay those penalties. I demand to see the person in charge!"

The people behind the counter look startled, and then they disappear for 10 minutes. When they return, their spokesman says "It's been arranged. You don't owe anything. You can board your flight now." Holy shit! I just learned something. In Russia, scream and shout that you know important people. I bet it works every time. Believe me, it never works in France, where a woman is taught to win by batting her eyes and wiggling her butt.

I'm back in my parents' apartment with less than a week to prepare for the U.S. Open. I bit off too much to chew, and I'm tired. But the travel was great. I open my bedroom door and find flowers from Larry. He phones daily. I go through my mail, and nearly throw out an envelope, believing it's from a department store in San Francisco called The White House. I change my mind and open it, and read the first line: "Pat and I want to congratulate you on your fine victories in the Wightman Cup." It's a letter from President Nixon. I'm not a fan of his, but it's still terrific to be acknowledged by the U.S. President.

At Forest Hills, I play well until the quarters, when I meet Virginia Wade. As I'm walking towards my court, Mom tells me that if I win this match, I'll be ranked Number One in the U.S. Why is she bringing up rankings on the way to the court? It's distracting, and I'm sure she wouldn't say that to any other player in the same circumstances. When I was 12, she told me that Number One is the only ranking that counts, and I guess the thought of me being the Number One woman in the U.S. is too exciting for her to bear. As it turns out, I have a much bigger problem: Virginia's huge serve, which is a major weapon on grass. Plus my tank is empty, from too much traveling and too many matches. The match is over all too quickly. After I beat her last month in Cleveland, I encouraged her to keep trying. I should have kept my mouth shut.

Soon after I'm out of the singles, Peaches and I lose to Billie and Rosie in the doubles. Actually, they massacre us. They must have decided to get back at us for our Wimbledon victory. But in the mixed, Torben and I have a good run. We win a few matches, and then in the quarters we convincingly beat Doris Hart (age 44) and Vic Seixas (age 46), two highly accomplished veterans who own lots of tournament hardware. It's exciting to reach the semis, but we're thumped by Margaret Court and Marty Riessen, the eventual winners.

I'm overdue for a rest, but I play one more tournament, at a resort that's under construction in La Costa, California. Match after match I play out of my head; everything I hit goes in. I play Peaches in the finals. She's the best at hitting hard, flat, and accurately. My usual tactics against her are to interrupt her rhythm with tricky spins and lobs, to make her miss. But today is different. I'm seeing the ball so well that I go toe-to-toe with her, matching her power with my own, and outhitting her. We're both in shock.

I finally take five weeks off, but then I head to London. To be closer to Larry, I play a six-week tour in Great Britain called the Dewar Cup. It's a fairly low-key circuit, no glitz or glamor, just good times. I end up with three wins over Ann Jones and one over Virginia Wade.

At the end of the tour, there's exciting news. Official world rankings don't exist, but several English journalists publish their own unofficial world rankings. It's been a helluva year:

WORLD RANKINGS 1969

	Lance Tingay, *London Daily Telegraph*	Frank Rostrom, *London Daily Express*
1	Margaret Court	Margaret Court
2	Ann Jones	Ann Jones
3	Billie Jean King	Billie Jean King
4	Nancy Richey	Julie Heldman
5	Julie Heldman	Nancy Richey
6	Rosie Casals	Rosie Casals
7	Kerry Melville	Kerry Melville
8	Peaches Bartkowicz	Peaches Bartkowicz
9	Virginia Wade	Virginia Wade
10	Lesley Bowrey	Lesley Bowrey

My 1969 tournament season ends in Stockholm in late November. I beat Rosie Casals, lose a tight one to Billie Jean in the finals, and I'm done! Larry flies over for a two-day excursion to Copenhagen. We register in Larry's name, but a tournament promoter still tracks me down by tipping the Stockholm concierge to find me. She's on the phone from halfway around the world, pushing me to commit to playing in Philadelphia in February. So this is what happens when you keep winning.

It's December, freezing in London and New York, but balmy by the Florida beaches. The promoter George Liddy has invited me to play an exhibition against Margaret Court in Fort Lauderdale. I tell him I'll accept if he'll pay Larry's airline ticket from London. We spend a few glorious days at the beach, and then Margaret and I go at it, pummeling each other mercilessly. At the end of an hour and a half, she wins the first set 9-7. All tuckered out, I quit. The audience understands. We gave them their money's worth. I get $500!

I return to New York. Larry goes back to London. We plan a March wedding.

CHAPTER 39
I HATE JACK DANIELS

My romance started so well. First in the spring of 1969, and then again and again and again, he said "I love you."

Then: "Marry me. I can't live without you."

Then in maddening, hiccupping succession: "I'm married, but you are my Funny Girl. We can make this work."

"My wife is a Spanish Catholic, and her family and her church will block a divorce."

"You and I are meant for each other."

"We must marry, but we can't unless I get a divorce, and that's impossible."

"This is hopeless."

In January 1970, Mom consults CK's brother, Uncle Eddie, a New York lawyer who's the family's fixer. He suggests a divorce in Mexico, where Larry won't need his wife's consent. Sensing a way out of the morass, Larry agrees. Within days, Uncle Eddie prepares the paperwork, so Larry flies in from London and we catch a flight to El Paso. I stay in a dumpy motel while he takes a taxi across the border to Ciudad Juarez. There he signs the unilateral divorce papers and returns stateside a divorced man. Sort of.

He says: "I don't know if I can marry you. My wife will be devastated."

But then he adds: "I need you."

And then he returns to London, still yo-yoing around.

Mr. Hoxie called me the Tiger because when things got rough on the tennis court, I tried twice as hard. I haven't changed. So my reaction to Larry's insane tumult is predictable. I grit my teeth and fight through one crisis after another. I talk Larry through his indecision. I organize caterers and flowers and a classy location in New York City. Mom drops her father's name to procure a New York judge, only to discover that the State of New York doesn't honor Mexican divorces, so we scramble to move the event to Connecticut.

One week before the wedding, my parents' best friends, Joe and Sue Cullman, throw a party at their estate in Westchester for the happy couple. Only Larry doesn't make it. He blames work, promises he'll show up for the wedding. His words are a blur, just blah, blah, blah.

Friends are already flying in from around the country. Carl Borack arrives from California the night before the party and sleeps on our couch. Mom says it's too late to cancel the party, so out we drive, Mom, Dad, Carl, and me. Carl's a good looking guy, and he's the hit of the party. Guests keep congratulating him on our impending nuptials. I can't breathe.

And then the final insult. Four days before the wedding, Larry says "I just can't go through with it." I'm stunned but not surprised. He wants me. He loves me. But he's weak.

Larry has been my present and my future. For months I've focused only on what *he* wants, what we would do *together*. Now a giant cosmic rubber band has snapped in my face. There's no present, no future.

Just deeply unpleasant practicalities. First I have to contact all the guests, tell them not to come, mumble my gratitude. Cancel the flowers and the caterers. I spend hours at my parents' dining room table sending thank you notes and returning all gifts—except the silver tray engraved "Larry and Julie Hodgson, March 1970", which I cover up and leave in a corner. Let's look on the bright side. At least he didn't actually leave me standing at the altar. And although we lost all our deposits, we didn't have to pay the Justice of the Peace.

Mom reveals that a few months ago, CK smelled a rat and hired an English private detective. Early in our relationship, Larry told me he'd attended Cambridge University, but apparently that was a lie. This is staggering news, not only because Larry lied, and my family spied on him, but also because my family left me in the dark. They thought Larry was a bad guy, but they let the marriage go ahead and they even facilitated it by arranging a Mexican divorce. I've been betrayed by my entire family and by Larry.

Cascading pain. I can't remain in New York. I phone Linda van der Meer, who rescued me once, when I arrived on her doorstep in a hippie van. "Dennis is giving a tennis clinic in Hawaii, so why don't you come hang out with me by the pool?" I accept greedily and tell Mom.

Last year at this time, when I was riding high, Mom was thrilled. Now that the problem had ripened into disaster, she says "At least you can leave town. I'm left here with the social embarrassment."

A gate inside my heart slams shut. She's my mother. No one can take a mother's place. Mothers are supposed to help. And now she's turned on me. I'm in intense pain, tumbling towards rock bottom.

I do the unthinkable: I break the rule about not confiding in Dad. I tell him what Mom said, but he doesn't believe me. He's on her side. Always.

I have to leave, so I steal away to Hawaii. A 12-hour flight. A hotel in paradise, another pool, another restaurant, a kind friend. But no relief from the horrifying unraveling of my love life. I last two days. Another 12-hour flight back to New York.

There's only one more person to call.

I phone Larry. His voice is so happy, so bright. He says "I love you. Come to London." He doesn't need to ask twice. I hop a flight. A mere seven hours on the jet. Like old times we go over to the King's Whistle and down a few lagers. "Come live with me," he says, so I catch a flight home to pack my bags. I fly through the front door and bound into my room, brimming with joy. There's a note on my bed: "Larry called. He said to phone him right away." He tells me not to come. He's changed his mind. I hang up. Breathe. Call him again. He sounds so unhappy. I just want to comfort him. I'm sure he'll want to take me back. I tell no one about this final indignity.

In a blind rush I pack my bags, throwing in flannel and wool clothes to fend off the freezing English spring. I fold in my tennis clothes, just in case. I don't know how long I'll be gone, or when I'll start to play again. I leave a note where Mom is sure to find it—in the foyer next to the scotch. I rush to the elevator before anyone can try to stop me.

The doorman calls me a cab. I stuff my luggage and my five rackets in the trunk. The Long Island Expressway is dark and rainy. I cry all the way to JFK. I'm counting down the hours 'til I see him.

I snag a reservation on Pan Am's inaugural flight of its monster Boeing 747 jet from New York City to London. The plane's huge, but it's crammed. I'm smack dab in the middle of a five-seat row, stuffed between two large men who spill over into my space. They've co-opted the arm rests, and there's no place to lean my head, so once we take off I recline my seat as far as it'll go and lean my head against the side of my neighbor's seat.

I close my eyes, but I still can't sleep. I've barely slept in weeks. Hours pass. My neighbor shakes me. The stewardess is standing in the aisle with my dinner. I don't want dinner. She gives me a foul "Everyone is supposed to eat dinner" look and I close my eyes again. I have a vision of Larry's button nose. His rich, dark sideburns. Of the way his eyes sparkle when he sees me. The man behind me gets up, leaning all his weight on my seat back. I'm jolted back, then slammed forward like a catapult.

I finally nod off for a few minutes, waking to the announcement that the stewardesses are coming through the cabin with our duty-free purchases. Larry drinks beer in pubs, but at home he prefers whiskey, which I hate, because it reminds me too much of Mom's evil scotch. In the States, he fell in love with Jack Daniels. So I'm bringing him a bottle. Maybe I'll like that better. I'll try it with him.

At customs, the agent says "I loved watching you at Wimbledon," and lets me breeze through. At least something's going well. Outside customs I phone Larry. The English pay phone does its annoying "pip pip pip," and I plunk in the coin. The BBC operator says Larry's out to lunch. I leave a message and take a cab to the Brompton Hotel. They know me there. I get a porter but warn him my bag is very heavy. I bring my life with me in my luggage. I'm more at home on the road than in my parents' apartment.

I love the Brompton. It's cozy, unpretentious, and affordable. American tennis players hurting for money fill it up during Wimbledon. It's a maze of corridors connecting to doors opening onto stairs and more corridors. Not modern or efficient, but from 7 to 9 AM they serve you a nice boiled egg with a rasher of bacon. And the hotel is one Tube stop away from the Queen's Club, where we practice.

Again and again I ask the hotel operator to phone Larry's numbers. I can't go back home. Mom's ashamed. I'm ashamed too. I'm a failure.

It's dark out when I finally reach Larry. I tell him I need him, and I brought him Jack Daniels. From his end there's an unbearable silence.

Then "I told you not to come."

Then "Go back to New York. My wife is so upset."

He hangs up.

I'm trapped, with nowhere to turn. Too little sleep. Too much pain. Too many flights. In 10 days, New York-Hawaii-New York. New York-London-New York-London.

I make sure my door's locked, and I screw open the Jack Daniels. Dull with shock, I take out the bottle of sleeping pills I got last summer for my long flight from New York to Moscow. I take a slug of booze. It's as bad as scotch. I swallow five pills. A longer slug and several handfuls of pills. I finish half the pills and half the Jack Daniels. The bottle of pills looks fuzzy. I call the hotel operator and ask her to phone Larry's number. Sleep is overcoming me. I tell Larry what I've done and lay down the phone.

I hear knocking at my door, then nothing.

✳   ✳   ✳   ✳

Hazy gray sunshine filters through the curtains. The pounding in my head is excruciating, my mouth is beyond parched, and my throat feels raw. I'm lying in a narrow bed. I sit up, look around. Other women in narrow beds. Lots of them. It's a hospital ward, but devoid of nurses. I wait forever. Finally a young doctor stops at my bed. I ask him how I got there.

"An ambulance brought you. We had to pump your stomach. You shouldn't have done this. You have to take control of your life." Very helpful. He walks away, stopping at each bed, dispensing the same advice. I wonder how many men go through this much pain.

Finally, a friendly face appears. It's my buddy David Gray, the tennis correspondent for *The Guardian*. He's always been kind to me. He's Oxford educated, a fine writer with a good knowledge of tennis—a rarity—and a lovely touch of humor. On the road I sometimes join him and other journalists for dinner. English tennis writers aren't paid that well, but they get to see exotic places on small expense accounts.

"Would you like to stay with my family for a while?" He doesn't pry. He's very English.

I can't speak, so I nod. I wonder how he knew I was in the hospital. I guess Larry called him. Anything to get rid of me. David hands me my carry-on bag, which contains a change of clothes, and says he'll wait for me in the lobby. I remove the clean clothes from the bag and stuff it with the sweater I was wearing last night, which is wadded by my bedside, reeking of vomit. I stuff it in my bag. I don the clean clothes.

We ride in silence to his house in Putney, just a hop, skip, and a jump from Wimbledon. I'm shivering in waves. He pulls my suitcase and rackets out of his trunk. I wonder if they had to break down the door to my hotel room.

David's house is small. And bone-chilling cold. There's no central heating, just a few portable heaters they move from room to room. David's wife Margaret has prepared a Sunday roast beef. I've never met her or their two young children. They're well-scrubbed, well-mannered, and pink-cheeked, maybe because they're always cold. Margaret is lovely, clearly smart and educated, but reticent. So English. Lunch is exceedingly awkward. Then I retire to my room, where I think of phoning Larry. Finally I sleep. My brain has been so deprived of dreams that they fight their way through, spattering my unconscious with demented fragments.

The next morning I take my turn in the frigid bathroom and then I eat breakfast with the family. I have to figure out what I'll do next. Tennis is all I have now. No family. No Larry. Humiliated. Broken. I decide to go for a run. I open the door and I'm slapped with icy rain. I don't go far. I'm exhausted, and I'm not fit. All winter and spring I've been distracted. A failing love, not tennis, was my first priority. I've had no energy to train with Suad. I don't turn to him for advice. He's a coach, not a bosom buddy. Nor have I turned to my other New York friends. Too much shame.

I've been staying with the Gray family for three days. I need to do something else. I ask David for the tennis calendar, and I discover that the Nice tournament will start in a few days. I make a last-minute entry with a special request to postpone my first match until Wednesday, and they agree. I'm ranked five in the world. They're happy to have me. I fly out on Sunday, leaving myself a few days to practice.

In my first match in Nice, I play a low-ranked French woman. I'm slow and frequently off balance. My Wilson T-2000 steel racket is great for power, but requires my natural speed and the terrific control I learned at the Hoxies. I trip and hit a forehand off center. The vibrations shoot up my arm. I've injured my elbow, which hurts when I hit forehands. But I don't quit. I have nowhere else to go. I soldier through.

I play Nice and Monte Carlo in a fog. I can't concentrate. I'm the Tiger without her fangs. I win some matches on experience, but my distraction is paramount.

The rhythm of tennis tournaments takes over. Eat, practice, shower. Eat, play matches, shower. Eat, sleep, start over. When I first played in Europe five years ago, I swore by *Europe On $5 A Day*. Now that I've won some big matches, tournaments put me up in hotels with Michelin stars, fluffy duvets, and concierges who expect fat tips.

Oh god oh god. I forgot I'd entered the Italian Open as Mrs. Larry Hodgson, and now the organizers have issued an international press release saying Julie Hodgson would defend her title. My private tragedy has turned into public shame.

I check in at the tournament desk, and in my best pigeon Italian I ask them to change my name back to Heldman. "I was supposed to get married, but I didn't."

I see David Gray every day, and we're friendly but superficial. I'm grateful that he rescued me in London, but neither of us mentions what happened there. Not one word. I assume David is equally tight lipped with others. I know tons of people on the tennis tour, but now they're awkward around me. Sure, we say "Hi, how are you?" or "Ciao come stai?" Or "Bonjour, ça va?" But none of the other players, writers, or various hanger-onners ever mention anything at all about The Marriage That Wasn't.

My parents write, and I write them. I send back jokes and gossip, but no mention of The Marriage That Wasn't. I wonder if David spilled the beans to Mom about the Night at the Brompton and the Hospital. I guess I'll never know.

Rome is a boisterous city of excitable Italians, terrific restaurants, and unique ambiance. One's dinner companions include spectacular architecture, classic marble sculpture, and the occasional wandering gigolo. In previous years, I loved dining out with David and a few other English writers. This year I buy yogurt and apples and cookies and eat in my room. I don't cry. I don't listen to much music. I just sit there in stultifying pain.

Last year I rode into Rome on a tidal wave of victories, and I took the title, the biggest of my career. This year I'm slow and stiff, constantly fighting wars on many fronts: the practical ones on the court, the suffocating trauma of the last few months, and the deep pain in my elbow. Luckily the competition is much weaker than last year, and to my great surprise, I reach the finals, where I'm trounced by Billie Jean. I play really badly. Blearily I stand through the trophy ceremony, leave the courts, and return to the hotel without showering. I win $300. I don't even bother to count it. Onto the next tournament, the next matches.

Last year Larry sent me flowers at every stop on the tour. This year there are none. Why doesn't he phone? Did his love just die? Mine didn't.

Onto the biggest tournament of the spring, the French Open. As in Rome, fortune smiles on me, and I get a good draw and reach the semis, where I run into a very dominant Margaret Court. We walk proudly onto the enormous stadium court, and I proceed to play abominably, winning just a handful of points. I phone Larry. He pours out his love for me. We talk. He begs me to stay at his house during Queen's and Wimbledon. He lives in Wimbledon, not far from the All England Club, so I'll be relieved of the stress of fighting London traffic.

I see Larry's house for the first time. As Suad would say, it's shit. It's tiny with thin walls and a postage-stamp garden. He doesn't even own the house; it's in his wife's name. He says she's at her parents' home in Marbella.

Arms around each other, we talk of our future. Not much to say there.

I try to get keyed up for Wimbledon, but my energy is sapped. Larry works. I'm alone for hours each day in his wife's house. What are my choices?

On paper I'm having a great year—I reached the finals of the Italian Open and the semis of the French. A career year for most players. But it's a lie. I'm playing on reputation and with a lot of luck. But maybe now that Larry and I are back together my inner star will shine.

At Wimbledon, once again 1970 brings me another great draw. If I reach the round of 16, and if I can just get by Frankie Durr—who isn't a grass court specialist--I have a shot at the Wimbledon semis. Frankie and I meet on Court One. Twice last year I shone on this court. I was loose and newly in love, and each time I hit a good shot, I grinned and the crowd roared. This year I'm tight as a board, and the crowd emits barely a sound as my game slides down the drain. No question Frankie's a terrific player, but I play like a 10-year-old. Balls go flying off my racket totally out of my control. It's a mess.

After my ignominious loss, I leave the court, and as I wind my way through Wimbledon's labyrinthine staircases towards the members' changing room, my head hung low, I hear my name. I turn around, and there's Mr. Aks, my adored Dalton School music teacher.

He says "I don't know why you lost. You're a much better player than your opponent."

"I guess it just wasn't my day."

"I've been waiting years to tell you that I understand why you quit the chorus to play a tennis tournament. I play tennis all the time now, and I realize it takes a great commitment."

I try to think of something to say, but my mind's bouncing between sorrow and emptiness. So I murmur "It's great seeing you, but I'm sorry, I have to go."

I bathe and meet Larry in the players' tea room. Above the bar, the BBC is showing snippets of the Wimbledon highlights of the day. The announcer intones "Today there was an upset on Court One. Let's turn to that match now." The next announcer says "Miss Julie Heldman, the American Number 5 seed, is struggling . . . ." You ain't just whistlin' Dixie darlin'.

After Wimbledon, I play a few more tournaments, because I don't know what else to do. But my elbow is getting worse, and I realize I must attend to it. I make an appointment with a Harley Street specialist—the crème de la crème—who tells me I've torn a muscle, and a blood clot is resting between the muscle and the sheath of the bone. There'll be no tennis for quite a while. I start ultrasound and physiotherapy.

Larry invites me to stay with him while I rehab my wounds. But his house belongs to another woman. Is his wife coming back? Will Larry still want me if she does return? He can't make up his mind between us. I can see it's a losing cause. Every day I love him less.

I phone my parents. Dad's being transferred again, this time back to Houston, where Shell has moved its U.S. headquarters. I offer to help them move from New York to Houston. I pack my bags and return to New York.

Once again I'm stuck in traffic on the Long Island Expressway, which feels perpetually gray and sad. I'm a wounded Tiger, crawling back to her lair. The U.S. Open is only a few weeks away, but I'll be injured for months to come. I don't want to face the tennis world. Or my parents.

I have no fight left.

CHAPTER 40
THE POWER BROKER

When Mom started *World Tennis* in 1953, she wrote most of the articles and performed almost every task necessary to publish a first-class publication, including licking envelopes, inking the addressograph machine, and pasting up the layouts. In the circulation "department," she did everything from opening the mail to making stencils for new subscribers, to filing them. She only interrupted her highly focused attention when cash came in the mail, which she giddily stuffed in her bra. She filed the stencils of so many subscribers, first by state and then by name, that she could recite the 48 states of the union alphabetically.

Mom developed systems for circulation and filing, and as the magazine grew, she hired employees and taught them her systems. That left her freer to sell ads, grow the magazine, and occasionally run a tennis promotion. By 1960, she hadn't done any filing for so long that she was rusty at reciting the states, and when she tried, she forgot Hawaii and Alaska, which had joined the union in 1959.

World Tennis lost money during its first decade. But in the early 1960s, the magazine began to hit its stride. The issues grew larger, sporting more pages with four-color advertisements. And Mom kept working on the magazine's quality. She bought photos from the game's best photographers. And she improved the magazine's writing by hiring several great English tennis scribes, including David Gray, Rex Bellamy, and Richard Evans, and the effervescent American, Bud Collins, all of whom traveled with the tour and knew it well.

Before 1961, Mom rarely took up causes in *World Tennis*, other than her own promotions. Instead, she gave Gar Mulloy carte blanche to puncture pompous officialdom, and she usually left the subject of tennis politics to Ned Potter, the magazine's sage elder, whose monthly column "Passing Shots" thoughtfully considered the major issues in the world of tennis. Occasionally she'd insert long treatises about racism or tennis politics where they really didn't belong, in the "Around the World" column, nestled between announcements of marriages and births.

In March 1961, Mom started writing editorials, which at first were careful, understated, and diplomatic, as if she didn't want to step on anyone's toes. But by the second half of the 1960s, she'd dropped her guardedness, and her language was sometimes tough and even combative, when she used her editorials to fight for causes.

As Mom's magazine evolved during the 1950s and 1960s, so did her promotions. Before she rescued the 1962 Nationals, she had a broad view of how to fix the event, like a high-level executive. Simultaneously, she worked non-stop, often completing menial tasks.

By 1968 and 1969, she had become transformed, and she was able to step up in a big way.

Mom's new role emerged soon after the very first U.S. Open in 1968, held at Forest Hills. She had fought hard for open tennis, and she was happy when the ILTF approved it in early 1968, but like pretty much everyone else in the tennis world, she was disturbed by the initial rules that were promulgated. Six months later, those rules would contribute to problems at the 1968 U.S. Open. In fact, the tournament was a disaster, and in her editorial after the event, she lashed out at the USLTA:

"[T]he early days of the Open ... were slow-moving and poorly attended. ... It was obvious that the USLTA felt a major international Championship, supposedly the second biggest in the world, could be played without commandeering the best Europeans and Australians, that the scheduling could be made by a non-professional, and that the acquisition of the world's best pros was sufficient to guarantee success. ... It would have taken only $35,000 to have brought in the best amateur and registered players in the world, but the penny-wise USLTA felt the expenditure was unwarranted."

At the end of her rant, Mom offered suggestions for improving the tournament, including importing Captain Mike Gibson, the Wimbledon scheduler. But she soon realized that more drastic changes were needed, because the USLTA couldn't be trusted to run the 1969 U.S. Open. Earlier in her career, Mom would have micromanaged a revolution. In late 1968, she instead went to work behind the scenes, this time not as a promoter, but as a power broker. She carefully selected highly qualified individuals, and then fought hard to get them appointed.

Mom began by inventing the title of Chairman of the U.S. Open, or possibly Mom and Joe Cullman made it up together. It was tailor-made for him. She believed that his skills—and his company's money—would be instrumental in improving the event. But because Mom had no official position, she couldn't make the decision. That was up to the incoming USLTA President Alastair Martin, and Mom needed to convince Alastair to appoint Joe.

Joe wasn't a hard sell. His business acumen was well known, as he had grown Philip Morris into a tobacco industry leader. And everyone knew about the $167,000 Philip Morris had spent to erect a giant, electronic scoreboard in the Forest Hills stadium, which blared, in enormous letters, "Come to Marlboro Country." And then, because Marlboro was a huge advertiser on CBS, Joe had easy access to its CEO, William Paley, a fellow titan of American business. Joe suggested to Paley that the network should cover tennis at the U.S. Open, and sealed the deal by committing Marlboro to be the major sponsor of the telecasts. Paley agreed to the arrangement, and CBS television began covering the U.S. Open in 1968.

Based on all of Joe's contributions to tennis, Martin rapidly appointed Joe as the Chairman of the 1969 U.S. Open.

With Joe in place, Mom's next aim was to find a seasoned and successful tournament director, who would avoid the bonehead errors made by the USLTA in 1968. During the first years of the open era, the mentalities of most tournament organizers remained mired in the amateur era, and very few professional tournament directors existed. Amongst them, one stood out. In 1966 and 1967, South Africa's Owen Williams had turned his country's national championships into the second most financially successful tournament in the world, after Wimbledon, despite having to import most players from halfway around the globe and having to operate in the political system of apartheid. Mom had seen his success first hand, when Owen had invited her to Johannesburg in 1967 to play mixed doubles. She was long past her playing days, but Owen wanted the editor of the world's most powerful tennis publication to see what he was doing. When she returned to New York, she wrote a long, glowing, and detailed editorial, naming his tournament, the South African Open, the fourth most important tournament in the world, after Wimbledon, the U.S., and the French. She reported that Owen worked incredibly hard, snagged big sponsors, and exploded with marketing ideas, way ahead of his time. He built a club for the patrons, which became a focal point for tournament goers wishing to eat and drink. He erected tents where sponsors could entertain their guests. And every day of his tournament had a name, such as Ladies Day, when there were contests and fashion shows and celebrities galore. All of these plans would one day become commonplace in big tournaments, but back then, they were exciting and fresh.

Owen's tournament ranked high with the fans and the sponsors, but also with the players, whose needs he understood, as he'd been a top player in the early 1950s. Mom was convinced he was the best tournament director for the U.S. Open, but the decision was up to Joe and Alastair, not to her. Joe flew to Johannesburg to meet Owen and see for himself. They got along so well that Joe offered him the job on the spot, details to be worked out, which Owen heartily accepted.

The devil was definitely in the details. In New York, Owen told Joe, Alastair, and Mom that he had to have complete control, which meant no one—not even Joe or Alastair—could second guess him. That nearly killed the deal, because Joe and Alastair were miffed. In stepped Mom, who sat Joe and Alastair together in a room and said "He has probably forgotten more about tennis than the two of you will ever know. Give him what he needs. Otherwise you will be dealing with the interference of the USLTA and the West Side Tennis Club."[5] Joe was a powerful and decisive business executive, but when it came to tennis, he said he "felt like a puppet on a string," with Mom as puppet master. After her determined admonitions, Joe and Alastair conceded and gave Owen complete control. Owen signed a five-year contract to be the tournament director for the U.S. Open.

Joe sweetened the deal with first-class treatment for Owen: a double suite in a premier hotel in Manhattan; a corner office in Philip Morris's Park Avenue headquarters; and even a chauffeur to take his family everywhere. In return, Owen converted the 1969 U.S. Open into the prototype of a highly successful, modern tournament, with its own U.S. Open Club for wining and dining members, and several specialty days, including Fashion Day. The USLTA had botched the first U.S. Open. The management team that Mom put into place brought excitement and organization to its second year.

Very few people know that Mom put together the team that ran the 1969 U.S. Open. She never publicly took credit for her role, and of course she didn't take a dime. Her actions were so hush-hush, that even when I played the tournament, I didn't know what she'd done. I only uncovered her accomplishments when I read Owen Williams's book, *Ahead of the Game*, in 2013. He wrote "Billie Jean King often gets more credit for creating Open Tennis these days than Gladys, but for

---

5 Williams, Owen *Ahead of the Game* page 194

those of us who were around, 'Gladioli' was the prime moving force that opened up the game in America, and not just for the women!" [6]

How was Mom able to change from a brilliant micro-manager to a person who adroitly exercised real power? During most of the 1960s, I had already left the parental nest, so I didn't see her changes up close, and I can't explain them all. But one thing is clear. Once Joe Cullman became her great friend and then her collaborator, she became more successful at delegating responsibility and wielding power, both in her editorials and in the tennis world at large. Joe was charming and sophisticated, and he had great instincts. He was also a good judge of people, and he built a formidable company, by leading from the top and delegating. He taught Mom how to do the same.

During the past few decades, several players from the 1960s and 1970s have confidently told me that it was common knowledge that Mom and Joe had an ongoing affair—although no evidence has ever surfaced. Certainly no one told me back then, and I was so clueless that the idea never crossed my mind. To me, Joe and Sue were my parents' close friends. Recently, I've learned more details about Joe. He was married to his first wife Sue from 1934 to 1974, and soon after they divorced, he married Joan Straus (the ex-wife of a Century member), so he wasn't a "free" man for long. He was also known for having a wandering eye for women. Mom and Joe enjoyed each other's company, but were they just friends and business associates, or something more? When I was younger, Mom pontificated that the French had better marriages than the Americans, because the French had both a spouse and a lover. But I don't know if Mom was all talk or if she ever actually took a lover. I personally don't believe she and Joe were intimate, due to Mom's need to be in charge. It's hard for me to imagine her putting up with a lover who had a penchant for chasing skirts. Owen Williams, who spent a great deal of time with both Mom and Joe when he was living in New York, and who was closer to them than almost anyone else, said he really wasn't sure if they were an item. I guess I'll never know.

At the end of the 1969 Open, Owen wasn't sure if he'd honor his contract and return the following year as tournament director at the U.S. Open. He had walked away from enormous business and personal commitments in South Africa, which he needed to tend to. Mom pressured him to decide right away, but he

---

[6] Williams, Owen *Ahead of the Game* page 191

eventually decided to return to South Africa. Once again the power broker, Mom immediately tapped her old cohort, Bill Talbert, to take over Owen's job. Talbert knew every aspect of the tennis world, and moreover, he lived in New York City, so unlike Owen, Talbert would be more likely to stay in the job for years. Mom presented her choice to Joe, who already knew Talbert, and appreciated his worth. Talbert remained the tournament director of the U.S. Open for most of the years from 1970 through 1987, leaving Mom's imprint on the event for years to come.

CHAPTER 41

RUMBLINGS

It's August 1970. The last time I flew across the Atlantic, I was heading towards London and disaster. This time, I'm returning to New York, barely managing the emotional pain that fills me. But once I open my parents' apartment door, I'm relieved to see a giant mess, because that means there will be plenty for me to do. I need to keep busy.

My parents have lived in New York City for 17 years, and soon they'll move to Houston, leaving the city for good. It's been quite a run. Our first apartment, at 200 East End Avenue, was smallish. We didn't have much room for visiting tennis players, but during tournaments, Dad and Laura lugged our mattresses under the dining room table and into the living room, where tennis players could sleep, and Carrie and I slept on our box springs. In 1961, after eight years in our first apartment, Mom and Dad bought Penthouse A on the 23rd floor of 180 East End Avenue, a few yards from our old apartment building but a big step up in the world. They've lived there ever since. The new building is fancier than the old one, the new apartment has three bedrooms instead of two, and we're on the top floor, so Mom no longer blows a gasket every night, as she did whenever the old upstairs neighbor made a racket. In Penthouse A, tennis guests have the luxury of their own bedrooms. And to top it all off, the roof has a swimming pool and a rec room, where Mom can hold her annual party during the U.S. Open.

Penthouse A doesn't look very fancy at the moment. Half the furniture is gone, and the walls are lined with boxes. Mom hates clutter, but there's no escaping the chaos. I open my closet door, and Putty the cat unexpectedly shoots out. He never hides in there. He must be petrified with the commotion. Sixteen years ago, Mom found Putty, then a kitten, in the pet department of Macy's on 34th Street. He was shivering in the corner of his cage, traumatized by the blaring noise and constant bustle. He's never really recovered.

I yell "Mom!" and walk into her room. She says "'Tis 'Tis," and like a good performing monkey I carefully give her a kiss on the cheek (She doesn't kiss me.). It's been ingrained in me since I was little that I must touch her gingerly. She's worried she'll bruise.

As usual, Mom doesn't ask how I'm doing. So I launch into practicalities, and I ask her the plans. She says: "Dad, Laura, and you will fly to Houston four days after Forest Hills, and I'll stay in New York a few days longer to meet with advertisers and tie up some loose ends."

"What about Putty?" I ask. "He's already scared, and I'm worried about how he'll react on the plane to Houston. I could get him a travel carrier. That should help. And should I take him to the vet to get a sedative?"

"How could you? How could you? I will not have him take medicine. He could die from it." Uh oh. Mom gets unhinged over anything medical, her words spilling out so rapidly that they run into each other.

She continues "It's cruel to put him under the plane in a cage."

I say: "But I can't carry him on my lap without a carrier. I'd be scratched to bits and he could escape."

Mom picks at her bright red fingernail polish, a sure sign that her wheels are turning. "I have an idea. I'll ask Dad to get the Shell Oil executive jet. That way Putty will have his own jet and his own staff." Mom's panic is sending her into dream land, blinding her to Putty's real needs. And she's clearly oblivious to my stultifying grief. So Putty and I are both wounded, but we'll survive as a team. I'll focus my love and attention on a creature who's even needier than I am, hoping he'll be less frightened because I'm there.

Forest Hills is almost upon us. No players are staying chez Heldman this year, due to the rampant disarray. Nonetheless, while the tournament is being played, Penthouse A will remain a hub of the tennis world. During the day, Mom will attend the matches, while hanging out with friends and correspondents from all over the world, *World Tennis* advertisers, and tennis stars. Away from the matches, she's a working machine. She's had the magazine for 17 years, and she still works as hard as ever, day and night, doing the job of many mere mortals. This week, she's added to her monster work load, because she's organizing the family's move to Houston.

Dad also holds down two jobs. During the day, he's the very first Jewish vice president of Shell Oil, a major accomplishment in a company that's not known to welcome Jews. At night, he works for *World Tennis*, as he has for 17 years, completing tons of detail work and writing his longstanding "Styles of the Great" series, in which he lovingly and precisely explains the technique and strategy that made famous players tick, starting in the early 1930s with Ellsworth Vines, Don Budge, and Alice Marble, all the way up to current greats like Rod Laver and Margaret Court.

All of my parents' hard work on the magazine comes to a screeching halt on the Tuesday night of Forest Hills, when Mom throws her *World Tennis* party. This is the ninth and last party she's held in the rec room on our roof. The event has quite a history. In the beginning, Dad, Laura, Carrie, and I bought drinks at the corner store and filled huge metal tubs with ice, beer, and soda. Then Dad drove Mom's Cadillac to the Madison Avenue Delicatessen, at 86th and Madison, halfway across town, to buy deli meats, potato salad, and cole slaw. Twice in the early years of the party, we ran out of food while we still had hungry guests, so Dad and I had to dash out in a taxi to stock up. After the first time, the rule was always "FHB" (Family Hold Back), which meant no food for the Heldmans until everyone else was fed. This year we're expecting over 100 guests, and Dad and I are thrilled that the party is being catered, which means that we can eat like regular people.

Quite an assortment of tennis people shows up at Mom's party: First and foremost, competitors at the Open. But Mom loves all kinds of players, so there's also a sprinkling of friends she plays with at the Town Tennis Club in midtown Manhattan and at the Century Country Club. Other revelers include *World Tennis* advertisers and contributors, USLTA execs, and some of the most important people in the tennis world. Of course Joe Cullman is there. He fits into so many categories: friend, tennis player, *World Tennis* advertiser, and due in large part to Mom, a major contributor in the tennis world.

I can't help it. I'm still checking that there's enough food to last through the night. But there's no reason to worry. We make it through the party unscathed, without even one player being tossed into the swimming pool.

The chaos at Penthouse A and the happy commotion at Mom's party are matched by the current upheaval in the tennis world. Open tennis began two and a half years ago, and the once-stable amateur tennis world is a thing of the past. Now money is king, with numerous groups fighting for territory on the tennis landscape. Loads of tournaments that had been around forever have collapsed, and new tournaments pop up. The old amateur tournaments were usually co-ed. Most of the new tournaments are for men only.

So top-flight men players are making more and more money.

And top flight women are being screwed.

The fallout from the implosion of the tennis calendar has left fewer tournaments for women players, and even those have puny prize money, barely enough to survive on week to week. And some weeks are empty, a disaster for those who have nowhere to go and no place to stay. Early in the year, *World Tennis* twice contributed $5,000 in prize money to women's tournaments, to fill holes in the tennis calendar. And Mom has been railing against these injustices in *World Tennis*, but the cards seem stacked against us. You'd think the tennis associations would come to our rescue, but they're not fighting for us. Maybe we should have known that would happen. Just look at the people running the associations. The USLTA: all men. Other national associations: all men. The International Lawn Tennis Federation ("ILTF"): all men.

You'd think current or past men players would extend a helping hand, but several top American men, including Arthur Ashe, Stan Smith, and Marty Riessen, are adding to our woes. Ashe, who won the first U.S. Open in 1968, is the most disappointing. He's a black man and a civil rights advocate, and on most subjects he's high-minded and beyond reproach. We'd all hoped he'd understand the women players' plight and try to help us out. No such luck. He thinks women shouldn't get **any** prize money in tournaments where men are competing, due to his antiquated notion that only men are bread winners. "Men are doing this for a living now. They have families, and they don't want to give up money just for girls to play." A quick look at Billie Jean King, Margaret Court, and their husbands should set him straight. Both women are the bread winners in their families.

Of course the women players hope that tournament promoters will do the right thing. Take Jack Kramer, an icon in the tennis world. He knows what it's like to struggle against the establishment. After he won three majors in the late 1940s as an amateur, he turned pro and grappled with the USLTA from the outside, first as a barnstorming pro player and then as the promoter of his own pro tour for most of the 1950s. He's known throughout the tennis world for his accomplishments and also because he's charming, good looking, extremely knowledgeable about tennis, and a fine broadcaster, and because most American weekend players use the Wilson Jack Kramer wood racket, the most popular model ever.

But Kramer won't help us. Instead, he's leading the charge against us.

He's running the Pacific Southwest, the Los Angeles tournament that Perry T. Jones started in 1927 and turned into a perennial powerhouse where top men and women players competed, and Hollywood stars cheered from the box seats. Although Jones is quite old and gravely ill, he's still the titular head of the tournament. But everyone knows Kramer's in charge. He's responsible for raising the prize money and fixing the prize money breakdown, which was announced just before Forest Hills began. Believing that women players don't sell tickets, he's skewed the purses wildly in favor of the men. The men's winner will make $12,500, and the women's winner will make only $1,500. The total prize money for the women will be $7,500, and very little money is allotted for the early rounds. The whole thing is insulting.

To put the Pacific Southwest prize money in perspective: At Wimbledon, the ratio between the men's winner and the women's winner is 2 to 1. At the U.S. Open, it's about 2.6 to 1. But at the Pacific Southwest it's over 8 to 1. No other tournament gives the women such a raw deal.

What's more, the women are stuck, because there's no other tournament that week.

Something has to be done. Forest Hills has begun, and the women's locker room has become a focal point for the players' distress.

As always, Mom attends the matches every day, but this year, I spend most of my time back at Penthouse A, padding around in slippers, sporadically packing boxes left handed. I have a lot of recuperating to do. My right elbow needs rest and no heavy lifting. And my profound and lasting gloom often brings me to a dead halt. Since those terrible days last spring, no one has mentioned the events that devastated me. Friends and family have acted as if everything is normal, which is far from true. I've sometimes wished that even one person would acknowledge my grief by hugging me and saying "I know it's hard." But that hasn't happened. Instead, I spend much of my time alone.

When Mom returns home on the first day of Forest Hills, she reports that discontent is brewing among the women, but no one has come up with a viable plan. Billie Jean King and Rosie Casals feel the loss of their livelihood as acutely as any other women players. From the spring of 1968 until the spring of 1970, they were signed as "contract pros" with George MacCall, who reportedly guaranteed Billie Jean and Rosie $45,000 and $25,000 a year, respectively. Now that their contracts are up, and the women's circuit is being decimated, their prospects have dropped from healthy to impoverished, and they have become activists. Although Billie Jean recently had knee surgery, and isn't competing at the U.S. Open, she and Rosie have taken the initiative, and they're circulating a petition for all women players to boycott Kramer's tournament. A boycott will work only if everyone signs, effectively shutting down the women's event. But the women players are far from unanimous about the boycott. Some say they're happy to play for nothing. Others don't want to commit. A few, like Nancy Richey, ranked Number One by the USLTA in 1968 and 1969, cannot sign, because she never entered Kramer's tournament in the first place. The boycott looks dead.

Although Nancy can't sign, she's equally as angry and perplexed. She asks her father, who is also her coach, for advice. He says "Get Rosie and Billie and go talk with Gladys. If anyone can help you gals it will be her." Nancy follows his advice, and the three women approach Mom, who invites them to lunch on the Clubhouse terrace. She has her two double vodkas, and then they all eat sandwiches amidst the tinkling glasses and the loud conversation of the other diners. Nancy, Billie, and Rosie ask for help.

Surely a person who is less energetic and less capable than Mom would bow out gracefully, saying "I'm already too busy running the magazine and organizing the family's move to Houston." Instead, she tells them she'll work on the problem. Once she returns home, she gets on the horn, all the while wearing her dark glasses, chain smoking, and worrying her fingernail polish. She knows a whole lot of people in the tennis world, and, because Mom and Dad are moving to Houston, where we used to live, she seeks out her old contacts there. A few days later, she enters the locker room and tells the women: "I've put together an eight-woman invitation tournament in Houston." It will be held during Kramer's Pacific Southwest.

After her announcement, the locker room buzzes with excitement, because there's a glimmer of hope.

To ensure the success of the Houston tournament, Mom zooms into high gear. The event is barely three weeks away, not much time to put together a quality event, so she hits the ground sprinting. After a few false starts, she finds a home for her tournament, to be called the Houston Women's Invitation, at the Houston Racquet Club. She recruits Jim Hight, president-elect of the Texas Tennis Association, who in turn brings in Delores Hornberger, the head of the Houston Racquet Club Women's Association. Within days, Delores and her group sign up volunteers, ball boys, and ball girls, acquire bleachers and box seats, and start selling tickets.

The next hurdle is to obtain a sanction from the USLTA. A tournament with a USLTA sanction counts towards a player's ranking. But if a player enters an unsanctioned event, he or she risks being suspended, which means being banned from all other USLTA sanctioned events, and many international events that are governed by the ILTF. So a sanction is basic to every tournament. And the failure to get a sanction is a disaster.

Mom's first step in the quest for a sanction is to gain approval from the Texas Tennis Association, which is a snap, because Jim Hight makes it happen. But the Texas association must in turn apply to the USLTA for a sanction. Fearing that Kramer would try to stop the Houston tournament from obtaining a sanction, Mom approaches him at Forest Hills and asks him if he'd oppose the sanction. He says "No, I'm not that kind of guy." That was easy.

As Forest Hills draws to a close, Mom works at getting the best possible lineup for the Houston tournament. Billie Jean, Rosie, and Nancy immediately agree to come, although Billie, still recuperating from knee surgery, will play only the pro-am doubles. She's even contributed $500 as prize money for that event. Margaret Court is a strong possibility, and the Houston organizers are gnawing their knuckles, praying they'll get her. She's the best player in the world this year. And she just made really big news by winning the U.S. Open and becoming only the second woman in history, after Maureen Connolly in 1953, to take the Grand Slam by winning all four majors in the same year.

Besides King, Court, Casals, and Richey, Mom has put together a powerhouse group: three other world top tenners, Kerry Melville and Judy Dalton from Australia and Peaches Bartkowicz from Hamtramck, Michigan, plus two other top American players, Patti Hogan and Val Ziegenfuss. I'd love to be part of the event, but my injury makes that impossible.

During Forest Hills, Mom keeps after Dad to secure the use of the Shell executive jet, so that "Putty can have his own plane," and somehow Dad pulls it off. After that, the trip falls into place, and we're ready to leave Penthouse A for good and fly to Houston. Dad, Laura, Putty, and I take a taxi to the Teterboro Airport in New Jersey, and we drive right up to the plane, which is surprisingly tiny, with only six seats. Putty's wrapped in a thick towel, and I hold him tight as the engines rev and we take off.

The noise is deafening and unrelenting. At full volume, I ask Dad why that's so. He says "It's a prop jet, not a pure jet." I don't understand what the difference is, but talking is impossible, so I give up. Putty is shaking all over. We refuel in Nashville, and I let Putty down for a moment. Big mistake. He burrows under a seat, beyond our outstretched hands, and we can't extract him until an hour after takeoff. He's beside himself with fear. This whole idea stinks.

Finally, our agonizing trip comes to an end. I snatch Putty, and we take a taxi to Mom and Dad's new home, at 109 Timberwilde Lane, barely a mile down Memorial Drive from the Houston Racquet Club. Our first job is to get Putty situated. He always sleeps with Mom, but she's not here, so we take him to Dad's room, where he scampers as far as possible from human hands. We leave food and his litter box nearby, so that he can hide as long as he wants.

Dad, Laura, and I take a deep breath and look around. The new Heldman household is a large, rambling, one-story ranch house, with two giant master bedrooms at the far ends of the property. Both have oversized round beds. The previous owners left some items of dubious taste—a bathtub where the water pours out of the mouths of brass swans and lamps with blackamoor statues holding up the lights. Kitsch is a good word. Out back, I take a first glance at their new tennis court and amoeba-shaped swimming pool. I walk through the house again and realize that the boxes we filled in New York need to be emptied in Houston. Ugh. Lots of work. We roll up our sleeves and get started.

Mom is still in New York working on the magazine when she receives word that Margaret Court has pulled out of Houston. Having lost to 15-year-old Chris Evert in a tournament in Charlotte, Margaret complains of a sore ankle, which is more likely a sore ego, and she's returning to Australia. So Mom replaces Margaret with Kristy Pigeon, the next available player down the ranking list, who's a former U.S. and Wimbledon junior champ. Nine women have signed up to play—eight singles players and Billie Jean.

CHAPTER 42

INSURRECTION

It's Monday, September 21, 1970, and the start date for the Houston Women's Invitation is two days away. Dad's away on a business trip, so I'm the only Heldman available to answer the phone. In the early evening, it rings, and I answer. It's Val Ziegenfuss. She says she got a call from Stan Malless, the chairman of the USLTA Sanctions committee, threatening her with suspension if she plays Houston.

I have no idea what to do. I'm here to work hard and soothe the frightened cat. I say "Mom is currently on an airplane, flying here from New York. Just hold on a few hours. She'll fix things."

Soon after we hang up, another Houston entrant calls, and then another, reporting the same thing. Something has gone very wrong.

When Mom walks in the door, I explain the crisis. She retires to her room and starts making calls, as usual chain smoking and fussing with her nail polish. One after another, she calms the players down, telling them to fly to Houston, and she'll cover their airfare. After an hour or so, we talk. "Kramer's made an about face," she says. "He told Malless he would oppose our sanction." So now we have two powerful guys against us, Kramer and Malless.

Every year, the USLTA publishes a yearbook, which contains lots of information, including its rules. Very few rules pertain to sanctions, and none of those rules cover this situation. So USLTA officials make up rules on the fly, and now we're faced with volunteer officials wielding unrestrained power, beholden to no one. The result is a perfect breeding ground for discrimination against the women players. Malless cites a few bogus arguments. The first is that the USLTA won't give sanctions to two major tournaments in the same week. Which is a lie. The USLTA previously did exactly that for the Houston and Charlotte tournaments. His second argument is that two prize money tournaments cannot be played simultaneously, but there's no basis for that assertion.

As if making up rules wasn't bad enough, something more sinister is happening. Kramer is running the show, telling Malless what to do. Kramer won't give more prize money to the women, but he wants to be sure they can't make money elsewhere. He had said the women's prize money was low because they couldn't sell tickets. If that's true, why would he care if they play anywhere else?

It seems like their goal is to keep women powerless.

Mom finds out that Kramer sent a telegram to the USLTA, signed by Perry T. Jones—who is terminally ill and couldn't possibly have written it—arguing that the Houston tournament shouldn't have a sanction. No one is fooled by this attempted subterfuge. Kramer has turned against us, but is unwilling to admit it, so instead he uses the name of a dying man.

Kramer had originally said he wouldn't oppose a sanction for Houston, because "I'm not that kind of guy." Now he's opposing the sanction. Yes, he *is* that kind of guy.

And Malless certainly isn't a prince. In 1968, Nancy Richey won his tournament, the Westerns, in Indianapolis, while it was still just for amateurs. After he presented her the trophy, she asked for her promised "expense" money. The maximum allowable per diem was $28, but this upstanding USLTA official had agreed to pay her $350, almost double the legal amount. Usually that type of transaction takes place in an office. Instead, Malless took her behind some large bushes at the side of the clubhouse and tried to grab a kiss. Yuck.

Mom's old pal, Alastair Martin, currently the President of the USLTA, is backing up Malless. Mom wires Martin, to find out where he stands. No reply. She tries again. No reply. Nancy calls him, and he tells her that any player who competes in the Houston tournament will be suspended. That makes three very powerful men who are against us.

The next day is Tuesday, and the players arrive. The USLTA comes up with a new wacko idea. They'll give Houston a sanction only if there's no prize money. But players will still be allowed to take "expenses" under the table. They want the women to revert to the old, nonfunctional amateur world while the men are making more and more money. Again, there's absolutely nothing in the rule book to support a decision to give a tournament a sanction only if it won't give prize money.

The Houston players are under siege, and they need help. Suddenly, Mom makes a blockbuster announcement. Virginia Slims, a relatively new women's cigarette brand from Philip Morris, has agreed to sponsor the tournament.[7] The company is contributing only $2,500, but it's providing a highly sophisticated public relations capability and the strength of a powerful corporation. This is a real shot in the arm for the women players and the tournament. With the approval of Jim Hight and Delores Hornberger, the tournament changes its name to the Virginia Slims Invitational of Houston.

It's Wednesday morning. September 23, 1970. The women pros are at the club, giving a clinic, and I'm at home with Putty and Laura, working on the house. Mid-afternoon, I figure I might as well see what's up. I've agreed to cover the finals of the tournament for the *Houston Chronicle*, so I need to keep an eye on the whole event. I drive down Timberwilde, past several sprawling mansions, and then I turn left onto Memorial Drive towards the Houston Racquet Club.

When I saunter into the clubhouse, I find out that the women's tennis world has been turned upside down.

After the clinic, Mom and the players met with the tournament organizers in a room in the clubhouse. The USLTA's threats to suspend the players could impact their entire tennis careers. And the USLTA has also threatened to suspend the club, which could harm its ability to run the many other tournaments it plans to hold every year. Mom came up with a bold plan to protect everyone. Clearly, the USLTA had to be taken out of the equation. George MacCall and Lamar Hunt, the two most successful tennis promoters, are not beholden to the USLTA, because they've signed their players as contract pros, so Mom decided to give the Houston players the same option. She offered them a one-week contract with *World Tennis* for $1. If they signed and became contract pros, the USLTA wouldn't be able to harm them. All but one of the players agreed on the spot.

---

[7] **A note from the 21st Century**. I believe that Mom had the Virginia Slims card up her sleeve all along. Joe Cullman wasn't in the U.S. during the crisis at the Houston tournament. He'd previously scheduled a shooting safari in Africa, where he'd be unreachable, starting a few days before the tournament. Mom and Joe met in New York before he left, where I believe they put together a plan to involve Virginia Slims in the Houston tournament in the event of an emergency, such as the one that later arose. I believe that Joe gave the project the green light before he left for Africa, for three reasons: First, tennis was Joe's pet project; no one else at Philip Morris in 1970 had such a strong interest in the game. Second, Joe had a strong personal connection to Mom; I know he would have gone out of his way to help her. And third, Joe's approval made everything easier. If he hadn't given clear approval in advance, Mom might not have known which executive had the authority to make the decision in Joe's absence. Because of the plans Mom and Joe made, once the crisis occurred, Mom made a call to a pre-arranged person at Philip Morris to say that the time was ripe for Virginia Slims to make an entrance. And history was made.

Unfortunately, no one can predict what the USLTA might do after the end of the one-week contract, when the players would no longer be contract pros. If the association would decide to suspend the players—even without a proper reason—the women could be prevented from playing at home and abroad. Patti Hogan found that risk too great to bear. Talented but tortured, Patti was raised in Southern California by an abusive father, but over the past few years she's been headquartered in England. To protect her ability to play there, she pulled out of the Houston tournament, although she made it clear that she supported the cause by entering the pro-am, which will raise money for the tournament, and by acting as the scribe for the meeting and writing the contract that every player signed.

Once Patti dropped out, the tournament was one player shy. There were only seven players entered in the eight-woman singles field. Billie Jean, bum knee and all, stepped up and filled the last spot.

With everyone in agreement, Mom and the players left the room and entered the club's lobby, where the press and photographers were waiting. All the players were handed a $1 bill, and then they were posed, four standing behind a couch and four seated on it. The women held their dollar bills proudly, as a sign of their independence and in defiance of the USLTA's mistreatment. Sitting down front on the far right of the photo, wearing her ever-present dark glasses, was Mom, the woman who engineered this marvelous moment.

I've always regretted that I wasn't in this iconic 1970 photo of the Houston players who rebelled against the men who ran the USLTA.

When I arrive at the club, the players tell me about these revolutionary events. I know right away that I have to take a stance.

I quit playing tennis four years ago because my emotions were too fragile to withstand the pressure I lived under. I returned to the tour 18 months later because I wanted to travel, and tennis gave me that opportunity. Like Patti, I enjoy playing tennis tournaments in far-flung places. If I stand beside the other players in Houston, I risk losing the freedom to travel wherever my tennis racket will bring me. But the choice is clear. I have to do the right thing, to subordinate my personal needs to the greater good. I have to join my fellow players against a threat to our careers and to all of women's tennis.

So I sign the $1 contract. My elbow prevents me from playing a whole match, but I agree to play one gentle point, out of solidarity. Then, if the other players are suspended, I will be too.

Mom tells everyone that when I received my $1, I said "Does this mean I have to wash the dishes?" That's her fantasy, not the truth. The truth is very serious.

Billie Jean offers to play me the one point that I committed to. I hurry back to my parents' new home, change into tennis clothes, return to the club, and walk onto a side court with Billie. She serves softly, and we pitty-pat the ball back and forth, again and again, until she says "Don't you think that's enough?" That makes sense, so I hit the ball into the net, we shake hands, and I become a contract pro.

The Virginia Slims Invitational of Houston is a success. The matches are excellent, showcasing quality players who have a variety of styles. The event gets tons of free publicity, starting when the photo of Mom and the eight women with their $1 bills is published in the *Houston Post*. I'm not in the photo. Too bad. I wish I was.

Although Billie Jean is the most famous player here this week, she loses in the first round to Judy Dalton, the "Old Fruit." In the Saturday afternoon finals, it's Rosie Casals, fresh off a runner-up finish at Forest Hills, against the Old Fruit. Rosie, despite being only five foot nothing, has a high potency, dynamic style. Her wondrous array of shots shows off her magnificent talent. Judy's a real character, a cheerful chatterbox off the court, but on the field of battle she's a relentless attacker. The crowd erupts in cheers as the players vie to reach the net first. Rosie squeaks out a win, 5-7, 6-1, 7-5.

During the tournament, Mom contacts tournament promoters around the world, scoping out their interest in running women's pro tournaments. She tells several of the Houston competitors that she's planning more women's pro tournaments. Their feedback is enthusiastic.

Billie Jean's husband Larry arrives during the week. Apparently Billie had called him and told him to hurry down to Houston, because it's full of opportunities. In January of this year, he had made a preliminary effort to get involved in women's tennis by sending a letter, which he'd typed while he was still in the army, to eight top players, including me. In it, he outlined a proposal for an all-women's tour. I don't know if anyone other than Billie or Rosie showed any interest, but I sure didn't. For one, he wasn't proposing any tournaments, just glorified exhibitions. And he clearly stated that he didn't have any sponsors lined up. Now he's in Houston trying to carve out a place for himself in the future of women's tennis.

Saturday night, after the conclusion of the tournament, the Heldmans throw a dinner party for the players. Laura gets out her biggest pots and we have her specialty meal of salad, spaghetti with tomato sauce, and boiled fresh corn. The house is looking better, although there are still plenty of boxes.

Billie Jean and Larry attend the dinner, and after we finish eating, he asks to speak to the women who signed the $1 contract, so we pile into one of the giant bedrooms. Some of us sit on the huge, round bed, others are scattered about. He says he wants to run a tour just for women pros, and he wants to present his case. He says that Gladys can present her case after him. My anger begins to boil. He came to the Heldman house as a guest, with the goals of pushing Mom aside and running all of women's tennis. Not cool.

I leave the room to find Mom. She's sitting alone in the living room. I tell her what Larry said, and I ask her to speak to the women.

She looks stricken. Her words are agitated and frantic, showing she can't function. "I can't do it. I can't do it. You'll have to do it for me."

Only Mom could have made this tournament happen through her creativity, her thoroughness, her connections, and her steel backbone. But at this moment she's shut down. From time to time throughout my life, I've had to do her dirty work. This is one of those occasions.

I really don't want to do it, but there's no choice. I say "OK. What do you want me to say?"

"You'll have to decide."

I return to the room, and after Larry speaks, it's my turn. "My mother asked me to speak for her. The truth is that Larry doesn't have much experience running tournaments, and he's had failures. Mom has only had successes. She successfully ran the U.S. Indoors in 1959. She revitalized Forest Hills in 1962. She knows everyone in tennis, and she brought in Virginia Slims. She's the best person for the job."

I've spoken the truth, and I said what I needed to say. But using the word "failures" was very harsh. Through no fault of my own, I was thrown onto the hot seat. I had no time to figure out how to soften the blow.

We adjourn for the players to decide what to do. Nancy calls her father, who says "Absolutely no question about it. Vote for Gladys!" Peaches asks Nancy, who repeats her father's advice. Billie Jean and Rosie quietly confer. And then it's time to vote. Someone finds a large sheet of paper and rips it up. We each get a little piece, on which we write either "Larry" or "Gladys." We drop our scraps of paper into a little glass bowl, which is then dumped onto the huge round bed. The scraps are counted, and Gladys has won. Nancy says "This is where women's pro tennis was born, with Gladys as our leader."

CHAPTER 43

THE HOLY TRINITY OF WOMEN'S TENNIS

In 1970, the world thought that women tennis pros couldn't make it on our own. We were overjoyed to show them they were wrong. We succeeded because we had an unbeatable combination of leaders, our Holy Trinity, who were all deeply committed to the success of the women's pro tour:

> **Gladys Heldman**: A promoter with a 100% success rate; a bully pulpit, as the editor and publisher of *World Tennis*, the world's largest tennis magazine; a fanatical work ethic; a never-back-down attitude; and she knew everyone in tennis.
>
> **Billie Jean King**: A charismatic champion; a dedicated feminist; an extraordinary player who drew crowds; and a gifted communicator with the public and the press.
>
> **Joseph F. Cullman 3rd**: Gladys's close friend and the money man, Chairman and CEO of Philip Morris. From the outset, the tour's major sponsor was Virginia Slims, a Philip Morris brand marketed exclusively for women.

Behind the leaders were legions of high quality women pros, who were eager to join the new tour and fiercely dedicated to its success. Along with Billie Jean, they worked incessantly to ensure the tour's triumph.

And we had the force of luck and destiny. Philip Morris's worldwide success was based on the unregulated advertising and sales of tobacco, and the company poured money into on-air commercials. But as evidence about tobacco's harm came to the forefront, Congress began to take notice. In 1970, Congress passed a law prohibiting cigarette advertising on television, to begin on January 2, 1971, three and a half months after the Houston tournament. That left tobacco companies searching for alternate ways to promote their brands. Joe Cullman spotted a golden opportunity in the struggle for women's pro tennis. The partnership between Virginia Slims and the women pros proved immensely successful for both sides. Because of Philip Morris's money and its marketing clout, the tour was able to survive and thrive. Because of the synergy with the women's pro tour, Virginia Slims sold more cigarettes.

The women pros went to bed with the devil, who saved us.

CHAPTER 44
THE FLEDGLING TOUR

Mom has been elected the leader of a tour that must start from scratch, under siege from the men who run tennis. Many observers are deeply skeptical that the women can succeed. It's up to Mom to scrabble together tournaments, so that women's tennis can survive and thrive.

As always, Mom uses her giant bed as an office. There she holes up, catapulting into high gear, attacking the daunting project from many different angles.

First, she phones Barry MacKay, an old pal and a former U.S. Number One player, now the tournament director of the Pacific Coast Open, the Northern California tournament that's due to start in just a few days. Mom's timing is perfect, because Margaret Court, whom Barry had banked on, has dropped out, leaving him without a female star. Mom tells him that if he increases the paltry women's prize money ($3,400 for the women versus $20,000 for the men), she'll deliver the Houston stars. She reminds Barry that the women have become contract pros, in response to the USLTA's threats of suspension. He doesn't care. To save his event, which is open to both pros and amateurs, he rapidly finds a new sponsor, who triples the women's purse, and Mom and Barry strike a deal. The result is excellent for the Houston players, who now have a place to compete, and for the tournament, which gets positive publicity, plus names with star quality. The outcome is terrific, with 22,000 paying fans, the best in the tournament's history.

Score one for the women. But many more tournaments are needed, so Mom delves into her wondrous Rolodex, seeking tournament promoters, whether or not they have previously run a women's tournament. She remains involved in most transactions, connecting potential promoters with sponsors, and then going to bat for the promoters with Virginia Slims, whom she talks to frequently, and whom she draws further and further into her web. Mom knows that the Houston players' careers are on the line, so she also remains in close contact with them, keeping them informed of her progress, and even asking them to help find tournament promoters in their home towns. And she reaches out to top women players who didn't compete in Houston, inviting them to join our fledgling group.

Simultaneously, she's running *World Tennis* magazine, where she keeps up her usual pace, writing articles, corresponding with tennis people all over the world, and making the daily decisions that make the magazine tick. She doesn't stint the magazine just because she's running a whole new tour.

Mom is so amped up that she fails to notice that I'm doubly wounded, with a fractured psyche and a painful elbow that keeps me from playing tennis. She knows about the elbow, and that I'm not ready to play tournaments, but she never asks if it's getting better. And she avoids dealing with my emotional issues, which she called a "social embarrassment." So I revert to my childhood way of dealing with her. When she's around, I wear a happy face and I try hard to amuse her, knowing she cannot and will not help me.

I'm also bored. I'm without tennis, which usually organizes my life. Plus I know absolutely no one in Houston. People tout the city's shopping centers, but they're giant indoor malls, which I hate, and anyway the nearest one is 15 miles away. I'm itching to do something, but I don't know what. Then I get an "Aha!" moment. I'm in Texas, which is cowboy country, the perfect place to learn to ride a horse. In the Yellow Pages, I find a horse stables with a sense of humor, called Avis Rent-a-Horse. It's comparatively close to home, so I reserve a time, and off I go. I'm a rank novice, and I'm hoping to find some good instruction, but my teacher is a minimalist. He hoists me up, pushes my boots in the stirrups, and says "Go." My horse doesn't move. The instructor says "Kick him!" I give the horse a thump or two, but he isn't impressed. After 10 minutes of struggling, the horse has traveled barely 50 feet, just to the edge of the pasture, but as soon as the instructor dismounts to open the gate, my steed does a 180 and zooms back to the barn. No matter what I do, my horse knows that I'm a novice, and that he's the boss. This isn't what I had in mind.

A few days later, I give up on Houston and return to New York, where I move into Mom's new pied-à-terre. For 17 years, Mom ran *World Tennis* from Manhattan, and numerous fibers of her success are intertwined with its city blocks. Many *World Tennis* advertisers call Manhattan their home base, and so do a large portion of Mom's friends and acquaintances, including Joe Cullman and Dick Savitt. When Dad announced that he was being transferred to Houston, Mom realized she'd have to return to Manhattan regularly, so she leased a small apartment in a boutique hotel on 37th Street, near Park Avenue. It's my new home base.

Two weeks after the Houston tournament, Mom calls a press conference in Manhattan to announce to the world that the *World Tennis* Women's Pro Tour is under way and that Virginia Slims will sponsor at least five tournaments, starting in Richmond, Virginia in early November. Billie Jean, Nancy Richey, and I are at the podium, representing the players. The three of us are thrilled with Mom's progress, and we smile broadly, often breaking into laughter. I'm brilliant at faking happiness. No one behind the podium or in the press section could possibly know that I'm suffering.

When Mom's in New York, we lead separate lives, but we both sleep in the small apartment. When she returns to Houston, I'm free to read or smoke pot and play my favorite albums on the stereo I bought with my first tennis earnings. When I venture out, I often go alone to the nearby Sam Goody record store to buy albums, or I enjoy the luxury of catching an afternoon movie, or I return to the Museum of Modern Art, my favorite haunt. I'm licking my wounds, and they're beginning to heal, although I still have a few months to go before I can compete.

Mom keeps wrestling with the tour's schedule, an ever-moving target. One day, Chattanooga's in, and Baltimore's a maybe. Another day, Philadelphia is firm and San Juan, Puerto Rico is interested. She's always been adept at making instant changes, as the circumstances dictate.

The status of the players on our tour is unstable and precarious. The USLTA has never actually suspended us, but they've also never been supportive. The Australian association is in full attack mode against our two Aussies, Judy Dalton and Kerry Melville, because they've committed to our 1971 tour, whose early months conflict with the Australian Open and the tournaments leading up to it. In December, their fight comes to a head, with the Aussie association declaring that Judy and Kerry are ineligible to represent their country, because they're contract pros. Mom supports Judy and Kerry by sending them frequent letters and cables, assuring them that there will be plenty of tournaments on our tour.

She also gets them some money, via endorsements from Wilson rackets (believe it or not, for using the model bearing the name of their rival, Billie Jean King). And while Mom's at it, she obtains a dress contract for Nancy Richey, which is a big deal, as Nancy's always worn shorts.

Nancy, Billie Jean, and Julie announcing the new tour.
Julie feigns happiness brilliantly.

On September 26, 1970, finals day at the Virginia Slims of Houston, the 1971 women's schedule was a blank slate. One month later, Mom sends all the Houston players a letter. In such a short time, she's gained firm commitments for seven new tournaments, and a few more maybes, starting in January 1971. This is beyond extraordinary.

The first full year of the *World Tennis* Women's Pro Tour starts in San Francisco. Politics intrude yet again. When the Houston 9 signed the $1 contract, they became contract pros, but few tournaments outside the tour admit contract pros. Mom has lobbied Bob Colwell, the incoming president of the USLTA, to reinstate all of us as independent pros. In early 1971, he raises a flag of peace, but it's tainted. He offers to reinstate all the Americans—except Billie Jean and Rosie--as independent pros. His excuse for leaving out two of our top players is that they were already reinstated once, in 1970, after their contract with George MacCall ended, and the association is balking at reinstating them for a second time. Yet again, the USLTA has fashioned a novel theory which isn't based on any actual rules. At a meeting in January 1971, the women pros turn down the USLTA's offer, voting to stick together and to require the USLTA either to reinstate all of us, including Billie and Rosie, or none of us. Faced with such a strong stand, the USLTA backs down and reinstates everyone.

Billie Jean's husband Larry is the promoter of San Francisco and Long Beach (Billie Jean's home town), the first two tournaments of 1971. Larry came to Houston wanting to run the tour, but he took his defeat in stride and instead became a promoter, working alongside my old coach Dennis Van der Meer. They're ready to go and so are the other players, but I'm not. My elbow is still healing slowly, and I haven't yet started to practice. I remain in my New York cocoon, mostly alone, waiting impatiently.

Billie Jean has fully recovered from the knee surgery she had last summer, and she's now playing the best tennis of her life, winning the first five events on the tour. One reason for her great run is the speed of the court we play on. Every week, we use the same surface, a carpet that travels with the tour. The tour has two identical carpets. While one is being laid at the new tournament site, the other is being shipped to the following event. The court plays fast, which is perfect for Billie's serve-and-volley style. Time and again, she sprints to the net and puts away volleys. The speed of the court also helps her cover up her forehand weakness, which is most evident when she's trapped in the back of the court. On the tour's carpet, she can "chip and charge," basically hitting an abbreviated stroke as she's speeding forward. On court, Billie exudes confidence, flair, and charm, which audiences love. Before the tour, she was a star who'd won the Wimbledon singles three times. With each passing week, her fame becomes ever greater.

The tour has a packed, three-month schedule, but the tournaments were established in such a hurry that some are a bit of a shambles, desperately lacking spectators and often with miserable working conditions. Still, the players dive in to help. A tournament in Chattanooga is held in a hard-to-find location, so a group of players stand on the street, showing spectators where to go. In a different city, the scoreboard hangs so low over the middle of the court that lobs are next to impossible, forcing the competitors to create new patterns of play. In other arenas, the lights are weak. Often linesmen are missing. But the world doesn't know about these hiccups, because the Virginia Slims PR machine glosses over the problems. The main story is "Billie Jean King wins again!"

After five weeks of sitting out the action, I'm finally able to join the tour in Philadelphia, the sixth tournament of the season. I enter the locker room unsure about what I'll find. I hear "Julie!" and my pals Kristy Pigeon and Denise Carter come rushing up for a hug. They say "You can't believe what's happening!" The players' lives have changed dramatically from the old days of competing in country clubs. Now, besides playing their matches, the players have to work hard giving clinics, doing interviews, and chatting up the local sponsors at cocktail parties. Billie Jean is toiling the hardest of all, both on the court, where she's winning all the singles and doubles, and off the court, where she's spectacular with the press, who always want a piece of her. So she's busy all the time. But while everyone respects her for her commitment to the tour (many of the top players, including Margaret Court and Virginia Wade, have refused to join us), Billie Jean has become a real pain in the ass. She tries to get her way all the time, on and off the court, and because she's the star, many people give in to her, which further fuels her overbearingness.

I try to ignore these problems, because I'm here to play, even though I started practicing only a few weeks ago, and I'm not really ready. I just couldn't wait any longer. So it's no surprise that I lose in the first or second round of my first five tournaments. I keep practicing, but I can't find a rhythm. For one thing, I was injured for 10 months, and didn't touch a racket for seven of them. Another reason is that most of the tournaments have only 16 players, compared to regular tournaments, which usually have 32, and to Wimbledon and the U.S. Open, which have 96. In larger tournaments, you have a better chance of meeting a lower ranked player in the opening rounds, and getting more match play. But with our tour's small draws, you can't help but run into a really good player way too soon.

Interestingly, the one-court, small-draw tournaments give an advantage to the players who are already playing well. They're scheduled at night, when crowds come to watch, and they get to practice at the arena before they play. So they get better practice, more match play, and more fun with the crowds, and as a result their lives are less dreary and difficult.

The players on the fledgling tour worked hard to ensure its success, teaching clinics, giving interviews, and helping out when needed. Here, Rosie Casals, one of the tour's top stars, is pitching in as a ball girl.

Another reason for my poor play is that the new tour isn't much fun. In the frozen north, we play in indoor arenas that have only one court, so we have to find practice elsewhere, unless we arrive at the arena at the crack of dawn or wait until the break between the day and night sessions. As a result, players rarely hang around the arena during the daytime, and the locker room is gray, empty, and lonely. I have a long-term, love-hate relationship with tennis, and I play my best only when I'm having fun both on and off the court. Losing again and again drains me. And to top it all off, there's often nowhere to go. Even dinner spots are limited, and sometimes Denny's is the only option, but it's a lousy substitute for the leisurely dining I enjoy in Europe.

On the other hand, the camaraderie on the tour is very special, and the players have a unique bond. Like soldiers in a trench, we're constantly under fire, and we rely on each other to build women's professional tennis. We've all taken a big risk—that we'll be excluded from important tournaments and that our tour might fail—but we believe we'll succeed. We also place our trust in Mom, our leader who runs the show from her round bed in Houston, and in Billie Jean, our star, to pull us through. This is our present and it's the future of women's tennis. We'll do this together.

Finally, in St. Petersburg, my sixth tournament, I catch fire. I startle everyone by convincingly beating three women in the world's top 10: Ann Jones, Kerry Melville, and Rosie Casals. In the finals, I meet 16-year-old Chris Evert, who has improved exponentially since I beat her two years ago in Fort Lauderdale. This time, she makes mincemeat of my game with her uncannily accurate groundstrokes and her comprehensive defense. Because she hits everything back, I start aiming closer and closer to the lines, and I can't believe it when nearly every forehand I smack is called "Out." I become furious, certain that everyone, including the linesmen, is against me. That's not a recipe for success.

When Mom first announced the 1971 tour, it ended in early April. Still, she kept searching for other tournaments, and up popped Caesars Palace in Las Vegas, which promised the largest prize money of the season. Of course she put it on the schedule. All the other tournaments have had prize money in the $10,000 to $15,000 range, but Las Vegas is paying out $30,000 for a 16-player draw. That's big bucks. But the resort's tennis complex is incomplete, with virtually no protection from the wind. In the first round, I play Kerry Melville in a howling gale. At one end, I barely touch the ball, and it flies into the opposite fence. At the other end, I slam the ball with all my might, and it barely reaches the net. Fortunately, the tournament checks with the weather bureau and finds that the wind is whipping at 45 mph, so they pull us off the court until the conditions become more civilized. I've stopped plenty of times for rain, but never before for wind. When we start again a few hours later, the wind is still a big factor, but at least we can play a little bit. I win because my topspin forehand makes the ball drop, unlike Kerry's flat or sidespin shots, which the wind can carry into the fence.

In the quarter-finals, I beat Frankie Durr, another good win. So far, I've earned $2,400, my biggest payday ever. But that's the end of my good run in Vegas, because Billie Jean beats me badly in the semis.

When I come off the court after being thumped, I'm surprised to see a guy I dated at Stanford, and we celebrate my return to form by drinking and carousing deep into the night. The next morning, after imbibing Alka-Seltzer, my trusty hangover cure, I join Val Ziegenfuss and Kristy Pigeon on a flight to San Diego, for our next tournament. We're staying in a complex that proudly announces that it has a gym, so we visit it, to work out. As it turns out, the term "gym" is an overstatement. It's a small room, with just a few machines. I try one that says it's for pushups, but after I push the bar out, I run out of strength, probably as a result of last night's overindulgences. When I let go of the bar, it snaps back hard and slams into my nose with a crunching sound. This is bad. There's blood everywhere. So Val and Kristy drive me to the nearest hospital. We ask for an ice pack while we're waiting, but they don't have one, so they plop me in a wheelchair and get creative by placing a surgeon's glove, stuffed with ice, over my nose. Once they staunch the bleeding, they take an x-ray and tell me the obvious: my nose is broken. I get an appointment for the following day with an ear, nose, and throat specialist. The doctor is a tennis fan—of men's tennis—and he chatters happily as he stuffs yards of cotton up my nose and then completes his handiwork with a cast that covers the center of my face. When I ask him if I can play the tournament, he has no objection, so Kristy and I head out to practice. She's fun to be around, a real character, a woman who loves being outrageous. Her remedy for over-population? Women should eat their babies. She's also a helluva tennis player, with a wonderful, free-swinging lefty serve. And she's an artist. After we finish our practice, she offers to improve my appearance by painting my cast. Luckily, she travels with an artist's colored pens, and I stay still while she performs some magic. When she's done, I look in the mirror, and I'm startled, because there's a psychedelic vision in the middle of my face. This should be interesting: a player with a broken nose, a cast on her face, and a psychedelic painting is competing in the Virginia Slims of San Diego. Unbelievably, encumbered with my strange mask, I reach the semis, where I lose again to Billie Jean, as expected.

I decide to watch the finals, between Billie Jean and Rosie, but the place is standing room only, so I position myself behind the chain-link gate at the back of the court. Rosie's playing great, running away with the match, 6-4, 4-0, until Billie Jean throws a fit. She slings her wood racket towards the umpire's chair, and screams "I can't play with this racket!" (the Wilson Billie Jean King model). She then walks around the net post towards her opponent's chair, picks up one of Rosie's steel rackets, and turning to Rosie, she asks "Can I use one of yours?" Rosie nods, and then she folds, because Billie Jean has gotten into Rosie's head. Billie Jean wins 4-6, 7-5, 6-1.

Bill Tilden, America's great tennis star of the 1920s, and Jean Borotra, one of the French tennis Four Musketeers of the 1920s, were both famous for their gamesmanship, making innocent-sounding remarks to throw the opponent off his game. Billie Jean's actions and her remark to Rosie were in that same vein. She "owns" Rosie on court, beating her nearly every time they play. Most probably, had Billie Jean not asked to use Rosie's racket, Rosie would have closed out the match routinely. Billie Jean's remarks sounded innocuous, but their impact was serious. She showed that she believed Rosie had the advantage because she was using a steel racket, and she asked Rosie to give up that advantage. It's unlikely that any other player would have acceded to Billie Jean's request. But Rosie couldn't say no to Billie Jean, so Rosie lost.

I don't know if Billie Jean's actions were conscious, or if she just got so mad that she blew her cool. What I do know is that Billie Jean has changed in the last few years, since we were on the winning Federation Cup team in Torino in 1966. Back then, she was already determined and focused, but far more open and outgoing. While the tour has increased her stardom, it is also sucking her dry. To a large degree, as the biggest winner, she bears the responsibility for the tour, and that's a heavy load. As a result, she's largely devoid of friendly banter with all but Rosie and a few others.

Billie Jean, Rosie, and a few of their friends form a clique on the tour, but there are no other cliques. Some of the split is natural: they're winning everything, and they're always playing at night. Most of the rest of us struggle earlier in the day. But even if we're all in the same room, Billie and her clique gravitate away from the others. Billie Jean used to be quite friendly to me, but this season I've barely had a happy word from her.

There's a more devastating problem. When Billie Jean is interviewed, she's often asked "How did you start the tour?" She doesn't say "Actually, Gladys Heldman started the tour and I'm proud to be a player." Instead, she usually says something like "I've worked hard to make this tour succeed." And sometimes she even sounds likes she's claiming responsibility for starting the tour. Billie Jean's statements bruise Mom deeply, and Mom is constitutionally incapable of speaking up for herself, which is incongruous coming from such a powerhouse in the business world. So night after night, Mom calls me in tears, complaining that Billie Jean is trying to take credit for Mom's work. I grow to dread those calls. There's nothing I can do but listen and tell her I know how much she's done, and how wrong Billie Jean is for not giving her credit. On the one hand, I feel badly for Mom. I know how hard she's worked to create a tour out of whole cloth. On the other hand, when she calls me in tears, I feel used. I know all too well that my job is to take care of her, but that she won't do the same for me.

CHAPTER 45
OUTCASTS

After the San Diego tournament, I return to Mom's little apartment in Manhattan. I immediately hit the Sam Goody store to buy Joni Mitchell's "Blue," a poetic expression of a single woman's struggle for love and fun. I also purchase new albums by Carole King and Elton John, which I copy onto cassette tapes, so that I can bring them with me. Then I fly to London, where we'll play a tournament at the Hurlingham Club. The event isn't part of the tour, but Mom has negotiated excellent prize money for any woman player who's good enough to be accepted. The draw includes Margaret Court, which should be interesting, as many of our players are furious at her for raking in the bucks with huge, secure, under-the-table payments instead of taking a risk to help all of women's tennis. If she'd join us, that risk would be smaller for everyone, as solidarity would bring strength.

I certainly wish Margaret would join the tour, even though I too am angry at her. But my anger is deeply muted by her generosity to me eight years ago, when I was 17, after I'd won the National Juniors. As I entered the clubhouse in Longwood, Massachusetts, to play the National Doubles, Margaret strode across the room to congratulate me. No one else—not even my parents—made a big deal about my victory, yet Margaret, who had just won Wimbledon, went out of her way to be kind to me. That meant a lot.

Even still, many of Margaret's current statements are hard to swallow. Time and again she speaks out against our tour, proud that she can make more money taking guarantees and adamant that she "wouldn't want to play the same people all the time" on the tour. In one of her worst outbursts, she says: "I don't think women should be paid the same as men, even outside tennis. We aren't equal." This reflects a profoundly confused world view. According to her, a husband should be paid more than a wife, because men are superior. Yet Margaret earns all the income in her marriage. She travels the world playing tennis, and her husband Barry's role is to accompany her as her consort. So who is superior? And why does someone have to be superior, anyway? Every time I read one of her quotes, I think: "gibberish."

On the second day of the London tournament, Margaret starts spouting again, telling a reporter that the women on our tour won't talk to her. Oh no. Alarm bells go off in my head. I have to stop these remarks from spreading. I rush to the reporter and tell him it isn't true. "We're not angry at Margaret. She's a great champion, and we'd love it if she'd join our tour."

Following my intervention, the story deflates and rapidly peters out. But the British press, ever ready to drum up drama, start referring to me as the spokesperson for the tour, which of course isn't true. I just tried to reduce the rancor so that we could go about our job of playing tennis.

But as soon as one crisis is resolved, another pops up.

Last year, when women players began to protest the disparity between the men's and women's prize money, some of the top men players attacked our right to earn a living, with one even saying that we were taking money from their families. Now that we have our very own tour, that claim is obsolete. Instead, the men have turned to spreading poisonous rumors. In London, we're told that the men players are saying that many women on our tour are lesbians. It's true that several top women tennis players are lesbians. Although I'm not close friends with Billie Jean and Rosie, and I've never spied on their private lives, it's common knowledge on the tour that both are lesbians, even though Billie Jean is married. But we try to keep that information hush-hush. No one wants to bring it out in the open, because public knowledge of homosexuality on our tour could be ruinous, and it could undermine all our good work. The men haven't yet gone public with their accusations, but we're concerned that they might. But there's something much worse, at least for me. The men have circulated a list among themselves, naming many names, including mine.

When I find out that they're calling me a lesbian, I feel like I've been slammed in the solar plexus.

My body reverberates with the echoes of Mom warning me about lesbians when I was a child. The first time was when Mom took Carrie and me (we were 11 and 10) on Mom's annual trip to the tennis tournament at the Caribe Hilton in San Juan, Puerto Rico. On our first day, she dropped us off by the pool around noon. I had a dreary day. I didn't know how to swim, Carrie wouldn't talk to me, and we were surrounded by adults who were strangers. Plus Mom hadn't given us guidance about surviving in the tropical sun, so when she picked us up at 5, we were burnt to a crisp. The following days remained boring and endless. Finally, a ray of hope descended when one of the women competitors started talking to me and making me giggle. After her match, she invited me up to her room, so I asked Mom, who said yes. Nothing amiss happened, but that night, Mom told me I couldn't hang around the woman anymore, because she was a lesbian. Mom explained that lesbians had sex with other women, and that was very, very bad. I was deeply disappointed. Finally, someone had been nice to me, and I really liked her, but she was off limits. I was a child, so I was confused. Because I liked the woman, did that mean I was a lesbian?

Despite Mom's cursory explanation, I didn't understand anything about lesbians. At the dinner table Mom often talked about people having sex, but most of it went over my head, as I didn't know the mechanics of what a man and a woman did together. And I certainly didn't have a clue about what two women would do. Mom's extreme discomfort about lesbians left me confused and upset.

The subject arose again several months later. One night after dinner, I was sitting in the living room, trying to concentrate on my homework, when I heard Mom emerge from her room. She rarely came into the living room at night, but when she did, she was often pissed off about something and looking for a reason to attack me. That night, she started joking, so I figured I was off the hook. She even complimented me, saying that, now that I'd played at the Hoxies for two years, I'd begun to show that I'd inherited Dad's athletic ability. "But you need to walk like a model." So she strolled up and down our small living room in her "model" walk, legs glued to each other, swishing and swaying. That walk has always looked ridiculous to me. Time and again she's tried to change my walk. Although I knew that contradicting her was forbidden, I've consistently refused—wordlessly—to mimic her walk. My own walk is more natural. I spread my legs just slightly for better flexibility, and I bounce gently on my toes. Unfortunately, my silent rebellion has caused me untold grief. That night in the living room, she started by doing a lousy, exaggerated version of my walk, and then she lowered the boom. "You walk like an athlete. Gym teachers walk like athletes and they're lesbians." Because I'd clawed one small piece of my own identity away from her, she'd attacked. And from that night onwards, whenever she got on my case for my athletic walk, she compared me to a lesbian. And in *World Tennis*, she took other veiled swipes at me. She praised the women players who swished and swayed, referring to them as "feminine" or "lovely" or "pretty." Never once did she use those words about me, and she never explained why. But I understood. She was getting back at me, because I had staged my own mini rebellion, and I wouldn't stop.

Mom's persistent attacks on my sexuality, starting when I was so young, have left me with a deep wound, which the cruel rumors of the men tennis players have pried open. I want to scream "I'm not a lesbian. I've never been a lesbian," but I can't say anything. Any response from me would be fanning the flames, and might look like I was protesting too much. Instead, I'm stuck with the same label that came directly from Mom, the leader of the Cult of Gladys, whose words I wasn't allowed to contradict. She was deeply afraid of lesbians and she said I acted like a lesbian. Even though I don't have sexual feelings for women, Mom's words have instilled in me a profound fear that I am, in fact, a lesbian, because she said so.

Notwithstanding that fear, I've never cared what my fellow players do behind closed doors. My main concern is whether or not they treat me well. In my late teens, I played doubles with a woman named Tory, one of the nicest people you'll ever meet. We traveled and roomed together and told each other our joys and our woes. We practiced hard and ended up being ranked Number Two in the U.S. in doubles. One night, with the lights out, she confessed that she was beginning to prefer women over men. Not once did I feel threatened by her heartfelt admission, because she was honest and genuine. Yet what I accepted in her, I dreaded for myself, a murky fear that was hard to expel, because it had been implanted in me when I was very young.

Lesbians are outcasts. Apparently, so are women tennis pros, at least according to the press. To sports editors, men play sports and women apply lipstick. Most sports reporters have grown up following baseball and football, but not women's tennis, about which they're quite ignorant, and many consider covering women's tennis a demotion. Because the reporters need to be educated, our players have become adept at sidestepping strange questions while leading the reporters back to the subject at hand. One day, the local newspaper sends a fashion reporter to interview me, probably because she's the only female reporter on staff. She's never seen tennis, and she doesn't even know what tennis dresses look like. So I spend a hilarious half hour pantomiming tennis strokes, and then filling her with personal tidbits about the players—their nicknames, home towns, playing styles and the occasional anecdote—so that she can write a fun article and entice fans to come on down and watch us.

On-air interviews, nearly always with male reporters, have their own idiosyncrasies. I've become adept at spotting a blank look or even panic in the interviewer's eyes, because he doesn't know what to ask. I've learned not to let him twist in the wind, and when necessary, I take over, launching into a monologue in which I enthusiastically describe the players on tour and the upcoming matches, and then I culminate with a suggestion that listeners should come down to the arena, where they'll have a great time.

The attacks by the men tennis players, coupled with the media's perplexity about us, have convinced me that the world sees women tennis pros as outcasts, and it got me wondering why. It must be because we're flying in the face of society's vision of how women can use their bodies. In the media, which is run by men, women are treated as inferior and as sex objects, whether they're selling cigarettes on television, starring in the movies, or being the obedient wife who supports the breadwinning husband. The women pros don't fit that mold. Every day that we suit up to play, we buck the male preconceptions of womanhood by proudly earning a living using our muscles.

I've always loved my muscles, perhaps because both Dad and Mr. Hoxie made me proud of my athletic ability and of the hard work that has built my strong body. Still, many of the players—including me—fear that if we work too hard at building muscles, we'll look like a man, something we dearly want to avoid. Interestingly, Margaret Court, who rails against most of what we stand for, has apparently never feared looking masculine. Since she was a teen, she's trained in a gym and built a strong and heavily muscled body that has propelled her to the top of the women's game. Thus, another one of her contradictions: She spouts women's inferiority to men, but her force of personality and her strong body defy the male establishment's view of women with muscles.

Because of my body type, I'll never look big and strong like Margaret or masculine like the men pros. Yes, my legs are sturdy and durable, but I have small bones in my arms and torso, and no matter how hard I train, the top half of my body looks petite. The Stanford Medical School, which had recently started studying sports medicine, sent researchers to our tour's Northern California tournament to measure our muscles and bones. The results showed that I had the greatest difference of all the players between my right and left sides. Because I trained intensely while I was growing, the bones in my right arm grew to meet the demands of my muscles. So even though I don't look big, my right arm is so ripped that it's nearly impossible for me to find a long-sleeve blouse that can slide past my bulging muscles.

CHAPTER 46

MY SVENGALI

After a commotion-filled week at the Hurlingham Club, I'm dying to get out of London. Next up on the tennis calendar is the French Open, where players on our tour, including me, were almost excluded. In any other year, my entry would have been automatic. But for the last eight months, since September 1970, the USLTA has been intent on pounding the women's tour into submission by threatening to suspend us. If they'd followed through, we would have been ineligible to play the French. Fortunately, we're currently in the USLTA's good graces, and the French have opened their doors to our rebel group.

I phone Ingrid, and we agree to share a hotel room in Paris. When I first played in Europe, we often roomed together, practiced together, and shared meals with friends. In 1969, she became Mrs. Jan Bentzer and had a baby, but she returned the following year. Now it's 1971, and we've both been competing, but on different continents. While I was slogging away for increasing amounts of prize money in large industrial cities in the U.S. frozen north, she played on the Riviera. I would have loved to travel with Ingrid and experience her friendship, her hilarious sense of humor, and her European sophistication. And she would have loved the bigger prize money in America. During the week that I earned $2,400 in Vegas, Ingrid garnered the piddly sum of $18 for reaching the women's doubles finals in Beaulieu, France. Ingrid and other women players around the world are praying for our tour to expand, so that they too can start making money. And like me, spending it.

In my amateur days, my greatest pleasure was traveling, and although I earned bupkis (in Yiddish, nothing), I could find happiness by visiting exotic locales. That kind of traveling has been missing on our new tour, so instead of focusing on experiencing joy, I aim to make money, which makes me feel like a big shot. But I'm not content just to watch my bank account swell. I want to spend some of my earnings, and I've developed a yen to buy a car. I've decided to pick one up overseas, drive it around for a while, and then ship it home after Wimbledon as a used car, so I'll pay less customs. On my first day in Paris, I amble up the Champs-Elysées, window shopping for a car. In the Fiat store, my heart goes out to a cute little orange sports car, called a Spider, which I can snag for around $3,000. That will suck up a huge chunk of my earnings, but that's OK; I'm trying to buy some happiness. I phone Dad and ask him to wire the money from my bank account to Fiat. In a few days, the adorable car will be mine.

Meanwhile, I begin competing at Roland Garros. When I was younger, with nearly limitless energy and concentration, I had a clay-court mentality: I was patient and willing to hit lots of shots to set up a winner. But my patience has been fading away, due in part to playing indoors on the tour's fast carpet, which requires a more aggressive style. All too often, I try to end the point quickly, a dangerous tendency on European clay. In Paris, I play well enough to reach the third round, where I meet an ambidextrous Dutch player, who smacks hard, flat forehands from both wings, a rare style that's difficult to get used to. I know I should play long points, waiting for the inevitable error from her flat strokes, but instead I'm impatient and erratic, and I lose. Damn it, I hate losing.

The next morning, Ingrid and I are in our room, packing our tennis bags to head out to Roland Garros, where I'll tie up some loose ends before picking up my little sports car and taking off for England to play the grass court tournaments leading up to Wimbledon. When the phone rings, I assume it means that the tournament transportation has arrived. Instead, an English-speaking voice asks for me. I respond, using the proper grammar my parents always insisted upon: "This is she."

The caller stutters "My name is Vuh Vuh Vincent Hanna. I've read that you're the spokeswoman for the rebel women's tour. I cover both sports and labor relations for the London *Sunday Times*, and your story intrigues me, because you fit into both categories."

Once I set him straight that I'm not the spokesperson, we chat briefly, and I agree to wait an extra day before leaving France, so that he can interview me tomorrow at Roland Garros.

Vincent Hanna and I sit on a bench near Court 5, separated by his tape recorder. He's about five feet ten, maybe 30-40 pounds overweight, wearing a light-blue suit and sporting slightly disheveled, flaxen hair. He's obviously done his homework, because he understands the roles of the holy trinity of the women's pro tour: Mom, Billie Jean, and Joe Cullman/Virginia Slims. He starts with an unexpected question: "Has the tour encountered any prejudice because your mother and Joe Cullman are both Jewish?

I reply "None that I know of."

Then he throws me a bigger curve: "It's too bad the tour has to depend so heavily on Virginia Slims, because the company sells sickness and death." Rarely does anyone state that fact so baldly. When he asks me to respond to his fiery rhetoric, I politely decline. I silently agree with him, but I don't want to get drawn into that conversation. The last thing our tour needs is someone dissing our biggest sponsor.

So he turns to another subject: "I've read what you've said about the importance of solidarity. You sound like the foreman of a labor union."

"All the men in American tennis have been fighting us, and many top women players refuse to join our tour. Plus we have to struggle for legitimacy, to overcome being treated like outcasts. We have no choice but to hang tough together."

"I know how it feels to be marginalized. Although I went to college and law school at Trinity College in Dublin, I'm a Catholic who was born and raised in Belfast, Northern Ireland, which the Protestant British have occupied for 50 years. They treat us like second-class citizens. So many of us, including me, have rebelled by joining the IRA, to demand our dignity and our country's freedom."

Vincent's stutter is intermittent, but when he launches into his commitment to Northern Ireland, it disappears, so I bet myself that he'll keep talking about that subject. Instead, he pivots and moves on to something new. "How do you feel about women's lib?"

"I rarely think about it," I say. "I just focus on making a living playing women's pro tennis. Women's lib is such a huge issue. My mind works better dealing with smaller, more concrete problems."

"You may not admit to being part of a larger movement, but I have women friends who see the players on your tour as symbols of women's freedom, and yes, women's lib."

Our conversation keeps batting back and forth, from my view of women athletes and their muscles, to my tennis career, to my education at Dalton and Stanford, including my six months at Stanford in France, and then to his work at the *Sunday Times*, his goal to do more documentaries for BBC television, and even his pride in playing the 12-string guitar well enough to be a studio musician for a famous folk singer.

Vincent checks his watch and discovers that we've been talking for two hours, an inordinate amount of time for a tennis interview. It was quite a wild ride, and

I loved it. As he packs up his tape recorder, he asks me where I'll be next week, in case he has any more questions, and I tell him that Ann Jones and her husband Pip have invited me to stay with them for a few days at their home in Birmingham. I've known Ann for years, first as an insurmountable clay court opponent, and once I started to beat her, as a rival, a friend, and a partner on the practice court, where we slog away for hours. But now she's pregnant, so we won't do much practicing. I don't know Pip that well. For most of his life, he was a businessman from Birmingham who volunteered in the tennis world. He was in his late 50s when he married Ann, and ever since, he's traveled with her on the tour. In January of this year, he became our first tour director, and he does a fine job managing the players, the schedule, the carpet, and pretty much everything else.

The day after my interview with Vincent, I cross the English Channel, and once I'm at ease driving on the left side of the motorway, I lean on the accelerator, to feel the power of my little car, hugging so close to the road. When I arrive at Ann and Pip's house, she tells me that some guy with a stutter phoned and said he'd call back later. Within an hour, Vincent phones again, and asks me what I think about Billie Jean's announcement that she wants to reach $100,000 in prize money this year, a first for a female athlete.

I say "I think it's brilliant. Billie Jean is a born publicist. She knows that 'Joe Six Pack,' her term for the American sports fan, loves to measure athletes by the amount of money they make. By setting such a high monetary goal, she attracts hordes of ordinary Joes and keeps them rooting for her."

The next morning, Vincent calls again, and admits "I'm running out of questions, but I loved talking to you so much that I keep listening to the tape, and now I want to hear you talk again. Besides, you ruined my trip to France. I went there with a girlfriend, but she got fed up with me listening to your interview, and she cut our trip short."

I don't know what to say. He's funny, brilliant, and knowledgeable about a variety of subjects, and I learn something whenever I talk to him, but he seems to want me desperately, and I don't feel the same for him. I mumble a few words and then say goodbye.

After a few lovely, quiet days with Ann and Pip, I play a small tournament in Nottingham, which I win, and then I drive to London, where I've rented a flat, which I'll share with Ingrid during Queen's and Wimbledon. After we meet at the flat and dump our luggage, we hightail over to the Queen's Club to practice, only to find Vincent, who insists that, when Ingrid and I are finished, he'll take me to dinner at his favorite trattoria. Afterwards, we drive the Spider to his teeny house in a working class neighborhood just off the City Road, which he bought because it's inexpensive and convenient to Fleet Street, the headquarters of most London newspapers, including the *Sunday Times*. Because the property is quite narrow, there's just one room on almost every floor, with the kitchen in the basement, the living room on the ground floor, Vincent's bedroom on second floor, and the bathroom and a tiny extra bedroom at the top. As we sit in his pint-sized living room, Vincent plays tunes from his favorite albums and then sings me a few Irish ballads, accompanied by his 12-string guitar, which he plays like an angel. And then he seduces me. And I still don't know how I feel.

I concentrate on the Queen's tournament, which is one of the most unpleasant events of the year, because the grass courts are awful, the umpires are the worst, and the ball boys and ball girls seem completely untrained. Still, almost everyone plays Queen's, because it provides grass court practice the week before Wimbledon, which everyone needs. Plus the club's eight indoor wood courts come in handy during England's frequent rain.

In the third round, I meet Virginia Wade, which is never fun. Her big serve and low-skidding, sliced backhand give me fits on court. Off the court, I hate her arrogance and dismissiveness, which remind me all too much of the way my sister treated me when we were younger. As our match unfolds, the umpire repeatedly makes mistakes. In fact, everything's a mess. After three or four bad calls, Virginia hits a shot that lands on my sideline, producing a puff of chalk. The umpire calls "Out."

I say "No, actually that was good. You should give her the point."

Then both of us start overriding the umpire, which is never done in tournaments, but it seems to be the only option in this match, until deep in the third set, when Virginia hits a ball outside my sideline, but the umpire remains mum, meaning that he's calling it good. I say "That was out."

Virginia responds "How did you call that?"

She didn't use the word "cheat," but that's what she meant. Instantly, my insides explode, and I silently become consumed with fury. A few games later, the match is over, Virginia having won. I trot up to the net, and as I shake hands, I say "If you call me a cheat again, I'll kill you."

Still boiling, I bolt towards the locker room, where incoming players report that Virginia is telling all the journalists what I said, and now the news of my threat has reached every corner of the club. Surely it will spread to the afternoon newspapers, which delight in a good fight. I anticipate three-inch headlines. I want to hide.

I shower and change, and meet with reporters, admitting that I did in fact say what Virginia has been reporting. Leaving the club, I glance at the afternoon papers. I was right. I'm Julie Heldman, villain.

Why did I blow up so colossally? I've never done anything like that before. I hadn't realized I was so close to the edge. Looking back, I can see what led to my explosion. At 20, I quit playing competitive tennis, to escape the pervasive pressure in a world dominated by Mom. I returned to competitive tennis at 22, hoping to find joy in traveling the world, and trying to convince myself that winning wasn't important. But my formula was unstable, because it was based on a lie—winning has always been way too important to me—and after a failed romance, I tried to take my own life. At 24, I joined the other eight Houston players in standing up for women's tennis. I knew that our cause was more important than my well-being, so I consciously relinquished my freedom to travel to fascinating places. Now, instead of enjoying the sunshine in Rome or on the Caribbean circuit, I've been competing in cities like Oklahoma City and Detroit in the dead of winter, where my days and nights are often nasty and grueling. I try to look, sound, and act normal, but underneath that false exterior I'm crumbling, succumbing once again to the pressure to win, rarely offset by opportunities to enjoy life. Plus once again I'm living in a world dominated by Mom. I can't escape either her pervasive authority or her frequent phone calls in which she complains about Billie Jean and the USLTA. I feel trapped.

After Virginia questioned my line call, I snapped. I don't want to snap again, but I have no idea how to subdue my rage.

The next day, the morning newspapers have a field day on my outburst. I'm embarrassed and worried that I could get into trouble. Still, I need to practice, so I sheepishly return to Queen's. As I enter its giant public rooms, I hear someone calling my name. It's Pancho Gonzalez, smiling at me from across the room. He's now 40-something, but throughout the 1950s and 1960s, he ruled pro tennis with an unbeatable serve and an unmatched competitive spirit. He was also famous for his growling temper. Pancho stands up, and as he keeps his eyes trained on me, he silently pulls a black glove onto his right hand, clenches his fist, and raises it high. It's a salute from one rebel to another. Thank you Pancho.

The Queen's Club tournament ends on Saturday, and Vincent's article in the *Sunday Times* comes out the following day, on the eve of Wimbledon. The main theme is the conflict between Billie Jean, our tour's activist star, and Margaret Court, our staunch opponent. They're the world's top two women players and last year's Wimbledon finalists, and both remain contenders this year. Their contrasts make a compelling story. So does Vincent's description of our fledgling tour and his respect for the women rebels.

Vincent doesn't write much about me, but in one compact sentence he shows his respect and affection: "Julie Heldman is a Stanford history graduate whose playful exterior hides a mind like a honed razor." I love those last words. I want to drink in his belief in me, but compliments, especially ones about my intelligence, don't stick to my bones. I've never been able to dislodge the feeling that I'm not smart enough. To the outside world, I'm the person who skipped two grades and succeeded academically, yet the little person inside of me can't stop thinking that I'm a dummy. And now, Vincent has shouted to the world that I'm brilliant. He hasn't budged my entrenched self-image, but maybe his encouragement will help me on my way.

Vincent is determined to pull me into his world. He introduces me to his friends Mickey and Yvonne, who publish a journal about labor relations. In the same way that my family lived and breathed tennis, Vincent and his pals are absorbed by the crazy world of English trade unions. English industry is afflicted with the blight of over-unionization, and some auto factories have nearly a dozen different unions. One worker's grievance can spread like wildfire from his own union to all the others, shutting down an entire factory. Every day, Vincent, Mickey, and Yvonne spend hours discussing arcane labor laws and the personalities of the most powerful union leaders, trying to make sense out of a dysfunctional system. They blather on endlessly, without stopping to fill me in on the background, while I sit there like a lump. Maybe they think I'm just the jock (the "bra?") who is smart, but only about tennis.

I reach the third round at Wimbledon, and for the first time, I'm scheduled for the Centre Court, to play 19-year-old Evonne Goolagong, an Australian of Aboriginal descent, with a sweet personality and a wonderfully fluid playing style. The first time we played was at Bournemouth last year, where I was favored, but I lost in a nail biter, 13-11 in the third set. Today, she's the heavy favorite, having swept through the field to win the French. From the start of our match, she's swinging loose and free, while I'm tied up in knots, overwhelmed by the mix of my inner turmoil and the atmosphere of the most famous tennis stadium in the world. Two years ago, I too felt loose and free on Court One, Wimbledon's second biggest arena, because I was filled with joy, an emotion that's currently missing from my life. Today, I go down in flames, and I feel miserable. When I come off court, Vincent says: "You were so nervous that you looked like a crab scuttling across those famous lawns." Is that supposed to help?

After my loss, Vincent asks me to live with him and says he wants me with him all the time. I accept his offer, even though I'm not wildly in love with him. He keeps drawing me into his world and telling me he loves me, but I can't overlook his 30 extra pounds and his casual cruelty. Growing up, I absorbed a bellyful of meanness, which I had to swallow, without recourse. On the tennis court, I've always battled ferociously. Off the court is another matter. I wish I could confront Vincent's nasty remarks, but I'm incapable of doing so. Standing up for myself remains too scary. Still, he believes in me, and he's giving me a home base that's far away from Mom. But I don't open up to Vincent, and I never reveal my attempt to end my life. I can't bear to speak the words, not even to him.

Vincent and I plan that he'll come with me when I return to the States to compete. He also wants me to remain by his side while he's working on projects for BBC and the *Sunday Times*. His next project is to land an interview with Lee Trevino, the world's hottest golfer, who just won the U.S. Open and is coming to England to compete in the British Open golf tournament, to be held at Royal Birkdale the week after Wimbledon. Growing up in Ireland, Vincent played enough golf to understand many of the game's nuances, so when he reaches Trevino, he schmoozes about the American's choice of clubs and then turns to questions about prejudice in the U.S. against Hispanics. The conversation goes so well that they set a date for the full interview. Vincent invites me to tag along, but I don't want to go. I hate golf. Actually, I've never watched it, but my parents always treated golf as the competition to tennis, and thus the enemy. Plus I'd rather rest than drive for four hours and then be bored as they talk about golf. But Vincent keeps pressuring me. Finally he says: "I'll teach you about golf. Besides, we'll take the Spider, I'll drive, and we'll have fun." I give in.

We start out early, with Vincent driving faster and faster. Soon, he asks: "Have you ever gone 100 miles per hour?"

"No, I wouldn't dare." I'm a baseliner. I don't take big risks.

"Let's try it!" As he pushes the Spider towards its limit, he screams over the wind and the roaring engine: "Isn't this great?" I say nothing. He's scaring the bejesus out of me. I keep my eyes trained on my feet.

To my happy surprise, Trevino is delightful, filled with jokes, quips, and reminiscences about learning to play golf on public courses while almost all golfers had more privileged backgrounds. On the first day of play, Vincent and I follow Trevino for nine holes, with Vincent explaining every stroke and lie of the ball. The experience lifts me out of my doldrums and shows me a different world.

A few weeks later, the women's tennis tour starts up again in Venice, Italy, and the players get to see the storied city, with its canals and gondolas, and to sip espresso at the Piazza San Marco. This event has an all-too-rare combination of good prize money and European charm. Oh how I miss this kind of travel.

The next tournament is in Houston, where Mom has pushed the promoters and Virginia Slims to increase the prize money to $40,000, a new "all-time high" on the tour. The biggest surprise is that Margaret Court will participate. Mom made a lightning visit to Wimbledon to meet with Margaret, and showed her that she could make more money playing for our large purses than with all the under-the-table guarantees she was raking in. Apparently dollars and cents have trumped her previous misgivings about women's roles in society. When she committed to Houston, the USLTA threatened to suspend her too, which is ridiculous, because they have no authority over her. I guess once she decided that the money was big enough, she became willing to withstand the kinds of attacks that we've been subjected to for a year.

By the time Vincent and I reach Houston, Margaret has pulled out because she's pregnant. Oh well.

We're staying at my parents' house, along with Ann and Pip. On the first day of the tournament, August 9, 1971, we're lollygagging about in the living room, when the radio reports appalling troubles in Northern Ireland. In dawn raids, British troops stormed into Catholic neighborhoods and arrested nearly 400 without trial, almost all of them members of the IRA. Pip, ignoring Vincent's distress, says "They had it coming." Vincent marches out, and I follow him into our room, where he explodes, furious at Pip's prejudice and at the British government for stomping on the rights of his countrymen and countrywomen. He also bewails his own helplessness because he's so far away from the troubles.

He spends hours on the phone trying to reach friends and family in Northern Ireland. But there's little he can do.

Once the Houston tournament starts, I win one match but succumb to the flu before I can play another. Vincent and I both want to get out of town, so we catch an early flight fly to Cleveland for the Wightman Cup, the annual competition between Britain and the U.S., to be held in a temporary stadium at a high school in Shaker Heights, a fancy Cleveland suburb. The USLTA has chosen me for the team because Billie Jean, Rosie, and Nancy Richey have opted out, angered by years of the association's poisoned dealings. I too am incensed with the USLTA, yet I jump at the chance to play Wightman Cup, not due to any nationalistic tendencies on my part, although I believe that our country, warts and all, is the best there is. But after my bleak and lonely childhood and adolescence, I crave the kind of camaraderie I've found on national teams. Two years ago, at the height of my deliriously happy summer, I played so well in Wightman Cup, on the very same court we'll be playing on this year, that I was named the MVP. I'd love to reach those same heights again.

Vincent is certain that he's an expert on almost every subject. Because he's interviewed English soccer stars and watched them train, he's sure he can help me become more fit. The day before play at the Wightman Cup begins, he puts me and Kristy Pigeon through sprints on the grass field next to the stadium. Sprint, stop. Sprint, stop. I see no benefit in these exercises. But *what the hell*. No harm done.

But the surface we'll play on is iffy. It's a rubber carpet that was made by Uniroyal and then laid on top of an outdoor cement court, although the rubber surface had never previously been tested against the vagaries of Ohio's midsummer rains and extreme heat. During the week of practice, the surface keeps bubbling, heaving, and coming apart at the seams. Why the promoter didn't just use the plain cement court is beyond me.

Our team boasts 16-year-old Chrissie Evert, the youngest player ever to represent our country. She's up first, and with no sign of nerves, she crushes Winnie Shaw, Britain's Number Two. I'm next, against Virginia Wade. I've recovered from the Queen's Club brouhaha, and I'm ready to battle Virginia on behalf of my country. I start out well, and at 4-all, I break serve. On the first point of the 5-4 game, I serve to her forehand, which she smacks deep down the middle. I turn to my right, but my left foot catches on a bubble in the rubber surface, and as I turn, I feel a ripping sensation in my left knee. It hurts like the devil, but I try to hide my pain. I do such a good job that at the next changeover, our captain, Carole Graebner, who is sitting on the court, doesn't know I'm hurt until I tell her. I never think of quitting, and I keep on fighting, even as seven games in a row slip away from me. By now, the damage must be obvious, because during some points the pain in my knee is so intense that I can't stand on it, so I hop around on my good leg. And on the changeovers, Carole rubs my bad knee with icy towels, which is well meaning but useless. When I'm 5-2 down in the second set, perilously close to losing, I win three games in a row, due to a combination of my will power and Virginia's errors—it's really hard to concentrate when you're playing someone who's injured—and I catch up to 5-all. But that's my last gasp, and I lose 7-5, 7-5. Still, I won five games in the second set while playing on one good leg. That's nothing short of a miracle.

After the match, my knee is so swollen that I can hardly walk. Vincent organizes a ride to a nearby hospital, and as he's helping me into a car, Pip approaches me and says "I knew you'd hurt yourself doing those sprints." That's it. Not a word of empathy or concern. Just blamefulness. I'd like to strangle him.

At the hospital, they take x-rays, which are inconclusive, and then they drain my knee and give me crutches. I want to keep playing in the Wightman Cup, but the damage is too great.

Back from the hospital, I phone my parents, which means Mom, as Dad never answers. I tell her about my knee, and she says "Oh dear," but she's distracted and doesn't ask any questions, not even about the pain or the seriousness of the injury. In reaction to her lack of concern, I feel bereft, and I begin to doubt the severity of my injury.

Vincent is covering the Wightman Cup for the *Sunday Times*, so he turns his attention to Chrissie, who is determined and focused beyond her years. On the final day of the Cup, she plays her second singles match, against Wade, under impossible conditions, with the rubber surface requiring attention every few points. The situation certainly distracts Virginia, but Chrissie remains clear and calm, and she tromps her older opponent 6-1, 6-1. It's a startling international debut. Everyone attending the matches in Cleveland knows that a star has been born.

After Cleveland, I face the fact that I have nowhere to go. My home is now in London, not in the States. Houston is out, because I can't deal with Mom ignoring or belittling my injury. During last winter and spring, I spent my down time at Mom's Manhattan apartment, but that no longer feels like an option, because my knee is so bad that I frequently need help. I'll need Vincent, but he can't come to New York before the U.S. Open, because he'll be doing a documentary for the BBC in Florida. So I decide to tag along with him. Every few days, my knee swells to monumental proportions, and then I get it drained.

Vincent is covering Forest Hills for the *Sunday Times*, so I'll have to be at the Open. I figure, *what the hell*, I'll enter the tournament and conceal the extent of my injury. Hobbled and in pain, I flame out in the third round to someone I've never lost to before. Still, I've clearly pulled the wool over the eyes of the *World Tennis* reporter, who writes that I seem to have regained my mobility after the Wightman Cup. Not true.

Although I've never enjoyed large parties, Mom does, and she invites Vincent and me to sit at her table for 12 during the U.S. Open's annual ball, where she buys a table every year. During a lull in the music, Mom starts talking about how she treats black people well. Vincent asks what she means, and Mom says she's color blind when it comes to hiring employees at *World Tennis*.

Out of nowhere, Vincent loses his cool and goes after Mom. "I'm a Catholic from Northern Ireland, which means I'm a member of a group that is constantly being discriminated against. I think it's great that you give a few minorities a job, but you have absolutely no idea what minorities really need."

A deadly silence descends over the table. No one ever raises his voice at Mom. Or tells her off. I don't even think his point is that good, but I'm thrilled that he fearlessly criticized her. I wish I could do that, but her rules have been ingrained in me since I was little. I remain mute.

I don't know if I love Vincent, but I'm delighted that he shut Mom up.

After Forest Hills, Vincent and I return to London, and he takes me to the fancy Harley Street office of a well-known knee surgeon. At the beginning of the examination, the surgeon points admiringly to the muscle on the medial side of my bad knee and exclaims: "What a superior vastus medialis!" I take that as a compliment. Then he moves my knee around and says "If you could play on that knee at the U.S. Open, you aren't ready for surgery. Keep playing, and come back and see me when your knee tells you it's time."

This doesn't make sense. My knee is in terrible shape. I wish I could convince the surgeon of that reality, but I become stymied, unable to speak up for myself. Afterwards, I turn to Vincent, begging for understanding, but he only makes the situation worse: "Some American football players play on a broken leg. You're as tough as they are. You can keep going."

I don't understand why Vincent's so keen on me continuing to play on a damaged knee. Maybe he's diminishing the extent of the injury because he feels a twinge of responsibility. The defective court in Cleveland was the direct cause of the damage to my knee, but Pip Jones keeps hammering at me that Vincent's wind-sprint training also harmed me. If that's true, Vincent has harmed me doubly, both as a tangential cause of the injury and by preventing me from getting better.

Vincent then pushes me into signing up for the Dewar Cup circuit, five tournaments to be held in the British Isles. I'm not looking forward to playing another indoor circuit in winter, mostly in smallish towns, where there's nothing to do. Vincent comes with me to the first leg of the circuit, in Edinburgh, where we begin chatting with Evonne Goolagong, who's on her first trip away from Vic Edwards, her strong-willed mentor, coach, and surrogate father. This year, Goolagong won both Wimbledon and the French, and for sure she'll be ranked Number One in the world. Wherever she goes, people rush out to watch the new star. As usual, Vincent delves deep into her essence, asking about her Aboriginal heritage and trying to convince her to stand up for her people's rights. Over drinks, Evonne and I agree to play doubles on the circuit, and from the start we have a rollicking good time. At each tournament site on the mini-tour, the sponsors place a four-foot tall, empty plastic bottle shaped like a bottle of Dewar's scotch. Before our first doubles match, I sneak the bottle off court and fill it with the yellow fluid I use to fight cramps and the heat. As Evonne and I walk out for our first doubles match, I cart the huge thing back on court, and at each changeover, I lift up the bottle and pour a delicate glassful for the both of us, as if we were drinking scotch. The crowd can't stop laughing. As always, Evonne is easy going and goes with the flow. Because of that, and because she's a great player, playing doubles with her is a joy.

The second tournament on the circuit is held in Billingham, in Northeast England, where we play on a rubberized court laid over an indoor ice rink. In the semis of the singles, against Evonne, I face another disaster. The arena's de-humidifier is on the fritz, resulting in a thin film of water covering the rubberized court, which makes it exceedingly slippery and quite dangerous. I don't care; my left knee is already shot. So while Evonne moves gingerly, careful to protect her future career, I career around the court, falling four times, bleeding in various places, and I win.

During the entire circuit, I play with an ace bandage around my knee. As far as I can tell, no one knows the extent of the damage, because I try not to make a big deal about it, plus I make up for the decrease in my speed with an iron will and great hand-eye coordination. I reach the semis or finals of almost all the singles events, and Evonne and I are either finalists or winners in all the doubles events.

My most incredible victory on the circuit is over Evonne in the semis of the concluding tournament, the Dewar Cup finals, which is played at the Royal Albert Hall in London, an arena that's far better known for chamber music recitals. Her second serve isn't working well, so time after time I tee off on it with my forehand, which gives me lots of free points. I win the match with the craziest possible score: 6-0, 0-6, 6-1. The next night, I lose the finals to Wade. I haven't beaten her in two years, and it's getting into my head!

Soon after the Dewar Cup is over, BBC Radio invites me to be interviewed during a First Division soccer game at the Arsenal stadium—just a few miles from Vincent's house. I'm a soccer fan, so that sounds like fun, and I accept. I've done so many interviews about tennis that I can do them in my sleep. Vincent takes this interview as a new opportunity for me, because he believes I could be a dynamite broadcaster. Before the game, he teaches me crucial information about the Arsenal players, which I greedily absorb, and when we go on air, I start by answering a few questions about tennis, and then I launch into my newly acquired expertise about soccer. I keep expecting the BBC reporters to say "Thank you very much" and politely escort me away, but they never give me the hook. Even at half time, the director asks me to stick around to talk some more. I'm a hit, because Vincent packed me full of information, which enabled me to soar.

The tournament season is over, so I practice less, hoping my knee will heal, which it doesn't. Instead, I become domesticated, and most nights I cook. I decide to invite Teddy Tinling to dinner at Vincent's house. Whenever I've eaten a meal with Teddy, he holds court with outrageous quips, to the delight of all. Now I want to show Teddy my new world with Vincent.

We carefully prepare for Teddy's visit. We don't have an official dining room, but we cover the kitchen table with a starched white table cloth, and because Teddy's so tall, Vincent saws a few inches off the legs of the chair where Teddy will sit. I devote two days to cooking, and delicious smells pervade the house. We also invite Vincent's friends Mickey and Yvonne, and the conversation at dinner is lively, although more about labor relations than tennis. Shortly after the main course ends, Teddy stands up to go, without an explanation. I don't know what went wrong. A few days later, while I'm practicing at Queen's, a mutual acquaintance tells me that our dinner table conversation infuriated Teddy. I still don't know why. But I can guess. I think Teddy's like Mom in several ways. For a start, he likes to talk only about tennis. Equally important, they enjoy only a few types of people: ones with a tennis pedigree, an inherited title, or lots of money. Vincent, Mickey, and Yvonne have none of those attributes.

Coincidentally, a few weeks later, I find out that Mom, who adores Teddy and his dresses, got him a job as the official tennis dress designer for the Virginia Slims tour. When Vincent discovers that the designs will display the tour's "Ginny" logo, a flapper with a tennis racket in one hand and a cigarette in the other, he convinces me that a line has been crossed, and that I must take a stance against wearing cigarette advertising on my body. Soon afterwards, a "fluff" piece appears in the London *Times*, showing Teddy's designs and stating that I refuse to wear his clothes, without explaining why. Infuriated, Vincent dashes off a letter to the editor of the *Times*, in my name, saying that I won't wear dresses that "are designed to advertise cigarettes." The language in "my" letter doesn't sound like me at all. But I agree with the stance he's taken on my behalf.

Soon after the letter is published, I spot Teddy at the Queen's Club, but he turns away when he sees me. And Mom never mentions "my" Letter to the Editor. Clearly, they're giving me the silent treatment, in retaliation for my public stance. Theirs is an attempt to whitewash the underlying dilemma of women's pro tennis: our chief sponsor is Virginia Slims cigarettes. Smoking cigarettes is harmful to everyone's health. The company's main goal in sponsoring our tournaments is to increase sales of Virginia Slims cigarettes to women. More sales mean more ill health. The women's pro tour is harming women by having a cigarette company as its main sponsor. I refuse to make smoking cigarettes any more tempting by wearing the Ginny on my tennis clothes. But even I am compromised, because I don't boycott the tour.

Virginia Slims has told the players what to say if anyone asks about having a cigarette company as our sponsor: "Virginia Slims never told me to smoke cigarettes. And I don't tell anyone else to smoke. But if you do smoke, you should smoke Virginia Slims." That's a clever but disingenuous statement. By wearing cigarette advertising on their tennis dresses, the players tacitly endorse smoking cigarettes, especially the brand that is sponsoring the tour.

Besides, my reasons for opposing smoking are personal. When I was little, and our family lived in rural Texas, Dad smoked, even though he was an asthmatic. One day, he had so much trouble breathing that he was carted away to a hospital in an ambulance, placed in an oxygen tent, and told never to smoke cigarettes again. Throughout my childhood, I too struggled with asthma and bronchitis, and his episode impacted me deeply. I knew I'd never smoke. And I haven't.

Gladys wearing a Tinling dress that advertises
Virginia Slims cigarettes.

When I first met Vincent, I was firmly against speaking out against our main sponsor. Six months later, I'm doing that very thing, and it's all because of him. Like the fictional Svengali, he has insinuated himself into nearly every aspect of my life, and taken over. He drew me in by believing in me and taking me to his bed, and then he introduced me to many new areas of interest. Most recently, he's been teaching me to improve my writing, using his very own—and very salty—recipe for writing an article: "You must stand in your reader's shoes. When you read a draft of your article, you must say to yourself: 'Why the fuck would I want to read this article?' After the first paragraph, you must say 'Why the fuck would I want to continue?' And at the end of the article, you must say 'What the fuck did I just read?'" After Vincent's tutelage, I write several articles for the London Sunday Times, which, in part, owe their snappiness to him.

Vincent's overriding message is crystal clear: I should expand my horizons far beyond tennis, and he's the domineering force who will guide me there.

Teenage Martina Navratilova wearing a t-shirt
advertising Virginia Slims

CHAPTER 47
MISERY

It's the beginning of January, and I've arrived in San Francisco to play the first tournament of the 1972 women's pro tour. I'm here because I have nowhere else to go and nothing else to do, and because Vincent keeps pushing me to compete despite my deteriorating knee. In the first round, I get stomped by Wade, yet again! I play so badly that I want to quit tennis altogether. Then out of nowhere, a ray of hope descends. Vincent hears of a doctor in town who has a machine with a new technology, called an arthrogram, which uses a special kind of x-ray technology to see inside knees. The very next day, I'm in the doctor's office, yearning for him to pronounce me ready for surgery. He prepares for the test by filling the knee joint with fluid, which is quite painful, and then he tries to turn on the equipment, but just my luck, it's a dud, and it won't start. So instead of gaining some hope, I spend an uncomfortable night with a swollen knee, caused by the failed arthrogram procedure. I tumble into despair.

I stick around the tournament to practice, but at first I'm wary to talk to the other players, in case they've seen "my" letter to the London *Times*. To my surprise and relief, no one mentions the letter, probably because other newspapers didn't pick up the story. Mom also never mentions the subject to me, which isn't surprising. She's allergic to dealing with emotionally charged issues.

After San Francisco, I bump along, playing three tournaments in a row. With hampered mobility, I can win matches only if my anticipation and hand-eye coordination are extraordinary. Occasionally I beat a top-quality player, but more often, I'm moderately awful.

Virginia Slims has assigned quality public relations people to our tour (now called the "Virginia Slims Tour"), and they spread the story of women's pro tennis across the airwaves and into newsprint. In each stop on the tour, we get great coverage. We've all become seasoned interviewees, looking and sounding professional. Occasionally, fans get an inflated impression of our abilities and our sophistication. In Oklahoma City, I stay with a couple in their 30s in a comfortable suburban house. The morning after I arrive, the three of us eat breakfast together, and once the husband goes to work, the wife and I chat happily in the living room. Out of nowhere, she says "Julie, you're a free woman. Do you think I should divorce my husband?"

Free woman? Not with Vincent stage-managing my life. She must think I'm knowledgeable about men, because I'm unmarried and living with a guy. Or that, because I've stood up for a cause, I'm sage enough to advise her about standing up for herself. I wish I were. I try to let her down delicately: "I'd love to help you, but I know very little about marriage and divorce." She looks crestfallen, and there's nothing I can do.

At the Washington D.C. tournament, I stay with the Hollander family, who are far more sophisticated than my Oklahoma City hosts. Bernj Hollander is an antitrust lawyer, and his wife Joan plays classical piano duets. Their rambling three-story house in suburban Chevy Chase, Maryland once accommodated four children, but the three older ones are grown and have fled the nest. Only Ellie, who's 18, remains at home while she's finishing high school. Her older brother Jonathan is a modern dancer intent upon making a mark in New York City, the center of the dance world. He's injured his knee and returned home to see the family doctor, who makes a house call. After the doctor examines Jonathan, his mother says "Julie's knee doesn't look good. Would you examine hers too?" He does, and then he says "Jonathan has a strained ligament. He needs rest and some physical therapy. But Julie's knee is much worse. I don't know how she runs on it. She'll need an operation in the very near future." Finally, someone has confirmed my self-diagnosis. I was beginning to lose hope that anyone would ever believe me.

The next day, I'm due to play Billie Jean King, who's trapped in a political fire storm. Last month, *Ms. Magazine* published its premiere issue, which contained a list of 53 well-known women, including Billie Jean, who're sticking their necks out by admitting that they've had an abortion, which is illegal in most states. Before Billie arrived in Washington this week, the *Ms. Magazine* article hadn't caught on with the press. But then a *Washington Post* reporter interviewed her and wrote an article headlined "Abortion Made Possible Mrs. King's Top Year," arguing that she was only able to make fame and fortune because she crassly decided to have an abortion. Billie Jean is the top star on our tour, and she's an emerging presence in the women's movement. Her worlds collide during a press conference, when she spots the *Post* reporter who wrote the article and demands that he leave the room. When he refuses, she storms out.

What a tough week for Billie Jean. Not only does she have public tribulations, she also has no idea that Vincent has prepared me to combat her rat-a-tat, foot-stomping maneuvers, which she's been using over the last few weeks to trick her opponents into believing that she's rushing the net. The first time she does it, I catch the ball after it bounces, turn to the umpire, and claim distraction. Ironically, the result is that Billie Jean becomes distracted, the very thing she was trying to do to me. After that, she loses her edge for a few games, so I jump ahead and win the first set. With Ellie and her mom screaming for me after every point that I win, I take the first set. Billie Jean fights back to win the second set, but my cheering section boosts my energy, and I run away with the third set, 6-1. After the match, Ellie and her mom smother me with hugs. I wish my family was like theirs.

A few days later, Billie Jean complains in a press conference that she has an injured knee and an infected toe. I'm sure they hurt, but it sounds like she's making excuses for losing to me. Still, I know what I've done. I beat the tour's biggest star while I was hobbled by a swollen knee that delivers constant, thudding pain.

Every ball I hit in practice, and every match I play, takes its toll on my knee, but I keep trying. Finally, in March, I split sets against two top-10 players, and then flame out 6-0 in the third, when I can barely move. That's it. I've had enough.

During the eight months I played on a ripped-up knee, I had five wins over women in the world's top 10: two over Goolagong, and one each over Melville, Masthoff, and King. In every match I played, I ignored the discomfort, gritted my teeth, and gave it my all.

I fly back to London and immediately meet with the surgeon. He sits me on a high table, with my legs dangling. He holds my left thigh down with one hand, and then, without warning, he grabs my left foot with the other hand and jerks it up until my leg is straight. The pain is fierce, but I hold my tongue. He looks pleased with himself. "Most people scream when I do that test. You didn't, but I can tell it hurt a lot. That proves that you have a torn meniscus and you need an operation."

I'm ready. The surgeon gives me a choice about where to have the surgery, either in a private clinic in London or in a public hospital in Croydon, a largely commercial district on the city's outskirts. I ask "Where can you operate first, and where will you be most available after the surgery?" Croydon wins on both counts, and we schedule the operation for the next day, March 17, 1972. Both the surgeon and Vincent promise to visit me every day.

After the surgery, I wake up in a private room, alone and sporting a cast from mid-thigh to mid-calf. When I lie completely still, my pain is modulated and dull. But if I try to move even the smallest amount, the pain kicks up to excruciating, far worse than before the surgery. My first priority is a raging thirst, but there's no water and no bell for the nurse near my bed. I try yelling "Hello!" but no one comes. Finally, I spot the bell, but it's five feet away, and I don't know how I'll get there, because rolling over to get off the bed spikes the pain off the charts. I wait quite a while, and then I move slowly and gingerly to reach the bell. After a while, a nurse appears, and she brings me water, but she places it on a table that's hard to reach, so that even getting a sip of water is painful. No one offers me any medication. Throughout the afternoon and night, I remain almost completely alone, and although I occasionally ring for help, the pain levels remain at a 10.

Night time brings its own trauma. My room overlooks the Croydon High Road, where motorcycles and other loud vehicles roar up and down throughout the night, as revelers celebrate St. Patrick's Day, and their noise bounces loudly around my room, interrupting my sleep. I'm living a nightmare of neglect, isolation, and pain.

Once the vehicle noises subside, I doze fitfully for a few hours, but when I awake in the morning, I'm still alone. I try calling Vincent, but I can't reach him. I ask a nurse when the surgeon will come see me, but I find out nothing until late in the day, when I'm told "He'll be here tomorrow." So much for their promises to be available.

When the surgeon finally makes an appearance, his report is confusing. "I've rarely seen a knee as bad as yours. It was so swollen that I couldn't figure out which side to go into first, so I made my first cut on the medial side." That makes no sense. Everyone knows my injury was on the lateral side. The surgeon continues: "When I made my cut on the lateral side, particles of debris exploded upwards. But I was able to remove the meniscus, so you'll be fine."[8]

"When can I go home?"

"Anytime you want to."

---

[8] 38 years later, I visited an orthopedic surgeon in California, for a consultation about having a partial knee replacement. When I told him what the London surgeon did, the California surgeon started shouting: "He did what? What? He cut you twice in the same operation? That's terrible!" I'll use the word that the California surgeon was implying: "Malpractice."

So I try to track down Vincent, first by phoning home, and then by calling everyone I know in London. When he returns my call a few hours later, I swallow my anger and tell him he needs to drive me home. After two more hours, he comes to pick me up, looking harried. He makes no apologies for his absence, or for not keeping in touch when I needed him by my side. This makes no sense. He's always told me that he wants me near him, but when I needed him the most, he vanished. Could he have been off with another woman? That's too horrible to countenance, so I bury the thought and focus on healing.

My cast will remain in place for six weeks, and I plan to recover in Vincent's teeny house, which will be extraordinarily difficult. I spend most of my time in Vincent's bedroom, on the second floor, and to reach the bathroom, I have to sit on a step and scoot my butt up one step at a time. Going downstairs is even clumsier. Who knew that the simple task of going to pee would be so difficult? And most of the time, I'm alone in the house, without any help. Vincent works all day and comes home at night, and Florence Nightingale he certainly isn't.

When I'm released from the cast, my muscles have atrophied, so I'll need to work hard for months to build them back up. I don't despair. Instead, I decide to dedicate myself to rehab. There's a gym a few miles away, near the Arsenal soccer stadium, so I buy a bicycle and ride there twice a day, rain or shine, and then I work out for as long as I can. Recovering muscles is a slow and arduous process. The physical therapist tells me he's never seen anyone work as hard as I do, but my recovery is hampered because I played so long on the knee that the surgeon screwed up.

Smack dab in the middle of my recovery, Vincent plans a car trip to Northern Ireland, with Mickey, Yvonne, and me. I love the idea of seeing his birth place, so I prepare to go. As I'm adding the final touches to my small suitcase, I lean over, and the camera hanging from my neck slams into my poor tender knee. For the first time since I ripped the meniscus nine months ago, I melt down, howling and crying with frustration and pain. Vincent treats me like a wimp, because I totally lost it. He doesn't understand that a person can only take so much misery.

The first stop on our road trip is Londonderry—which the Irish call "Derry"—where the IRA has taken a foothold since January of this year, when British troops shot 26 unarmed protesters in a massacre called "Bloody Sunday." Vincent's IRA roots are pulling him to investigate what's happening there. On the way, our drive seems endless. Always heading west, we cross England to Liverpool, where we take a ferry, and then we drive across Northern Ireland to Derry. After so many hours in the car, my knee is stiff and cranky, but I say nothing. When we reach the wall surrounding Derry, Vincent tells me: "Mickey, Yvonne, and I are going inside, to see how the revolution is progressing. Your knee probably wouldn't hold up to the walking, so why don't you stay here and wait for us?" And there I sit for hours, fuming. Upon their return to the car, Vincent drives for an hour to his parents' house in Belfast, where once again I'm marginalized, shipped to a small single room, because Vincent doesn't want to tell his father that I'm his girlfriend, as I'm Jewish.

Barely two years ago, I tried to take my own life, and I hope never to feel that badly again. 1972 is coming close. It's early May, and this year is already one of my worst ever.

Back in London, I tell Vincent that I'm unhappy. I stop short of telling him how often he's been the culprit, but he has to know. Instead, I say "Nothing's going right."

In response, he declares his love for me and says "I want you to have my baby." I'm astounded. We've never discussed that possibility, but now that he's planted the idea, I spend days floating on a cloud, dreaming of motherhood. And then, in record time, I become pregnant.

When I excitedly tell Vincent, his reaction is instant and negative: "You'll have to get an abortion." I don't understand. It was his idea to have a baby! He gave me hope, but now that I'm pregnant, he's yanking it away. I'm devastated.

Abortions are legal in England, but that doesn't make them less difficult, and it certainly doesn't reduce the sadness I feel about removing the growing life from within me. Vincent couldn't manage to help me after my surgery, but he wants me to have the abortion so badly that he organizes all the details. He makes an initial appointment for me with his doctor, and then he signs me up for the procedure. He drives me to the bus filled with other pregnant women, some of whom are chatting together. We're taken to an unpleasant, antiseptic-looking building, filled with uncommunicative, antiseptic-looking doctors and nurses. At the end of the day, the passengers once again board the bus and return silently to London. I suspect that, like me, they're impacted both physically and emotionally.

I grieve.

Once again Vincent pushes me hard, this time to play Wimbledon. I'm gaining strength, but I know my body, and my knee is clearly far from ready for competition. Yet I cave. I just can't defy Vincent. I guess I'm a lot like Dad. Both of us can be pugnacious on the tennis court, but away from the game, in our personal lives, we let strong personalities walk all over us. My years in the Cult of Gladys taught me not to stand up for myself, not to show annoyance or anger at a powerful figure, and not to cry when I'm hurt. When Vincent came along, I gave way to him, just like I did to Mom. He's my Svengali, who pulls the strings of my life. He opens doors for me but he pushes me deep into physical and emotional pain. But I can't leave him. Like Dad, I stick it out, no matter how tough the road. Besides, I have nowhere else to turn.

So I try to figure out how to get ready for Wimbledon, which is barely a month away, when I've been out of the cast for only 25 days, and I haven't begun to practice. Then a small miracle happens. My buddy Denise Carter, who quit the tour after getting married, invites us to stay with her at the hotel where she's teaching tennis in Southern Spain, near Marbella. Vincent is thrilled: "Let's do it!" So I call Ingrid, who's at the French Open, and I tell her about the invitation, and I invite her to join us, so that we can practice and have fun. She jumps at the opportunity.

When Vincent and I arrive, Denise is lovely and welcoming, but her place is too small to accommodate us, so we'll have to pay for a room at the hotel. When Ingrid arrives the following day and finds out that she too will have to pay, she goes ballistic. The rooms aren't cheap, and Ingrid's strapped for cash, so I understand her distress. I wish I'd called her the moment we found out about the accommodations. But I didn't, and I blame myself.

Ingrid and I try to make the best of the situation by practicing at least once a day, but even that turns out badly, because my knee is stiff, and it's far more painful than before the operation. I can barely keep the ball in the court. We try playing some points, but I'm truly awful, and when I miss five or six shots in a row, I can't stand it anymore. For the second time during my recovery, I implode, screaming and crying, mourning the horrors of the last eight months, blaming myself for screwing up, and hating the fact that my tennis is so unbearably awful.

Then comes yet another trauma. I get an infection from the abortion, which leaves me in constant pain. There's no choice but to return to London, get some antibiotics, and curl up in bed for a week, another seven days when I'll be unable to practice.

Once the infection is gone, I return to the gym, and I start practicing regularly.

I enter the Queen's tournament, where I lose in the first round 7-5 in the third to a player I think I should beat—if I had two strong knees. Given my condition, I'm encouraged that I at least put up a battle.

When Wimbledon starts, I know it's crazy for me to play, but I do it anyway. Before my first match, I decide to unravel the tape that binds my knee, hoping for increased mobility, but as I walk on court, I fret that I've screwed up yet again. Once the match starts, I'm determined to play my heart out. My opponent is a good, young American, and we fight tooth and nail, but early on I bend low, as I always do on grass, and I scrape my knee on the turf, causing one of the incisions to bleed, which scares the hell out of me. But I keep on fighting for hours. I want so badly to win, but I lose 10-8 in the third.

Since the operation, Dad has phoned regularly, and Mom has phoned occasionally, but neither has shown much interest in the details of my recovery. So when I find out that Mom is planning a two-day, lightning trip to Wimbledon on tennis business, I try not to get my hopes up that she'll pay much attention to me and my wounds.

Vincent gets a splendid idea. He knows how much Mom loves the trappings of the rich, so he hires a chauffeured Rolls Royce to drive her around, but all we tell her is that we're sending a car and driver to meet her at Heathrow Airport. When the chauffeur leads her to the Rolls, she's exhilarated. Our plans have a potential flaw. Her Wimbledon tickets are being held in the referee's office at the All England Club, inside the club's gates. We don't know if the persnickety guards will stop her from entering the grounds because she doesn't have a ticket. But when they see the Rolls, they usher her right in. Apparently, in England, a chauffeured Rolls Royce works as well as a Wimbledon ticket.

Mom spends her visit packing in meetings with players and the tennis elite. When we get together, she's preoccupied with her work and barely mentions my knee. I can't help lamenting that she doesn't care.

After Wimbledon, Vincent scores yet another great interview, this time in London with Russia's Boris Spassky, who will soon go to Iceland to play the American Bobby Fischer for the 1972 World Chess Championships. Vincent invites me to the interview. Before we arrive, I read that Spassky was the latest of a long string of Soviet world chess champions, who all grew up in the Soviet political system, so I expect him to be a stereotypical bureaucratic type. Boy was I wrong. He's quite charming, warm, and comfortable, the kind of guy you'd like to sit next to at dinner. A few days after the interview, Spassky flies to Iceland to compete against Fischer, who is brilliant, boorish, and eccentric. He hasn't changed much since he was 14, when he was already a chess prodigy, and his mother phoned Mom, looking for a healthy, athletic outlet for her chess-crazed son. Carrie and I, who were about Bobby's age, played tennis with him for an hour on the upper court at the Heights Casino. Halfway through, we vowed "Never again," because he was so obnoxious. He hasn't changed. In Reykjavik, he beats Spassky by making brilliant and surprising chess moves and by making his opponent's life miserable.

In August, I return to the women's pro tour, albeit somewhat cautiously. I still have to get stronger, so I add 30 pounds of weights to my already heavy suitcases. At airports, I seek out porters to carry my bags, but before they pick them up, I warn them: "Watch out! They're really heavy." Most of them scoff at me, try to pick up my bags, and then say something like: "Oof! Is that thing filled with bricks?" The weights are essential to my recovery. Three times a day, I sit on a bathroom counter, strap them onto my left foot, and lift them 30 times. My regimen also includes running up and down hills, forward and backwards, to build up my endurance. I keep getting stronger, slowly.

And I learn to play with a different kind of pain in my knee. It's sharper than before the surgery, although less severe than immediately after the operation. But pain remains my constant companion, particularly when I hit a forehand. I know my form is correct when my knee hurts.

Several weeks into the summer swing of the tour, during the Denver tournament, Vincent makes a disappointing film for the BBC about the women's tour. It's both inaccurate and misleading. He says the women players run their own tour by having regular meetings, and that I'm the spokesperson and the "shop steward" (labor leader), who negotiates with the tournaments and with Pip Jones. All of that is wrong. Pip runs the tour, not the players. If it were otherwise, we'd have anarchy. And not only am I not the spokesperson, I don't have any official position with the tour. Then Vincent, my Svengali, cajoles me into saying something outrageous in his film, so I describe several women players in the amateur era as whores, because they exchanged sexual favors for under-the-table expenses. I cringe when I see that portion of the film.

During the summer, my results are erratic, just what you'd expect from a player who's still on the mend from big-time surgery. In the fall, I play the Dewar

Cup once again. My progress is intermittent, although I have one huge win, over Wade! But my tennis life takes an interesting turn. During the Edinburgh tournament, Jimmy Jones, an ex-player who runs the magazine *British Lawn Tennis*, approaches me and says "You've recovered from your operation, and you're fine now, so you should stop favoring your leg." It sounds like he thinks I'm a complainer, and that I don't really have pain, which is obviously not true. But his remark makes me doubt myself, as I'm hard wired to doubt my own experiences, especially when someone accuses me of malingering.

Jimmy continues: "In 1956, I coached Angela Buxton when she reached the finals of Wimbledon. Angela and I now work together, and if we start coaching you this winter, you'll get better quickly." He outlines their methods: They work outside, summer and winter, so that I'll get used to playing with distractions. That way, in a tournament, nothing will disturb me. And he strongly believes in working on patterns that I'll use to finish points at the net. In particular, he will teach me to hit high volleys with a full swing—just like my forehand—in place of the traditional jab volley or the overhead smash. Very few players use the swing volley, but it sounds like it's made for me!

Jimmy's making sense, so I decide to try out their team-teaching approach. In November, we begin meeting at a public court near Hampstead in North London. The days are frigid, so I wear two layers of track pants, which keep my legs warm, but my hands are freezing, because I can't play tennis with gloves. I need to feel the racket's grip. I work hard, and as I run and jump and twist, even my hands warm up, and I actually feel good. For the first time in an eternity, I can lean on someone with tennis knowledge. I'm gambling that, if I keep my mouth shut about the pain, Jimmy and Angela will help me rebuild my game, regain confidence, and recover from my prolonged misery.

CHAPTER 48
SPIRALING OUT OF CONTROL

During 1972, while I was trapped in a cocoon of injury and sorrow, professional tennis was undergoing momentous changes. With the advent of open tennis in 1968, a revolution had started. U.S. promoters, drawn to professional tennis by the prospect of lining their pockets, found sponsors, who funded tournaments, which attracted players and spectators. By 1972, tennis's popularity in the U.S. had increased dramatically, due to galloping growth in prize money, expanding television coverage, and a passel of home-grown players with star quality, including Billie Jean King, Chris Evert, Arthur Ashe, and Stan Smith.

In this new world of professional tennis, the amateur associations that had held sway for nearly a century became increasingly irrelevant, yet they clung to their fading power. As a result, they clashed frequently with promoters and players, and tennis politics became ugly. On the men's side, Lamar Hunt's WCT group had gobbled up most of the top men stars. Because Hunt's players were "contract pros," the old national associations had very little dominion over them, except during a few weeks a year, when the associations retained the right to decide who would compete in the Davis Cup and in the four majors, the Australian Open, the French Open, Wimbledon, and the U.S. Open. In 1972, the power struggle between the old and the new forces in men's tennis reached a crescendo, when the International Lawn Tennis Federation (the "ILTF") banned all the WCT pros from the Italian, the French, and Wimbledon. After Wimbledon, peace was established, but the men players, fed up with ceding authority over their careers to promoters and part-time volunteers, established their own group, the Association of Tennis Professionals (the "ATP"), which became their advocate.

The women pros had an even gnarlier path, because the national associations were run solely by men, who showed little interest in women's professional tennis until Mom jumped in. She tried to work within the USLTA's rules, but the association was determined to hold onto power over the women.

Mom's determination to create a professional tennis tour solely for women was revolutionary, and so was her commitment to future players. For the first time in top-level tennis, a two-level, feed-in qualifying event was held before every tournament, providing opportunities for second-tier players and future stars. She also established a slush fund for players who needed help with expenses, and she opened her heart and her wallet to struggling players, including women of color, who'd previously had few opportunities in big-time tennis. Because she reported to no one, she could burst forth with ground-breaking ideas and bring them to fruition in record time, unfettered by outside forces.

During the tour's first year, Mom turned the dream of women's pro tennis into a reality. Yet hardly a week passed without a threat from the USLTA.

Early in the tour's second year, Joe Cullman, who was disturbed by the ever-present hostility between the USLTA and Mom, put out peace feelers. He asked Donald Dell, tennis's first super-agent—and my Peugeot driver in Italy six years ago—to broker a peace, and to everyone's surprise, he succeeded. In February 1972, Mom and the USLTA agreed that she'd become its Director of Women's Professional Tennis. Her roles were to manage the women's pro tour and to administer the women pros' involvement in the Grand Prix, a multi-national series of tournaments that awarded points to players based on matches won, with a big payday at the end of the year to the women with the highest number of points.

Mom's position with the USLTA was a great idea in theory, but it couldn't last. She'd always needed to be in charge, but now she had to report to men whom she didn't trust and whose decisions were often flawed. From the start, the Grand Prix was the sticking point. Virginia Slims tournaments paid the most money into the Grand Prix pool, but its players received fewer points per tournament than those who competed overseas for less money. The situation blew up in mid-summer 1972. U.S. women's tournaments had set aside a total of $18,000 for the 1972 Grand Prix, which Mom was holding. Throughout her life, she'd been fastidious—bordering on fanatical—about following every rule and paying every bill. Before 1972, she would have paid the $18,000 and then written an editorial about the unfairness of dealing with the Grand Prix. But by the summer of 1972, she had become highly committed to women's causes, long before that was fashionable. She started by rebelling against handing over the money, arguing that because there was no female representation on the Grand Prix committee, it had no right to govern the women pros. She bought some time by asking the tour's players to vote about the fate of the $18,000. They backed her up, electing not to deliver the money to the Grand Prix and choosing instead to divert the funds to the Virginia Slims year-end tournament in Boca Raton.

Mom had a long history of making sound decisions, but her actions surrounding the Grand Prix $18,000 were ill-advised. She never explained why she began to lose her bearings, but she was obviously living through impossible dramas that would have put anyone under: the killer pace she'd been maintaining for two years, running both her magazine and the tour, and the constant fighting she'd had with the USLTA. The combination of all those factors led to a mountain of pent-up frustration and anger, which was hidden to the casual observer. She still worked endlessly on her giant round bed, wearing dark glasses day and night, smoking two-to-three packs of cigarettes a day, and consuming vast amounts of liquor. She still complained constantly about Billie Jean, both to me and to anyone else close by. And she still delighted in telling dirty jokes and making outrageous comments while lunching under the gazebo in the backyard of her Houston home, close to the tennis court where she adored playing.

But worse problems were on the horizon. The USLTA and the ILTF, strident in their certainty that the $18,000 belonged to the Grand Prix, threatened Mom that if she didn't hand over the funds, they'd sue her for it and withdraw the sanctions for the tour's two $100,000 tournaments, Boca Raton and the Family Circle Cup.

The risk was too great. Mom had never been involved in a lawsuit, and she was afraid that she'd lose. She also didn't want to jeopardize the tour's two richest tournaments. So she handed over the money, but she also quit her position at the USLTA, saying in a press release that the association should take over the tour, which was "tremendously time-consuming and expensive. I cannot neglect *World Tennis* magazine," which she called her "baby."

Mom's resignation was met by an immediate howl of protest from the players, the tournament promoters, and the Virginia Slims executives. They begged her to return, believing that she was the only one who could carry the torch for the women's tour. She'd never stopped wanting to run the tour—it too was her "baby"—but she needed to be in charge, and she'd had enough of the volunteer bureaucrats. So shortly after resigning, she basically did a massive about face. While she was still under contract to the USLTA, she agreed to take over the tour again, but on her own behest, not under the auspices of the USLTA. In September 1972, she prepared contracts for the 1973 tour, covering 18 tournaments and over $600,000 in prize money. Nowhere else was this kind of money available for the women pros, so within two months, 64 players from all over the world signed the contract. In *World Tennis*, Mom pointed out that, in the winter and spring of 1970, before she started the tour, the total prize money for women pros in the U.S. was $2,000 (other than the prize money contributed by *World Tennis*). She had turned women's pro tennis from poverty into wealth.

After the contracts were signed, Mom's next step should have been to apply to the USLTA for sanctions, which she'd always done in the past. But in late 1972, she refused to do so. That was clearly a bad decision, a sign that she was spiraling out of control. Her excuse was that the USLTA wouldn't have given the tour sanctions anyway. Even if that was true, she would have looked better had she applied for sanctions. But she was already heading towards more revolutionary territory, a new world of women's pro tennis completely devoid of the old national associations. She formed a new entity, the Women's International Tennis Federation ("WITF"), with herself as the leader. Her vision was that her federation would consist solely of women, and it would be equal to the most powerful tennis association in the world, the male-dominated ILTF, not subservient to it. No longer would women pros be governed by groups comprised solely of men. Under Mom's WITF, women would be in charge of their own fate at all tournaments except the major championships, where unfortunately they'd probably be barred. That was the huge weakness of the WITF, because Wimbledon and the U.S. Open were extremely important to Billie Jean and to Margaret Court, who was returning to the tour after pregnancy leave. Because they were Mom's two biggest stars, the WITF's future was shaky at best.

Angry that Mom had taken back the tour, the USLTA retaliated by starting its own competing tour, to be held between February and April 1973. Its tournaments had smaller prize money and weaker competition than the Virginia Slims tour, but the USLTA tour boasted two legitimate stars in the wildly popular Chrissie Evert and the delightful and talented Evonne Goolagong. They committed to the new tour because the USLTA scared the daylights out of Jimmy Evert, Chrissie's father, and Vic Edwards, Evonne Goolagong's mentor, with threats that if Chrissie and Evonne played the Virginia Slims tour, they'd be excluded from national teams and from the four major championships.

When the USLTA first announced its new tour, it tried to co-opt the Virginia Slims tournaments, but almost all of them preferred to remain with Mom's organization. One important tournament, however, jumped ship. George Liddy, the promoter of the Virginia Slims of Fort Lauderdale, needed Chrissie Evert, his biggest drawing card and the home-town favorite. When he discovered Chrissie wouldn't compete on the Virginia Slims tour, he walked away from his Virginia Slims contract and signed with the USLTA tour instead.

Furious at Liddy's gall in cavalierly discarding his commitment, Mom wanted to sue. But before she moved ahead with a lawsuit, her life turned in a new direction.

No one—except maybe Dad—could have predicted that during an ordinary phone call with Donald Dell, Mom would blurt out: "I'm mad at everybody in tennis, and I want to sell the magazine. I want you to find a buyer." This was absolutely extraordinary. From the day Mom started *World Tennis*, she poured every ounce of her energy into making her "baby" a huge success. Throughout my youth, I sat at the nightly dinner table as Mom talked endlessly about the tennis world and her magazine, without ever mentioning the possibility of selling it. And just a few months before she decided to sell, she'd issued a statement in which she chose *World Tennis* over the tour. So when Mom told Donald to find a buyer, he too was flabbergasted, and he said he tried to get her to change her mind, but she wouldn't budge. Maybe she realized that working at warp speed was unsustainable and that something would have to go, either *World Tennis* or the tour. She must also have been influenced by the tennis boom, which was responsible for increasing the value of everything related to tennis. Whatever her exact reasons—which she never revealed—she was intent upon barreling ahead. After Donald made just a few calls, he reached CBS Publications, which owned a number of magazines and jumped at the opportunity to buy the world's most influential tennis publication. They rapidly settled on a price of $2.4 million, and when the deal closed in December 1972, Mom reaped $2 million, after paying taxes and Donald's fee. Once it was all done, she called me with the shocking news, giddy about the money: "I took the check to the bank, and I told them: 'Deposit a million in checking and a million in savings.'"

After the sale closed, Mom revisited the possibility of suing Liddy. First, she needed a lawyer. She played tennis at the Town Tennis Club in midtown Manhattan with many high powered men who surely must have known terrific lawyers. But she didn't ask them. And apparently she didn't ask Joe Cullman, who would have been a wonderful resource. Instead, she turned to Dad. Why she did so is unclear. He was a scientist and a businessman, not a lawyer, and although he managed the patent lawyers at Shell USA, they weren't experts in lawsuits involving business contracts, so the best they could do was ask around, and they found a law firm in Chicago, even though the trial would be held in New York. Mom hired that firm, apparently without checking their experience or their credentials. Her new lawyers' first act was to convince her that the USLTA was the real culprit, and that instead of pursuing Liddy, she should sue the entire USLTA, and start by requesting a preliminary injunction, a special kind of lawsuit that asks for immediate action, in this case to stop the USLTA from interfering with Mom's "business opportunities," including the "promotion of professional tournaments." They filed suit in New York City on January 9, 1973, and the trial began 17 days later, on January 26, 1973. Trials for preliminary injunctions happen in a helluva hurry.

Mom's lawyers did a dreadful job from beginning to end. The entire foundation of the lawsuit was so flawed that it bordered on ludicrous. There was no way that the USLTA could cause Mom to lose "business opportunities," i.e. money, because she never took money for running women's pro tennis. But her lawyers never brought out that fact, likely out of fear that it would sink their ridiculous case. The lawsuit was doomed from the start.

Yet while Mom's lawyers were woefully deficient, the USLTA's lawyers, who came from an elite Wall Street firm, were excellent. They badgered her on the stand for two days, making her look like a two-faced money-grubber. And the judge also chimed in to question her decisions and demean her character. Afterwards, she would always say: "Those were the worst days of my life."

Mom's lawyers attempted to bolster their case by adding Billie Jean King as a plaintiff. She testified that she would lose money because the USLTA was preventing her from competing on its tour, but its lawyers destroyed her effectiveness by showing that she had plenty of opportunity to make money on the very rich Virginia Slims tour.

A few days after the end of the trial, the judge ruled against Mom and Billie Jean on all counts, saying that their evidence was insufficient. In fact, Mom's lawyers admitted to the judge that they hadn't proved **any** interference with business opportunities, the very basis of the case. In a preliminary injunction case, a necessary element is that the plaintiff act in good faith. The judge ruled that Mom hadn't done that, pointing to her decisions to take back the Virginia Slims tour from the USLTA while she was still under contract with the association, and what he called her unwarranted "cries of distress" that the USLTA would render Virginia Slims players ineligible for the majors, a situation that he said Mom could have cured by applying for a sanction. Had Mom's lawyers been competent, they would have highlighted all of the USLTA's past threats, to explain so many of her actions. Instead, the lawyers just plain blew it.

Everything about the trial was a disaster for Mom: She lost, she was mortified on the stand, and then she had to reach deep into her own pocket to pay her lousy lawyers.

But Mom also failed herself. For many years, she'd had one success after another in the tennis world, but not in 1972, when so many of her actions were self-destructive: As always, she was unable to deal with issues that were emotionally charged. Perhaps the biggest issue was that she didn't know how to extricate herself from crushing overload. So she kept harming herself, until everything finally blew up.

There is another factor that may have led to Mom's uncharacteristic behavior in 1972 and 1973. Perhaps she was so close to the edge that her brain chemistry went awry. I'm suggesting that she suffered from bipolar disorder, which in that era was called manic depression, although she was never diagnosed with it, and she never sought treatment for any mental illness, in part because she hated and mistrusted the entire medical profession. But a number of factors point to that possibility.

For a start, bipolar is often passed along genetically, and I've been diagnosed with bipolar, so it's likely that I inherited it from her. And many of her characteristics fit squarely within the clinical definition of bipolar.

To be diagnosed with bipolar, a person must have two different kinds of episodes during his or her life, mania and clinical depression. Mania involves extremely high energy, a reduced need to sleep, and often racing speech. Mom had all of that for many years. She buzzed through life at such a high speed that she said she needed to drink a great deal of liquor for its sedative effect. Currently, that would be called self-medicating.

For discrete periods of times, mania can be highly beneficial. For many famous artists with bipolar, including Vincent Van Gogh and Virginia Wolff, mania fueled their creativity. And for many other highly successful people, including Mom, mania vastly increased their productivity.

But while mania can be thrilling and positive, it can also turn into out-of-control behavior such as wild spending sprees and sexual excesses—although there's no evidence that Mom had either of these—or into terribly bad judgment, which Mom certainly had during 1972 and 1973. Worse, when a person can no longer continue at mania's frantic pace, clinical depression can take over.

We all go through spells of sadness that we call depression, but clinical depression is significantly worse, as it involves prolonged bouts of intense melancholy. Mom had plenty of those. For decades, she was obsessed with hurt about Billie Jean. Years after Billie Jean had stopped talking out of line, Mom still couldn't let go of her indignation. In the late 1980s, when I began to stand up to Mom, she shifted much of her hurt and anger away from Billie Jean and towards me. She never confronted me, of course, because that wasn't in her nature. But every day for years, she called my sister, crying and lamenting "Why does Julie M hate me?" I believe that Mom's prolonged, inconsolable episodes of sadness rose to the level of clinical depression, and that her emotions were in part fueled by her brain chemistry misfiring.

Still, we'll never know for sure if Mom's precipitous slide in 1972 and 1973 resulted solely from too much work and stress, or if there was a brain chemistry component, or if there was something else we don't know about. We do know that for months she acted totally out of character by making one mistake after another, which the judge highlighted in his opinion.

Soon after Mom's dramatic loss in court, Joe Cullman once again tried to bring about peace. This time, it was harder to achieve. Mom insisted that the women pros should continue their fight for autonomy from the national associations, but the players were reluctant to continue the fight. The most devastating problem, however, was that the USLTA leaders insisted that they would come to the table only if Mom was out. In May 1973, a deal was signed. Starting in 1974, there would be only one women's pro tour, without Mom, under the auspices of the USLTA.

For decades, Mom had been a major force in tennis. She ran *World Tennis* and the Virginia Slims Tour, but after the events of 1972 and 1973, she was no longer in charge of either. After selling *World Tennis*, she remained the editor for a year, and the publisher for several more, but she no longer wielded power as she had before.

In 1973, Mom was only 51, but her era at the very top of women's pro tennis was ending.

CHAPTER 49
A FRESH START

I've just turned 27, and I'm still playing competitive tennis. I never thought I'd keep it up this long. As a kid, my goal was to win the Juniors and then do something else. But once I discovered the joys of traveling, I kept competing and seeing the world. And then I joined the women's pro tour. Although my days on tour are often grim, my bank account has continued to swell, even after I endured a terrible injury, followed by a brutal operation. Now, as I begin the 1973 women's pro tour, I still struggle to heal my ravaged knee, reconstitute the broken pieces of my career, and leave all that misery behind.

When I arrive in San Francisco for the first tournament of the tour, I'm hopeful, because my coaches, Jimmy Jones and Angela Buxton, have made me fitter, and they've helped me finish points at the net. Still, my knee presents a challenge. I used to rely on my speed afoot, but now I have to learn new tricks to overcome my hampered mobility. Plus I play my best tennis when I'm happy, and there's not much joy in these bones. Nonetheless, I try hard, struggling to improve, but I lose lamely in the first round of the singles in the first two tournaments. Doubles is a different story. Billie Jean and Rosie have been a dominating team for years, but Billie's currently injured and off the tour, and Rosie needs a short-term substitute. I'm not generally lauded for my doubles prowess, but when Rosie spies my improved net game, she asks me to be her partner, and we win two titles in a row. Once Billie Jean returns, I become a singles specialist again.

As the weeks go by, my play remains bumpy. Three times I take a set off of Margaret Court, a rare feat, as she's winning everything this year, almost always in straight sets. But winning one set means very little. Beating her is what counts, and I haven't been able to pull that off. My best victory this season is over Nancy Richey, in a titanic late-night match that's so grueling that my body aches for days. But I've also lost to beatable players, and I'm still working on regaining accuracy and confidence.

Vincent's busier than ever. In London, he continues to write articles for the *Sunday Times*, but he frequently travels to the States to scare up interviews for the BBC. In his quest for a documentary with high impact, he sets his sights on Jimmy

Hoffa, the Teamsters leader with ties to the mob. But Hoffa's refusing all interviews, and he's in hiding. Trying to track Hoffa down, Vincent takes a complete flyer. He phones my old pal Carl Borack, who recently visited Vincent and me in London. Vincent asks Carl for help finding Hoffa, which is downright peculiar, as Carl's an Olympic fencer and a movie producer, without any ties to Hoffa or the mob. But out of the blue, Carl strikes gold while sweating buckets in a trendy Los Angeles steam bath. He starts chatting with a likeable and funny guy named Gaby, who turns out to be a Teamsters organizer. Carl jumps on the opportunity, and Gaby opens the door to Hoffa's handlers. As a result, Vincent gets his interview, a huge coup.

Since the day we met, Vincent has never stopped believing that I could succeed in other careers. For years, I've written articles in *World Tennis* and a number of newspapers, but he keeps pushing me to strengthen my journalistic acumen by taking more risks and being more controversial. But that just isn't me. I feel uncomfortable divulging personal details about myself or another player, and if I reveal too much, I end up feeling squirmy and embarrassed. Vincent also keeps nudging me to become a TV broadcaster, which I'd love to do. But opportunities are scarce, because other than Wimbledon and the U.S. Open, women's tennis is rarely televised. This spring, there will be a new opportunity, when NBC broadcasts a tournament called the Family Circle Cup, sponsored by the eponymous magazine. Vincent's on my case to get the job.

The tournament is being held at a resort on Hilton Head Island in South Carolina. When I arrive to compete, I organize a long practice on the green clay, which used to be one of my favorite surfaces, until my knee impeded my ability to play long points. After the practice, Johnny Moreno, one of the tournament owners, introduces himself by saying "Your dad and I grew up playing each other in Southern California. I hated his lefty serve, which was so loaded with spin that it kept yanking me off the court." I love Johnny's obvious respect for Dad and the joy he takes from tennis. Johnny's easy to talk to, so we spend a few hours together, as he describes the wild-and-wooly route he and his partner Jack Jones took to develop the tournament.

Most promoters have deep ties to the community where a tournament will be held, and they draw on local sponsors, clubs, and volunteers. But not Jack and Johnny. Their mission started in Southern California in early 1972, while they were watching men's tennis on TV. Jack became bored with what he called their "bang bang" points. He preferred the longer, more intriguing points of women's tennis, and he decided then and there to bring women's pro tennis to TV. Jack asked Johnny, "Where do we start?" so Johnny called Mom, the wife of his former rival, and she said: "Come on down to Houston with a check for $15,000," which they did. During their first meeting, on Mom's giant round bed, she said, "If you hold a women's tournament with $100,000 in prize money," (at that stage, the largest women's purse ever), "you can buy the rights to women's tennis on TV with your $15,000 check." So, in a flash, they'd procured the tour's rights, but they still needed network TV, a sponsor, and infrastructure. Jack began by shopping all the networks, who were all unwilling to spend money on women's tennis. So instead of taking the traditional route of selling the broadcasting rights to the networks, he made the unique decision to give the rights to NBC, but retain the rights to sell commercials during the show. Then Johnny found the resort on Hilton Head and Jack convinced Family Circle Magazine to become the lead sponsor, by showing them that they could sell plenty of ads in the tournament issue by giving away a trip to Hilton Head with each ad. All the pieces came together, and the tournament was profitable from the get-go. I doubt that any tournament has ever had such a circuitous route from the germ of an idea to fruition.

Central to Jack and Johnny's zeal was their determination to showcase women's tennis on television. When I ask Johnny if I can do the commentary, he responds, "We'd love that. But NBC will also have a say in the matter, and their decision will depend on who else is available."

Unfortunately, I become available right away, by losing badly in the first round in one of the worst matches of my career. I have no idea why I was so awful. But I stick around the tournament, at the figurative stage door, hoping to do the TV commentary. My hopes are dashed when Rosie beats Billie Jean in the semis, making Billie available to do the TV, and NBC is dying to have her for the broadcast. Several hours later, my fortunes improve, when Johnny calls to report that NBC and Billie are having trouble reaching a deal. "We may not know until the last minute, so you should get your hair done and be prepared, in case you get the call." I make an appointment with a hairdresser, and then I look in the mirror, something I rarely do. I hate what I see—long, stringy hair that hasn't been cut in three years. I guess I stopped caring how I looked once my marriage to Larry fell through and I lost my zest for life. Besides, Vincent likes my hair long. But now I need to look special, so I spend a couple of hours getting all done up.

At mid-morning on finals day, I get the call saying I have the job. I wear my nicest outfit and appear at the platform where I'll do the broadcast with Jim Simpson, an unassuming guy with a great sports broadcasting resume, and Bud Collins, a bubbly tennis enthusiast, whose main gig is writing a column for the *Boston Globe*. As we're about to make our opening remarks, the director asks me if I have any makeup, which I don't. I frantically rush around and borrow some from another player, feeling ashamed that the director doesn't like the way I look. But once the match gets underway, I'm completely at ease. I grew up bantering about tennis, and I enjoy describing what I see both journalistically and anecdotally. Luckily, the match between Rosie Casals and Nancy Richey is a humdinger. Their styles contrast wonderfully, with Rosie rushing the net whenever possible, and Nancy mostly hugging the baseline and crunching groundstrokes. The outcome is settled when Rosie executes a perfect and totally unexpected dropshot, and wins 7-5 in the third. Jack and Johnny are thrilled with the match and my performance, and the NBC producer is also highly complimentary.

I fervently hope that broadcasting will be my next career.

I doubt that Billie Jean worried for a moment that she didn't get to do the Family Circle Cup broadcast. She's involved in so many undertakings that she must hardly sleep. One of her biggest projects is World Team Tennis, which she and Larry founded. It's a coed league of 16 teams, each representing a different city. Team Tennis differs from regular match play because substitutions are allowed, and the scoring is different—the sets are truncated, and the points are called 1, 2, 3, instead of 15, 30, 40. Team Tennis's goal is to maximize fan involvement, and to give tennis fans what baseball and football fans already have, home teams they can support. Even though Team Tennis play won't begin for another year, the teams have been sold, and the owners have held a draft. I've been drafted as the Number One woman for Chicago, but I don't pay much attention to the process, because playing Team Tennis would be too risky for me. The season will consist of near-constant travel for four months, mostly to play one-night stands. All of that is hard on the body, and I can't afford any more damage. I'll have to give Team Tennis a pass.

After Mom was booted out of running women's tennis, everyone hoped that the constant strife in professional tennis would subside. But that hasn't happened. Sure, women's tennis calmed down, but Team Tennis, the new kid on the block, is scaring the daylights out of the national associations, who are threatening to bar Team Tennis players, once play starts in 1974.

Why don't the associations just stop?

Instead of stopping, in 1973, the Yugoslav national association suspends its top player, Nikki Pilic, for playing a lucrative tournament in Las Vegas instead of representing his country in Davis Cup. Wimbledon fans the flames by honoring the suspension and barring Pilic from The Championship. The ATP, which has been itching for a fight, votes to boycott Wimbledon. All but three ATP members refuse to compete in the Championships. The men's event goes on, but with a weak field. The ATP has won a huge power struggle.

Billie Jean King wants an equally strong association for the women, and she establishes an entirely new entity called the Women's Tennis Association ("WTA"), to be run by the players. She holds a meeting at the Gloucester Hotel in London in June 1973, a few days before Wimbledon, which I attend, along with about 60 other women. I support it wholeheartedly, but Mom doesn't. When I call her from London, she says "I already have an association. There's no reason for Billie Jean to form a new one." Mom is missing the point. In her association, the WITF, the players aren't autonomous, because they report to her. Plus her WITF is already warring with the national associations and the four major championships. The WTA represents a new beginning, free from disputes and the bad feelings that have been boiling over for years. But I suspect that Mom's real issue is deeper. She used to be in charge, and now power has shifted away from her, towards Billie Jean and the WTA. I bet that rankles.

I prepare for Wimbledon by playing several tournaments and training with Jimmy and Angela. At Queen's, I recover some of my former moxie, beating Chris Evert in the quarters. Damn it feels good to see the ball so well! But my bubble bursts in the next round, when Goolagong thumps me. At Wimbledon, I win a few rounds, and once again I meet Chris, who gains her revenge by trouncing me on Centre Court.

During my victory over Chris, I had a bounce in my step, but that was a rare occasion. Mostly I'm dead serious. I envy players who love what they're doing. I don't. I compete for the money, because I believe in the need for the solidarity of women's tennis players, and because I've committed to the tour, but most days I feel like my life juices have been sucked out of me, even on the hallowed Centre Court.

After Wimbledon, I play a small grass-court tournament in Newport, Wales, where I meet Australia's Dianne Fromholtz, a 16-year-old wunderkind, who is 11 years younger than I am. She beat me a month ago, so I know how well she can play. My knee problems have affected everything about my game, and I've even lost my service rhythm so badly that sometimes I get the yips, and I can't even toss the ball in the air. When that happens, I've resurrected an old Hoxie artifact—my underhand serve—but now I hit it with lots of spin, to make the ball move and swerve. Against Dianne, I'm serving at 10-9 in the third set, 40-30— my match point—when the yips attack. So I serve underhand, but with so much spin that the ball bounces and takes a sharp right turn, low to the ground and out of Dianne's reach. I win the finals of a women's international tournament on an underhand ace. That must be a first.

Back in the States, women's tennis achieves yet another milestone. For a year, Billie Jean has been campaigning for equal prize money at the U.S. Open, without success. In mid-summer 1973, an angel named Dick Gelb appears out of the ether. As chairman and CEO of Bristol-Myers, he directs his company to contribute $50,000 to the women's prize money at the Open, so that it will equal the men's. The tennis public knows little about Gelb, but Mom and Joe Cullman do. Gelb is a member of Century Country Club. Yet another Jewish scion of industry has stepped forward to help the women pros.

This is true progress, but it's just the first step. None of the other three majors has equal prize money for the women, so while this is a momentous occasion, we still have a long way to go.

Forest Hills has always been played on grass, and until recently, so were many other tournaments leading up to it. That's all changed. With the evolution of open tennis, there's only one women's professional grass-court event before the U.S. Open, held in Newport, Rhode Island. Vincent and I had planned to meet there a few days before the tournament starts. I arrive on schedule, but after several days he still hasn't shown up. I get antsy, because he hasn't called for a long while, and I have no idea where he is. Wondering if he's had an accident, I phone his friend Yvonne in London, who says "Don't you know?" Apparently all of his friends, except me, have known for a while that he has a new girlfriend. He didn't even have the guts to call me.

During our two years together I was the unhappy recipient of many of Vincent's mean-spirited jibes. I suppose I should have known that one day he'd treat me heartlessly, but I didn't. I just went along passively, pleased that he was in charge, but largely blinded to his downside. In many ways, Vincent was similar to Mom. Both treated me with casual cruelty, total dominance, and a barbed sense of humor. And both of them belittled my illnesses, injuries, and emotions. He was my Svengali, who controlled me, influenced my thoughts, and largely kept me apart from tennis people. That in turn rendered me isolated and alienated, echoing my childhood aloneness. Now that he's made such a spectacularly unpleasant exit from my life, I feel devastated but at some level relieved.

Now I can make a fresh start in the tennis world. My first job is to win some matches in Newport, Rhode Island. I begin by ramping up the agility training that Jimmy and Angela taught me. Then I extend my practice sessions. I eat healthy meals of lobster and clam chowder. And I give myself a lecture: Do not think about Vincent during matches. That's easier said than done.

Starting with my first match in Newport, I play as if I were shot out of a canyon, running like a demon and rushing the net so effectively that I beat Rosie Casals in the quarters and Kerry Melville in the semis. Although I lose to Court in the finals, I've regained a sense of purpose, and I feel my confidence creeping back.

At the U.S. Open, I nearly lose in the second round in the intense heat, but with a little luck and a lot of determination, I squeak out the match. Next is my encounter with Billie Jean King, whose fame is more like a streaking comet, now that the huge match against Bobby Riggs is almost upon us. No one thinks I'll beat her, but I stay the course, and she quits, storming off the court in a huff while I'm 4-1 up in the third. The score is messy, but the victory is mine, although many reporters crucify me, for no good reason. Maybe they're swayed by the angry look on Billie Jean's face, but the truth is that she was breaking the rules, and she was angry at me for querying the umpire about that. After enduring months of sadness and despair, I lack the emotional wherewithal to deal with the reporters, the craziness, and Mom. I tumble out of the tournament in the following round.

Still, since Vincent failed to show up in Newport, I've had spectacular success, which is proof that I'm on the right path. But on certain issues, he gave me good advice, such as pointing me towards a career as a broadcaster. I'm determined to follow that path. After my loss at the U.S. Open, I stand once again at a proverbial stage door, trying to get a broadcasting gig. This time, I'm hoping to be hired by CBS to do the semis and finals of the U.S. Open. Yet again, the tactic succeeds. I'll do the broadcasts with Pat Summerall, a former NFL star, and Tony Trabert, a tennis player who was twice ranked Number One in the world in the 1950s. My broadcasts go well, because I'm lively and informative. But I begin to catch a glimpse of the more sinister world that's hidden behind the scenes in television.

Frank Chirkinian, the CBS golf producer who's best known for making the Masters tournament a lively on-air success, has been hired to do the tennis, and according to everyone, he's a mean sonofabitch. I've heard stories of him screaming viciously at his co-workers, creating a nasty and unpleasant atmosphere in the broadcast truck. Fortunately, he has no time for me, and I make sure to stay out of his way. In the broadcast booth, Summerall is unfailingly friendly and helpful, and Trabert seems OK. But Johnny Moreno warns me that Trabert is bad-mouthing me behind my back, saying I don't know anything about tennis. First of all, that's mighty peculiar, because I know a whole lot. But I also wonder why he doesn't have the guts to be straight with me. He's a full-grown adult. He should act like it.

In quiet moments, I begin to think about my changed circumstances. At first, Vincent's betrayal devastated me. But with every passing day, I rejoice in my renewed freedom, and I realize that, now that we're apart, I'll be able to travel more freely. For years, I've wanted to watch Brazilian soccer up close, and when I hear about a three-tournament circuit in Argentina and Brazil, my interest is piqued. I seek out the promoter and take whatever deal I can get. Money isn't my driving force. I'm trying to retrieve the joy I once had. I begin to wonder where else my racket can take me.

I also decide to spiff up my style. Soon after the Open, I stride down Madison Avenue to the Vidal Sassoon hair salon to have my hair cut. I give myself over to the hairdresser, closing my eyes as he snips away. When he says "It's done. Have a look," I open my eyes. Oh no! This certainly isn't what I expected. My hair is barely an inch long, which makes me look like a boy. I want to hide. As I leave the salon, I hunker down, slinking close to walls, hoping no one will notice me. After a few days, I get up the gumption to meet with friends, who say "Wow! You look cute!" Their kindness is well-intentioned, but I'm still horrified; my hair is just too extreme. But it's certainly a break with the past.

During the 11 days between the end of Forest Hills and the Battle of the Sexes, everyone's talking about the match and taking sides. ABC, which has paid exorbitantly for the broadcast rights, plans a similar battle in the broadcast booth. The producers choose Rosie Casals to cheer for Billie Jean and Jack Kramer to cheer for Bobby. The ever erudite Howard Cosell will sit between them and pontificate. But in an aggressive exercise of power, Billie Jean tells ABC that she won't play the big match if Kramer's in the booth. The bad feelings between Billie Jean and Jack began in 1970, when he tried to undermine the first women's pro tournament in Houston. And their mutual distaste accelerated in 1971, when Billie and Rosie walked off the court in the middle of their singles finals in Kramer's tournament in Los Angeles. They'd asked for a linesman to be removed, so the umpire called Kramer, who was the tournament referee, but he refused to come down to the court from the broadcast booth, which meant that no one could make the decision, and Billie and Rosie were stuck waiting. When they decided to leave the court, they took the rap as the villains, although Kramer had placed them in an impossible situation.

Billie Jean's determination to get Kramer axed from the Battle of the Sexes broadcast is round three between them, which she wins. ABC replaces Kramer with Gene Scott, a Yale graduate and former Davis Cup player, who is intelligent and moderate. During the match, Rosie hogs the airwaves with frequent pot shots at Bobby, leaving Scott struggling to say anything at all. Although I withheld my enthusiasm before the big match, after Billie Jean wins decisively, I'm thrilled, like most women in America. She brushed aside Bobby's disparagements of women, and she's shown women everywhere how to overcome adversity and reach for the stars.

In October, I return to London, to find that Vincent has taken all my possessions out of his house and dumped them into a new flat he's rented in my name. Vincent's actions are so bizarre. He's removed me from his life, but he still hasn't told me why.

After I spend a few days arranging my new flat, I start my Dewar Cup campaign in Wales, where I reach the finals, losing to Wade. Then I fly to Edinburgh, for the second Dewar Cup event, but I begin to feel a crushing heaviness. Too many bad things have happened to me. Vincent's abrupt departure, coupled with his erratic and despicable behavior. The attacks by the press after my victory over Billie Jean. My disastrous new haircut. Moving alone into a London flat that I did not choose. I begin to feel sick. Within a few days, a nasty cough develops, which blossoms into a full-blown bronchitis. I still reach the Edinburgh finals, but at the following tournament in Billingham, I come to a dead halt, and I default early, which is rare for me. I quickly return to London, where I ask a friend of Vincent's for a referral to a doctor. Within an hour, Dr. David Jackson arrives at my door. He's 50-something and handsome, as well as smart, charming, and medically astute. His main practice is through the British Health Service, but on the side he does house calls. I tell him I need to get well quickly. The Dewar Cup finals, to be held once again at the Albert Hall, will start in five days. "No problem," he says, and kicks into high gear. Every day he comes to my apartment to give me injections of antibiotics and Vitamin B-12, which work like a charm. I reach the finals against Wade, where I come so incredibly close to winning—just two points away—but I can't close the deal, and I lose 7-5 in the third. I owe so much to David. Not only did he heal me, he also shored up my spirits, which I needed so badly.

Before I leave for South America, I call Ingrid and ask if she wants to come too, and she jumps at the opportunity. I can't help her with the Argentine portion of the trip, but I call the Brazilian promoters, and they're game.

Buenos Aires hasn't changed much since I was here in 1968. It retains its wide, tree-lined boulevards and restaurants that serve meat at almost every course. I also have fun on the tennis court, where I win the singles, doubles and mixed, a rare triple. Then I fly to Rio, where I meet up with Ingrid, and we stay at a hotel a few blocks from Ipanema Beach. When we leave the hotel in the morning, music from every corner and every café washes over us, and wherever I look, bodies sway to the rhythm of samba. Ingrid cannot resist any opportunity to get a tan, so we hit the beach, where we're surrounded by vendors, soccer and volleyball players, children, and lovers. Even on the beach, music is everywhere, and many sun worshippers are dancing. The Cariocas, as the residents of Rio are called, really know how to enjoy themselves.

But the tennis is a problem. The club is far away, and it has very few courts, so practice is hard to come by. And I hate the balls. Instead of flying straight through the air, they dip and swerve. When I play Ingrid in the finals, I get angrier and angrier, loudly complaining "The balls aren't round!" I behave like an absolute jerk, screaming in between points, but I can't stop.

After I squeak out a three-set win, I get my trophy, and then I shower and change. Outside the locker room, a ruggedly handsome man approaches me and proclaims "I love your fiery spirit!" I figure he's crazy, because there's nothing positive to be said about my misbehavior. But we begin to chat. His name is Alejandro, pronounced "Aleshandro."

I tell him "I've always wanted to watch Brazilian soccer. Do you know how I could do that?"

"I can take you," he says. "I have tickets for today's game, so get your stuff together and let's go."

As we drive to the stadium, he excitedly talks about all his girlfriends, one who's blonde and beautiful, another who loves to dance, another who dresses with flair. He loves them all. I've gotten myself into an interesting pickle. I want to watch Brazilian soccer, and he wants to seduce me. We end up doing both. I revel in the flair and artistry of the players, in the 200,000 fans who chant and sing and sway during the match, and in the Maracanã stadium itself, the largest in the world. On the return trip, we stop at a motel and enjoy each other, just for fun. At this moment, Vincent is a distant memory, and I'm having a great time.

The following day, the players leave for Sao Paolo, Brazil's business capital, which feels sterile, compared to the richness of Rio. What Sao Paolo does have is knuckle-gnawing traffic. After a few days, it also has Alejandro, who comes to visit me. He brings passion to every aspect of his life. For a long time, Brazil has been under military rule, which he despises. Once, after he spoke out against the government, the police arrested him and brought him into a small room, where they ordered him to cease and desist. Alejandro brims with emotion as he recounts how he spat in the policeman's face. Alejandro escaped a disastrous outcome only because he knew some men in power, who got him released, but he lives on the edge.

After I win the tournament in Sao Paolo, it's time to say goodbye to Alejandro and Brazil and continue my travels. I've been asked to represent my country in the Bonne Bell Cup, a relatively new women's team competition between the U.S. and Australia, sponsored by a cosmetics company. I always love team play, and I've never visited Australia, so I accept instantly. I'll have a few free days before the event begins in Sydney, so I decide to savor my freedom and avoid jet lag with two layovers: one night in Lima, Peru and two nights in Moorea, Tahiti, where I've uncovered an exquisite resort. There, I sleep in a thatched over-water bungalow, surrounded by blue and shimmering water. I decompress by listening to Brazilian music on my boombox and watching the sunshine shimmer off the waves.

When I arrive in Sydney, I bring my boombox to our first team meeting, and I serenade my teammates with all kinds of music, especially Brazilian. None of them are interested. Oh well. I am.

Our captain is Peachy Kellmeyer, a former high-quality player turned tour director of the women's pro tour. She has her hands full. Her three top players, Chris Evert, Nancy Richey, and I, are all over the place. Chris shot straight to the top of women's tennis when she was 16, becoming an instant super star. But now she's 19, and she recently announced her engagement to another young tennis megastar, Jimmy Connors. Nancy Richey is 31 and struggling with a difficult marriage. And although I was recently dumped by Vincent, I feel like I'm in my prime. I just celebrated my 28th birthday, and I'm bubbling over with excitement, as I march to the beat of a different drum.

Peachy, originally from West Virginia, has a low-key style, and she tries to make everyone feel at ease. But I'm so hyped up that nothing can slow me down, and I beat everyone in practice. Nancy's been one of the best players in the world for two decades, but because she isn't playing her best, Peachy makes the controversial choice to play me ahead of Nancy. In my first match, against Goolagong, I start out on fire and take the first set, but then games rapidly slip away from me. At a set apiece, Peachy, who's sitting on court, calmly says "You're fine. Nothing has changed. There's no reason you can't play the way you did in the first set." Never has a captain's intervention worked better. I relax and cruise through the third set victoriously. Unfortunately, the magical feelings I brought with me to Australia don't last, and the following day, I lose to Melville.

The next event is the Australian Open, played on grass at the Kooyong Club in Melbourne. Although Australia has been tennis mad since the beginning of the 20th century, and this event is one of the four major championships, the tournament needs work. Because the women's prize money is weak, the temperature can be oppressive, and the grass courts are just OK, very few women foreigners take the exceedingly long trip Down Under. Worst of all, Australia is highly chauvinistic, and the men who run the tournament seem largely indifferent to women players. My round of 16 match is played way the hell away from any spectators, which infuriates me. In the press room after the match, I give them a piece of my mind. "The men are scheduled on the front courts, but you send the women down in the boondocks, which is outrageous." I don't think the tournament referee cares one iota about what I say, but my words hit the wires around the world.

In the quarters, I get what I wished for, to play in the stadium, where my opponent is the Australian Lesley Hunt. At one stage, we have to rush off court due to gale-force winds, heavy rain, and the temperature dropping 30 degrees. When we return to finish the match, the court is soaked. I win in three sets, but as we're about to walk off court, the referee tells the crowd that a men's singles match scheduled for our court will be moved to an adjoining court in the center of the stadium, because our court was "not fit for a men's match." I grab the court-side microphone and implore the crowd: "What are we, second-class citizens?"

The referee doesn't issue an apology. Perhaps he really believes that women don't deserve to be treated as well as men.

I've reached the semis, and once again I play in the stadium, this time against Evert. Sadly, she calmly plays her usual focused, accurate, and error-free game, and she dismisses me summarily.

I've scheduled two more tournaments, one in Sydney and the other in Auckland, New Zealand, but I've ripped through all my high-strung energy and ground to a halt. I'm spent. It's time to return to my lonely flat in London and rest.

CHAPTER 50
ALMA

It's January 1974, and I'm having an extended rest in London, four weeks without a tournament. I lead a lonely, domestic life, eating mostly at home, rearranging my few pieces of furniture, searching for antiques, attending movies, and of course practicing tennis, either indoors at Queen's or outdoors in the freezing cold with Jimmy and Angela. I also begin to search for a new flat that will be truly mine, free of memories of Vincent, where I can move once my current lease is up.

One day, I get a phone call from Dr. David Jackson, asking me to lunch. I'm glad he wants to be my friend. He picks me up in his car, and we have a tasty meal at a nearby bistro. But on the return trip, he shocks me by saying "I've made an appointment for you tomorrow with a psychological counselor named Alma Traub. I've written her address on this piece of paper. You should go."

I know nothing about psychology, except it's the only college course that I nearly flunked. I also don't know why David's doing this. I see no reason to go.

So I don't go. The time for my appointment comes and goes, without me leaving my flat. But David doesn't let me off easily. Later that day, he phones and says "Alma says you missed the appointment, and you didn't call. That wasn't polite. I'll make you another appointment, but you'll have to go this time."

With my *London A to Z* map book in hand, I find Alma's tiny studio apartment, a two-room basement bedsit nestled in a quiet square. One of the rooms is a minimal kitchen with barely enough space for a table for two, and the other is a multi-purpose room, where she sees patients, with just enough space for a single bed, a desk, and two chairs. Alma welcomes me kindly, speaking with an Austrian accent. She's small and dressed warmly, to overcome the lack of central heating, and she makes a pot of tea, which we drink as we get acquainted. She asks what I do for a living, and I describe my life of playing tennis and traveling. Then she enquires about my parents, and I explain that they're highly educated and successful, and that they're both experts about tennis. By then, the hour is up, so we agree to meet again.

At my second appointment, on a Friday, Alma asks about my childhood, and out of nowhere, a floodgate opens. Story after story come pouring out: That I was sickly but rarely cared for; that until I was seven, I wasn't around other children, and I never went to other people's houses; that even after I was seven, I rarely saw other children, except when I sat with them in class or I competed against them; that Mom frequently screamed at me and humiliated me; that I had to deliver her nightly double scotches at exactly the prescribed moment; that she never, ever cooked for me, but I had to prepare her meals and make sure she got the best food; and that she worked endlessly on *World Tennis* magazine, attending to even its smallest details, but neglected nearly all of my needs.

As my memories spew forth, Alma remains silent, but when I stop, she says: "You probably don't know that if you had a different mother, you wouldn't have had to suffer the way you did."

When the hour ends, I go home, feeling no extraordinary effects from the session. Once I'm alone in my flat, however, I begin to cry, and I can't stop. I badly need to talk to someone, but who? Not Mom; she's the culprit. Nor Dad, who'll never say anything against Mom. Not Vincent or any of his friends, who are out of my life, and besides, they wouldn't understand. And not David, who'll probably tell me that I'll feel better if I keep going to Alma. On Sunday, after two solid days of crying, I stop sobbing for a few minutes and call Ingrid at home in Sweden. I tell her that I'm seeing a therapist, and now I'm crying constantly about the way I was treated as a child. Never before have I told Ingrid about my childhood, so she's flabbergasted. She enjoys Mom's sense of humor, and like everyone in the tennis world, she respects Mom's contributions to the game. So when I begin to describe what Mom did to me, Ingrid can't take it in. "You're fine now," she says. No, I'm not. And Ingrid isn't helping. I desperately need to be understood, but she can't comprehend what I'm going through. So I say goodbye and hang up, and the tears come flooding again.

Monday morning, I force myself to stop crying, to prepare for a training session with Jimmy and Angela. I work hard with them, and I say nothing about the raging tumult that has engulfed me. I hide my distress so well that they can't possibly know what I'm going through.

How could I tell Jimmy and Angela, anyway? From the first time Jimmy offered to train me, he declared that my knee had healed, although it hadn't, and he made it clear that the subject was closed. So I adapted by never telling him about the constant, low-level pain I endure. And neither Jimmy nor Angela has shown any interest in my emotional state, so I hide that too. My relationship with them is only about tennis, so I obviously can't tell them that I'm seeing a therapist. Plus what I'm going through feels like a mystery to me, so I couldn't possibly explain it to them. It's better for me just to clam up.

The next time I see Alma, I tell her about my extended crying jag, and she tells me I can phone her anytime. That's a relief.

I also tell her I don't know what caused me to cry so long and so hard.

"You've had a lifetime of bottling up some intense emotions. While everyone in the tennis world was praising your mother, you had a different reality, which you couldn't tell anyone, not even your father. You've had to swallow a mountain of grief."

I cry again.

I still don't understand all this crying. Mom says I cried all the time when I was little, but those tears dried up long ago, largely because Mom made fun of me for crying. So why are my tears returning with such a vengeance after a few short sessions with Alma?

Once again, Alma helps me understand: "All your life, you've hidden your sadness from the outside world and from yourself. It's sad and scary to examine those emotions closely."

My stories keep pouring out. But even though I'm confident that they're accurate, I often doubt myself, and Alma points out that I've apparently made a lifelong habit of doubting my own truth. Because Mom always played down my illnesses and injuries, I have trouble believing that I'm sick. Even if I get a high fever and bronchitis, I worry that I'm exaggerating my illness. And when I tell Alma a painful childhood incident, I fear that she'll say "So what. That isn't a big deal." Although she never does. And most of all, I worry that if I tell anyone else about the way Mom treated me, they'll either diminish my concerns or refuse to believe me. Or, like Ingrid, they might say "You're fine now."

The emotions I feel when I cry are complicated. When I recount my childhood woes to Alma, the pain that surfaces rips me apart, but it also brings some relief, because I can finally speak the truth and be believed. Yet even that relief is tinged with fear that Mom will get back at me (even though she's thousands of miles away). She often told Trixie and me an allegory called "Zou Pushed Me," whose unspoken moral was "Never tell on your mother." In the tennis world, I've always been the "good daughter," proud of Mom's accomplishments but hiding from the world—and largely from myself—all the ways she abused me. Never before have I mentioned the actions of Mom that I'm supposed to hide. But that's precisely what I'm doing, in Alma's basement flat.

In early February, I fly to Florida to play my first tournament of the year in Fort Lauderdale. After weeks of sessions with Alma, I feel battered by conflicting emotions. But I've practiced a lot, and I'm ready to compete. Ingrid's here, which means I have a pal, and we laugh a lot and talk up a storm. At meals, we play off one another, and sometimes other tables of players even join in the gaiety. Yet one subject is strikingly absent: the phone call in which I begged Ingrid for support because I'd been crying nonstop. She's my good friend, and if she avoids the subject, I figure everyone else will too, so I tell no one that I'm seeing a shrink. No one will understand.

My first round opponent is 17-year-old Martina Navratilova, from Czechoslovakia, who last year played in the States for the first time, but on the rival USLTA tour. News of her talent spread fast, although she undermined herself by binging on junk food and becoming pudgy. When we walk on the court for our match, I don't know what to expect, because I've never seen her play tennis. This tournament's on green clay, where almost everyone plays long points, but she attacks the net constantly, which rarely works on this surface. Clearly, she has lots of talent, but she misses too much, and I pass her at the net and lob over her head enough to win in three sets. But that's my only good result. In the next round, I lose to a lesser player. Ditto in the next tournament.

From the tour's earliest days, Mom wanted us to play every single tournament, to guarantee the fans the best possible fields. Now that the USLTA has taken over the tour, we can come and go as we please. So after just two tournaments, I return to London, where Alma begins to focus on my life on tour. I describe the fun I had with Ingrid, but I confess that I usually struggle to get through the day.

Alma says "Your life sounds lonely and grueling. I think you need someone to travel with, either a coach or a friend, who can provide companionship and also help you with all the details you have to take care of." Alma wants to understand and protect me, which feels strange and unnatural. No one has ever done that before. "I'm also worried about your injuries," she says. "You should think about playing fewer tournaments, to protect your body."

I reply: "I wish Jimmy Jones was different. He's a really good coach, but he doesn't understand my injuries or what I'm really like. I wouldn't want him to travel with me. And I don't know anyone else I'd want to travel with."

"You need to work on finding someone. You'll feel a lot better if you're less alone." Starting when I was eight, Mr. Hoxie called me the Manager, because I could manage difficult situations alone. I was proud to be so resourceful. I'm still proud of that, but now Alma's trying to convince me that I can and should ask for help.

CHAPTER 51
HIGHS AND LOWS

In 1969, I was ranked Number 5 in the world, but after that, I had three years marred by injury and suffering. With the help of Jimmy Jones, last year, in 1973, I returned to the world's Top 10. Now my goal is to climb closer to the top, but that will be unattainable unless I improve my current form. I'm hampered by the tough fields, where I usually win a round or two and then lose to a seed. I could improve if I got to play more matches.

In May 1974, World Team Tennis starts, which will change everything. Many women pros have signed with Team Tennis, which means they'll be absent from tournament play for four months. That could give me more opportunities to shine.

Even the Federation Cup, held this May in Naples, has been decimated. All the U.S. big names are absent. Billie Jean King, Rosie Casals, and Nancy Richey Gunter are playing Team Tennis, and Chris Evert is having a rest week. The USLTA selection committee has chosen me to play No. 1 singles and doubles, but they had to reach further down the rankings to fill out our roster. Still, our team is good enough to reach the finals, where we lose to a stronger Australian team, which is led by Evonne Goolagong.

The French Open draws are also weak, and I have little trouble reaching the quarters, to play Chris Evert. The day before the match, I phone Jimmy Jones and ask him to fly to Paris for the day, to help me. This year Chris has been invincible on clay, crushing everyone, even the top stars. But I'm not asking Jimmy to invent tactics that would magically help me beat her. More than anything, I need moral support. Even though I come close to begging, and I offer to pay him, he refuses. He's always been a good coach, but this coaching relationship is way too flawed. When Chris and I walk onto the stadium court at Roland Garros, I know I'm all alone. In the first set, she squashes me like a bug, but I take her to 7-5 in the second set. That's at least respectable.

Since the beginning of open tennis in 1968, the tennis world has been consumed with in-fighting. Although World Team Tennis is currently warring with the national associations, I'm hardly affected. And when I attend the second annual meeting of the Women's Tennis Association, I expect few controversies. Instead, I'm shocked when Billie Jean announces that going forward, membership in the WTA will be limited to women ranked in the top 20 in the world. I stand up to protest: "This makes no sense. Instead of shrinking our numbers, we should be opening our arms to invite more players, including qualifiers and juniors. That's the road to the future." I expect a roar of approval from the packed room, but there's only light applause. I really don't get it. I wonder why the players being excluded don't protest more. After the meeting, I call Mom in Houston, to tell her about the meeting. During her years in charge of the tour, she always insisted on having plenty of qualifying tournaments, to provide opportunities for as many players as possible. Billie Jean's announcement appears to be going in the opposite direction. Mom says: "This isn't right. I'm going to find a sponsor who will support all levels of the tour."

Wimbledon is starting right away, but I still haven't found someone to travel with. At Alma's instigation, I phone Vincent to ask if he knows anyone. His first reaction is to make fun of me, but then he says "I'll look around." The next night, he calls back. "I've found someone. Her name is Sally Hay, and she's a production assistant at the BBC. She's capable and reliable." He gives me Sally's phone number, and I call her immediately. With Wimbledon nearly upon me, I'm too busy to meet right away, but I decide to give her a tryout at the tournament in Newport,

Wales, that takes place after Wimbledon.

At dinner the first night, Sally's pleasant, and I like her, although I don't think we'll become best friends. Then she drops a bomb: "I need to be truthful. Vincent was my boyfriend for a short while last year. Your clothes were in his house, but you were away playing in the States."

Vincent's a scoundrel.

At least Sally told me the truth. I don't hold a grudge against her. I ask her to travel with me.

In early August, Sally and I hit the tournament trail, with stops in Indianapolis, Toronto, and Newport, Rhode Island. The weaker draws mean that I get more matches, and I start playing better. Another reason for my improvement is that Sally is supporting me, which takes a load off me. She helps organize my life, and I feel less lonely.

Next up is the U.S. Open at Forest Hills. I struggle in the first round, but I don't worry, because I'm feeling match tough. Afterwards, Sally and I eat crab stew at a bistro near our midtown Manhattan hotel, but we both wake up around 4 AM with stomach cramps and the runs. Once again I've gotten food poisoning. My next match, against Martina Navratilova, is scheduled for noon, so Sally and I set the alarm for 9 AM and catch a few more hours of sleep. When the alarm goes off, I call the tournament committee, tell them my predicament, and ask them to refer me to a doctor. I remember that Dr. David Jackson's Vitamin B12 injections helped me a lot, so at my 10 AM appointment, I ask the doctor to give me one. He obliges, and at noon, Martina and I walk on court. When I beat her earlier in the year, it was on clay, but Forest Hills is on grass, which should favor her attacking style. Even with the injection, I'm not operating at full strength, and I know I can't last three sets. I'll need to jump out to a quick start. I quickly ramp up my concentration; playing sick or injured usually helps me focus. From the start of the match, she madly rushes forward, but she leans in too close to the net, and nearly every time, I carefully loft a lob over her head. Fortunately, she never changes her tactics, and I win quickly and efficiently, 6-4, 6-4. I clearly dodged a bullet.

The next round is the quarter-finals, against Nancy Richey Gunter. My match against Billie Jean King at last year's Open was relegated to the Clubhouse Court, and this year, Nancy and I don't do any better. We're shipped to a different kind of Siberia, a court in the middle of nowhere. What a strange decision for a match between Nancy, who has frequently been ranked Number One in the U.S., and me, who has twice been ranked Number Two. The tournament director must not know that after the last few weeks of matches, I'm seeing the ball big and my confidence is soaring. Nancy and I are both known for our groundstrokes, so we have long, punishing exchanges from the back of the court, which I break up occasionally with a well-placed slice, a dropshot, or a darting foray to the net. The match is close, but I win in two sets, 7-5, 7-6.

Now I've reached the semi-finals against Billie Jean King. This is the first time I've come this far at Forest Hills. Although I usually keep my pre-match warm ups to 20 minutes, I'm having so much fun playing well that I keep going for 45 minutes. Too long. That was stupid. In front of a jam-packed stadium crowd (which holds 14,000), I start out playing great, and I win the first set 6-2. But the good times don't last. Fatigue strikes me, and Billie Jean takes over by reaching a higher gear and winning 6-1 in the third.

I'm doing the CBS broadcast again, so when my match is over, I run as fast as I can up the path to the Clubhouse, where I shower and change, and then, with my hair still damp, I run back to the Stadium to call the other semis, between Goolagong and Evert, which has already gotten under way. Not long afterwards, the skies open up, rain pours down, and the match is postponed until Saturday.

Saturday morning, Sally buys the papers, and I thrill to the words of Rex Bellamy of the *London Times*, acknowledging how well I was playing: "Julie does not hit the ball; she talks to it. She does not play rallies; she composes them. When things are going well (as they were), her ball control faithfully observes the dictates of a shrewd tennis brain—which is to say that her opponents can be teased into all kinds of trouble. She often toyed with Billie Jean . . . ."

Such a luscious tribute to my unique way of playing.

I show up to do the broadcast on Saturday morning at 10. It's still raining, and the weather forecast calls for rain all day long. If that happens, the tournament will have a ton of expenses and very little income. To avoid a financial debacle, the tournament director cancels the whole day's play at 11 AM. Ridiculously soon after the announcement is made, the rain stops, and the sun shines brightly. But there's no turning back.

Frank Chirkinian, the CBS producer, is stuck without a live match, so he decides to play a tape of my match against Billie Jean, which I'll analyze. It's extremely rare for a player to commentate on his or her own match. But on this sunny day in Forest Hills, that's what I do. Normally, the "talent" sits in the open broadcast booth, which is halfway to the top of the Stadium, but today, Pat Summerall and I will be ensconced on the ground floor in the covered Marquee, in case the rain reappears. The crew places a monitor in front of us, and we go live. I tell the country what it felt like during the match: how great a player Billie Jean is, why I served to her forehand, how she dominated the net, how I was seeing the ball well, and then . . . how she turned the tide and took over the match. Throughout the broadcast, I try to be honest and clear. Only once do I take a little potshot at Billie Jean. As we go to commercial when I'm 4-1 down in the third— the reverse of the score when she walked off the court last year—I say "Right now, I'm thinking of quitting." That was snarky, but I couldn't help myself.

Back at the hotel after the broadcast, a stream of people phone me, gushing at my performance. Only one man complains to me about the show, saying: "No one should ever broadcast her own match."

At the end of the day, I tell Chirkinian that I'll be available tomorrow for the continuation of the Goolagong-Evert semi-final, but not on Monday, the new date for the finals. I've agreed to be the playing captain of the U.S. Bonne Bell Cup team, and I owe it to the other team members to arrive in Shaker Heights, Ohio, as scheduled on Monday.

By midday Monday, Sally and I arrive in Ohio, ready for our first team meeting. We're a rag tag group, definitely the underdogs. Our only marquee name is Evert, but we have Chris's younger sister Jeanne, not the superstar herself. From the moment we get together, there's fun, excitement, and commitment. Kristien Kemmer, a member of the team, was just on the winning World Team Tennis team, and she's still stoked from their victory. I'm pretty darned thrilled that I'm playing so well, and I'm flushed with the belief that we can pull this off. So we feed off of each others' energy, and we have a blast.

But this won't be easy. Most of the Aussies are ranked higher than us, and they'll be led by Evonne Goolagong, who beat Chris Evert in the Forest Hills semis, and then barely lost to Billie Jean in the finals, 7-5 in the third.

Day 1 we lose both of our matches. Never mind, we'll do better tomorrow. Day 2, I win a singles match and a doubles match with Kristien, and at the end of the day, we're up four matches to two, just one match away from victory. Day 3 starts with me playing Goolagong. In the first set, I play attacking tennis, and I win 6-3. Everyone knows the expression "Never change a winning game." But I choose otherwise. From the start of the second set, I use a different style, giving her no pace, and I win 6-1. When the umpire says "Game, set, and match," I yell something like "Whoopee" and run forward with a broad grin to shake hands. Evonne looks at me askance and mockingly mimics me. I immediately feel sorry about my noisy celebration. She's such a nice person, and I don't want to upset her.

But after that moment at the net, I can't help hugging everyone in sight. We beat the Aussies. We did it! When our team gets together for the last time, we're drenched in happiness. This victory was special.

The next morning, I'm flooded with words of praise, about my success as a captain and my own play. One journalist wrote "Julie reached an emotional and physical peak to produce the most awesome and beautifully orchestrated tennis of her career."

The next day, Sally and I fly to Orlando for a clay court tournament. Ingrid's there, so we'll play doubles together. I'm still seeing the ball great, so I fly through a few rounds, and in the semis, I meet Billie Jean, who beats me often. During the first set, it's business as usual, as she dominates the net, but the tide turns in the second set, and I'm hitting the ball so well that victory is mine. After the match, the *Orlando Sentinel* reporter tells me that Billie Jean, who is avoiding interviews, was reportedly upset that I had "questioned several line calls." The reporter also tells me that in the other semi-final, between Frankie Durr and Martina Navratilova, both of the players questioned calls, and some were reversed. In fact, **most** players— Billie Jean included—argue about line calls. Maybe my intense determination makes me seem more ferocious than other players, but I don't knowingly break the rules. Billie Jean also said that I "disputed a line call after the point was played" (not that I remember), and that she didn't protest because she was "too tired." I think fatigue was probably a bigger issue for Billie Jean than disputed line calls. She'd worn herself out playing four months of World Team Tennis and then sapping every bit of her energy to win the U.S. Open, in a supreme effort of will.

Instead, Billie is claiming that I'm the culprit. I can't handle being unfairly attacked. For over a month, I've felt strong, both emotionally and physically, but now I feel my insides collapsing.

On the morning of the finals, I read the *Sentinel*, hoping to be showered with praise. The reporter complimented the way I played, but I focus on a quote from Martina: "I've always wanted to play Billie Jean in the finals. . . . I played Julie at Forest Hills and I understand what Billie Jean went through. I was disappointed in her." I assume she means she's disappointed in me. The words explode in my head.

It's yet another attack, this one so vague that it feels like a blanket condemnation. I read the quote again, and I become enraged. Ingrid tells me I'm overreacting, but I can't settle down, even during the finals, which Martina wins in straight sets.

The next day, we fly to Denver, where the next tournament is being played and where Trixie lives. We lead dramatically different lives. In the seven years since I graduated from Stanford, she's continued playing the bass guitar in a rock 'n roll band called the Anonymous Artists of America. They started out in the hippie world of Haight Ashbury, but after a few years, the group pulled up stakes and moved to a commune in the mountains of Southern Colorado. The band couldn't make money in the mountains, so they moved to Denver and tried to scratch out a living.

Although Trixie and I get along better as adults, our differences remain huge. I tell her that something inside me has snapped, and I'm having trouble coping. But she's quiet and withdrawn, and unequipped to help me as I slide further and further into distress. I play the tournament, but I lose badly, and I leave as quickly as I can. When Sally and I land in London, we go our separate ways.

In London, I still can't recover. I've split with Jimmy Jones, so I have no coach. Why do I stay in London? Maybe I should pack up and return to the States. But I need Alma. I go to her, hoping she can help me recover from this crash, but even she is having trouble helping me dig out of this hole. The suffering continues.

In the end of October, I'll play the Wightman Cup, to be held indoors, in Cardiff, Wales. I've been named the playing captain, and I'll be joined by several of the women who played by my side in the Bonne Bell Cup last month. In Cardiff, I'm up first, against Virginia Wade. It's a seesaw battle of three very close sets, with the outcome depending on just a few points, which I lose. Normally, I'm able to shake off a loss, even a close one, but not this time. I'm devastated, certain that I've let my team down. Even after I shower and change, I'm so distraught that I struggle to leave the locker room to sit on court with my players. In this condition, I'm not much use to them, and we dig ourselves the biggest hole ever: six matches for them, none for us. I even lose to a woman ranked far below me. In the last match, we barely resurrect some dignity by pulling out a lone doubles victory.

I decide our terrible loss is all my fault, and I wonder how I could have screwed up so badly. I torture myself by thinking that the Bonne Bell Cup victory was just a fluke, and that the nightmare in Cardiff was the real thing.

Back in London, I find a new flat on a fancy street in the Holland Park

350 DRIVEN: A DAUGHTER'S ODYSSEY

neighborhood. It's much larger and airier than the one Vincent leased for me, and it's a handsome abode, the ground floor of a Georgian house that has been carved into four flats. I hire movers, and once they bring my possessions, it becomes obvious that I don't have enough furniture. I want to decorate the place and fill it up, but I don't know how. I've spent so much of my life on the road that I've never watched flowers grow and bloom, and I've never built a nest of my own. I buy a few pieces of furniture, but I leave most of the place empty, including my giant living room, which resembles a long, wooden bowling alley, masquerading as a place to live.

The night of my move, I get a phone call from Fred Barman, an American promoter, who says "I'm holding a tournament in Japan, and we need another player. Can you come next week?"

I don't know why I accept. Maybe because my self-worth is so disastrously low that I'm thrilled that anyone wants me at all. But I have lots of boxes left to unpack. And I'm still suffering aftershocks from the comments made by Martina and Billie Jean and from my disastrous failure of leadership in the Wightman Cup.

I don't feel strong enough to go to Tokyo alone, but Sally isn't available, so on the spur of the moment, I ask Vincent's pal Yvonne to travel with me. We rapidly get our tickets and our visas, and a few days later I pour my exhausted body onto the plane, and we wing away to Tokyo, a 12-hour flight and a 9-hour time change. We're scheduled to refuel in Moscow, but as we approach the city, the captain announces: "Moscow is socked in with fog, so we have to turn back to Stockholm, where we'll sleep overnight." This is terrible news. I have no idea when I'll get to Tokyo. In our Stockholm hotel room, I phone Barman and say "I won't arrive until late tomorrow at the earliest, so I'll be unable to play until the following day."

He responds: "You'll have to play tomorrow. You're playing Sawamatsu," the Japanese Number One, who's an excellent player. "And your match will be broadcast live on Japanese TV."

"But I won't be able to get there in enough time. Please reschedule me." I assume he'll get some sense, so I decide to continue onto Tokyo. But when we arrive, he hasn't changed a thing, and I'm due on court in a few hours. I should just tell him I refuse to play. But I don't have enough emotional strength to fight him. In a fog of fatigue and gloom that began months earlier, I start the match, and I play quite well for one set. But then I hit the wall. I'm totally sapped, I can hardly move, and I lose the match. Because there are no changing rooms at the courts, Yvonne and I return to the hotel in a taxi, with me still wearing my dirty, sweaty tennis clothes. In our room, I collapse onto the bed fully clothed and fall sound asleep. But the respite doesn't last. A few hours later, I'm awakened by my bed shaking forcefully. We're in the middle of an earthquake.

The last year has slammed me around. Towards the end of 1973, my trip to Brazil filled me with energy and joy, which spilled over into my tennis. For the following months, my life was relatively calm. Starting in August, I began playing great tennis and imbuing my other pursuits with a golden touch. Yet way too soon, I had a huge crash, which hit me much harder than the Tokyo earthquake.

I desperately need to recover.

WORLD RANKINGS 1974

	World Tennis Magazine	Bud Collins Encyclopedia
1	Chris Evert	Billie Jean King
2	Billie Jean King	Evonne Goolagong
3	Evonne Goolagong	Chris Evert
4	Olga Morozova	Virginia Wade
5	Virginia Wade	Julie Heldman
6	Kerry Melville	Rosie Casals
7	Rosie Casals	Kerry Melville
8	Julie Heldman	Olga Morozova
9	Nancy Gunter	Lesley Hunt
10	Martina Navratilova	Francoise Durr

CHAPTER 52
NEW WORLDS TO CONQUER

When I return to London from Japan, I'm swamped with fatigue and feeling perilously close to the edge. I crawl into a shell, sleeping way too much and avoiding everyone but Alma, who helps me rekindle my life force. After a few weeks, I recover most of my energy, and I gain a measure of peace. I even start practicing at Queen's.

But my sessions with Alma have changed, in a distressing way. When I began going to her, I looked forward to our appointments, because they gave me relief. I used to leave soon after the hour was over, but now she fixes us a pot of tea, and we talk, but mostly about her life, and she's even begun to turn to me for advice and consolation. This doesn't feel right. I want her to take care of me, not vice versa. She still helps, but now my visits are tinged with dread.

With the onset of more energy, I turn to writing. Last September in New York, I got a contract to produce a tennis instruction book aimed at women who have never played sports. My goal is to be extremely upbeat and to soften my readers' fears about entering a world heavily dominated by men. Each morning, I sit down at the typewriter, hoping to complete a few pages. S+ome days, I zip along, but on others, the blank white page feels daunting. I try to stay upbeat, but I can't make the words come out fast enough. I'll have to work hard all year to meet my commitment.

In the beginning of January, I prepare to join the tour in San Francisco. Sally can't come along anymore, because she's started a full-time job. I don't know who else to bring. So I'll just go it alone.

From the first point of the first tournament, I play pretty well, relying on the excellent hands and fine tactical sense that never seem to leave me. But I'm on autopilot, and I lack the desire that could make me one of the very best players. Tournament after tournament, I win a few matches and flame out. Still, I make plenty of money, because the tour's purses keep escalating. I know many players would change places with me, but I used to do better, and I hate watching myself deteriorate.

Alone in a hotel room, I realize that I'm killing time until I can figure out what to do with the rest of my life. This is 1975, and I'll turn 30 in December.

That's too old to be playing tennis. Should I stop now? Most players teach tennis after they stop competing, but that's not for me. My knee still gives me chronic pain, and I can't imagine standing on my feet for hours every day. Plus I crave new challenges. I've already laid the groundwork for new worlds to conquer: writing, broadcasting, and doing public relations for companies. But so far, those jobs aren't paying enough to permit me to walk away from competing on the tour.

I've brought my manuscript with me, and every day I set aside time in my hotel room for the book, but I discover that writing during tournaments is nearly impossible. The stresses of the tour syphon off all my energy. Instead, my manuscript lies dormant, a silent accusation that I should be doing more.

In mid-March, I play a tournament in Houston. During my second-round match, I get a sudden, sharp pain in my shoulder. It comes and goes, attacking mostly when I serve, but also sometimes when I hit a backhand. I finish the match, which I lose. The tour now has a trainer, a luxury we never thought possible in the tour's opening days, but I've never asked her for treatment, because her constant companion is a player who has sometimes treated me callously in the past. I have no concrete reason to believe that the trainer would be less than professional with me, but since my childhood, I've been inordinately sensitive to attacks, and I avoid situations where they could possibly occur. So even though the pain is often sharp, I stay away from the trainer. Going to a doctor would seem to be the next logical choice, but who? And where? I don't know where to turn and who to ask. When I hurt my knee, I let Vincent take over choosing a doctor, and everything turned out terribly. For many people, this would be a time to call their parents. But not for me. Mom thinks all doctors are evil and out to get you. Dad also avoids doctors, although I'm not sure why. He's had shooting pains down his leg for years, but instead of seeking medical help, he shovels down a dozen or more aspirins a day.

I keep playing tournaments, waiting for clarity.

At the Family Circle Cup, which has moved to Amelia Island, Florida, I win two matches and reach the quarters, this time against Navratilova, who smothers me, 6-2, 6-2. My tennis is stalling while hers is revving up. Last year I beat her twice, but this year she's "owned" me, and now she's one of the best players in the world. The baton has passed to the next generation of tennis stars: Evert, Goolagong, and Navratilova.

Once again, I approach the tournament owners, Johnny Moreno and Jack Jones, offering my services as a broadcaster. On my behalf, they contact the

NBC team, who agree to hire me. Once again, I'll work with Jim Simpson and Bud Collins. It's always fun working with Bud, who's knowledgeable and often outrageous in front of a microphone. This year, the Family Circle broadcast will have three parts. First, Jim, Bud, and I will call the match live. Next, the director will edit the match down to an hour, including commercials. And finally, Jim, Bud, and I will do the voice over in an NBC studio in New York.

My schedule complicates matters. After the Family Circle Cup, I'll fly to London to see a doctor about my shoulder. The following day, I'll head out to Aix-en-Provence, where I'll be the captain of the U.S. Federation Cup team. Once I'm finished there, I'll fly back to New York for the voice over, an inordinately long commute.

In London, the doctor gives me bad news. "You've torn fibers in five muscles around your shoulder. You need to take a long time off, to let them heal."

I say: "I can't do that." Once again, our Fed Cup team is missing all the top U.S. stars, largely due to Team Tennis, leaving me to play Number One for the U.S. An exceedingly immature 18-year-old girl will play the Number Two spot. Without me, our team won't have a chance.

I say: "I'll have to play."

"I strongly advise you not to do that. You'll make your shoulder worse."

I arrive in Aix, determined to compete. Before I see the draw, I run into Ingrid, and I tell her that my shoulder is in miserable condition. Once I see the draw, I realize I should have kept my mouth shut. I'll probably play her in the second round, when the U.S. meets Sweden, and my confession about my shoulder may well distract her, because it's really difficult knowing your opponent is injured. And that's exactly what happens. Because of the pain, I play lousy and lose my singles to the Swedish Number One, a bad loss. But I don't give up, and everything comes down to the doubles, with me and my partner against Ingrid and hers. They come agonizingly close to beating us, and at match point for them, I direct a forehand at Ingrid at the net, but she bunts it long. We go on to win the match 8-6 in the third. I wonder if my confession broke her concentration. I put her in a terrible position.

Edy McGoldrick of the USLTA is in Aix-en-Provence to watch the Fed Cup. After our team barely defeats Sweden, Edy and I sit down to chat, and I tell her about my shoulder, and that I've frequently been sick and injured throughout my life. I say "I wonder if my root problem is psychosomatic." Later, I can't believe I said that. In fact, just a few days ago, the London doctor went to great lengths to explain why my shoulder is so bad. I'm confused and worried that my foolish statement could come back to haunt me. So I phone Alma, who interprets the situation: "Even though your illnesses and injuries have been very real, your mother always treated you as if you made them up. In your conversation with Edy, you blurted out your mother's message, as if it were the truth, which it isn't."

Our Fed Cup team reaches the semis, where once again we lose to an Australian team led by Goolagong.

Off I go again, to New York to do the voice over. It starts smoothly, but then I find an error while I'm analyzing a slow motion replay of Virginia Wade's serve. When the replay finishes, it starts all over again, a clear mistake. I hold up my hand, explain the problem to the director, and say "Don't worry. I can fix it. Just run it again."

On the second go around, I start by explaining one aspect of Wade's serve, and then I say "We should look at that again, to understand why hers is the best serve in women's tennis." Viewers probably won't spot the mistake, because I made it look completely normal.

I'm on a roll. I love being a broadcaster, and I know I can do the job extremely well. I desperately hope that broadcasting will be my ticket out of playing competitive tennis.

Once we wrap up the show, I bounce back across the Atlantic for the Italian Open. Not to play it; my shoulder is a wreck. In fact, I have nothing scheduled in Rome. I'm going there on spec to try to get hired for this week's NBC broadcast. Meanwhile, back in New York, unbeknownst to me, Teddy Nathanson, the director for NBC tennis, went to bat for me. When I see him in Rome, he says "You're doing a fine job, and you need an agent. Here's the number of my agent, Bob Rosen. He's in New York, and he's a really good guy. He's waiting for your call."

I immediately phone Rosen, who's friendly and knowledgeable, and he wastes no time in opening doors for me. He gets me a contract for the Italian and French Open broadcasts, with first-class expenses and really good money. "How about Wimbledon?" he asks.

I say "I'm not sure. I may want to play the tournament."

On the Saturday of the Italian Open, I begin my new broadcasting job. Jim, Bud, and I sit in the booth for hours, commentating on the best matches played on the Campo Centrale (the center court). When we finish, the production team drives to the center of Rome, to edit the tape in the studios of RAI, the Italian TV company. The plan is for RAI to broadcast the tape at 10 PM Italian time (4 PM in New York). But when everyone reconvenes at the Foro Italico at 9 PM Italian time, we're slapped with the bad news that the RAI studios have lost electricity, so we'll go live without any video to show. We confer about what to do, and I suggest a plan. I'll give the viewers a clinic on how to play on Italian red clay, a surface I know so well, but which is rarely found in the U.S. I've given so many clinics on the women's pro tour that I'm an old pro, so everyone agrees. At 10 PM, Bud and I stand in a lighted spot in the middle of the darkened stadium, describing how to slide on red clay, and how it differs from other surfaces. I know viewers would have preferred to see the matches, and we certainly wanted to broadcast them. But we had a crisis, and I did the best that I could. The next day, our broadcast glides along without a hiccup, and American viewers get to watch our very own Chris Evert beat Martina Navratilova in the finals.

Next stop, Paris. My shoulder hurts less, so I wonder if the torn muscles have healed. I decide to test it out by playing the tournament, hoping to win a round or two. Instead, I lose ignominiously in the first round to a journeyman player. I think long and hard about whether or not to play Wimbledon, and I come to the conclusion that I won't do myself any good by playing badly. So I check in with Rosen, and he gets me two more deals: Wimbledon and the World Team Tennis All Stars. This is exciting. My new career is blossoming.

After the French Open, I spend a few quiet days in London. I'm about to turn out the lights one night when the phone rings. Foregoing the niceties, the caller says: "Heldman! What the hell did you do to Billie Jean?"

"What?"

It's Rosen, calling from New York. "I just got a call from Chet Simmons, the President of NBC Sports. He said Billie Jean and her husband Larry have contacted NBC five times to get you off the air. What did you do to them?"

I'm dumbfounded, a rare state for me. "I can't think of anything I've done. Billie Jean and I have been at loggerheads for a long time, but I have no idea why she and Larry are coming after me now."

"Did you do anything to her in the past?"

"We've definitely had our issues. Five years ago, when the Houston players were voting for the first tour leader, I spoke for Mom and against Larry. I said that Larry had had failures, and after I spoke, Mom won the vote. That could certainly have pissed them off. And I only beat her a few times, but each time I did, she got angry, especially my victory at Forest Hills just before her match with Riggs. We've also had a few petty spats. But I can't believe she'd use personal issues to try to get me fired."

"This could be a problem. Chet turned them down, but I know he wouldn't like it if they keep going after you. So you better be on your best behavior."

"Got it. But this is coming out of nowhere."

I hang up and think: *Could this really be true?*

If it is true, I wonder why Billie Jean and Larry didn't say anything to me directly. But Rosen has no reason to make this up. Plus his reputation is pristine, and both Teddy Nathanson and Bud Collins sing his praises and trust him implicitly. And even though Bob's been my agent for a very short while, I think he's great, because he's been nothing but kind, helpful, and straight. And as to the President of NBC Sports, I sincerely doubt that he'd fabricate such a story. This is the last kind of problem he'd want to deal with.

I struggle to figure out what might have happened. Then I realize that Billie Jean and Larry might be trying to protect their "baby," the World Team Tennis All-Stars, which I'm slated to broadcast. Maybe Billie Jean and Larry are upset because I decided not to compete in Team Tennis, and they're worried I might say something harmful about it during the broadcast. I wouldn't do that. I have nothing against Team Tennis. The owners are paying the players really good money. In fact, the team that drafted me offered $50,000 for the initial four-month season, a sum far larger than I could have made anywhere else. I would have loved to take that money, but my body is fragile, and I need to protect it. I skipped World Team Tennis out of fear that its one-night stands would place me at risk for further damage.

But I'm just guessing that World Team Tennis is the issue. Billie and Larry haven't told me why they've gone after me.

There's one solid reason to believe that Billie Jean tried to get me removed: Two years ago, she did something nearly identical when she got Jack Kramer axed from the ABC broadcast of the Battle of the Sexes. But in that case, Billie Jean and Jack were bitter enemies. Is that how she sees me? If so, that's just plain wrong. Sure, we've been at odds from time to time, and there's definitely some bad blood, but I've been on her side on all the issues that have united our tour. Moreover, I've never said a bad word about Billie Jean publicly. In fact, in press interviews and during TV broadcasts, I've always spoken about her admiringly because I wholeheartedly believe that she's a great player, and that without her leadership and charisma, the women's pro tour wouldn't have such early success.

Thoughts are whirling around in my head. I can't magically make this problem go away. And I don't want to cause worse difficulties by confronting Billie Jean and Larry or bothering the suits at NBC Sports, who've already stood up for me. So I'll try my best to get on with my job and hope that somehow this crisis will subside.

So when Wimbledon starts, I'm on my best behavior. Our tiny booth, which overlooks Centre Court, gives us a unique and intimate perspective of the matches. In the Ladies' Singles finals, Billie Jean proves she's one of the best grass court players of all time when she slaughters Evonne Goolagong, now Mrs. Roger Cawley, 6-0, 6-1, to earn her *sixth* Wimbledon singles title.

Interviewing the great Rene LaCoste for NBC.

I'm also a member of the broadcast team for the men's finals, which is a big deal, because I'm the first woman to broadcast men's pro tennis. The match is fascinating, because it's between Arthur Ashe and Jimmy Connors, who are polar opposites. Connors is white, Ashe is black. While Ashe is always composed, Connors is usually rowdy and boorish. Connors has refused to participate in Davis Cup, while Ashe is committed to playing for his country. And Ashe was the previous President of the Association of Tennis Professionals, which Connors is currently suing.

At 23, Connors is the Number One player in the world and the prohibitive favorite. At a few days shy of 32, Ashe is past his prime, but he has a plan. He's always played slash-and-burn tennis, but this time he decides to employ a style he's never used before, to hit dinks and slices to screw up Connors's rhythm. The tactic catches Connors off guard, and it works. During play, I'm calm and contained, but when we go to commercial, I come close to screaming "Go, Arthur!" The crowd roars when Ashe wins in a big upset. I'm thrilled, although I know not to show it in public.

After Wimbledon, I fly to Los Angeles for the Team Tennis All Stars. I stay with friends of my parents, Edward and Cynthia Lasker, who live in a large house in Bel Air. Cynthia loves fashion and style, and I'm weak in those areas, so she takes me under her wing, carting me off to a fancy Beverly Hills salon, which does my hair and makeup. But when I return to the Laskers' home and look closely at my face in a mirror, I come close to tears, because my face is caked with what looks like thick mud. When Cynthia sees how upset I am, she calms me down and rubs off half the makeup. The result is startling. I'm really attractive! At the All Stars, plenty of tennis people compliment me on my looks. I'm happy, but focused on the job, and I get caught up in the Team Tennis excitement and the great players who are on display. I speak for a moment to Billie Jean and Larry, but they reveal nothing about their efforts to get me removed from the broadcast.

Even though I'm beginning to do more and more broadcasting, I still haven't decided if my tennis career is over. After nearly two months of rest, my shoulder hurts less often. So I decide to give it one last shot. In August, I play three tournaments, followed by the U.S. Open, which has now converted from grass courts to green clay. In all four tournaments, I play significantly below par. The pain is way too intense. I play my final match in the Forest Hills Stadium, a doubles against Chris Evert and Martina Navratilova. One point stands out. I charge the net alongside my partner, but Chris lobs over my head. I tear after it and twist to throw up a lob, but the movement results in pain so fierce that I double over. That's when I decide "Enough." My days of competing in tennis tournaments are officially over.

After Forest Hills, I fly to Cleveland, where once again I'm the captain of the Wightman Cup Team. I was also chosen to play, but I can't, which weakens the team. We have one superstar, Chris Evert, but the only matches we win are her two singles. Over the decades, the British have rarely beaten the Yanks in the Wightman Cup. Under my watch, the British have won the Cup two years in a row. Ouch.

The following week, I stay in Cleveland, to go to trial. Four years ago, while playing under the auspices of the USLTA, I ripped up my knee playing in the Wightman Cup right here in Cleveland. Vincent asked the USLTA to pay for my medical bills, but they inexplicably turned me down. Two years ago, with the statute of limitations running out, Vincent helped me hire Tom Heffernan, a Cleveland lawyer, who filed suit on my behalf against Uniroyal, the company that made and laid the court that caused my injury. I don't know why the lawyers didn't sue the USLTA also. Tom's been working hard to prepare for trial. He deposed Virginia Wade, who testified about how dangerous the court was. He also tried to depose Chris Evert, who played on the Uniroyal court that week, but she was only 16 at the time, and her father still won't let her get involved.

Now I'll have my day in court. During the proceedings, I sit silently, not understanding much of what's going on, as if I were a spectator in a theater of the absurd. Tom has arranged for Carole Graebner, our captain when the injury occurred, to fly in from New York to testify on my behalf. On the tennis court, she was a relentless competitor who rarely got nervous. In the court room, she looks flustered and keeps making mistakes. First, she testifies that she saw the injury occur, which wasn't true. Then she says "I told Julie not to play." Also untrue. When I take the stand, Tom asks me about how the injury occurred, how long I was out of commission, and how much my results were harmed after the injury. Then Uniroyal's lawyer cross examines me, but draws no blood. Finally, Tom calls an economist to the stand, to prove how much money I lost due to the injury. The economist's conclusion sounds useless to me: "I can say with 90% certainty that she lost somewhere between $30,000 and $90,000." That's an awfully wide range.

At the end of four days of trial, the jury awards me $67,000. How they arrived at that number is beyond me. I think they looked at the wide span of the economist's figures, split the difference, and then gave me a few thousand more. No matter. I feel vindicated. Uniroyal will have to pay me the earnings that I lost. Tom's work will bring me enough money to sustain me for quite a while.

But soon after the trial is over, Uniroyal appeals the judgment. I won't get any money until the appeal is decided.

I return to London to make a last-ditch effort to finish the book. After a year of sporadic writing, I've finished the table of contents, four solid chapters, and a bunch of snippets, but I haven't come close to completing it, and I don't love what I've written. I'm flummoxed. On the one hand, I made a commitment, and I really ought to finish the project. On the other hand, I'm hanging onto the project by a thread.

A phone call from Rosen changes everything. He offers me a wonderful prospect, to write the scripts for a series of tennis instruction videos that he's producing. Bud Collins and I will do the on-camera teaching, along with John Alexander, a handsome Aussie tennis star. And to ensure the quality of the project, Rosen has hired NBC's Teddy Nathanson to direct the shows. I accept right away. This is much more fun than the book, which I permanently set aside. Filming of the videos will start next month, in January 1976, so I immediately dive into the task.

CHAPTER 53
A DREAM DENIED

This is 1976, the first year in a very long time that I won't be competing in any tennis tournaments at all. I quit tournaments "forever" in 1966, but that retirement lasted only 18 months. This time, my retirement is most definitely permanent, a decision that's dictated by the chronic, severe pain in my shoulder. My biological age is 30, but my wounded parts—my shoulder and my knee—feel like they're 80. I'm putting my aging joints out to pasture, but I'm doing so quietly, without making an announcement. Younger players will take my place on the tour.

I thought I'd be thrilled to call it quits. I looked forward to scads of free time, without having to practice and play matches, but instead I feel flat and drained. I sleep endlessly, day and night, escaping the intense pain in my shoulder and the feelings about quitting tennis after 22 years of competition.

Still, my life is loosely tied to the tour. I have a contract with the National Tea Council to give a clinic at every tournament on the tour, and I write articles—mostly for *World Tennis*—about the women pros. I'm also writing a column for *Seventeen Magazine*. My first effort, titled "Should You Beat Your Boyfriend at Tennis?" was my best. My answer was "Yes, if you can, but if your boyfriend misbehaves because you beat him, then you should find a new guy." That's a howl, me giving advice about boyfriends. My record with men hasn't exactly been glittering. Last year, *Seventeen* also hired me to give a keynote speech at the banquet wrapping up its annual tournament in Mission Viejo, California, where nearly 100 girls from all over the country converged to compete in three age divisions. My 40-minute talk went so well that the magazine has invited me back for a repeat performance.

When I'm not occupied with those jobs, I hole up alone in Mom's New York apartment—Mom comes here less since she sold *World Tennis*—scribbling madly to finish the script for Rosen's videos. Tennis instruction can be overly technical and deadly dull, and I'm trying to avoid those outcomes. I light on the idea of making Bud Collins the goofy, comic relief. On the air, he refers to himself as a "hacker," although he's actually a very competent player, but in the videos he'll act dumb and sometimes swing and miss. I hope he's OK with that. With barely a few days before we begin filming the videos, Rosen calls again, and he's close to giddy, reporting an NBC offer that's the opportunity of a lifetime. They want Bud and me to broadcast all of their tennis this year, including the French, Wimbledon, and WTT All Stars, but also an eight-man, made-for-TV, men's event, called the Avis Challenge Cup. The tournament will last nearly four months, because only one match will be played per week. Every detail draws me in: The prize money will be a whopping $320,000; the event will be played in Kona, Hawaii and broadcast live to the Mainland by satellite, using cutting edge technology; NBC will broadcast 10 of the tournament's 15 matches; and the tournament's stellar roster will include Rod Laver, Ken Rosewall, Arthur Ashe, John Newcombe, Ilie Nastase, and the 20-year-old Bjorn Borg, who's already won the French Open twice.

I accept instantly.

But accepting means rearranging my priorities. I'll fulfill my commitment to do Rosen's videos, but I rapidly pull out of everything else: the clinics, the articles about women players, and the *Seventeen* magazine columns and speech. By doing so, I leave some people in the lurch. I wish I didn't have to do that, but broadcasting is my dream, and I hope it's my future. Besides, I'll spend many weeks resting and relaxing in paradise.

As I put the final touches on the scripts for the videos, I worry that I've left something out, but once we start filming at a resort in Austin, Texas, Bud and John Alexander, who are consummate pros, take my script as a starting point, and improvise masterfully. Bud manages to be both self-mocking and knowledgeable, and John plays the straight man who wants to teach great strokes. I jump in and out between my roles as writer and teacher, and we finish in two days, with a terrific product, to be shown on HBO.

In March, Bud and I fly to Kona on the Big Island, where life slides by at a leisurely pace. During the beginning of each week, very little happens, and I continue sleeping away my days and nights. By Thursdays, activity speeds up when we travel with the NBC crew around Hawaii to film teaser videos, to be shown at the beginning of each upcoming broadcast. Every Friday two great players fly in and practice. Bud interviews them, with me standing nearby, listening but not talking. Throughout my youth, many famous players visited or stayed with our family, but I was ignored and treated like the wallpaper. Since then, great players have always felt unapproachable to me. I wish I could get over that.

Bud and I make the broadcasts lively and fun. We let the tennis be the main show, and we never talk over the points, but neither of us likes to be too serious. Bud has a nickname for every player, and even a fake name for the net-cord judge, whom he calls "Fingers Fortescue." In the world of TV sports, there's a persistent undercurrent of sexism, which I sometimes try to undermine. For instance, TV cameramen delight in spotting random buxom babes in the stands, whom they show for no apparent reason. I never comment on that sexism, but I sometimes turn it upside down, by admiring Borg's "cute butt" or Newcombe's "magnificent mustache."

Bud has had plenty of broadcast partners, ranging from sober tennis aficionados to famous comedians, but I'm shocked when he tells me I'm his all-time favorite. I don't get much feedback from NBC, although Dick Auerbach, the producer, and Teddy Nathanson, the director, seem to like my work. However, I've heard a rumor that some men pros don't like me doing the commentary, but I don't know whether they disagree with my analysis or they reject me because I'm a woman. Or both.

In Kona, I rarely stray far from the hotel. But during our eighth week on the Big Island, a resident invites us to go snorkeling on his private boat, and I leap at the opportunity. I've hardly swum since I was seven, and I can barely stay afloat unaided, so they strap me into a life preserver, and I jump into the warm tropical water, where for the first time I get to see schools of breathtaking, multi-colored tropical fish. After only 15 minutes of unadulterated joy, I get the chills, and I have to return to the boat. By the time we return to shore, I'm running a high fever, which continues throughout the night, along with a ferocious diarrhea. In the morning, I visit a nearby doctor, who is clearly concerned: "Your fever is very high, and your blood pressure is way too low." He gives me an antibiotic and Kaopectate with opium. Between the illness and the opium, I fall in and out of delirium. The next day, Trixie calls from the Mainland to chat. When I hear her voice, I slur *"This is weird. I just had a vision that you'd walked into my room."*

The illness grips me like a vise, but despite massive fatigue, I continue doing my job. I fly to the Mainland for a different broadcasting gig, and then I return to Hawaii, for my final stint there. Next, I fly to Rome for the Italian Open. We spend several days scouting the matches, and one day Bud joins me in the stands. We talk a little tennis, and then, out of nowhere, he asks "Will you marry me?" My first reaction is: This is weird. We haven't dated, nor have we been the teeniest bit romantic. I think he's one of the nicest guys in the world, and I'm flattered, but I like him as a friend and a broadcast partner, not as a potential husband. I thank him, and I try to let him down gently.

On the final weekend in Rome, I still feel under the weather, but I'm committed to doing my job. We spend hours baking in the broadcast booth, commenting on how fabulously Italy's Adriano Panatta is playing and how much support he gets from the crowd. Once we wrap up, I accompany the cast and crew as we head to a fine restaurant downtown. But soon after the first course is served, I become woozy and fall forward, barely missing my soup. They send me out to the limo, where I collapse in the back seat, waiting for everyone to finish, so that we can return to the hotel.

I'm frustrated and scared. I've seen doctors on three continents, but none of them has diagnosed my illness. Determined to be healthy for the French Open broadcast, I spend a few days with friends in the South of France, and then I rest in bed in a Paris hotel for several more. I even forego scouting matches, an essential part of being a good commentator. On the final Saturday, I show up for work, sounding chipper and feeling fine, but during a men's semi-finals, I once again become depleted. But I'm a fighter, and I hold on until we go to commercial, when I fold over and collapse, neither awake nor unconscious, in a land between shadow and substance. Once we're back live, I sit up and work. Ten minutes later, I'm struck again, and I nearly pass out, but I continue working. On Sunday, the men's finals pits the American Harold Solomon against Panatta, who, even without the help of his home crowd, adds the French title to his collection during his magical spring. I survive the match without an incident, for which I'm thrilled. I desperately hope my health is turning around.

Monday morning, the NBC entourage arrives at the Charles de Gaulle airport for our flight to London, but after passing through customs, I come to a screeching halt. I drop my carry-on bag, crumple to the floor, and cry. I can't move. Auerbach orders a wheelchair, and I'm taken to the plane, where I can't stop crying. On board, he orders another wheelchair, to take me from the Heathrow gate to the limo at the curb. When we arrive at my flat, he has the limo wait as he phones Dr. David Jackson and waits for him to arrive.

David appears rapidly, and after examining me, he says "You're young and in good shape. This shouldn't be happening to you. I'd say you have either tuberculosis or typhoid." He sends me to a lab for testing, where the attendant looks at me like I'm crazy and says "This is ridiculous. No one gets typhoid."

When the tests come back, David's diagnosis is confirmed. I have typhoid, a horrifying disease, which if left untreated, kills 30% of its victims. For those of us who survive the disease, exhaustion is a major symptom, after the initial onslaught of fever and diarrhea. But combating typhoid has been unbearably difficult, because the disease is so uncommon in the U.S. and Europe that few doctors know how to spot it. In my case, seven doctors in two months misdiagnosed me. I'm incredibly lucky that David, my savior, is a brilliant diagnostician and knows me well.

Finally, I know what's wrong. But my worries aren't over. David says "There's only one medicine that cures typhoid. It's an old antibiotic, but it's really tough on the body, and there's a risk that you'll get aplastic anemia, which can be incurable. So I'll have to watch you closely."

Once I begin the medicine, I feel worse than at any time since I initially came down with the illness. I can barely move.

One month ago, I offered my London flat for the NBC pre-Wimbledon party. The building's spacious backyard is a perfect spot to hold an outdoor summer event in London. Little did I know that I'd be unable to help prepare for the party, or even attend it. When the guests arrive, I knock on my neighbor's door and collapse on his couch, where I spend the entire evening.

I finish the antibiotics on the day Wimbledon starts, but I'm still laid flat. David draws some blood and confirms that I'm anemic, but fortunately it's the curable variety.

I should be walking around the hallowed grounds of the All England Club, but instead I lie on a chaise longue in my giant but otherwise empty living room, sporadically sleeping and watching the tennis on the BBC. My flat is large, so I have enough room to host two Wimbledon players, Ingrid and Val Ziegenfuss, but we don't spend much time together, because their days are filled with practicing, playing matches, hanging around the tournament, and going out to dinner. Neither seems to fathom the enormity of my medical calamity.

With two days to go before NBC's first broadcast at the 1976 Wimbledon, I desperately want to believe that I'm well enough to do my job, so I undertake a trial run. An NBC limo picks me up at my flat and drops me off near the broadcast truck, on the edge of the All England grounds. My goal is to watch a few matches and talk to some folks, but I get only as far as the Players' Tea Room, where I crumple into a chair. I wait for a resurgence of energy, without luck, so I realize I have to return to the limo, which is parked by the NBC truck. Walking that relatively short distance seems unfathomable. A few feet away, I spot Virginia Wade, never my best friend. When I approach her, she looks surprised, and then disbelieving when I lay out my problem: I'm recovering from typhoid fever, I need to walk to the NBC truck, and I don't know if I can make it. "Will you please walk with me?" Still looking askance, she agrees to my request, and we saunter very, very slowly. I don't collapse, but several times I stop to lean against a bench. When we reach our destination, I thank her. She helped me with my lawsuit, and now she's helping me when I'm sick. I owe her, big time. Before the limo drives me to my flat, I tell Auerbach and Teddy Nathanson that I tried, but I'm not well enough to do the broadcasts this weekend. Later, I phone Mom with the same news. She barely reacts. She seems not to get what I've been going through.

So during Wimbledon's first weekend, I sit in my flat, all alone on my chaise longue, instead of holding forth in the teeny booth overlooking Centre Court. My days alone on the chaise give me too much time to cogitate. I conclude that I don't have much of a life in London, and there's very little reason for me to keep renting this flat. I made London my home base five years ago, when I moved in with Vincent. When he left me two years later, I stayed on because he rented a flat for me, and because my coaches, Jimmy Jones and Angela Buxton, were based here, and so was Alma, my therapist. Two years ago, I split with my coaches, but I remained dependent on Alma. But now I'm rarely in London anymore, and I'm ready to stop seeing her, in large part because it feels like she's become dependent on me. I feel confident in my ability to strike out on my own.

London is a wonderfully livable city, although I hate its gray skies and its frequent rain. But it's clear that I don't belong here anymore. I decide to move out right after Wimbledon. I call a moving company and get everything started.

During Wimbledon's second week, my energy increases enough that I can walk around the tournament a little bit. And I'm able to broadcast the women's and men's finals. In both matches, the younger generation takes over. Billie Jean's retired from singles play, so in the Ladies' Singles, the baton has passed to Chris Evert, who beats Evonne Goolagong (now Mrs. Roger Cawley) in a tight, three-set match. In the Gentlemen's Singles, Bjorn Borg, who's barely 20, and is mobbed by hordes of adoring teenage girls, faces Ilie Nastase, who's a few days shy of 30, yet he remains an extraordinary talent, a wacko, and often an unpleasant human being. Throughout the Championships, Borg has struggled with stomach muscle tears, and he's received at least three cortisone shots to control the swelling and the pain. Before the broadcast, I interview an orthopedic doctor, who takes me step by step through the medical implications of the shots, which I pass along to our viewers, resulting in effusive praise from Bud. Borg crushes Nastase in three straight sets, to adolescent shrieks of joy.

Wimbledon ends on a Saturday, and the movers show up in force the following Monday. I'm too tired to make decisions and too tired to help them. I tell them to take everything, and then I fall back onto the chaise. Later that day, two of the movers ask me if they should pack the canned food in the kitchen. I can't even decide that, so I just repeat my previous order: "Take everything."

Once again, I'm massively depleted, which brings another problem. I'm supposed to fly from London to San Francisco, to broadcast the World Team Tennis All Stars in Oakland. I've taken plenty of long flights before, but never in my current condition, and I can tell I'm not up to it. So I pull out of the broadcast. Even though I have no choice, I feel awful about canceling obligations.

I'm now officially homeless, and I don't know where to go next. My first thought is to settle in at Mom's apartment in Manhattan, but I don't feel strong enough to get by on my own. So I fly to Houston to stay with my parents, hoping someone will take care of me. But from the start, nothing goes well. A few days into my stay, I feel miserable, and I'm filled with questions. Why has the fatigue lasted so long? Could anemia be the culprit? Or a new illness? I ask Mom to find me a doctor, and she does, but he's useless. He ignores my history and proclaims that I have a heart murmur. David Jackson never heard one. Boy do I miss him. Mom doesn't help either. My sleep schedule is chaotic, and sometimes I sleep all night and other times most of the day. Anyone hearing my saga would understand that I need tender loving care. Mom instead becomes blameful. She tells me that my upside down sleeping habits prove that I'm completely well, and all I need is to play tennis with her as my partner, against two Japanese visitors. In other words, she wants to show me off. This is crazy, but I'm not allowed to tell her "No." So I suit up and stuff down my anger as we play two sets in the oppressive Houston summer heat. And then I feel worse.

Last year, Colgate Palmolive signed me to do promotional work and broadcasting for the 1976 Federation Cup, which Colgate is sponsoring. The event will take place next month in Philadelphia, in conjunction with the U.S. Bicentennial, and I've been looking forward to the job ever since. But it requires lots of travel and commotion, and I'm not strong enough to do it. I call my contact at Colgate and cancel my commitment. I get a call from Edy McGoldrick of the USLTA, who's heavily involved in the Fed Cup, and I tell her that PR tours aren't worth much anyway. When I hang up, I realize that was really stupid, that I've just dug myself a hole.

Within a few days, a good friend who knows the Colgate people well calls to tell me I've made some enemies with my remark. Plus Edy is telling everyone that I'm not sick, that whatever illness I have is psychosomatic. Psychosomatic typhoid. That's a new one. But it's my own fault, because of my dumb remark about PR tours and my equally ridiculous statement in Aix-en-Provence that my shoulder pain was probably psychosomatic. But the upshot is that Edy is spreading venom about me, and I'm feeling vulnerable and attacked. With nowhere else to turn, I tell Mom what's happening. Bad decision. Instead of helping me, she launches into an extended rant about how Edy was horrible to her three years ago. She doesn't even bother to address my situation.

I have to get out of Houston. I came here because I desperately needed help, which has been sorely lacking. Why didn't I know that would happen? Why doesn't it occur to me that Mom might harm me? Because I don't protect myself, I keep reliving my childhood agonies. I decide to pack my bags and fly to New York. Being alone there will be better than being misunderstood and mistreated in Houston.

In New York, I listen to music, catch up with old friends, and hungrily read page turners. I can't believe that I'm still exhausted five months after I fell ill.

After the Open, I get a call from Rosen. I look forward to his calls, because he's a friend, and he's been the bearer of good news. Not this time. "I just got off the phone with Chet Simmons. NBC won't be using you anymore. He told me you 'have enemies in high places.'"

Stunned, I hang up. I had no warning, no sign that the NBC higher ups were displeased with me. Which "enemies" is Chet referring to? My first thought is Billie Jean and Larry, because they came after me last year. Could they have done so again? Or has someone new, such as Edy McGoldrick, thrown fuel on the fire? Or maybe the NBC suits are fed up with me canceling commitments. But what if Chet's statement is actually a smoke screen for some other reason to fire me? There's no way to know, and no one's talking. My job with NBC was a dream, and far too soon, that dream has been denied.

This terrible news arrives as I'm about to embark on a week-long vacation in Haiti. I had high hopes for the trip, partly because I was banking on a resurgence of my strength. But it's hard to have a good time after such a slap in the face.

When I return to New York, I finally feel well. In Mom's apartment, I discover a barrage of messages, some from Bernie Weiss and others about him. I met him three years ago on a short flight from London to Edinburgh. He was unavailable at the time, because he was married. His situation must have changed, because Mom, Rosen, and Bernie have all told me to call him. Although we previously met for only a short time, I remember liking him a lot, largely because of his devotion to his two sons, which touched me deeply. So I phone him, and he tells me he's recently separated from his wife, who's moved to Los Angeles with the kids. So he's free, and we agree to go out tonight. Forty-five minutes before he's due to arrive, the doorbell rings, and I look through the peep hole to find out who's there. I recognize Bernie, who's a tall and burly guy with curly brown hair and eyeglasses that are askew. When I open the door, he says "I hate driving in Manhattan, because I always get lost. So I arrived early and started driving around. But the traffic is awful, and I gave up. So here I am." I was beginning to be annoyed that he was early, but I'm taken in by his delicious, broad smile. Inside the apartment, he hands me a package, saying "They're Dianne von Furstenberg scarves. We have an eyeglasses company which has a license to sell her frames, and we give her scarves away with every purchase." I have no idea who Dianne von Furstenberg is, but I keep that tidbit quiet.

Bernie's going through a tough time, torn between wanting to be near his boys, wanting to live out his fantasy of becoming the Casanova of Manhattan, and wanting to find me. He started the latter quest by calling the Information operator in Houston, because he'd followed my tennis results in the newspapers, which listed Houston as my home town. The first Heldman he dialed was Mom, who gave him Rosen's number.

On our date, we go to a nearby restaurant, where we have a bunch of drinks and laughs, and then he draws the nearby tables into the hilarity, so that everyone has a rollicking good time. Afterwards, partly due to the excess of alcohol in his system, he stays the night. In the morning, we say goodbye, but soon afterwards, the doorbell rings. It's Bernie. He doesn't have enough money to get out of the garage. I hand him a $20 bill, and he says "I'm flying to Las Vegas today, so I'll call you from there."

The next day, he sends a telegram saying "I BET YOUR $20 ON ROULETTE. LOST IT, DOUBLED IT, AND LOST THAT. YOU OWE ME $40" This guy is unlike anyone I've ever known: warm, caring, goofy, and crazy funny. He's a keeper.

CHAPTER 54
APPLYING TO LAW SCHOOL

From the start, Bernie and I are drawn together like powerful magnets. His company is located an hour outside Manhattan, but he keeps returning to the city to spend all his free time with me. With previous boyfriends, I've felt a range of emotions, from excitement to betrayal, but with Bernie, I feel something entirely new, the profound sense that we belong together.

With the Christmas holidays approaching, he invites me to go on a vacation with him. "A friend is loaning me a chalet in the Swiss Alps."

"That sounds great!" I say.

The next day, he reports that the chalet is no longer available. "But there's a lovely hideaway in the Caribbean."

"Wow, that's terrific!" I say.

The next day, he bears more bad news. "Our schedule doesn't work. The house isn't available the week that I'm free." I try to hide my annoyance.

One more time, he calls, barely able to contain his excitement because he's made a reservation at a resort in Aspen. An hour later, he calls back. He has to cancel. There's no snow there this season.

We end up in Santa Monica, spending the first night of our vacation on his wife's (they're separated, not divorced) couch, while she escapes to Palm Springs.

The following morning he lays another surprise on me: "I have an unexpected business trip to San Francisco today. Will you watch the kids?"

For breakfast, I take the boys to an International House of Pancakes. As we eat, I discover that Seth, age 12, isn't happy that his dad has a new girlfriend. Darren, age 9, is deaf and has a wild excess of energy, so he needs to be watched closely. And the two of them fight frequently. Our time together is strained.

The next day, Bernie's sister Myrna takes the kids, leaving us free to move into a motel by the beach in Malibu. But it isn't much fun, because Los Angeles, which usually enjoys mild weather, is being deluged with torrential rain, and we're mostly trapped in our room. When we board the plane for New York, Bernie's sad to leave his kids, and all I want to do is get away from him and his whole family. At the JFK Airport, I stay with the luggage while he goes to retrieve his car. Forty five minutes later, he steps out of a taxi in front of the terminal and says "Don't say a word. Just get in the cab." We had flown separately from New York to L.A., and he'd forgotten that he'd left his car in La Guardia. That's it. I've had enough. Too many things have gone wrong. When he drops me at my apartment, I curtly say goodbye, expecting never to see him again.

Two weeks later, I'm in Fort Lauderdale, staying with friends, when the phone rings. It's for me.

"Don't you love the sunny weather in Florida?" It's Bernie. He's flown down here to make up to me. Never a dull moment.

When I'm not cavorting with Bernie, I try to plan how I'll make a living. I've quit playing tennis competitively and I've been shut out of NBC broadcasting, which is a huge problem, because the company airs most of the big tournaments. I toy with the idea of broadcasting something other than tennis, like the nightly news, but I'd have to pay my dues by starting in a small market, then building a reputation so that I could snag a job in a medium-sized market, and then I'd need to keep chipping away to move up in the business. That doesn't appeal to me. I've been on the road for so many years that all I want to do is lay down roots.

Mom is dipping her toes back into women's tennis. She's organizing a four-week tour called the Lionel Cup, to be held this spring, and she offers me the job of tour director. I'm wary of working with her, but I accept, because I need the money, and I have further qualms, because the tour will star Renee Richards, the transsexual tennis player. Before her sex change, she was Dr. Dick Raskind, a renowned pediatric ophthalmologist who starred on the Yale tennis team and then played men's tournaments back east. But now that she's a woman, she wants to compete in women's pro tournaments. Last summer, when she was outted, there was a hue and cry, and many women pros wanted her banned. Mom and Billie Jean supported her, saying that she was a woman, and should be treated like one. They pointed to the fact that surgery has radically altered parts of her body, and they claimed that because she now takes estrogen, she's medically a woman. But their logic is faulty, because it fails to explain the impact of testosterone on her system during her formative years. She has the shoulders, legs, and feet of a man. Estrogen can't change that bone structure. She doesn't belong in a women's draw.

But I'm working for Mom, so I keep my opinion to myself, and in public, I support the Lionel Cup and Renee Richards's right to compete against women.

Several months before the Lionel Cup tour is due to start, Mom leaves town for a separate promotion she's running in Hawaii. She says "I'm leaving you in charge, to make all the decisions." During her absence, not much happens, but whenever an issue arises, I take care of it, and I enjoy feeling competent. But when she returns, she cuts me off entirely, never communicating with me or giving me anything to do. I feel undermined and close to distraught. I don't want to be treated like this. I'll finish this job, but I vow never to work for her again.

One door after another is shutting on me. I'm at a loss for what to do next.

Out of nowhere, the Dalton School invites me to give a talk to students on "Careers Day," which is perfect for me, as I've had many careers—tennis, journalism, public relations, and broadcasting. When I enter the school, I run smack into Miss T, one of my all-time favorite teachers. When she asks what I'm doing, I summarize my last 15 years, and I tell her that I've had enough of being subject to someone else's whims. To attain security, I'll need to return to college to learn a profession. I started Stanford pre-med, but I had to give it up. "I'd still love to be a doctor, but I'd be almost 40 before I could practice medicine. I can't figure out what else I could do."

"You've always had a logical mind," she says. "Why don't you become a lawyer?" Wow, I never thought of that! She's right. How could she remember me so well after 15 years? I'm really lucky.

When I return to Mom's apartment, I start focusing on law school. I'll have to take the multiple choice entrance exam called the LSATs, but I'm 31, and I haven't taken a test like that since I was 16, so I'll need help. Friends suggest that I sign up for test preparation classes at the Stanley Kaplan School.

I get help in an unusual way. Bernie and I take in a World Team Tennis match at the Felt Forum, the smaller venue at Madison Square Garden. Billie Jean King and Virginia Wade of the New York Apples are crushing Betty Stove and Joanne Russell of the Seattle Cascades, and when they reach 5-2, I say "This set is over. Billie and Virginia don't lose when they're up this far."

Bernie replies "I'll bet $20 on Stove and Russell if you give me 10-1 odds. If the New York pair wins, you'll get $20, but if the Seattle pair wins, I'll get $200."

"You're on," I say, feeling sorry for him for taking his $20. But from that moment forward, Stove and Russell blow through the next five games, barely losing a point. At the end of the set, I pull out my checkbook, and the fans around us, who've recognized me and overheard our bet, start ragging me: "Hey Julie, we want cash, no checks" and "He knew more than you did, Julie."

I hand the check to Bernie, who returns it to me, saying "Use it for your Stanley Kaplan course."

I should thank Billie Jean and Virginia for losing and helping me apply to law school.

The next day, I enroll at the Stanley Kaplan School. In my first class, I'm bored big time, so I walk out, and I concentrate instead on taking their many practice exams, which are very helpful. Some days, I inhale three or four of them. Once I realize that the LSAT exams are meant to trick you, my scores improve dramatically.

No matter how close Bernie and I become, he can't bear to be far away from his kids. So he quits his job and plans to start his own eyeglasses company in Los Angeles. I don't know what I'll do without him. I cry when he leaves, but I plan to visit him often.

In late June, I place my pursuit of law school on hold and fly to London, because NBC has hired me to broadcast the Wimbledon Ladies' Singles. But they make it clear this is a one-off deal, and they treat me like an intruder. I have no idea whose decision it was to exclude me from NBC limos and NBC meals. Fortunately, Bud's his usual friendly self, and we still work together well.

To celebrate the Centennial Wimbledon, Queen Elizabeth makes a rare appearance in the Royal Box to watch the Ladies' Singles final between Britain's Virginia Wade and the Netherland's Betty Stove. Stove is tall, hefty, and strong, and she overpowers Wade during the first set. But the crowd badly wants "Our Ginny" to win, and they boost her energy with their cheers. Time and again she dashes to the net to put volleys away. When she triumphantly takes the Ladies' Singles title for Great Britain, there's an almighty roar. Because I've played both players, I'm able to unravel the interplay of the players' personalities and tactics, yet even though the broadcast goes exceedingly well, NBC doesn't want me back.

When I return to New York City, I take the LSATs, and when it's over, I'm sure I nailed it. A few weeks later, I find out I was right. I have a really high score. That means lots of law schools will want me, but the question is where to apply. The choice is narrowed once I move to Santa Monica to live with Bernie. I need to be near him. We find a small bungalow that's close to the beach and close to his kids. I refuse to move away from Bernie for law school. I apply to the best two law schools in Los Angeles, UCLA and USC.

Living with Bernie means I've inherited a remarkable, extended family. Dinners often include his sister Myrna, her husband Richard, Bernie's wife Linda, with whom he's remained close, and the kids. Linda and I have also become friends. Darren spends nearly half his time with Bernie and me. We like to say that his custody arrangement depends on who has the best dinner that night. I learn how to speak clearly to Darren and how to teach him, and I become an important figure in his life.

Because my undergraduate grades were disappointing—I nearly flunked Psychology in my last quarter--I won't be a shoo-in at either UCLA or USC. I decide to ask my cousin Johnny Kaplan for help. He's an acclaimed law professor at Stanford, well-positioned to come to my aid. I call him up, and he invites me to visit, even though we hardly know each other. I discover he's kind, funny, energetic, and forever generous. He's such a great teacher that each year hundreds of students sign up for his undergraduate criminal law course, to hear his unique insights delivered in a lively, Brooklyn brogue. To meet the demand, the university broadcasts his lectures live on the Stanford radio station. His knowledge about most subjects is encyclopedic, but he knows nothing about sports, and he had no idea I was a successful tennis pro. Still, he rolls up his sleeves to help. He knows many professors at UCLA Law School, and he plans to talk to them on my behalf. He also comes up with a way for me to overcome my less-than-stellar grades. He explains that after I graduated from Stanford in 1966, professors helped students remain in college to avoid the Vietnam War draft by giving them significantly higher grades, a phenomenon called "grade inflation."

"You'll need to write an essay showing that your grades would have been higher if you'd been at Stanford during grade inflation." Brilliant! I return to L.A., spend a few days among the stacks at the UCLA Education Library, and write a killer essay that makes two arguments: one about grade inflation and the other that I was a competitive athlete, which distracted me from concentrating on my studies. Within a few months, a fat envelope arrives, telling me that I've been admitted to UCLA Law School.

I plan to use the $67,000 award from my lawsuit against Uniroyal to pay for law school, but I can't touch it until the appeals court makes its decision, which seems to be taking forever. Two years after the end of the trial, my lawyer Tom Heffernan finally calls to say that we lost the appeal, in part because my captain Carole Graebner testified "I told her not to play," which wasn't even true. The court also opined that because I was a professional athlete, I should have known the court was dangerous. So the court based its ruling on an untruth and a garbled fantasy that I was an expert in court construction.

The upshot is that I won't get the large chunk of money I've been counting on. Tom tells me I have two options, either to retry the case or call it quits, but his firm is pressuring me heavily not to return for another costly trial, because there's no guarantee I'll win, and Carole's statement will remain damaging. I'm reluctant to throw in the towel, but Tom convinces me by sweetening the deal. His firm offers me $15,000 tax free if I'll go away. Reluctantly, I accept. I hope I'll have enough money to carry me through law school.

CHAPTER 55
LOSING LAURA

I'm enjoying some leisure time in Santa Monica Canyon, sticking my feet up and watching the flowers grow outside our cottage. In one month, law school will start, and I'll be plenty busy.

The phone interrupts one of my reveries. It's Dad. He says "Laura's very sick. She has only a short time to live."

"Oh no." I need to see her.

Dad continues "She has lung cancer, and she's decided against chemotherapy. She said she doesn't want to take drugs that make her suffer.'"

"I'll come right away." I hang up and make a reservation for the next fight to Houston. Even though Laura's retired, Mom still pays her well, and Laura lives rent-free in her own house, a small, air-conditioned structure on my parents' property. Mom has told Laura she can live there as long as she likes.

As soon as I dump my luggage, I knock on Laura's door, something I've done all too seldom. She's always been sturdy, but now she looks fragile, and she's nearly bald.

"Hello, darlin'. It's good to see you. I hope you don't mind I'm not wearin' my wig."

I gulp. I didn't know she wore a wig. I know so little about her.

Laura and I sit down to talk. For the last decade, I've rarely asked her how she's feeling, because she'd rabbit on interminably about her many ailments. Most frequently, she'd say "I got de gas," or "I got de ah-thuh-ri-tis," and then launch into her symptoms. Today she simply says "I know I's almost at the end." She turns instead to happy memories, of the times when I was little and she cared for me. As always, she says "You was like my own true chaald."

I think of Laura fondly, but I regret so deeply that I don't love her. A piece of me is missing, and I wish I knew why. Laura's always been part of the family, but excluded from activities outside the home. My biggest regret is that she never saw me play tennis, either in practice or at a tournament.

Our conversation is short, because we don't have much to say. I give her a big hug, and I vow to see her tomorrow, knowing that I actually lost her long ago.

CHAPTER 56
LEARNING A NEW PROFESSION

It's August 28, 1978. The U.S. Open is heading in a new direction, and so am I.

After being ensconced at the West Side Tennis Club in Forest Hills for 60 years, the Open is moving to Flushing Meadows. The new site is barely three miles down the road, but it represents a wholesale change. Our country's biggest tournament will now be held in a public arena instead of a private club; the view from the Goodyear blimp will morph from a pleasant landscape of grass into a sharp-edged mix of cement and steel; and while the West Side Tennis Club has strained to keep up with the tennis boom, the Flushing Meadows site has plenty of room to grow and keep apace.

The changes in my life feel equally monumental. I'm leaving tennis, my life's focus since I was eight years old. I'm getting out because tennis has been a mixed blessing. While it fed my drive to succeed, it has also brought me enormous physical pain and emotional trauma, the latter largely due to Mom's overbearing presence. To forge my own path, I need to leave the game behind.

During the first day of play at Flushing Meadows, I attend orientation lectures at UCLA Law School. I've prepared assiduously. I've bought my books and read my assignments, and I've carefully chosen my notebooks and pens. Bernie thinks my detailed planning is hilarious. "You spent more time during one afternoon at the stationary store than I did when I was studying for all my finals." But I succeeded on the women's pro tour in part because I was a mistress of careful planning with a ferocious drive and an otherworldly ability to concentrate. Those traits should serve me well in law school.

On the second day of the Open, my law school classes begin. Most of my first-year classmates are 22 years old, having come straight out of college, and many are dreading the hard work ahead. I'm 32, desperate to leave my old life, and thrilled to begin my next career. I'll go until I drop.

While the tennis world carries on without me, I discover that I love law school. I enjoy exercising parts of my brain that I'd left fallow since college, and I also get a kick out of opening the morning newspaper to find the myriad ways that the law impacts our lives.

I study unremittingly, reading every page that's assigned, and I show up in each class prepared to participate. Most professors use the Socratic Method, asking questions meant to teach students to think for themselves, and assigning pages in casebooks that summarize actual lawsuits. I love reading their tales of woe and their insights into people's lives. It's easier for me to remember personalized stories than to memorize by rote, which is a pill.

I'm particularly fond of my early morning Contracts class. I enjoy puzzling out the answers to the professor's questions, and from my assigned seat in the front row, I'm totally engaged. I constantly raise my hand, and I'm almost always right, but one time I'm wrong, which leaves me mortified. Out of my mouth spill the words "I'm sorry. I'm sorry," the talisman I've always used (unsuccessfully) to protect myself from Mom's humiliations. After class, a student stops me in the hall and says "Don't be upset. We're thrilled that you're so active and eager to speak up, because it takes the pressure off the rest of us."

A few weeks into the semester, my cousin Johnny calls to check on me, but also to report that the torts (personal injury) casebook used at Stanford—but not at UCLA—describes the appeals court decision in *Heldman vs. Uniroyal*, my lawsuit. Johnny says the book included my case as an example of a really bad legal decision.

Before I started UCLA Law School, I read Scott Turow's book *One L*, about his first year at Harvard Law School. He described an unhappy place, where the professors were abusive, and many students were hyper-competitive. I worried that UCLA Law School would be the same, but I've been happily surprised with its pleasant collegial atmosphere. I tell Bernie: "There's much less pressure here than on the tennis tour."

My desperate drive to succeed has been transmuted from the tennis world to law school. I apply myself at a grueling pace, studying diligently throughout the semester, and raising my hand frequently in all my classes. At the end of my first semester, I have two finals, and I prepare for them by reviewing the reading and my notes, and by taking every relevant practice test in the law library. A week later, our grades are posted anonymously, with a code number instead of a name. I get an A and an A+, for which I'm momentarily thrilled, but the joy soon fizzles, and I call Bernie in tears: "I'm not Number One in the class. Someone has higher scores than I do."

He gently chuckles at my distress: "And you said there was less pressure in law school." But it's true! The pressure I feel comes from my internal fires, not from the school itself.

At the beginning of the second semester, Johnny Kaplan visits L.A. and speaks with some of my professors, who report that I'm doing really well. My criminal law professor is particularly impressed. He likes my final exam so much that he shows it to students who need to improve their test-taking skills. Johnny is especially pleased, as I'm family, and he went out on a limb to help me.

In the spring of 1979, Mom calls to tell me that she's being inducted into the International Lawn Tennis Hall of Fame. Everyone in tennis has known this day would come, because she's been such a key figure in the evolution of modern tennis, and no one has done more. On the phone, Mom downplays her Hall of Fame selection, although it's the most important honor in the tennis world. In fact, she never speaks of it again, and she even fails to invite me to Newport, Rhode Island for her induction ceremony.

May brings my remaining finals and their posted grades. Mine are still excellent, but I can't help feeling discouraged that they're not the very best. Still, I don't remain discouraged for long. I just put my head down and vow to keep trying. Determined to absorb the entire law school experience, I dedicate myself during the summer to becoming a member of the UCLA Law Review by writing a "Comment," the student version of a law review article. The first step is to find a topic. Some students contact their professors, who are aware of issues in their field that are ripe for comment, but I'm stymied. I just can't knock on someone's door asking for help. I don't want to be a bother. Instead, I find a topic on my own, while reading a newspaper article about police raiding a lawyer's office in San Diego. What if the police rifled confidential client files? This raises a host of privacy and constitutional law issues, and I'm off and running. I work on the comment for nearly eight weeks, and the final product is very long and good enough that the Law Review accepts me.

During the summer, I acquire another responsibility. While leaving the law review office one day, I run into Professor Steven Yeazell, who taught me first-year civil procedure. He says "I'd like to offer you the job as a teaching assistant for legal research and writing. I believe very strongly that legal writing should be clear, compelling, and free of jargon. I need three TAs, and I've already found two, but I'm having trouble finding a third. Two have turned me down, but I hope you'll accept." Wow, what a ringing endorsement. I'm way down on his list of candidates, and he doesn't even bother to say that he likes my writing. But I accept anyway. I really want to help others, and I agree with his philosophy about writing.

Right before the beginning of the fall semester of my second year, Yeazell organizes a session in which several UCLA graduate students in English train the TAs to teach writing. It's both a refresher course in grammar and a call to use as few words as possible. Time and again, they refer to the writing manual called *The Elements of Style*, by Strunk and White, in which the sentence most often used is "Use short sentences." Perfect.

In my first year, the legal research and writing course taught me a lot about research, but very little about writing. It's a pass/fail course, and the TAs rarely did more than give me a check mark. I decide not to fall into that hole. This year, the students' first assignment is to write one page about themselves, just to give us a sample of their writing. Mary O'Hare, the lawyer who's running the Legal Research and Writing program for all the first year students, assigns me 30 papers to review, and I'm fascinated, because I expected all the students to write well, and although some papers really are excellent, others are actually awful. Those students have a lot to learn. So I decide to teach them. I sit down at my typewriter and explain in detail what the student did well and what he or she needs to learn. Some of my responses are twice as long as their submissions, and I require nearly half of them to do a rewrite. I'm not just giving check marks. I want them to improve.

I agree to meet with any student who needs more help, and some of those encounters are intriguing. I'm amazed to discover that the best papers come from students with backgrounds in science and philosophy. While their writing may not be flowery, it's usually clearer and more logical than the writing of students with backgrounds in English literature.

Last year, I worked extremely hard. Now that I've added Law Review and being a TA, I'm on overload. To survive, I make adjustments. I still attend classes and take detailed notes, but I no longer read the assigned cases before class. There just isn't enough time. But I still do my rigorous preparation for finals, and that's when I catch up, delving deeply into the cases the professor emphasized in class. My method works well, and at the end of my second year, my grades remain high.

The summer after my second year is jam packed with activities. I have a job downtown with a prestigious law firm. The work isn't too taxing, as the firm's goal is to entice me to work for them after I graduate. I learn several important lessons: I don't like commuting downtown, and I don't like the unpleasant lawyer who supervises me most of the summer.

I'm also busy working hard at revising my Law Review Comment so that I'll be appointed an editor. Unfortunately, the Comment Editor assigned to supervise my work is lazy and dismissive, and he gives me very little help, other than to tell me that I've misread several cases that are core to my arguments. He leads me to believe that my Comment won't be accepted, and I won't become an editor. I don't give up; I just have to carry on alone, without much guidance.

I'm thankful that Bernie's an easy going guy who understands my fanatical need to succeed. Even though I work too hard, we always set aside time to be together, often with the kids. My relationship with Bernie feels deeper than anything I've ever had before. I want to stay with him, but I want a bigger commitment, so I decide to take a big step. I invite him to dinner at a small French bistro on Santa Monica Boulevard, and as we enjoy the fine food and wine, I ask him to marry me. He says "I'll get back to you on Labor Day."

That doesn't feel good, so I ask him what's up.

He says "You know I love you, but the decision isn't easy for me, because the breakup of my marriage was painful, and I don't want to cause you and the kids any more pain."

Four weeks later, in the late afternoon of Labor Day, I leave the Law Review office, and I return home, where I discover Bernie feeding the kids dinner, a rare event. When they leave for their mother's house, I ask Bernie if he's made up his mind.

"I'll tell you my answer tomorrow, when the deadline's up."

"The deadline is today."

"Uh oh. The truth is that I'm working on it. I brought the kids over to ask them how they'd feel if you and I get married. Seth said he likes the idea, because he doesn't want us to split up the way Linda and I did. Darren seemed completely comfortable with the concept, because you're like a second mom to him."

I say "That's all fine and dandy, but what's the answer?"

"The answer is 'Yes.'"

"That's fantastic, but I do I have one requirement. You have to get divorced."

"That's reasonable."

At the beginning of my third year in law school, the current board of UCLA Law Review editors appoints its future replacements. A list is posted, and my name is on it as a Comment Editor. I should be pleased, but tears keep rolling down my cheeks. Although my own editor tried to lower my expectations, I still harbored a fantasy that I'd be named Editor in Chief, the highest position. I understand that becoming a Comment Editor is an honor, but I feel diminished, because I'm not Number One. For several days, tears keep flowing, which harkens back to my reactions when I was a child and I lost a match. I'm now 34 and ashamed of my tears, which I try to hide.

In my third year, I work even harder than before. Mary O'Hare asks me to stay on as a TA for another year, plus I'm now a Comment Editor for half a dozen second year students who want to follow in our footsteps as editors, and I work hard to help them. Moreover, I take several seminars where I undertake lengthy essays. In Entertainment Law, I write an extended argument that television should provide closed captioning for the hearing impaired. Living around Darren has taught me how devastating it is to be deaf, so I write the paper for him and for others who are similarly afflicted. The Entertainment Law Journal gets wind of my work, and they decide to publish my article as "Television and the Hearing Impaired."

I work day and night, often in crushing pain from the shoulder I injured playing tennis. I also suffer from bad allergies, and I drip and sneeze day and night. I work harder in law school than I did as an undergrad at Stanford, when my intense drive hadn't yet fully evolved. I also work harder than I did as a professional tennis player. A tennis pro has clear physical limitations, which I ignore in law school. I go until I drop, then I push some more.

Other people work extremely hard in law school, but my brand of work is unusual, because I dedicate so many hours to helping others. Tennis required me—and most others—to be self-centered in order to succeed. I'm thrilled that I can now be of use.

I add to my busy schedule the job of getting Bernie divorced. I start by buying a book called *Do Your Own Divorce*, where I find the necessary forms to complete. I fill in everything except his financial arrangements for alimony and child support. I tell him "That's up to you."

I also decline to show up in court on the day of their hearing. I prep Bernie by explaining the documents and teaching him the magic words for ending a marriage in California: "irreconcilable differences" and "irrevocable breakdown." Once he's in front of a judge, however, Bernie stumbles to get the words out. Fortunately, he'd already charmed the judge, who interjects the phrases for him.

I need to plan my wedding, but I have no idea what to do. Into the breach jumps Trixie's close friend Mary Corey. Their lives have had many parallels. Mary was at Dalton just before Trixie, and years later they lived close to each other in communes in the Sangre de Cristo Range of the Rocky Mountains in Southern Colorado. Mary currently lives in her mother's house in Beverly Hills, and she magnanimously offers to design our wedding.

Bernie and I set the date for a week after my graduation, which I badly want Mom and Dad to attend. The wedding ceremony will be held in the hillside garden behind Mary's house. And we want a rabbi to marry us, but we don't know one, so Bernie leads the search.

But far too soon, Bernie and I realize that we can't afford the wedding, because our finances are crumbling. When we first met, he was the vice president of a major optical company, based in New York, where he earned a hefty salary. He left that job to move to California, to be near his kids, and since then, money has been harder to come by. He currently has to change jobs, and I've run through all the cash I'd set aside for law school. I call Mom and tell her our predicament, and she doesn't hesitate. "We'll pay for your wedding." She's always been extraordinarily generous with money.

Soon, Mary begins taking me on shopping trips, for a wedding dress, flowers, food, wine, and more. I'm glad she knows what she's doing, because I don't. I know a lot about tennis and studying law, but very little about the world most people live in.

A few days before graduation, I discover that I'm being showered with honors. Early this year, Mary O'Hare surreptitiously decided that the world needs to know how great a job I've been doing as a TA, so she started a campaign to get me nominated for two prestigious awards. She emphasized how many students I've helped and how much they respect me. Her favorite story came from a conversation between two students that she overheard while she was walking down the law school hallway.

One said "I have great news! Julie liked my paper!"

The other replied "She made me redo mine, and now I'm writing better."

I knew nothing about Mary's campaign until I received a congratulatory phone call from the UCLA Law School Alumni Association, which has named me the Outstanding Graduate, Class of 1981. A few days later, I get another call, this one from the UCLA Association of Academic Women, which has named me a Graduate Woman of the Year. I'm also walking away from my law school career with a certificate from the Order of the Coif, the law school equivalent of a Phi Beta Kappa key. And of course I have my UCLA Law Review certificates, one for being a member, the other for being an editor.

Bernie tells everyone "Julie got every award UCLA Law School had to offer." I love his pride in me, and that he can crow about me on my behalf, but I was always taught not to boast, so I tuck away my law school awards in the back of a drawer, near my tennis medals. Besides, no matter how many awards I receive in law school, I know the truth: I wasn't Number One either in my class or in the law review.

Mom and Dad arrive in Los Angeles the day before my graduation, which they attend, at my request. The event lacks excitement, but I enjoy it, because I've been happy here. Once it's over, I walk out into to the bright Southern California sunshine, in search of my family. I find Mom, who says "Thank god that's over. I need a drink. Let's get out of here." I'd been living under the delusion that she'd be on good behavior this week. Foolish me.

During the following week, family and friends arrive from near and far for the wedding. Trixie has come from Colorado, Bernie's parents have flown in from Florida, and a smattering of friends, including Ingrid, have braved the long flight from England.

On our wedding day, guests enter Mary Corey's garden to the sounds of baroque music (as Bernie says, "as symbols of our financial condition"). Linda arrives, escorted by Darren and Seth, who look handsome in their new suits. Also in attendance are all the members of our extended family. The remainder of the guests represent many different worlds: tennis people, people Bernie knows through the eyeglasses business, law school friends, and an eclectic assortment of friends who have gathered to celebrate with us.

A handsome rabbi weds Bernie and me in a brief, touchingly beautiful ceremony. Afterwards, the question most often asked is "Is the rabbi single?" After the vows, neither Bernie nor I can stop grinning. Then it's time for hugs all around, followed by food, drinks, and dancing.

Mom and Dad paid for the wedding, but they're the first to leave. They don't say why. They just say "Goodbye," and then slip out a side door.

The night of the wedding, Bernie and I spend a "honey night" in a hotel, and then I dive back into work, preparing "Television and the Hearing Impaired" for publication. I don't buckle down and study hard for the California Bar until the last few weeks, but I trust in my ability to write essays. After three long days of testing, I figure I passed but I'll have to wait six months to find out.

Two weeks after I take the Bar, we finally take our honeymoon, a 10-day rafting trip down the Copper River in South Central Alaska. We chose the trip because of Bernie's love of the great outdoors. But the weather is wet and cold, the worst in 100 years of recorded history. I hide inside our tent, and all 10 rafters, except Bernie, have moments of despair. He blissfully glides through the physical challenges, hoping for more.

CHAPTER 57
"HI MOM, I'M PREGNANT!"

After Bernie and I return from our honeymoon, I begin a one-year clerkship with Judge William Norris on the Ninth Circuit Court of Appeals. A federal appeals court clerkship is a plum job, offered to students who excel in law school. The work is right up my alley. It's similar to law review, because we do research to help the judge make his decisions, and we write drafts of his opinions. Sometimes judges co-opt their clerks' work wholesale; other times they use only bits and pieces.

During my clerkship, I have far less work than in law school, but my path is rocky. The first draft opinion I write stays on the judge's desk for several months, and he refuses to talk to me about it. As always, I become distressed by anything below the highest praise, so when I ask him for feedback, and he gives me no advice, only a suggestion that I should learn from my co-clerk Susan, I feel diminished, and over time, I grow to despise him. Fortunately, Susan's a kind and generous soul, and we become good friends. I'm shocked and disgusted when she reveals that the judge, a married man, is making unwanted advances towards her. He's invulnerable, because federal judges are appointed for life, and she feels stuck in an intolerable situation.

So do I. The judge isn't hitting on me. He's just poisonous. I stay far away from him by retreating to the court's law library, where I read voluminously and work hard at tightening up my writing.

In December, I learn that I've passed the Bar. Before I graduated from law school, I thought about becoming a law professor, but the pay isn't terrific, and Bernie and I are hurting for money, so I decide that once my clerkship is over, I'll find a law firm where I can bring home a larger income. With my law school record, I'll likely have plenty of choices. I make a wish list for my future job: I want a short commute; a small to medium-sized firm with an excellent reputation; and a corporate law department. I don't want to be a litigator. I've had my fill of fighting **on** a court, and I figure that fighting **in** a court would be equally hard on me. Many people tell me to go into sports law, because I'd be a natural. But I've heard that sports agents have to do a lot of hand holding, even fielding calls in the middle of the night, which turns me off. I assume that business clients will let me sleep through the night, so I decide to become a corporate lawyer. I'm not fond of doing scads of interviews, so I ask a few law school friends if they have any suggestions, and several mention the same 20-lawyer firm in Westwood—a reasonable commute from home—which has a small corporate department. I apply there, and they offer me a job. I'll join them next August.

My life is changing dramatically, and so are the lives of Mom and Dad. In the early spring of 1982, Dad retires from Shell Oil, after 37 years on the job. His co-workers take him to lunch and present him with a watch. Engraved on its back are the letters "FOFWW," which stand for "Faithful Old Fart With Watch." At Shell, he got a job for life, a pension, and a watch. Mom went the entrepreneurial route, and instead of receiving a watch, she sold her magazine for two million bucks, after taxes.

Mom and Dad decide to pull up their Houston roots and move to Santa Fe, New Mexico, even though they hardly know a soul there. This decision leads to a bunch of real estate deals. They sell their house in Houston and their ranch in Conroe, Texas, an hour north of Houston, and they buy a house in Santa Fe, which has enough grounds for them to build an indoor tennis court that's sunken six feet into the ground, to comply with Santa Fe's building codes.

After these transactions, there's still money left over, so Mom calls me and offers to buy us a house. "Why don't you find an agent, and when you have some houses lined up, we'll fly out and look at them." This is extraordinary news. Since law school, Bernie and I have had a tough time scraping together our monthly rent. With our own house, we'll be vastly freed up.

I've recently been playing tennis at the Riviera Club with Johnny Moreno, Dad's old rival and a founder of the Family Circle Cup tournament. I really like him and his wife Tish, who's a real estate agent, so I put her on the case. She rapidly finds some houses, and after Mom and Dad fly out, we spend a Saturday morning examining all of them. I think they're all great, but Mom has legitimate concerns about several, because they're older and they might need lots of repairs. She really likes one of the newer houses, and she decides to make an offer, "but I want to buy the house with all of its furnishings, so that you can get rid of all your awful furniture."

Mom giveth and she taketh away. In the midst of her unmatched generosity, she belittles me and makes me feel rotten. I should be used to her put downs, but I never see them coming, so they always hit me hard. And I'm confused. Does her huge gift erase everything hurtful she's ever said? I don't have an answer.

Mom finally chooses an unfurnished, nearly new house in an area called Rustic Canyon, one of the loveliest corners of Los Angeles. And it's close enough to the house where Darren and Seth live with their mom.

We take our ratty old furniture with us to the new house, and when Mom and Dad move to Santa Fe, they send us their excess furniture, some of which is fabulous, although much of the rest is crap. Oh well. Until we get established financially, we'll have to live with a crazy, eclectic jumble.

Meanwhile, after working for Judge Norris for nearly nine months, I'm still trying to gain his respect. Towards the end of my tenure, I get a big opportunity, when he assigns me a case involving the exceedingly complicated interplay of several sets of laws. Determined to get this right, I camp out in the library until I understand all the laws, facts, and precedents, and then I write an opinion that I'm proud of, and I hand it in. A month later, at the end of my clerkship, he still hasn't discussed the case with me. I guess I'll never win.

Several months after I start working at my new firm, I get an unexpected package from the judge. He doesn't enclose a letter, just a signed copy of his opinion in the case I slaved over. He used almost all of my work, and he adopted many passages verbatim. Apparently, sending me his opinion is his version of a compliment.

I have high hopes for my first law firm, but it's a bust. Its litigation department is booming, but its two-lawyer (including me) corporate department is in a slump, and I'm rarely busy and often bored. Just as I'm planning to quit, a headhunter calls to entice me to change jobs. "There's a firm called Hill Wynne

Troop and Meisinger in the building next to yours. Its corporate department is doing exceptional work, and they're looking to hire right away."

In a blur, I interview, I'm hired, and in August 1983, I start at Hill Wynne. On my first day, they throw me into a public offering, but only as a grunt. I'm determined to work like hell to show my stuff, and I keep being rewarded with increasingly difficult projects, ongoing stellar feedback, and lots of respect. Along the way, I make new friends. On the weekends, Bernie and I drink, dance, and laugh with my fellow lawyers. Everybody adores Bernie. He's so funny and charming that people enjoy being in his presence, even when his humor is barbed.

It's June 1984. I'm 38, and I've been at Hill Wynne for almost a year. An incredibly exciting year. Although I'm just a second-year associate, and I've never run an initial public offering ("IPO"), I'm already doing 90% of the work on an intricate and innovative IPO, a job usually performed by an upper-level associate or a partner. In this project, a partner is theoretically overseeing my work, but he's too busy working on other deals, so I'm mostly flying solo. And working incessantly. In June, I bill 304 hours in 30 days, and I'm whipped. On July 4, Bernie brings me dinner at the office, and I work until I hit the wall at 3 AM, when I crash for a few hours on a partner's couch. I wake up early, slug down a few mugs of coffee, and return to my intense pace. A few hours later, Bernie shows up with breakfast, lunch, and a kiss. I thought my workload would lighten up in July, but we encounter some last-minute glitches before we can file with the SEC. Once we've filed, I discover that my July billable hours have once again topped 300. I'm operating at a high level and billing insane hours. That makes me a profit center and a darling of the partners.

I'd hoped for a few days' rest after the SEC filing, but the project took so long that, although I'm seriously exhausted, I have to get ready to cover the tennis in the 1984 Los Angeles Olympics, which are about to start. Several months ago, I agreed to be the *World Tennis* reporter for the Olympics, where tennis is once again a demonstration sport—just as it was when I played in Mexico in 1968. This time the event is limited to amateurs who haven't yet reached their 21st birthday. The first day of play, I wander around the site, watching a little bit here and there, when a pal grabs me by the sleeve and says "You've got to see this." On a side court, 15-year-old German Steffi Graf is winning easily, blasting unreturnable forehands. After watching her for just a few minutes, I'm dumbstruck by her skill and her concentration, and even more by her aura, which reminds me of the 16-year-old Chrissie Evert. I'm certain Steffi will be a superstar. She goes on to win the event, and the graceful Stefan Edberg wins the men's. In my story for *World Tennis* I shout to the world that Steffi Graf will soon be the best woman player in the universe. The editor who hired me for the job was replaced just before the Olympics by Neil Amdur, a renowned and well respected tennis journalist. When my article comes out, he's cut it to pieces and omitted any reference to Graf's future stardom. I'm seriously pissed off. But the tennis world is now a mere sideline for me. Law is my main gig.

After the Olympics, I take two weeks off work, but instead of resting peacefully, I cry fitfully, and I don't know why. I've been weepy before, but never without a reason, so I visit a doctor to find out what's wrong. After I describe my work habits over the last few months, he says "You've been going too hard. The body has limits." He has no medicine to offer me, no miracle cures. Just kindness.

I turn to Bernie's sister Myrna, who's a psychotherapist. She tells me I need therapy so that I can learn to slow down. Eight years ago, when I left London and split with Alma, I thought I no longer needed help. I guess I was wrong.

Myrna sends me to her friend and colleague Phyllis Rothman, who is tall, dark-haired, well dressed, and empathetic. I start by telling her I know I'm working too hard, but then I rapidly change the subject, and the same distressing childhood stories that I told Alma come streaming out of me.

I'm desperately careful to ensure the accuracy of my stories, yet they often seem alien to me, as if they happened to someone else. And while the stories tap into a deep sadness, my tears have dried up. Instead, I cross my arms in front of my chest, hold on tight, and shake. At first, the stories and the shaking are confined to Phyllis's office. But soon I can't control my fragile emotions at home, and I beg Bernie to hold me at night as I shake. Neither one of us understands the power of what's going on. Bernie says "Your mother can't hurt you. She lives far away, and she isn't in your daily life." But I'm compelled to tell my stories to everyone: family, co-workers, and even casual acquaintances. Most people look at me blankly, hoping I'll shut up and go away. But the spigot has jammed, and I can't shut it off.

In an attempt to contain my internal explosions, I rapidly ramp up to seeing Phyllis three times a week, and I feel better. She tries to impress on me that I'll need to maintain a slower pace permanently. But in the fall, once we receive the SEC's comments, I kick into high gear, and all over again I work long, intense hours, until the IPO goes live, and then on every new project I take on. The partners clearly appreciate quality work and lots of billable hours. Their approval seeps into my pores and makes me feel good all over. I keep seeking that praise.

After the Olympics, I slow down for two months, and I feel better. Phyllis tries to impress on me that I'll need to maintain that slower pace permanently. But once we receive the SEC's comments, I kick into high gear, and all over again I work long, intense hours, until the offering goes live, and then on one new matter after another. The partners clearly appreciate quality work and lots of billable hours. Their approval seeps into my pores and makes me feel good all over. I keep seeking that praise.

In December, the head partners give the associates their annual review. We sit in our offices, waiting for the phone to ring, which might happen right away, within hours, or another day. I have trouble working while I await that call. Finally, my phone rings, and I head down the hall for my review. No surprise, it's terrific. I've done great work and pushed myself to the brink. But then everything turns upside down. First, one of the firm's founding partners tells me I made a big mistake by telling our public offering client that I was exhausted from hard work. It turns out my firm was underhandedly billing me at a partner's rate—which is much higher than mine—but they failed to let me in on the scam. By casually mentioning my fatigue, I inadvertently blew the firm's cover. The partners' failure to tell me what they were doing and then blaming the backlash on me is downright disgusting.

Next, another partner, Bob Wynne, tells me he's angry because the previous month I hung up on his client. Wynne had asked me to write a contract, which I did right away, and delivered it to him to review. A month later, when the client called me, the contract was still sitting on Wynne's desk. At first, the client was merely nasty, believing that I had failed to do my job. I tried to buy some time, so that I could alert Wynne about the problem, but the client became increasingly belligerent and started screaming at me. I tried holding the phone away from my ear. I tried offering to check the status of the contract and then calling the client back. But he just screamed louder. I can't bear screaming. I had too much of that as a child. So when my ears filled with white noise, I slammed the phone down. I made a beeline for Wynne's door, but he was busy, so I left a message with his secretary and a voice mail on his machine. Soon afterwards, the client called Wynne, ranting about my rudeness. And now Wynne is reinventing the incident, laying the entire blame on me, and taking no responsibility himself. This whole thing sucks.

I'm supposed to be deferential to the partners, but instead my anger comes bubbling up. I blurt out that most of the associates are unhappy because they're working too hard. Everyone in the room looks pissed off at me, and then another partner chimes in to tell me that I don't dress well, and I need to look more professional. This is the first time I've heard this complaint. I'm embarrassed and hurt that he dislikes the way I look, and I walk out the door, leaving for my appointment with Phyllis without a goodbye.

In the car, the floodgates open, and I can't stop crying. In Phyllis's office, I sob inconsolably for the full session. Returning to work, the tears won't stop. Phyllis calls me, searching for a way to help. Nothing works.

I go home and call Bernie. We've had tons of fun with my fellow lawyers, but to please the partners—and because I'm so intensely driven—I work way too hard. I know that if I stay at the firm, I'll keep working until I drop. I don't know how to slow down. But Phyllis has convinced me that slowing down is essential to my health. How can I slow down without leaving the firm? I start crying again.

I phone Bernie, and I say: "I don't know what to do."

Bernie says "Why don't you come work for me?"

Sixteen months ago, Bernie launched a startup company, USA Optical Distributors, even though we were broke. His working capital consisted of a loan from our newly divorced neighbor and a small bank loan. His plan was to sell high quality, designer eyeglass frames to small optical offices, and to give away gifts with purchase ("premiums"). He vowed to keep his costs low by purchasing frames only after he already had orders to sell them and by telemarketing, which was heretical to optical industry insiders.

But Bernie kept at it, growing the company conservatively to keep it afloat. Its headquarters consisted of two small, low-rent offices on the second floor of a building in a seedy portion of Inglewood, located just south of Los Angeles, a short ride from the airport. Towards the end of each month, USA Optical received large shipments of frames from its vendors. Bernie and his employees removed the frames, repackaged them, and shipped them out again within a day.

When the UPS driver complained about having to run up the steps multiple times during the month-end heavy shipping days, Bernie instructed his employees to drop the boxes from the second floor walkway into the arms of the driver standing below. Fortunately, eyeglass frames are very, very light.

USA Optical has grown steadily, but it's still quite small. Bernie promises me I can start working with him once the company is solid enough to pay both of our salaries. If I go to work for Bernie, I'll stop practicing law, which I love. I'll miss puzzling through complex matters, negotiating deals, and schmoozing with my co-workers. But I won't miss the exhaustion from overwork, belligerent clients, or partners who pull dirty tricks.

When Bernie offers me the job, I get a flush of excitement. This could be a way out of my predicament, and I could lead a slower life. Then out of nowhere, I get a flash of insight. If I stop working like crazy, I could have a baby. Only once have I ever seriously considered motherhood, when I was with Vincent, and he snatched away my dream by making me have an abortion. But now that dream could become real. I recently turned 39. My biological clock is ticking insistently. There isn't much time.

I tell Bernie "I accept your offer."

The only people who know about my plans to leave the firm are Bernie and Phyllis. I don't want to blow my cover to the partners until we're sure that USA Optical can keep growing profitably. And I definitely say nothing to my parents about wanting a baby. Mom sometimes tells jokes to anyone, from family to strangers, about matters that are intensely personal to me. Nothing could be more personal than having a baby.

For six months, I wait for Bernie to tell me the time has come. In June 1985, he finally says "We're ready for you," and I become the newest USA Optical employee. My job doesn't start smoothly. Bernie is a master of sales and marketing, but operations aren't his forte. The systems he developed for tracking premiums is convoluted. He's delegated most of the responsibility for operations to Fred, his rogue office manager, who spends most of his time as far as possible from Bernie, so that he can operate without supervision. The other employees tell me that Fred is beyond sleazy, and that he keeps a couch in his office so that he can have sex with job applicants. But I can't fire Fred. He recently told Bernie he was gravely ill. Wanting to do the right thing, Bernie went overboard and guaranteed Fred employment for life.

Bernie is technologically challenged—he struggles with anything mechanical—but when USA Optical opened its doors in 1983, he agreed to computerize the company's sales and accounts receivable, even though personal computers are in their infancy, and there are many glitches. It's far too easy to delete all the data on a hard drive, or to restore the wrong backups.

Months before I started working at USA Optical, I bought a second-hand computer, to teach myself a few programs. On my first day at work, I bring the computer with me, expecting that I'll just hook it up and get started. Instead, I get a nasty surprise. My office is empty. There's no desk, no chair, and no bookcase. When I ask Fred where the furniture is, he wheels in a small chair and then disappears down the hall. I figure, OK, if I have to go it alone, I'll get started right away. I drive to a discount furniture store, buy what's needed, and haul everything back to USA Optical's tiny headquarters. Slowly, I lug my booty up to the second floor, and then into my office, where I sit on the floor and assemble the pieces. At the law firm, I had secretaries and word processors at my beck and call. My life has changed dramatically.

Bit by bit, I make my mark at USA Optical. I develop new systems for premiums and accounts payable. When I find out that Fred stopped paying a data entry clerk overtime, and justified his actions by bogusly changing her title to "manager," I reverse his order, because it's illegal. Soon it becomes clear that Fred's tenure at USA Optical has to end. I tell him "I know that Bernie promised you a job for life, but you aren't doing a good enough job, so I have to let you go." He leaves without a fight.

But there are some things I can't change. Bernie's best sales rep is often rude to me and inappropriate. I can't say anything. I have no authority over anyone who reports to him.

Even though I still see Phyllis three times a week, my emotional pain remains severe. Again and again I tell her stories showing how much Mom hurt me, but the memories rapidly disappear from my conscience until I tell them again. But telling them has made my relationship to Mom increasingly strained. I phone her less frequently, and then I stop calling altogether. I write her letters instead.

Now that I've slowed down, I can concentrate on getting pregnant, but the months seem to drag on endlessly. Finally, after almost a year, my tennis training comes into play. On the court, I had to trust my instincts and be aware of subtle changes in my body. When I wake up one morning, I know something's different, and I go straight to the doctor's office to ask for a pregnancy test. Several hours later, he calls. I'm having a baby!

I tell Bernie's side of the family the wonderful news, and then I call Trixie. But I can't just call Mom out of the blue. It's been nearly a year since we've talked. So I write her, explain that I have good news, and tell her I'll phone in three days, on Sunday, between 4 and 6 PM her time.

I phone at 4 PM. Their phone rings and rings, but there's no answer. So I phone again at about 5:50. Mom answers. Dad never picks up. To talk to him, I have to put in a special request.

"Hi Mom, I have great news. I'm pregnant."

"Oh how nice. But we have to go now. We're having dinner at La Fonda at 6. It's 5:53 now, and we'll have to leave by 5:55, so we won't be late."

Shocked, I say "Ok. Goodbye," and hang up. My loving mother. I'll be 41 in a few months. Trixie's 42. This is probably Mom's only chance to have a grandchild. She sure doesn't seem thrilled.

I won't let Mom ruin my pregnancy. There's too much to do. First, there's the problem of my aging eggs. The chance of a baby having a genetic deformity increases dramatically once the mother hits 40, so the doctor sends us to a genetic counselor, who presents us with the option of doing genetic testing very early in the pregnancy, using a test called "CVS" or chorionic villus sampling, which carries a 2% risk of harm to the embryo. We'll know the results almost immediately. We jump at the chance. I'm scared. I realize that I want this baby more than anything.

I call Mom and tell her I'm worried. She says "I'm sure it'll be fine."

I ask to speak to Dad. He says "The risk is very small, so don't worry."

They're both right, but I'm 40 years old, the health of my baby is on the line, and my fear is palpable.

I take the CVS test, and we find out right away that the baby's a girl, and she's genetically perfect.

I call Mom. "Isn't that nice." She just doesn't get it.

Then come the nausea and the fatigue, the constant companion of many a pregnant woman in her first trimester. I go to work and to Phyllis, but I do little else, other than spending hours at a time lying in bed watching the baseball playoffs.

Now that we know the baby is fine, we need to name her. The Jewish tradition is to name a baby after someone in the family who died recently. Bernie's father died three years ago, so we search for female names similar to William or Bill. Wilhelmina just doesn't cut it. Nor does Billie Jean. We buy a book of baby names, thinking we could still honor Bill by using the first letter of either William or Bill. Nothing. So we start over, looking at names in alphabetical order. We barely turn the page when we're drawn to "Amy." It's an easy name, and it means someone who is loved. And she might be just a spec in my uterus, but I already love her dearly. So from now on, we'll refer to that growing life as Amy.

During the first two months of my pregnancy, Mom phones occasionally, but without much enthusiasm. I call my sister, hoping she can explain our mother's behavior. Trixie has a theory. She had inadvertently told Mom I was pregnant before I did. (Why did Trixie do that?) So maybe Mom's jealous. Or maybe she's mad at me for writing her instead of phoning her. Who can tell? She holds grudges tight to her chest.

Still, I harbor the belief that Mom will help me during my pregnancy and love her only grandchild. How could she do otherwise?

Then, in December 1986, during my third month, Mom calls up excitedly. At first I'm thrilled that she's finally eager about the pregnancy. But she isn't. She says she's coming to Los Angeles at the invitation of Mike Franks, an old tennis pal who's being honored at a major banquet for his charitable activities. Mom tells me that Bernie and I are invited too. "And Dinah Shore has asked me to play tennis on her court earlier that day, so you can come watch." She doesn't ask how I feel and what I what I want to do, which is to rest most of the time. Besides, I hate watching Mom play tennis. Her flawed technique annoys me, but even more, she acts like a child by turning to me for praise. I decide to compromise. Carefully enunciating my words, I say "I can't do all of that. I'm exhausted and nauseous. I can do one event or the other, but not both." She doesn't respond to that, and after a few minutes, she ends the call. The next day she calls again, discussing plans for me to attend both events. I say: "I told you, I can't do both."

She hangs up. Bernie overhears the call, and he's worried. "You're going to be in trouble, because you sounded annoyed."

He's right. Mom often hides her anger behind silence. After she hangs up, she doesn't call back about her L.A. trip. In fact, she stops calling altogether. Apparently, my sin of showing annoyance is way too grievous. Months pass without any communication from either Mom or Dad.

During the fifth month of my pregnancy, after two months of silence, Mom calls Bernie and asks "Why does Julie M hate me?" And then "Does Trixie hate me too?" Bernie doesn't say much, because the situation is too difficult. I'm certain that Mom wants me to call her and apologize, but I won't do it. I did nothing wrong. Besides, she doesn't care about me. She didn't even ask Bernie how my pregnancy was going or how I was feeling.

During my eighth month, after five months of Mom's silence, Bernie and I go to Lamaze class, where he keeps everyone laughing. When the teacher demonstrates a flip chart showing the names of the parts of the female reproductive anatomy,

Bernie, who, at 49, is by far the oldest dad, says "That's funny. I thought the whole thing was just called a pussy." The room dissolves into hysterics. Except for me. I'm trying to hide the tears streaming down my face. The emotional pain is so stark that it feels like physical pain, and Bernie's flippant humor isn't helping. I keep thinking "Every other woman in the group must have a mother who cares about her pregnancy." Mom's ongoing silence slices right through me. And it's worse because I never saw it coming.

Five days before my June 15 due date, Dad phones me on Mom's behalf. "You can make it up to your mother by inviting her to be with you when the baby is born."

"Make it up?" Dad, in his role as Mom's mouthpiece, is telling me I'm at fault for everything. After enduring a pregnancy from emotional hell, I'm being asked to apologize and admit the errors of my ways.

They're both delusional, and I turn them down. "I can't do it."

I know my decision could cause angry repercussions, but I have to protect myself and Baby Amy. Dad offers no solutions. We hang up without harsh words, just an overhanging resignation. He's never stood up to Mom on my behalf, and I know he never will.

By June 15, I've gained 40 pounds, and I'm so large and swollen that I haven't been able to work for weeks. Finally, on Saturday, June 20, I start feeling contractions. Teeny ones at first, but they come quite often, all through the night. On Sunday morning, the doctor sends us to the hospital, but they dispatch us home, saying I'm not far enough along. I feel like such a fool. So we return to the hospital only when childbirth seems imminent. But progress is still excruciatingly slow, and my body just won't cooperate. Thirty-four hours after the first mild contractions, and 16 hours after the start of strong contractions, both mother and unborn child are exhausted. So, as a precaution, they wheel us into an operating room and extract Baby Amy with one doctor pushing, and the other pulling. Because I haven't even reached the pushing stage of childbirth, Amy's head never gets smooshed, and she comes out perfectly formed and gorgeous, a generous 7 pounds 11 ounces and 22 inches long. Bernie's so emotional that he can't use the camera we brought, so a doctor grabs it from him and takes pictures of the birth. Then the nurse snaps Bernie watching Amy being weighed. If you look closely at the photo, you'll see his thumb on the scales. He jokes that he learned to do that during all the years he worked in his father's butcher shop.

CHAPTER 58
A TERRIBLE CRASH

When Amy is six weeks old, Mom and Dad visit her for the first time. Our relationship is so strained that Mom requires moral support. She brings along another Santa Fe couple: Don Meredith, the famous ex-quarterback and broadcaster, and his wife Susan. Mom and the Merediths become sloppy drunk. As a result, conversation is difficult, but that hardly impacts me, because I spend much of the time in the bedroom, breast feeding Amy. Mom comes in to watch, but she makes me feel uncomfortable. I haven't gotten over the way she treated me during my pregnancy.

While Amy's tiny, I spend most of my days at home with her. But our employees call often, because I'm the only one who can troubleshot the idiosyncrasies of USA Optical's fragile accounting program. The very day that Bernie, Amy, and I return from the hospital, a computer glitch is causing havoc at the office. So I gently place Amy in her bassinet while I talk an employee through the fix. When I hang up, I return to caring for Amy.

I know very little about raising a child, but I have two indelible rules: Give Amy as much love as possible, and don't pass along the damage that was done to me. I enjoy nursing her, walking her in the stroller, dressing her, and recording all her milestones. When she's nearly a year old, I start taking her to baby gym classes, until one day, when the room is particularly noisy, she looks at me and says "Outside." So we leave. That's another rule. I listen to her.

When Amy is 15 months old, Mom and Dad visit for the third time. Mom plays with her for a while, with Dad looking on, but then it's time for Amy's nap. I take her upstairs to her room, lay her down in the crib, and turn on the baby monitor. Downstairs, I tell Mom and Dad that Amy may not sleep very long, as she's begun to rebel against naps. Sure enough, 15 minutes later, we hear her crying.

Mom says "Isn't that cute!" No, it isn't. Amy's cries rip right through me. Mom's remark reveals her lack of empathy towards Amy's distress.

Unlike me, Bernie works full time. When he started the business, he gave away a small premium with each sale, and sales ebbed and flowed depending on the popularity of the premiums. Now, he also offers Hawaiian trips and Caribbean cruises, and customers are eager to buy from us every single month, to earn the trips. Bernie is the tour guide, and he has the unique ability to ensure that every customer has a great time. As a result, business has improved significantly.

Bernie's the company's public face and its master of sales and marketing, while I remain in the background, developing systems to make operations hum along. When he leads the USA Optical trips, I stay at home with Amy. Besides, in the four years since I started therapy with Phyllis, I've uncovered many painful memories, which have left me emotionally fragile. It's hard for me to be around groups of people.

With USA Optical on solid ground, Bernie and I can finally take larger salaries, but we're not getting rich, mainly because the company is a wholesaler, so our profit margins are circumscribed. Bernie dreams that one day we'll be masters of our own fate by importing our own frames and selling them under designer names that we license. But the worlds of big business and licensing are foreign to us, so we don't know how to fulfill his dream.

In 1990, out of nowhere, we find the people we need. We're taking a rare trip without three-year-old Amy, who's staying home with Maria Elena Rivas ("Nena") who came to work for us on the very day Amy was born. Amy has two Moms, one born in the U.S. and the other in El Salvador.

Our trip is to Acapulco, and it's free, because the hotel wants our company's travel business. During the mandatory walk through, a man with bright blonde hair and short shorts approaches me and asks if I'm Julie Heldman. "I loved watching you on TV." His name is Bobby Fried, and over dinner, we learn that he lives in Los Angeles, and that he's a marketing expert with a specialty in licensing. When he hears about Bernie's vision to grow the company, Bobby assures us that he can help us reach our goals.

Back in L.A., Bobby introduces us to his team: Bob Zeichick, an advertising and marketing whiz, and Ron Costa, who does operations and finance. To grow, we'll need help in all of their areas of expertise, so we decide to hire them all. With Ron running my part of the company, I can spend as much time as I want with Amy.

One of Bobby's first jobs is to find a new name for our company, to match our emerging business. When Bernie founded the company, he pulled the name USA Optical Distributors out of the ether. In contrast, Bobby spends days doing research, and he comes up with several names, but everyone's favorite is Signature Eyewear. We'll keep the name USA Optical for a division of the company.

The first license targeted by Bernie and the Bobs is Wimbledon, because its name connotes quality and class, not necessarily because I competed in The Championships nine times. In fact, I'm not involved in the quest for the license, although our team does mention to the Wimbledon people that I'm Bernie's wife. Bernie and the Bobs develop a marketing plan that includes advertising, innovative sales techniques (thanks to Bernie,) and retail displays that reflect Wimbledon's colors. We're up against a much larger German company, but we're the surprise winner. To celebrate our victory, Bernie and Bobby fly to London for a celebratory dinner at a small, posh restaurant in Chelsea. As always, I remain in Rustic Canyon with Amy. Over plenty of wine, Bernie prods the Wimbledon people for information: "We've been wondering. Which part of our presentation swayed you? Was it the advertising? The marketing?"

"Actually, the Wimbledon Committee has always liked Julie." I had no idea that the Committee appreciated me, and I'm glad that I haven't been forgotten.

We all expected the Wimbledon line to succeed, but sales are disappointing. The frames are unisex, and the Wimbledon line is up against unisex frames from designers that are far more famous, such as Polo, Calvin Klein, and Giorgio Armani. Worse, as we're trying to figure out what to do, I discover that our company is receiving angry calls from vendors, who are screaming that Ron promised to pay them but never followed through. The deeper we look into Ron's work, the more problems we find. As a result of the Wimbledon disappointment and Ron's mismanagement, Signature is nearly broke, and our reputation has been sullied. I have no choice but to fire him and take over his job until we can find a replacement.

The situation is grave. We've grown too big for the bank that Bernie started with, but other banks aren't interested, because we're sinking in a financial swamp. And the timing of the mess couldn't be worse. For months, Bobby has been pursuing a license with Laura Ashley, and they've recently said "Yes." Our forecasts for the Laura Ashley line are much more promising than for the Wimbledon line, because we're positioning Laura Ashley as the sole occupant of the feminine niche of designer frames, so our direct competition will likely be flimsy. Our in-house designer has created some gorgeous frames, and the Bobs have produced stunning advertisements and retail displays, using Laura Ashley fabrics. Bernie has sealed the deal by making audio tapes to teach our distributors' sales reps around the country how to maximize their sales.

Signature is ready to soar, but we're out of money. Normal channels are closed, so we tap a shady figure from Bernie's past, who provides enough money for us to reach the next stage, in return for 20% of the company. Next, we hire Michael Prince to find a new bank. He'd helped Bernie start the company, and he has significant experience in business and finance. After several false starts, he finds a bank that is willing to back us, so long as Bernie and I guarantee the loan. This is a huge decision. If the business goes under, our personal finances will collapse, and we'll even lose our house. Mom gave us the house, but she acts as if there are still strings attached, so I don't tell her the risk we're taking. She might try to stop us. But we believe in our company and our people. Everything we're doing and producing is first class. We sign the guarantee.

From the get-go, the Laura Ashley line is phenomenally successful. Formerly sterile-looking optometrists' offices come alive with the Laura Ashley fabrics on our displays, and our frames sell through to customers. We surprise the optical industry by outselling Polo, Calvin Klein, and Armani. We're riding a winner, and money comes pouring into our coffers.

But while our finances have improved dramatically, my life has changed for the worse. After the Ron fiasco, I realized that I'd need to manage people more closely, to avoid a repeat disaster. We've brought Michael Prince on full time to be our Chief Financial Officer. He knows far more about finance than I do, but he'll report to me, because this is our company, and the buck stops here. The vice president of operations also reports to me, which means I'm indirectly responsible for data entry, customer service, the warehouse, and computer systems, as well as two new departments, human resources and frame purchasing. With our explosive growth, we move to new headquarters for the third time since Bernie started the company, and I oversee the move. My part-time job with USA Optical has turned into seven days a week with Signature Eyewear.

As a result, I have less time to spend with Amy. I still read to her every night and drive her to school every morning, but when I gave birth to her, this wasn't what I had in mind.

To reflect my increased responsibilities, Bernie appoints me President of Signature Eyewear, and he becomes Chief Executive Officer. But deep down, he regards Signature as his candy store, where he can do as he pleases. When I came to work for him, there was a clear delineation: he was in charge, and I cleaned up after him. Now I've had to take on much more responsibility, and even though I never interfere with his domain—sales, marketing, advertising, and design—he feels like I'm encroaching in his territory, which makes him angry. We're busting our britches with rapid growth, yet he resents me doing my job.

Years ago, I let Vincent walk all over me, but Alma and Phyllis have helped me learn to stand up for myself. Now, when Bernie says something hurtful to me, I often fight back. Our battles sometimes rage, and although we try hard to shield our co-workers from our anger, it's obvious to everyone that something's very wrong. Because Bernie is charming, friendly, and the head of the company, most of the executives side with him, against me.

I still visit Phyllis three times a week, and she helps me decipher what's going on. She's big on lists, so she counsels me to write down what's going wrong between Bernie and me. But when I bring up my grievances to him, he explodes.

Our anger also spills over into our own home. We try to hide it from eight-year-old Amy, which we can only pull off by screaming at each other behind our closed bedroom door.

By 1995, we're living with non-stop anger, and I've had enough. We decide to separate, but Bernie believes that we'll get back together in a matter of days, so he stays at the bed-and-breakfast hotel a half mile down the road. Our situation is unique. We work together every day, and he comes over every night to spend time with Amy, but he leaves to sleep in his rented room. As the days drag into months, we realize that we need help, so Phyllis sends us to Dr. Ernie White, a wonderfully empathetic couple's therapist. But while our marriage isn't as damaged as Humpty Dumpty after the fall, we do have lots of broken pieces to mend.

Once we separate, I begin a campaign to look better. I've picked at my face for years, a compulsion that I cannot stop, and which has repulsed Bernie and left me looking frightful. Phyllis gives me the name of a psycho-pharmacologist, who prescribes a medicine similar to Prozac. My face immediately clears up, but the doctor changes the medicine several times to help me manage my frequent emotional distress. When he starts me on Zoloft (also similar to Prozac), I get an unexpected response: I sob uncontrollably for hours on end. He tells me "You have bipolar disorder. Your reaction to Zoloft proves it."

This is monumental. I have a mental illness. I'll have to take medicine for the rest of my life.

The doctor prescribes an anti-seizure medicine often used for bipolar, but it mostly leaves me feeling completely blah. It doesn't help me deal with our wildly busy company, our damaged marriage, or my traumatic childhood.

After Bernie and I have been seeing Ernie for a year and a half, we still haven't made much progress, largely because Bernie is deeply resistant to opening up. So I phone Ernie, planning to quit. I say "This is going nowhere."

Ernie responds: "I think you should give it more time. Bernie is voting with his feet, and he comes to every session. I think one day he'll have a breakthrough."

Ernie's right, and the day comes when Bernie begins to buy into couple's therapy. Ernie teaches us how to talk to each other, and we start watching out for each other's feelings. It works so well that when Bernie and I disagree during an executive meeting, the others tease us, saying "What would Ernie tell you to say?"

While Bernie and I are repairing our marriage, Signature keeps rolling sevens. Laura Ashley remains a fairy tale story, with each new release of frames selling like gangbusters. We add a men's line, Hart Shaffner Marx, and then we enter into negotiations with Eddie Bauer. To finance the growth of the new brand, and to get Bernie and me off the bank's guarantee, we decide to take the company public. Michael Prince finds investment bankers who are charmed by Bernie and captivated by the company's story, and we complete our IPO in the summer of 1997. Bernie had negotiated to get our money up front, so he and I are now financially set for decades to come.

Being a public company changes us, however. Bernie loves to try out exciting new ideas, but our institutional investors focus solely on growing the bottom line. The constant pressure to grow profits leads us to change the company radically. Most of our success has been based on selling to optical wholesalers, who have their own sales forces, and to a few large chains. To improve our profits, we decide to sell directly to optical retailers. Instead of having just a few distribution customers we could have as many as 10,000 individual optical retailers. Every part of the company would be massively stretched. We'd need an entirely new computer system, a project that would consume us for at least a year. Instead of having a half dozen sales reps who work for the company, we'd have over 100.

But Bernie believes in going direct, and so do I. We have faith that Bernie's relationships with our distributors will help us weather such a massive change. So we decide to go ahead with the project.

We pick August 1, 1999 as the date we'll announce to our distributors that we're going direct, and we work hard to reach that goal. We acquire three new licenses, Nicole Miller, bebe, and Coach, our first high-end line. We'll have so many brands that we'll need two sales forces. These acquisitions are exciting, but it's hard to manage such massive change.

Meanwhile, Bernie and I have gotten back together, but everything else in my life is tough. My psychiatric drugs aren't helping much, so I change psychopharmacologists. At our first meeting, the new doctor asks "Do you ever have suicidal thoughts?"

"Yes, I do."

"How often?"

"Maybe 10 to 15 times a day."

He prescribes a hefty dose of lithium, which relieves the weight of my depression, but my hands shake big time. So he lowers the dose, and I'm back in the dumps.

I also decide that after 24 years, I can no longer bear the pain in my shoulder, which has migrated all over my back. I have seen several fancy shoulder surgeons, to no avail, because they don't listen to me, and they never find anything on their MRIs. In desperation, I visit a hand surgeon who sometimes does shoulder surgery, and he says "You shouldn't be having this much pain. I'll do exploratory surgery to look inside the shoulder joint and see if I can help you."

In July 1999, the surgeon operates and finds a tendon that's too thick. For 24 years, every movement of my shoulder pinched the tendon, often causing nerve pain. He shaves the tendon down with a laser, and he predicts that the joint will be fine. But even though the surgery is minimally invasive, it takes time to heal, and I barely return to work before our big announcement.

On August 1, Signature Eyewear announces that we're going direct, but the blow back is far worse than we could have imagined. We underestimated our distributors' ire. Most of them are furious, and several are intent on harming us.

Meanwhile, my mental condition has deteriorated, so the psychopharmacologist tries a medicine called Effexor, which instantly throws me into a massive depression. When I tell the doctor, he says "Double the dose." Never have I felt worse, but I don't know what to do. After another unbearable month, I return to the doctor, who says "Stop taking it altogether." That's when I start calling the medicine the "Evil Drug," because the withdrawal is even worse than the horrors I've been living through.

At the height of my distress, my sister and I visit our parents in Santa Fe. I'm in terrible shape, and I beg Trixie to help me. During dinner at a restaurant, I ask her to accompany me to the ladies room. There, I explain what I'm going through.

"I have an ongoing conversation inside my head. One voice says 'I want to die,' so I respond (to myself) 'that's just the drug talking.' Instantly, the conversation repeats itself, over and over, endlessly. Living with this barrage of voices is acutely distressing." Trixie tries to help me, but I'm too far gone. I'll just have to survive this appalling withdrawal.

I know enough not to tell my parents that I'm bipolar or that I'm in terrible straits. Mom has rarely helped me when I was sick, choosing instead to make light of my woes or lash out against all doctors. And I rarely talk to Dad about medical matters. That's always been Mom's domain, a frightening thought.

This whole year has taken a lot out of me, topped off by the Evil Drug. The withdrawal has sucked out all my energy and left me debilitated. In January 2000, I get a phone call from one of our outside members of Signature's Board of Directors. He's concerned because Michael Prince is upsetting our institutional investors by diminishing them to their faces. That must be true, because he also diminishes everyone in our company, and he won't stop. The director asks me to become the liaison with our institutional investors. Normally, that would be challenging, but doable, but given my condition, the thought of adding even one more task to my overloaded portfolio leaves me petrified and disturbed.

January and February 2000 bring bad news. The Coach people are arrogant and obstructive, and they refuse to approve our Coach Sunglass designs in time for us to meet retail deadlines. They've ruined our entire season, and they don't seem to care. From every angle, we're being bombarded. Our ex-distributors have returned massive numbers of frames. The computer system is flawed. And we're making mistakes all over the place.

My sap is draining. Towards the end of February, I dress in my most presidential red knit suit for a meeting I attend in Bernie's office with potential investors. I sit quietly for 45 minutes, but then I pull Bernie aside and whisper "I can't go on."

"That's OK," he says. "Why don't you go back to your office?"

"I can't get up and walk, because I'll cry. Something's very wrong."

Bernie calls a recess, and he sits with me as I sob. Finally, I pull myself together enough to return to my office, and then I head home.

The following day, February 29, 2000, marks the first leap year in the new millennium. It also brings a joyous event for our family. Darren, who graduated from the Culinary Institute of America in Hyde Park, New York, has just opened his own restaurant, Café Catalina, located in a strip mall in Redondo Beach, and

Bernie is holding an opening night party there for Signature employees. He sits at the head table, surrounded by buddies, and I'm at a table nearby, but after I try to settle in, I realize that I'm going to fall apart, so I stand up and leave wordlessly. I wander into the wide parking lot, and as I walk slowly around the periphery, I can't stop the sobs that wrack my body or the tears that stream down my face. I've had too much stress, too much bad medicine, and too much going wrong. But the biggest issue is my bipolar disorder, which is now raging out of control.

After the night in the parking lot, I hit rock bottom. I cry often. I cannot work. I cannot laugh. When I try to concentrate, my brain freezes, and I come to a dead halt. I often sit on my bed, holding my head as I rock back and forth and plead out loud to the empty room, "I don't mean to be this way."

I desperately want to function normally, but that's beyond my capability.

While I was working, I made dozens of complex judgments daily. Now, even the most basic decisions elude me. If I'm asked whether I prefer lemonade or orange juice, or if 'd rather have wheat bread or sourdough, my brain stalls, and I hold myself and shake until the crisis passes. Because I can't engage in normal conversation, and because tears and brain freezes always lurk around the corner, I cannot be around people. I hardly spend time with anyone other than Bernie, Amy, Nena, or Phyllis, and when I do go out, I clam up, unable to figure out what to say. As a result, very few people grasp my condition.

Our dog Binky, a Cockapoo, is a bright spot in my life. He used to sleep with Amy, but when he saw my condition, he became my nurse. He now sleeps on my bed, and he won't leave my side, even to pee, until he's sure I'm OK. We walk together in the mountains while I listen to books on tape, and he's my constant companion in the car, where he leans his head on my thigh and lets his small body hang down between the driver's seat and the door.

One month into my breakdown, Bernie calls Mom to explain that I'm in rough shape. To my great surprise, she starts calling and asking how I'm doing, for the very first time in my life. She even pays attention to my symptoms, such as "I'm glad to hear you sounding a little better today, and that you're not stuttering as much." I grieve that she wasn't this way earlier in my life, but I'm thrilled that she keeps calling me and caring.

For three months, I'm barely able to function, yet I always believe that I'm improving. I tell Bernie "I'm almost ready to return to work."

Bernie thinks differently. "I'm sorry, but I don't think that's going to happen.

You're maybe 3% better."

In June 2000, my psycho-pharmacologist prescribes Zyprexa, an enormously strong anti-psychotic medicine. I finally get a little relief, but the medicine impacts my physical dexterity; twice I fall head-first down a flight of carpeted stairs. I'm shaken, but amazingly, I'm not hurt.

Those falls wake me up to the severity of my condition. I can't do much, and the powerful drugs, which barely make a dent in my damaged mental health, are really hard to manage. With a nudge from the Signature Board of Directors, I officially retire.

At Signature, Bernie and I held the same core belief, that we should treat our employees well. We provided them with high quality health insurance, including dental and disability. We knew how important that might be to someone working in the warehouse. Ironically, I become the first Signature employee to take advantage of our disability policy. The insurance company requires me to apply to the U.S. government for disability, which I'm able to do successfully. I discover that while many tasks remain daunting, I can still pull off a few difficult tasks.

I try to do everything possible to protect 12-year-old Amy from seeing the symptoms of my mental illness, including my brain freezes and my episodes of shaking. I carefully garner enough energy to tutor her daily. I feel proud that I can help her. That's pretty much all I can do.

My recovery is breathtakingly slow and enormously bumpy, with more disappointments than celebrations. At each setback, the doctor increases my meds, which help temporarily, until there's another crisis.

In May 2002, I'm far from being a social butterfly, but Bernie, Amy and I accept Mom's invitation to a series of parties in Santa Fe to celebrate Mom's 80th birthday, Mom and Dad's 60th wedding anniversary, and their 20th year in Santa Fe. Amy, who is 15, has been hit hard by the events of 9/11, so she isn't up to flying to New Mexico, so we take the train. When I was in my teens and 20s, I enjoyed taking trains across the U.S. and all over Western Europe. But our train trip to Santa Fe is appalling, because the food is inedible, and the cabin is so cramped that I have trouble sleeping.

In Santa Fe, there's lots to celebrate. Mom and Billie Jean King have had their troubles, but Mom has invited Billie and Rosie, who fly in to honor her, which is wonderfully reparative. I spend some time with them, catching up on old times. I reveal that I've had troubles, but I don't explain their severity. In fact, I rarely tell anyone how hard it is to get through the day.

The next day, Billie Jean and Rosie, one of the finest women's doubles teams in history, play a set against Mom and her coach Claudia Monteiro on Mom's indoor court. The all-time-great pair feeds Mom soft balls, intending to help her enjoy being involved in every point, but not realizing that Mom is used to playing in harder-hitting games, and she secretly wants the stars to pick up the pace, so that she can show off how well she's playing. But as usual, Mom doesn't speak up for herself. Nonetheless, everyone has a good time.

After three days of expending all my energy being sociable, I can't wait to get back on the horrible train, bound for home, where I can hang out quietly with Binky.

CHAPTER 59
"OUR MOTHER SHOT HERSELF"

Today is June 22, 2003, Amy's 16th birthday.

Bernie, Amy, and I love to celebrate birthdays. For me, they have a special importance, because Mom and Dad rarely noticed birthdays. Amy loves to plan her parties and invite loads of people, but then she tends to get overwhelmed by the commotion. Last week, she celebrated her big birthday with a large party, paid for by Mom, at the Santa Monica Miramar Hotel. Amy has rarely seen her grandmother, but Mom has remained unfailingly generous with money.

Because today is Amy's actual birthday, I know she'll want to do something special. Bernie, our family funster, can usually be counted on to orchestrate merriment, but at 5:30 this morning, he wakes me with a kiss, says "I love you and I made coffee," and leaves for a week-long horseback riding adventure in Wyoming. So it'll be up to me to help Amy have fun, but that's a stretch. In the three years since my breakdown, fun has been rare.

After Bernie leaves, I remain in bed, half awake, as always stultified by the combined impact of long-term depression and bipolar meds, which leave me in a perpetual fog. At 6:50 AM, I patter across the house towards the kitchen, seeking a jolt of caffeine. On the way, the phone rings. That throws me. No one ever calls this early. I wonder if Bernie's plane is delayed.

I pick up the phone in the family room. It's Trixie, her voice sounding strained, as she says: "Our mother shot herself."

I can't figure out what to think or say. I wonder, did I miss something? Did she mean Mom is dead? I manage "What?"

Yes, Mom is dead.

I learn the story in bits and pieces. The first surprise is that Mom asked to see a doctor last night, which is big news, because of her lunatic hatred of doctors and hospitals. When Bernie and I first got together in the mid-1970s, he thought I was exaggerating when I described Mom's extreme views towards the medical profession. His disbelief evaporated during a dinner with her, when he casually mentioned a doctor. Out of nowhere, Mom exploded into a paranoid rant against all doctors. As always, the family sat silently until her spewing ran its course. Bernie learned his lesson. Never again did he talk about doctors or hospitals in front of her.

Mom began feeling sick early yesterday, first with an uncomfortable feeling in her chest, which she thought was indigestion. Marie Bustos, our parents' housekeeper, brought Mom a Coca-Cola, and after she burped, she felt better. But other problems cropped up. She developed pain in her chest and down both arms, but that didn't stop her from playing her regular Saturday game of doubles. Last night, Marie helped Mom and Dad prepare for a costume party, by placing a tiara in Mom's hair and tying Dad's bowtie for his tuxedo. But they returned home at 10:30 PM, well before the party ended, and Mom asked Dad to call their doctor, who made house calls. Dad tried, but the doctor didn't answer, and his service told Dad to take Mom to the hospital, which was against her wishes, so they both went to bed. Dad's room was next to Mom's, and during the night, he heard her moaning and groaning. At 7:15 AM, he entered Mom's room to wake her up. She said her chest pain was "excruciating," and that she had pain in both arms. She asked Dad to leave her alone. Thinking she wanted to vomit, Dad returned to his room, but 10-15 seconds later, he heard a gunshot. He immediately called 911.

Mom's symptoms were classic signs of a heart attack. Whether or not she was aware of that fact is unclear. In New Mexico, autopsies are required for all violent deaths, and the medical examiner arrived on scene by mid-morning. His report stated that Mom believed she was having a heart attack. But Marie never heard

Mom say that, and the police, who were the first to arrive on scene, didn't report say that either. Whether or not Mom believed she was having a heart attack, the pain was unbearable, and according to Dad, she preferred "to end it."

The autopsy confirmed that Mom had had a heart attack, and that all of her coronary arteries were in bad shape: two were at least 95% closed, two more were 75% closed, and the fifth was 65% closed. All those years of heavy smoking and drinking had taken their toll.

The most shocking aspect of Mom's death is that she used a gun. I had no idea she had one. Years ago, she acquired a hand gun in Houston, after an incident on her street. Their home was at the end of Timberwilde Lane, a suburban paved street, before it turned into a dirt road leading into the woods. On Saturday nights, teenagers piled into cars and went joy riding down the dark, dirt road. Once, a carful of kids shot up our parents' front door with a shotgun. That's when Mom insisted on buying a gun. We all thought it was a terrible idea, because she was very nearsighted, she always wore dark glasses, and she refused to take shooting lessons. Even Dad felt unsafe with her having a gun, and whenever he returned home after dark, and he turned his key in the lock, he shouted "Don't shoot! It's me!"

Trixie visited Mom and Dad far more often than I did, and unlike me, Trixie knew that Mom had brought the gun with her to Santa Fe. Trixie says that everyone remained wary that Mom might cause an accident. Surely no one dreamed that she'd turn the gun against herself.

Mom had prepared for her death. She must have read up on how to commit suicide with a gun, because she chose the surest way to succeed. She put the gun in her mouth, aimed upwards, and then pulled the trigger. How dreadful for Dad, who was so close by when she shot herself.

On the phone, Trixie tells me she wants to get to Santa Fe quickly, to be there for Dad. But she lives in Denver, and she has two large dogs. She obviously can't leave them alone, but she doesn't have a reliable kennel, so she's hunting down dog sitters. If she finds one, she can fly to Santa Fe immediately. If not, she'll have to drive for at least six hours, with the two canines in the back seat.

Trixie asks me if I'm coming to Santa Fe, and I tell her I'll try. I silently wonder whether I can pull it off, with Bernie being away. The arrangements feel daunting.

When Trixie and I hang up, it's still early in Santa Monica and my brain remains locked in its morning haze. In this condition, if I push myself, I risk going on overload, when I freeze up, and I stop being able to think or act. Sometimes

I even stutter or start to cry. I'm petrified that I might fall apart while trying to secure a reservation, so I sit for a while, drinking my coffee. Thoughts about Mom begin to seep into my consciousness. Her death came out of nowhere. She was 81, but she seemed in the peak of health, and she was still playing tennis five or six days a week. But this morning, she took her life violently, without writing a note, leaving us sputtering in disbelief.

Mom was a mass of contradictions. She was both generous and cruel, fearless in the business world yet frightened of personal confrontations. And although she was unwilling and unable to care for her own children, she was responsible for saving women's tennis and helping many individual players.

I've always dreamed of having a mother who loved me unconditionally, took care of me when I was hurting, and cheered me on when I succeeded. Until recently, Mom had been incapable of that brand of mothering, partly—or maybe largely—because she didn't get much of it herself. When she reached out to me soon after my breakdown, I entertained a glimmer of hope that she would become more of the mother of my dreams. Losing her means I have to relinquish that hope. But it also means she won't hurt me anymore.

Thoughts of Bernie push to the forefront of my mind. I need him terribly. Since my breakdown, I've leaned on him, and he's protected me. But now I can't reach him, because he's on an airplane. I don't know how I'll manage in his absence.

I look at the phone, pick it up, and call Southwest Airlines. I buy a ticket and call Trixie to give her my flight information.

She tells me that Claudia Monteiro and Blaire Bennett have offered to pick me up. A wave of relief washes over me.

Claudia is an adorable, kind, and funny Brazilian, an ex-pro doubles specialist who's been Mom's coach and confidante since Claudia came to Santa Fe in the mid-1990s. Throughout Mom's life, she resisted getting close to people or turning to them for advice, but Claudia broke through in a way that nobody else could, because she loved Mom wholeheartedly and told her so all the time; because she figured out what Mom would want and then gave it to her; and because she invited kind and friendly tennis partners into Mom's games, vastly increasing Mom's joy on the tennis court. Mom adored Claudia, admired her tennis skills, and let her teach on Mom's court. In this atmosphere of love and mutual support and admiration, Claudia taught Mom how to improve her serve, volley, and forehand, which thrilled her. In all these ways, Claudia, who was much younger than Mom, became the only true mother Mom ever had.

Blaire is Claudia's long-term partner, an artist, and also a loving and generous soul. When I was growing up, Mom was deeply frightened of women who loved each other, but once she came to know Claudia and Blaire, that fear disappeared. Claudia, Blaire, Mom and Dad became close friends, who often went out together.

After Trixie and I hang up, I make another call, this one to Wyoming, where I reach Bernie's wrangler, Belinda, as she's leaving to pick him up at the Cody airport. I tell her the awful news and ask her to have him phone me.

For decades, I've had trouble answering the phone and making calls, out of fear of being attacked, even when I worked as a lawyer or at Signature Eyewear, where the telephone was a necessary implement for doing my job. This morning, I've already made three calls, which have drained me. As I start to pack a small suitcase, I grind to a halt. After a rest, I find enough strength to finish packing, but I recognize that I can't negotiate the Los Angeles airport alone. So I phone Linda, Bernie's ex-wife, who's a good friend. She too isn't a morning person, but she instantly recognizes my distress and the situation's urgency, and she arrives at my home in minutes, without makeup. I've rarely seen her without flawless makeup. Today, she's obviously concluded that speed is more important than beauty.

While Linda waits, I wake up Nena and make sure she'll stay with Amy until Bernie and I return.

And finally, I rouse Amy, a natural night owl who hates getting up early. I plan to say something simple and soothing, but instead my words spill out in rapid-fire succession: "Sweetheart, I'm sorry, but I have really bad news. Grandma shot herself, and she died. I have to leave for Santa Fe. I'll call you as soon as I know more. I'm sad to be leaving you on your birthday." She looks upset and befuddled, but there's nothing I can do. The truth is very harsh.

At LAX, Southwest Airlines has two very long, outdoor lines, one for checking in and the other for security. Linda parks me at the end of the first line and says "Stay here until I call you," and then she marches to the front of each line and convinces the people in charge to let me move ahead of everyone else. The security people even let me use a hidden elevator that they save for emergencies. I thank Linda for all she's done, and then I walk to the gate to board my flight.

In Albuquerque, Claudia and Blaire are waiting by the luggage, where they hug me tightly. Blaire takes the wheel, and as she drives to Santa Fe, she assures me that Mom had long ago planned her own fate. "For years, Gladys insisted that life wouldn't be worth living unless she could play tennis, and she was positive that doctors would only harm her. So time and again she said 'If I fall down, and I'm very sick, let me die.'"

Claudia agrees, giving another version of Mom's instructions: "Gladys always told me that if she fell on her own court, 'bring me to Jules and don't call a doctor.'"

It's comforting to hear their certainty that Mom wasn't out of her mind.

When we reach my parents' house, Dad is sitting at the dining room table, trying to be his normal, dignified self in the face of such a calamity. A few visitors drop by, but otherwise an unnatural silence reigns. Marie has been here all day, tending to Dad's needs, but he's trying hard to remain self-contained. I spend some time with him, feeling our closeness, often just sitting in silence, but I can't assess how he's doing, because my own emotional frailty makes me focus almost exclusively inward. Soon, I retire to my room to rest.

Trixie has found a dog sitter, and she arrives during the afternoon. She's concerned about Dad, because he looks quite frail. He's 84, and he's been in bad shape for four years, since a 1999 car accident that left him barely able to walk. More importantly, he's just lost his wife of 61 years, and he has to face an entirely new reality.

All day, I've been waiting for Bernie to phone, but it never happens. To my great joy, he arrives at my parents' house in the late afternoon, having found his way from Cody. By now, more visitors are dropping in, leaving food for the bereaved family on the dining room table and in the kitchen. Mom had a terrific reputation in Santa Fe, and she'd touched many people with her generosity, but although most visitors look shocked and incredulous, and a few shed tears, the house is mostly quiet.

Over the next few days, Trixie and I attend to some necessary details. We both want to view the body, so one of our parents' friends makes arrangements with the mortuary. Seeing Mom with the life drained out of her impacts me profoundly. I say to myself "She did the best she could," and then I cry for just a moment. And then I cry no more.

Dad's lawyer comes to the house to explain the family's financial arrangements. All the investments and cash are in a family trust. The house passes directly to Trixie and me, although Dad will live out his days there.

Mom and Dad's estate planning was excellent, and she had carefully mapped out how she'd end her life, but there's no sign that she considered the awesome emotional consequences of her death. When she pulled the trigger, she wasn't thinking about the impact on her granddaughter, even though she knew it was Amy's big birthday. And apparently she wasn't thinking about Dad, Trixie, or me. I think she was too desperate. She had to stop the pain and leave this life before a doctor could intervene.

Mom was strong minded throughout her life, and it was just like her to take charge of her own death. She went out on her own terms.

CHAPTER 60
THE END OF AN ERA

Mom was a dynamo. Blessed with a brilliant, creative, and active mind, and seemingly boundless energy, she roared through life, leaving a trail of wide ranging accomplishments.

Her contributions to the tennis world were extraordinary. She started *World Tennis*, and by force of personality she made it into a "must read" by tennis fans and players around the globe. Her editorials heavily influenced the future of the sport. Long before open tennis arrived in 1968, she conceived of a tennis world filled with prize money, marketing, and sponsors, and she used her bully pulpit to fight for reform. She was also renowned for her dazzling tennis promotions, which displayed her creativity and a deep understanding of the needs of players, tournament organizers, fans, and the press. And of course she will always be best known for starting the women's pro tour in 1970 and running it through 1973. I don't think anyone else could have done that.

Besides editing *World Tennis*, Mom also wrote many of its articles, and in her spare time, she wrote several tennis books, including one with Pancho Gonzales and another titled *Pancho Segura's Championship Strategy; How to Play Winning Tennis*. In the latter, Mom captured the genius of "Segoo," the greatest tennis strategist of his era, and Dad always called it the best tennis book ever written.

Mom's 1979 induction into the International Tennis Hall of Fame demonstrates the tennis community's appreciation for all of her contributions to the game.

During her glory years in the tennis world, Mom was a whirling dervish, yet she always engaged in other activities, which hint at what she might have accomplished had she not taken up tennis.

Mom needed very little sleep, so for about a decade, she spent many a night working on an ambitious project to write an encyclopedia of Greek mythology. She read background material voluminously, took detailed notes, and wrote numerous chapters, although this was one project she never finished. Also during the night, she attended to her rare book collection, pouring over advertisements in the New York Times Book Review and corresponding with booksellers who specialized in first-edition novels and biographies. She purchased scores of books for the collection, and she always claimed that she read every one of them. Outside her main collection, she also obtained several thick tomes that were printed before 1500. She loved dropping big words, so she referred to those volumes as incunabula, their formal name. Over the years, the worth of her collection appreciated significantly, reflecting quality choices. The value of one book skyrocketed to $500,000. Towards the end of her life, she donated that book, and others, to charity.

In 1972, while Mom was running the women's pro tour, she organized a tournament in Japan. Mom and Dad accompanied the players, and there she fell in love with the Japanese language, which she decided to learn, an enormously difficult feat. The English language, with its 26 letters, is a piece of cake compared to Japanese, with its more than 2,000 characters, called kanji. Mom had always loved doing puzzles, and was such a whiz at *New York Times* crossword puzzles that she completed them in ink, as fast as she could write. Learning Japanese was like an incredibly complicated puzzle, which she enjoyed working on. For the final 30 years of her life, she spent an average of three to four hours a day learning Japanese. Speaking it fluently was prohibitively difficult for her, but she loved the challenge of reading books in Japanese, with the Japanese-English dictionary by her side, which she annotated in the margins. Her progress was startling, and Japanese people were always amazed at how much she knew.

In 1979, when Mom was 57, she became a published novelist, with *The Harmonetics Investigation*. The plot involved a sinister ring of doctors who promised to rejuvenate elderly women but instead took their money after disabling them with shock therapy and psychosurgery. (She really did hate doctors.) The book wasn't a masterpiece, but the mere fact that she got it published was remarkable.

While Mom and Dad were still living in Houston, she visited her bank one day, to close an account that was solely in her name. Later that day, a bank executive visited Dad at work, trying to convince him to stop Mom from carrying out her decision. Infuriated by the bank's misogyny, she wanted to complain to the women members of the bank's board of directors, but discovered that there were none. That fueled Mom's decision to get women appointed to the boards of directors of companies. As always, she went straight to the top, launching a campaign to put women on the boards of Fortune 500 companies. She gathered data about highly accomplished women and fought to have them placed in the highest corridors of power. But her brand of feminism was ahead of its time, and although she worked on the project for a number of years, she didn't cause any tectonic shifts in major board rooms.

Once Mom and Dad moved to Santa Fe in 1982, she threw herself into philanthropy. Dad had always loved music, but not Mom. Still, once the Santa Fe Symphony began in 1984, they bought season tickets, and when she realized that the Symphony was struggling, she decided to help save it. She raised money by leaning on all her friends, and she could be enormously persuasive and persistent. She also developed an innovative marketing concept, which she called the "symphony club." Members of the club held intimate events at their homes, where small groups of symphony musicians entertained the guests, who paid $1,000 each to attend. Her efforts sustained the symphony for decades, and she became a local hero.

Many of Mom's accomplishments, whether or not they were connected to tennis, were extraordinary, yet while she was a powerful woman in business, she rarely reminisced about her successes, and she never boasted. She just couldn't. Instead, she hoped that others would tell the world how much she'd done. Rarely did that turn out well, and she never became truly famous. Moreover, she suffered a mountain of hurt whenever someone failed to credit her for starting and running the women's pro tour. As the years went by, Billie Jean King would frequently protest that she'd been saying all along that Mom had started the tour, and Mom felt better that Billie was acknowledging Mom's efforts. But then someone else would say Billie Jean started the tour, and Mom would be wounded all over again.

Mom's frustration and hurt grew to monumental proportions in February 1984, when Virginia Slims placed a special section in *Tennis Magazine*, the other prominent U.S. tennis magazine. The section heralded the Virginia Slims Championships, to be held at Madison Square Garden in the end of February.

One full-page article, which purported to be the history of the Virginia Slims tour, is filled with errors and omissions. Most worrisome, it falsely credits Billie Jean with approaching Virginia Slims along "with publisher Gladys Heldman." That's the only time Mom's name is mentioned. Nowhere does the article mention how important Mom was in starting and running the tour. It's basically a fluff piece, written by someone ignorant of tennis history, touting Billie Jean and Virginia Slims. [9]

For Mom, it would have been bad enough had anyone other than Virginia Slims stolen her credit, but it was unbearably awful coming from the very company she'd brought into tennis. Further, she'd worked incredibly closely with the Slims people while she was running the tour. When Mom found out about the ad, she tried to reach Joe Cullman, who didn't respond; George Weissman, the Philip Morris President, who also didn't respond; Ellen Merlo, the Virginia Slims Brand Manager, who responded, but was ineffective; and Teddy Tinling, who offered to set the record straight by writing an article in *Tennis Magazine*. But the higher ups at Philip Morris instructed Tinling not to write an article, just a letter to the editor, which he did, but it was a feeble response to a gross injustice, because it was very short and buried between other letters. Mom, who was, as always, hobbled by the inability to stand up for herself, could only vent her anger and frustration in a letter to Cullman, Weissman, Merlo, and Tinling. And then she did no more.

From that day until the end of their lives, there was no contact between Mom and Joe. What a sad way to end their partnership. They'd been two of the grandest titans of the earliest days of open tennis, and two best friends and collaborators. Without them, women's tennis would not have succeeded the way that it did, and the tennis world would have been very different.

After Mom died in 2003, Joe established the Gladys M. Heldman Tennis Scholarship Fund at Yale, Joe's alma mater. Each year, a member of the Yale women's tennis team receives a scholarship in Mom's name. Although Mom would have appreciated the honor, I doubt that it would have healed her wounds. They were too deep.

Joe died one year after Mom, at 92. Their deaths marked the end of an era.

---

[9] The 2017 fictionalized movie Battle of the Sexes committed the same sin, when Emma Stone, portraying Billie Jean, says that she'll start a tour, to which Gladys, portrayed by Sarah Silverman, responds "Really?" Had Mom seen that scene, she would have been hurt all over again.

Gladys Heldman Associates

February 7, 1984

To: George Weissman
Joseph F. Cullman 3rd
Ellen Merlo
Ted Tinling

For 3½ years I sweated and fought to formulate and to keep together a strong women's pro circuit. As you well know, it was a great financial drain on me, and I took an inordinate amount of abuse from the USLTA. In early 1973, three Virginia Slims tournaments bowed out because of USLTA threats and pressure, and I was faced with the choice of going to court or tamely giving up the Circuit. While Virginia Slims and Philip Morris remained quietly in a neutral corner (as interested bystanders, one might say), I was further abused by USLTA lawyers and a Federal court judge. I thought those were the worst four days of my life, but they weren't. The worst came two weeks ago when I saw the full-page Virginia Slims Advertisemen crediting Billie Jean King with founding the Women's Pro Circuit.

At first I believed (as I was told by Ellen Merlo) that no one at Virginia Slims ever saw the copy for the Advertisement. However, if that were the case, Virginia Slims and Philip Morris could demand from the publisher of "Tennis" Magazine that the correct story be carried immediately in a full-page story. The publisher would have no choice but to agree. Ted Tinling told me twice over the phone that he was writing the article, and that it was to be an article (not a letter). Yesterday I was told by Ellen that the Philip Morris people had decided in favor of a letter.

My children and my husband have seen the Virginia Slims Advertisement. So have the players and fans who were reading "World Tennis" regularly in the early 1970s. I don't know what they think of your loyalty, gratitude or friendship. As for a million other readers who are new to the game, they now "know" who was the inspiration and creator of the most successful sports sponsorship ever--Billie Jean King.

Yesterday I tried to call all four of you. Ted was in England, and I did speak to Ellen. George and Joe did not return my call. That hurt deeply, too.

I never asked for the credit or a pat on the back for my efforts. However, I am stunned by your giving credit to a third party, then deciding to negotiate for a "letter" only for compensation.

It was a low blow unworthy of a company with an honorable reputation. Your lack of action will live in my memory forever.

Gladys M. Heldman

CHAPTER 61
THE GOLD DIGGER

During the years Mom lived in Manhattan, she was drawn to high powered, intensely competitive people like herself, not so much to caring souls. In Houston, her friends were less Type A, but she developed few long-term relationships there. In Santa Fe, however, she was the happiest of her life. Claudia relit Mom's love of tennis and brought her amiable tennis partners. Even off the court, Mom developed solid and lasting friendships.

But she still adored enormously successful people, especially the very rich.

Mom met Eddie Gilbert in Santa Fe, when he came to play doubles on her indoor court. He was in his late 70s, having twice made and lost a fortune in New York, and twice landed in prison for securities violations. In 1989, he moved to Santa Fe, where he started a business and became a billionaire real estate mogul.

Eddie and his wife Peaches became friends with Mom and Dad. The two couples shared lots of meals, and Peaches became Mom's style advisor. She took Mom shopping for clothes, and she encouraged Mom to get plastic surgery. Eddie sometimes flew Mom and Dad on his private jet to Las Vegas, where casinos treated the Gilbert party sumptuously, because in casino parlance, he was a "Whale," who gambled millions.

Throughout their lives, Mom and Dad prided themselves in being scrupulously honest and having upstanding friends, yet they overlooked Eddie's criminal convictions, because he made excuses that they believed, in part because they were dazzled by his extraordinary wealth.

After Mom's death, Eddie and Peaches frequently invited Dad to dinner, which seemed very kind. But Peaches also had an ulterior motive, and he never saw it coming. Peaches was at least 35 years younger than her husband. Her friend Melanie had also married a much older, wealthy man. Upon Mom's death, the entire Heldman estate—valued in the low eight figures—had passed to Dad. As a result, he was a prime candidate for a younger woman who, like Peaches and Melanie, wanted to latch onto an older, rich man.

Four months after Mom died, Peaches and Eddie invited Dad to a luncheon party at the Gilbert house, and sat him next to Melanie's best friend, Michele

Delacey (called by me and many others "the Gold Digger"). At the time, she was 46 and Dad was a frail 84. Soon, he was acting like a young boy consumed with puppy love. He couldn't stop talking about her, and when they were together, she sprinkled magic dust over him, and he got all goo-goo eyed.

Trixie was determined to take care of Dad in his old age, so she made plans for both of us to visit him frequently. But we soon discovered that conversations with him could be strained, because he was preoccupied with his new love, even though they hardly spent time together. He could no longer drive, and they lived an hour apart, because the Gold Digger was studying architecture in Albuquerque, so she couldn't just pop over. But even when she phoned him and scheduled a visit, she often let him down. He'd wait endlessly, and when the phone finally rang, she'd make excuses about why she couldn't get there. Several times, we discovered after the fact that she'd stayed the night with her pal Melanie, just a few miles down the road from Dad's house. The Gold Digger seemed to have little regard for Dad's feelings.

Almost all of the value of the Heldman estate derived from money that Mom had either inherited or earned. For decades, she frequently pronounced that Trixie and I would inherit the entire estate, once both of our parents had died. But after Mom's death, and the money was all Dad's, something transformed him. He'd lived under Mom's shadow for 61 years, and he must've been itching to break free. Instead of following through on the plan that he and Mom had agreed to, he acted like a rebellious young boy, who to a large extent betrayed his daughters in order buy the Gold Digger's love.

In 2006, just as he was turning 87, Dad and the Gold Digger snuck away to get married. The only ones who knew their plans were Peaches, Melanie, and their spouses, as Dad had stopped socializing with most of his other Santa Fe friends. Photos of Dad near the time of his 2006 wedding show him looking nearly like a cadaver. Four months later, he died of stomach cancer.

During the three years between the deaths of Mom and Dad, he gave the Gold Digger increasingly large gifts, including an expensive house in Santa Fe. And two days before he died, he changed his will to increase his gifts to her. All told, she walked away with cash and property valued at about $6 million.

Dad's excuses for gouging a huge hole in our inheritance were jumbled. He said he wanted to provide the Gold Digger with "the security I never had." True, he'd grown up in poverty, but "never had" is incorrect. He gained security at age 27, once he married Mom. He also said that, because Michele had recently had an operation for ovarian cancer, he wanted to be certain that she could pay her doctors' bills once he was gone, but $6 million is a wild overabundance of money to pay any such bills. I think Dad was probably unaware of the biggest reasons that he gave away our money: All the way to the end of Mom's life, she made the lion's share of all financial decisions, from transactions of stocks to keeping a detailed ledger accounting for all their expenses, and requiring Dad to account for every cent he spent. And although in theory both of them agreed to their charitable contributions, the reality was different. She made those decisions and then asked him for confirmation, which he always gave. Once Mom died, I think he desperately needed to be free from Mom's financial rules, even from beyond the grave, and he wanted to feel like a big shot. Giving away so much of his daughters' money was a strange and perverse way of achieving those goals.

Apparently, the $6 million Dad gave the Gold Digger wasn't enough. During the last hours of his life, while he was unconscious in an Albuquerque hospital with his "devoted" wife by his side, she sent two men and a truck to the house where Dad and Mom had lived for 21 years, with instructions to take away paintings and furniture. She must have believed that, while he was still alive, she could claim an ownership interest in his property, because she was his wife, although that was incorrect. When Mom died, the contents of their home became solely Dad's, and the Gold Digger had no legal right to any of them. Dad's housekeeper Marie fearlessly blocked the doorway to the house, screaming "You can't come in! The owner is dying!" Fortunately, the movers weren't foolish enough to force the issue, and they left empty handed. Of course the Gold Digger has never acknowledged what she did.

While Dad was still alive, Trixie was righteously furious, as were most of Dad's friends and, from afar, so was Amy. But I was too fragile to be mad at him. I forgave what I thought of as his foolishness, choosing instead to hold onto the memories of his many kindnesses to me when I was a child.

Two memorials were held for Dad in Santa Fe, one organized by the Gold Digger, and the other by Trixie. While the Gold Digger excluded us from her event, Trixie magnanimously invited her to ours. When the service was over, 19-year-old Amy made a beeline for the Gold Digger and spoke the words that everyone else was thinking: "I'll never forgive you for what you did to our family." The Gold Digger left the room, alone. The Gold Digger still owns the house in Santa Fe that Dad gave her, but we never saw her again.

CHAPTER 62
ANATOMY OF TWO BREAKDOWNS

Before my 2000 breakdown, I acted like a modern superwoman, juggling multiple complex matters at work, running the household with little help from Bernie, maintaining our finances, and organizing Amy's life. Since my massive collapse, I've had trouble functioning, which has changed everything. Bernie has started doing more, especially with Amy, and he's become much more important in her life. When I can't use the phone or deal with even the simplest situations, he jumps in and takes over. And while he can't manage the computer systems I've developed for paying bills, he's smart enough to hire someone I can supervise.

After several years, my improvement is minimal. My emotional and mental states improve maddeningly slowly, and then only after I've visited my psycho-pharmacologist in a state of distress, and he increases the dosage of my medicines. I remain plagued with fears of inadequacy, due to my childhood trauma and the deeply imbedded depression, and dragged down by exhaustion, due to the soporific effect of the drugs that shore me up.

I hate being so debilitated, and I mostly try to hide my condition. But even those who are aware of my struggles, such as my extended family, rarely ask me how I'm feeling. The stigma of mental illness looms large.

During the more than 20 years I spent competing on the tennis court, I fought hard, always seeking a way to win. Those old habits lead me to believe that I can overcome my mental illness by force of will, and that a cure is imminent. But this illness is a new kind of enemy, a beast that I can't trounce by trying harder. Still, I harbor the belief that I can turn the illness around and begin to experience ordinary life.

Hiking in the Santa Monica Mountains is one activity I've been able to enjoy, with either Bernie or Binky. In 2004, I believe that I'm well enough to accompany Bernie on a guided helicopter hiking vacation in Banff, Canada. We'll be in a group of eight, a comfortable size. In theory, it seems doable, but on the very first day, I feel the onset of emotional instability, although I say nothing, go to bed early, and hope for the best. The following day, I get a nasty surprise when we reach our final destination, where we join 30 additional hikers. The far larger group feels oppressive to me, and I begin to crumble. Two days later, when we're out on the trail, I fall twice, melt down, and cry unstoppably in front of a dozen hikers. The more I cry, the more I'm embarrassed and certain they must see that I'm crazy, which spurs on even more tears. Because I can't stop crying, a big guy picks me up, slings me across his back, and carries me across a narrow river, where a helicopter whisks us away. I'm deeply traumatized, and never again do we sign up for a tour.

Instead, Bernie, Amy, and I take urban vacations, first to Paris in 2006 and then to Rome in 2007. Those trips are a great improvement over the hiking tour, because when I become physically or emotionally fatigued, I can regroup in our hotel room while Bernie and Amy climb the Eiffel Tower or go window shopping along Rome's Via Veneto.

Back in Santa Monica, I rarely go out. Even when I can gather enough emotional energy to be social, I rarely function well enough to enjoy the festivities. On the way home after dinners with friends, Bernie often says "You were charming tonight," but I know I wasn't, because I barely spoke a word the entire evening. I was once a glib broadcaster, and often the life of the party. But now I can't figure out what to say.

In 2009, nine years after my breakdown, I start working out with a trainer for the first time in decades. Feeling my muscles come alive is a wonderful boost to my mood, but the knee I nearly destroyed 38 years ago severely limits my ability to exercise. The trainer gently nudges me to see a surgeon, who performs a partial knee replacement in 2010. Once I regain mobility, my horizons open up further. A few months later, I receive another boost, this one from my psycho-pharmacologist, who prescribes a drug to counteract my constant fatigue. It boosts my energy enough that I can sit down at my computer, where stories about my life come pouring out.

The excitement of writing comes to a halt in December 2010, when I find a lump in my left breast, shortly after a clean mammogram. In January 2011, I have a lumpectomy, which shows that I have Stage I breast cancer. At first, I'm scared, having grown up in an era when the word cancer was a death sentence. But all the cancer doctors tell me how I lucky I am that I caught the tumor early, and I soon learn that it hasn't metastasized at all, so I don't need chemotherapy. Instead, I fly smoothly through seven weeks of radiation, and I escape relatively unscathed.

Once the radiation is finished, I have a regular appointment with my psycho-pharmacologist, where I report that my lower jaw is jutting out repeatedly. He had previously warned me that I might get unwanted facial movements, called tardive dyskinesia, because Zyprexa, the anti-psychotic medicine I've been taking for 11 years, is known to cause the movements. Further, the larger the dose, the greater the risk of tardive dyskinesia, and in 2011, my daily dose is huge. Tardive dyskinesia is often irreversible, so I have to stop taking Zyprexa as quickly as possible and ramp up on Seroquel, a lower-risk anti-psychotic. The withdrawal and change of drugs lasts for months and is highly unpleasant, but nowhere near as bad as my 1999 withdrawal from Effexor, the Evil Drug. By late summer 2011, the unwanted facial movements have decreased significantly, and I feel more normal than I have in years, because the new drug is definitely more effective than the old one.

By August 2011, I've already had my belly full of tsouris (Jewish for "woes"), but then I get more potentially troubling news, when Phyllis Rothman, my therapist for 27 years, announces that she'll retire in six months. I've always wondered how I'd feel when she retires, but now that it's happening, I feel nothing. I've already decreased the frequency of my appointments to once every two weeks, without adverse effects, so it looks like I'll survive unscathed.

In September 2011, I start a drug called Tamoxifen, to prevent further breast cancer. It's known to cause unpleasant side effects, but I get through 2011 without any.

In October 2011, out of nowhere, my life improves dramatically. My fatigue miraculously melts away, and for the first time in many, many years, I can do everything from menial tasks to complicated processes like helping my stepson Darren get a mortgage for his new condo. I ask my psycho-pharmacologist if he knows why I'm feeling so much better, but he's as clueless as I am. I occasionally fear that the good times will disappear as quickly as they arrived, but more often, I focus on the excitement of being a functioning member of the world for the first time since 2000.

In April 2012, Bernie and I fly to Charleston, South Carolina for a reunion of the Original 9, the women players who competed in the 1970 breakaway Houston tournament. Everyone tells me how well and happy I look. No one realizes—because I don't tell them—that I've recently been released from a dozen years in an emotional prison.

In 2012, the other members of the Original 9 told me how well I looked. No one knew I'd recently been released from a dozen years in an emotional prison.

In Charleston, I also accept a posthumous award given by the WTA to Mom for being a mother who contributed to women's pro tennis. Trixie and I enjoy the irony of Mom receiving an award for being what we jokingly call the "Mother of the Year." But the WTA couldn't have known about Mom's deficits as a mother, because we've obeyed her rules and never revealed how she acted at home. At a dinner for several hundred guests, I deliver a speech that I've worked on for two months, about Mom's unique contributions to women's tennis, and at the end, the crowd rises to cheer. I'm proud of my speech, and thrilled to be savoring success for the first time in a very long while.

In the two months leading up to Charleston, I began to have painful and disruptive side effects from Tamoxifen. During the event, I discuss the problem with Bernie, and we decide that I should stop taking it. The side effects rapidly fade away.

When we return home in April 2012, Phyllis has retired, and I remain happy and energetic. I even have enough get-up-and-go to launch a campaign to get pensions for women pros who competed during the early years of the women's pro tour. For over a month, I work alone, making phone calls, developing Excel spreadsheets, and trying to puzzle out how much the pensions would cost. But in early June, I begin to cry easily. In July, enormous fatigue descends. In the beginning of September, after attending a family wedding in Las Vegas, I return to my hotel room, where I break down and cry uncontrollably. I had eight terrific months, but once again I've hit rock bottom.

My 2012 collapse isn't as all-consuming as the 2000 breakdown, but the impact is nonetheless immense. Once again, I have trouble coping, and I have frequent tears, brain freezes, and fears that I screwed up or that someone will be mad at me. And the voices of self-destruction that I first heard in 1966 reach a crescendo. Once again, I can rarely hang around anyone other than Bernie, Amy, Nena, and my psychological team. That nixes all social events, including family dinners and nights out with friends. This crash also delivers its own unique side effects: I can't watch TV, attend movies, or go clothes shopping.

Not for the first time, a psychotropic drug is the partial culprit. Nearly three months after the 2012 breakdown, a blood test shows that Lamictal, a drug that I've been taking since 2000, is harming my white blood cell production, which explains my recent excessive fatigue. My psycho-pharmacologist contacts an executive at the manufacturer, who reports that my reaction is extremely rare. Just my luck. So I suffer through a short-but-intense round of changing medicines, and I land on my feet in early 2013 when my psycho-pharmacologist once again adds Lithium, the original mood stabilizer, which brings me a modicum of much-needed peace.

Another unexpected cause of my 2012 breakdown was Phyllis's retirement. For 27 ½ years, she was a mother figure, teaching me how to protect myself and understand others. She counseled and supported me each time I worked too hard, during my pregnancy, when I was a new mother, when my marriage became troubled, and throughout my 2000 breakdown. Before Phyllis, I never had the consistent support that good mothering brings. After all those years under her care, I believed that I no longer needed her. I now know that's wrong. Due to my combined childhood trauma and bipolar disorder, I can't survive without an excellent therapist.

Back in Santa Monica, I turn to a trusted friend—my former 18-and-under rival Janie Albert Willens, who is now a therapist—for a referral. She sends me to Mariann Hybels Miller, who does both psychotherapy and psychoanalysis. When I first speak to her on the phone, she immediately understands—long before I do--how much the loss of Phyllis is ripping me apart. In her office, Mariann points to the empty seat next to me on her couch and says "Phyllis is always with you, sitting by your side." But identifying the problem is easier than solving it, because this most recent breakdown has at least temporarily stripped away much of the fragile progress I made with Phyllis, and once again I need to sort through events from my gnarly childhood. I'm in crisis, and I need to see Mariann five days a week, so I start intense psychoanalysis. It doesn't take long for her to decipher why I had those recent, glorious eight months. She attributes my energy and accomplishments during that period to a condition called "manic defense," which happens when a person, who is desperately running away from uncomfortable thoughts or feelings, copes by getting energized. That pretty well defines what happened to me after Phyllis retired. Instead of mourning her loss, I threw myself into being productive. But once I could run no more, in part because of the drug-induced exhaustion, I crashed.

I make a lot of early progress with Mariann, but I don't turn the corner until mid-2014, when I begin seeing a new psycho-pharmacologist, Dr. Shirah Vollmer. One of her first acts is to rethink my diagnosis. For 18 years, all my doctors assumed that I had bipolar II, the less severe form of the disorder, in which the patient has no psychoses (breaks from reality). Dr. Vollmer thinks differently, once I report that I sometimes have fearful visions, in which I believe that people—either nearby, far away, or even on the telephone or the TV—can harm me, even though I consciously realize that those fears are baseless. The fears derive, in part, from the terrors of my childhood, when I was constantly wary of verbal attacks. But Dr. Vollmer has also labeled those fearful visions "mini psychoses," because they're delusional, and she's treating them, but her label has bumped up my diagnosis to the more acute bipolar I, partially reflecting the seriousness of my condition. Dr. Vollmer's methods also differ from those of my previous doctors in another beneficial way. To minimize the side effects related to switching drugs and dosage, she makes only the smallest changes, and as a result, over the last few years, I've had far fewer difficulties with drug side effects.

Under the combined care of my psychological team, I've become increasingly stable and thriving, and I'm rarely laid low by a chemical imbalance.

My two breakdowns ran from 2000 through 2015, excluding the eight months of my manic defense during 2011-12. During most of those years, I struggled just to get by, and I had so many things going wrong that I couldn't see the big picture. Now that the beast within me has become far more manageable, the causes of my mental and emotional troubles have emerged more clearly. The four most significant culprits were: the terror I lived under as a child, the stress of competing in the highly charged arena of tournament tennis, bipolar disorder, and the harmful effects of some of the medicines. Each one of those factors could have led to a breakdown. Their combination has left me sitting on a powder keg, waiting to blow.

Childhood Terror. In the Cult of Gladys, I was isolated from outsiders and constantly under the threat of verbal assault, neglect, and humiliation. The resulting cumulative damage, often called relationship trauma, is so powerful that it impacts brain chemistry and often results in alcoholism and/or drug abuse. I'm lucky to have avoided those two fates. But I grew up with unstable emotional underpinnings, which have impacted me in every stage of my life.

Stress in the Tennis World. I achieved a great deal in tennis, but I also suffered, partly because Mom dominated the world that I inhabited. When I was little and just taking up the game, she placed me in impossible situations and then laughed at me when I failed. As I began to make a mark in junior tennis, she praised me for not needing help, but turned on me when I screwed up. And for the most important tournament of my young life, the National Juniors, Dad didn't show up at all, and Mom came for just one match and then sped away, without a thought that I might need support, because watching me made her too nervous. So in the tennis world, I was almost always on my own, literally and figuratively. Yet even as Mom's misdeeds added up, I never saw the next one coming, because she always had a different narrative than I did, and hers were the only words that counted. As a result, I never learned how to protect myself from emotional danger, on or off the court, and my life was fraught with upheaval.

The seven summers I spent in Hamtramck, Michigan made my relationship with tennis even more difficult. Although Mr. Hoxie was a straight shooter and an all-around good guy, he hammered home his belief that tennis was about winning, not about having fun. His formula helped me become a winner, but it added to my internal pressure cooker.

Bipolar Disorder. I have a chemical imbalance which, if left unchecked, impacts my moods and my ability to cope. The imbalance has two causes: bipolar disorder and the relationship trauma that I suffered when I was young. Those two factors are so intertwined that it's often difficult to unravel them, to determine which treatment is best.

Bipolar disorder can be hard to diagnose. It usually becomes evident when a person is in his or her late teens or early 20s, yet I wasn't diagnosed until I was 50, which is highly unusual. But when I look back, I see clear signs of it earlier. At 18, I had a prolonged depression while I was at Stanford in France. At 19, after I broke up with my first major boyfriend, I had another, far more acute episode, which I blamed on competitive tennis, so I quit the game. Five years later, at 24, I attempted suicide. Had those events occurred today, I would have been instantly shipped off to a psychiatrist. But in the late 1960s and early 1970s, I was largely on my own. My parents certainly offered no guidance. Alma helped me for a few years, but she couldn't prescribe medicine. Anyway, in that era, few psychotropic medicines had been developed. Mom hid her own pathology by self-medicating with alcohol. I didn't drink to excess, but I had her other coping mechanism. My drive turned me into a workaholic, which at least had a positive side, as my goal was always to achieve. I threw myself into accomplishments, first on the tennis court, and then in law school, at the law firm, and in business. Perhaps the years when I ran madly after success were in part a form of manic defense, in that I was trying so hard to escape my childhood (and later my tennis life) that I was flooded with positive energy. But during all those years, I also had bipolar disorder, so my feverish determination to succeed, while ignoring fatigue, injury, and normal limitations, was also fueled by bipolar mania. Interestingly, once I was diagnosed and began taking psychotropic medicine, I lost the coping mechanism of working frenetically and interminably, and I slid quickly downhill. Four years after I was diagnosed, I had my huge breakdown.

The Harmful Effects of Medicine. Psychiatry is an inexact science. For many medical disciplines, a doctor can turn to MRIs or blood tests to diagnose an illness. Not so for psychiatry in general or bipolar disorder specifically, where doctors rely largely on the patient's description of his or her symptoms. As a result, the diagnosis and treatment of psychiatric conditions is prone to error. And to a large degree, the doling out of psychotropic medicines is a crap shoot, which can lead to terrible side effects. A large number of psychiatric patients end up with tales of woe about their medicines. Even the best drugs can have a nasty downside, and no one can predict how a patient will react to a change in medicine or in dosage. My history reflects a multitude of hits and misses. I've tried 18 different drugs over the last 21 years, and many of them have produced harmful reactions. Effexor, the Evil Drug, tops the list, because it was so pernicious that it precipitated my 2000 breakdown. And two drugs that helped me for over 10 years, Zyprexa and Lamictal, eventually mounted stealth attacks, causing significant physical problems.

Since 2015, the four factors that make up my powder keg have become largely under control. Since then, my mental health has been improving consistently, and my life keeps getting better.

CHAPTER 63
A HAPPY ENDING

I now lead a quiet, limited, and very happy life. I see Mariann daily, and she manages both the reverberations of my past and the bruises of my daily existence. I visit Dr. Vollmer at least once a month, and we've settled on a drug cocktail that delivers substantial stability: Seroquel and Lithium at night, and Provigil to wake me up in the morning. I feel lucky to be living in an era when these drugs are available.

My good fortune also spreads beyond my psychological team. Bernie and I have been together for over 40 years, and at 80 years old, he's blessed with a rare combination of being playful as a child, wise as his age, kind to everyone, and a lot of fun. We talk a great deal, and we support each other in different ways. He's never fussed about my inability to go out and have a good time—I still rarely socialize and I never go out to the movies—and I take care of many of the details of his life.

I'm also buoyed by my love for, and pride in, our daughter Amy. She's been an animal lover since she was a one-year-old and a vegan since she was 15, a young woman whose actions are based on a broad, moral view of the world. Like Bernie and me, she's an entrepreneur. Like Bernie, she's hysterically funny.

And I have wonderful friends and family, who help me get by when I have a bad day, and understand my limitations. Now that I'm functioning better, I'm more able to return the favor and extend my own hand in friendship.

And I get great joy from our animal family—currently two dogs, a cat, numerous birds, and a desert tortoise—who have taught me that every living being is unique, and love can come in many different ways.

Writing this book has been one of the most important factors in my renewed stability. I've enjoyed pretty much everything about the process, even though I've had a lot to learn. At first, I was confident in my tennis memories, and I didn't think I'd need to do much research. But then I sent a chapter that revolved around a tennis match to Joel Drucker, the International Tennis Hall of Fame historian, who gently pointed out that I'd gotten the score wrong, which required me to rewrite large portions of the chapter to achieve accuracy. Since then, I've been religious about researching everything I can think of, mostly in *World Tennis* magazine—of course—but also in books, magazines, newspapers, and a variety of online sites. I've also conducted some interviews, and I've been amused to discover that I'm not alone in having an imperfect memory. Even clear-headed interviewees make mistakes.

In the early 2000s, long before I thought about writing a book, I took a class in short story writing for several years. I was never drawn to making up stories, so I focused on my life events, which I thinly disguised as fiction. Several stories that I wrote for the class later became chapters in this book. However, for the following decade, I lacked the physical and emotional stamina needed to write a book. But whenever I got a shot of energy, I was drawn to my computer, to write. Most of my stories were quite personal, so I showed them to just a few people. In 2010, I handed Bernie and Phyllis a chapter which told, for the first time, why and how I'd attempted suicide. I'd never been able to talk about it, but for some reason I could write about it. Revealing those painful secrets lifted a huge weight off of me and left me wanting to write more.

In 2014, I decided to dedicate myself to writing the book, even though I still had only a few good hours a day. I needed five months to finish the first chapter, but I loved every minute of it. Over time, my energy improved, and the book became a mainstay of my existence. It has profoundly contributed to my wellbeing.

Writing the book helped me develop confidence. When I started the project, I'd send out chapters to readers and then live in abject fear that they'd hate my work. Those fears have largely subsided, and I now look forward to readers' comments, although I still have to gird myself against the discomfort of having my flaws revealed.

Before I wrote the book, no one—not even I—understood what my home life was like when I was growing up. Writing has helped me uncover the truth about my isolation, Mom's abuse and neglect, and the ensuing trauma. Through research, writing, and psychoanalysis, I've learned to trust the truth that I've worked so hard to uncover. With each eureka moment, I've been able to take another step towards gaining freedom from the ill-treatment that pinned me to my sorrow.

Writing the book has also helped me understand what Laura meant to me. From my infancy through my childhood, her love and her goodness gave me the resilience to find my way in the world, an irreplaceable gift.

And most of all, I've loved the process of writing and constant editing, always trying to inch closer to what I really want to say.

*   *   *   *

From 2000 through 2015, I struggled to have good days. And I rarely dreamed that one day I'd feel well, because I knew that bipolar disorder is a life sentence, and that few people who are afflicted with it can find the right combination of medicine and psychotherapy. Plus I've been doubly cursed, as the wounds caused by my relationship trauma are also hard to conquer.

Until recently, stability was evanescent for me, hard to come by but easy to lose. The factors that created my powder keg would all too quickly re-ignite. But with lots of hard work, I've achieved ever-increasing stability. In analysis, I grapple to disarm the damaging impact of my childhood trauma. I'm vigilant about taking my meds and maintaining a healthy lifestyle, to help me combat my demons. And I know I must contain my drive, which has thrust me towards accomplishments, while simultaneously sending me careening towards disaster.

All that work is reaping rewards. For the first time since my bipolar symptoms began to surface in 1964, I've been consistently stable for over a year.

Now that I've achieved a one-year milestone, I allow myself to believe that I can do it again. Stability breeds more stability. I look forward to a better life.

ACKNOWLEDGMENTS

In 2000, I retired from business due to the impact of my giant breakdown. The following year, seeking activity, I decided to learn to write fiction, so I signed up for a short story writing class at the nearby Santa Monica College.. My first attempts at narrative description were pretty grim, but I began to improve once the teacher, Jan Cherubin, taught us to describe sounds and smells and textures, which was new to me, and I eagerly inhaled her instruction. In 2014, when I committed to writing this book, I naturally turned to Jan to be my editor, and she taught me much more, especially about the use of language and the flow of a book. She was unfailingly warm, knowledgeable, and supportive, and she helped me capture my own voice. That was quite a gift.

Once I had a complete draft, I turned to my great friend Amy Bookman, a former agent at Creative Artists Agency, who is uniquely perceptive. She gently told me that, although all the pieces of the book were in place, I sometimes repeated myself, especially at the ends of chapters, which was distracting. So I read and re-read the book, ruthlessly carving out repetitions. The narrative flow improved significantly.

The book contains quite a few details about my family's history, most of which came from my sister Trixie's oral history of our father. Over numerous long sessions during the late 1990s, when Dad was just entering his 80s, she typed as fast as she could while he reminisced about himself, Mom, the family, and science. I found out more about our family history by scouring contemporaneous accounts, and by reading nearly 20 years of *World Tennis*. Trixie and I had donated Mom's bound volumes of the magazine to the International Tennis Hall of Fame, but Trixie had held onto copies of Mom's early magazines, which she donated to me. Also, Lovey Jergens generously gave me her collection of *World Tennis*. For missing issues, the UCLA research library was a wonderful resource.

Trixie also helped me in many other ways. She read numerous chapters of the book, and she was able to give me invaluable feedback about our parents and the world we grew up in.

Besides doing written research, I interviewed a number of people whose personalities and memories added richness to the book: Claudia Monteiro, Blaire Bennett, Marie Bustos, Owen Williams, Sammy Giammalva, Donald

Dell, and Peachy Kellmeyer.

After I double checked every fact in the book, I turned to Donn Gobbie, the best researcher I've ever known. He was just finishing his thesis for a PhD in women's tennis history, so he meticulously set me straight on a number of points. I can now say, with complete assurance, that *Driven's* tennis history is astonishingly accurate.

Joel Drucker read every chapter in the book in its initial form, and he was unfailingly supportive, even while gently nudging me in new directions. Early on, he suggested that I add more emotion, and when I did, he was the first to cheer me on.

Richard Naughton has been a friend since we met in Sydney, Australia in 1973, and he too read every chapter of *Driven* along the way. Because he's the author of several tennis books and a law professor, his perspective is somewhat unique. I could always count on Richard to respond speedily, thoughtfully, and thoroughly, and I co-opted many of his suggested changes.

Cynthia Doerner and I both competed on the women's pro tour in the 1970s, but we didn't know each other well until 2015, when we started working on the project to obtain pensions for women pros who competed before 1989. I began sending Cynthia chapters of the book and discussing what I planned to include. When I somewhat sheepishly raised the issue of mental illness, Cynthia strongly encouraged me to write about it, saying "you're not alone, and you'll help other players who've gone through similar difficulties." Her words helped me leapfrog the stigma that I had held onto, and as a result, to understand more of my own truth.

Maxine Wolf was a double reader, in that she read every chapter of the book to a woman in her late 80s named Eva who wasn't interested in tennis. Maxine reported that Eva was captivated by many passages, but never by the ebb and flow of a match. That taught me to keep tennis descriptions pithy, to hang onto readers and listeners for whom tennis is a foreign language.

I'm also grateful to the following people for reading chapters and giving me astute comments: Rhonda Raider, Michael Heldman, Nancy Richey, Marilyn Katz, Carl Borack, Dorothy and Jim Fadiman, Janie Willens, Linda Weiss, Myrna Kettler, Richard Kettler, Nina Bomar, Phyllis Rothman, Toni Moss, and Alan Spatz.

Peaches Bartkowicz, my old Hamtramck doubles partner, gave the most succinct feedback. After I sent her chapters, I'd check back with her. With unabashed enthusiasm, she always said: "Send me more chapters!"

My poor hubby Bernie read every chapter numerous times, which led to a complex dance between us. First, he'd find a problem, and he was always right. Next, he'd suggest a fix, and I'd make a change, but rarely the one he suggested. So I'd write new material, and around we'd go again, until we were both happy with the outcome.

I spent about four years writing *Driven*, at first in sporadic bursts, but during the final long haul, from 2014 through 2017, I wrote for nearly four hours every day, with passion overcoming fatigue. Not once did Bernie complain about his absent wife. Instead, he was proud of me.

He really is a mensch.

ABOUT THE AUTHOR

Julie Heldman won 22 women's tennis tournaments, with victories over all the top stars of her era, including Billie Jean King, Margaret Court, Chris Evert, and Martina Navratilova. Julie represented the U.S. on two winning Federation Cup teams and at the 1968 Mexico City Olympics, where she won three medals, a gold, a silver, and a bronze. Her highest women's rankings were number two in the U.S. (twice) and number five in the world (twice).

Julie has been inducted into the International Jewish Sports Hall of Fame, the Stanford Athletic Hall of Fame, the Intercollegiate Tennis Hall of Fame, the Eastern Tennis Hall of Fame, and the Dalton School Hall of Fame.

Julie graduated from Stanford University in 1966. After retiring from competitive tennis in 1975, she worked for several years as a journalist and a tennis commentator on network TV. In 1981, at age 35, she graduated from UCLA Law School with honors and then practiced law for four years.

After law school, Julie married Bernie Weiss, and in 1985, at age 39, Julie joined Bernie's startup eyewear business, eventually called Signature Eyewear. Twelve years later, they took the company public.

In 1987, Julie gave birth to their daughter Amy.

In 1996, Julie was diagnosed with bipolar disorder. Four years later, she suffered a cataclysmic breakdown that lasted 15 years, with only one eight-month respite during 2011-12.

Driven: A Daughter's Odyssey is Julie's first book.

53693528R00264

Made in the USA
Columbia, SC
20 March 2019